Master the Physician Assistant National Certifying Exam (PANCE)

1st Edition

PETERSON'S
Publishing

PETERSON'S
Publishing

About Peterson's Publishing

To succeed on your lifelong educational journey, you will need accurate, dependable, and practical tools and resources. That is why Peterson's is everywhere education happens. Because whenever and however you need education content delivered, you can rely on Peterson's to provide the information, know-how, and guidance to help you reach your goals. Tools to match the right students with the right school. It's here. Personalized resources and expert guidance. It's here. Comprehensive and dependable education content—delivered whenever and however you need it. It's all here.

For more information, contact Peterson's Publishing, 2000 Lenox Drive, Lawrenceville, NJ 08648; 800-338-3282 Ext. 54229; or find us online at www.petersonspublishing.com.

© 2011 Peterson's, a Nelnet company

Bernadette Webster, Director of Publishing; Ray Golaszewski, Publishing Operations Manager; Linda M. Williams, Composition Manager

ISBN-13: 978-0-7689-3311-6
ISBN-10: 0-7689-3311-0

Printed in the United States of America

10 9 8 7 6 5 4 3 2 1   13 12 11

First Edition

By printing this book on recycled paper (40% post-consumer waste) 32 trees were saved.

Petersonspublishing.com/publishingupdates

Check out our Web site at www.petersonspublishing.com/publishingupdates to see if there is any new information regarding the test and any revisions or corrections to the content of this book. We've made sure the information in this book is accurate and up-to-date; however, the test format or content may have changed since the time of publication.

Contents

PART I: Physician Assistant Basics

PART II: Diagnosing Strengths and Weaknesses

PART III: Overview of Question Types

f www.facebook.com/CareerResource

PART IV: Two Practice Tests

PART V: Appendices

Contents

SPECIAL ADVERTISING SECTION

Before You Begin

OVERVIEW

- **How this book is organized**
- **Special study features**
- **Special advertising section**
- **You are well on your way to success**
- **Find us on Facebook®**

HOW THIS BOOK IS ORGANIZED

Physician assistants (PAs) practice medicine under the supervision of physicians and surgeons. PAs are formally trained to provide diagnostic, therapeutic, and preventative healthcare services, as delegated by a physician and as determined by law. The U.S. Bureau of Statistics reports that over the next decade, employment for physician's assistants is expected to grow much faster than average and overall job opportunities should be excellent.

To work as a PA all states require students to complete an accredited, formal education and pass a national exam—the Physician Assistant National Certifying Examination (PANCE), administered by the National Commission on Certification of Physician Assistants (NCCPA) and open only to graduates of accredited PA educational programs—to obtain a license. PA educational programs usually take at least 2 years to complete for full-time students. Most programs are offered by schools of allied health, academic health centers, medical schools, or 4-year colleges.

This book was carefully researched and written to help you prepare for the PANCE. The chapters in this book explain what it is like to work as a physician assistant and review important material that is likely to appear on the PANCE. Completing the comprehensive practice tests in this book will help you pass this exam.

To get the most out of this book, take the time to read each section carefully and thoroughly.

- **Part I** provides an overview of Physician Assistant basics. It offers information on topics like the type of education you need to become a physician assistant, responsibilities, where PAs work, salary and benefits, and tools and technology. Part I also outlines the steps you need to take to become a Physician Assistant, including preparing and applying to take the PANCE and how to become licensed.

- **Part II** is a diagnostic test that will help you to understand your strengths and weaknesses. Take this test under normal testing conditions; go to a quiet setting and time yourself. Use your score from the diagnostic test as a guide to what you need to study. Then, take the practice tests to see how you've improved. This section introduces you to the kinds of questions you will see on the PANCE, including questions about laboratory and diagnostic studies, history taking and performing physical examinations, formulating the most likely diagnosis, health maintenance, clinical intervention, pharmaceutical therapeutic, and applying basic science concepts.

- **Part III** is an overview of the types of questions you will see on the PANCE. A chapter is devoted to each subject area on the test. Each chapter begins with a review of the question type, tips for answering those particular questions, and practice questions with answer explanations. The multiple-choice questions in the practice exercises are just like those on the actual test. Complete the questions and study the answer explanations. You can learn a great deal from these explanations. Even if you answered the questions correctly, you may discover a new tip in the explanation that will help you answer other questions.

- When you feel that you are well prepared, move on to **Part IV**—the Practice Tests. The questions on the practice tests in this book are not the actual questions that you will see on the exam. If possible, try to work through an entire exam in one sitting. The actual test is administered in 4 blocks of 90 questions with 90 minutes allowed for each block. Do not look at the correct answer until you have completed the exam. Remember, these tests are for practice and will not be scored. Take the time to learn from any mistakes you may make.

- The **Appendices** offer additional information about recertification, accredited physician's assistant programs, and other possible careers in medicine.

SPECIAL STUDY FEATURES

Master the Physician Assistant National Certifying Exam is designed to be as user-friendly as it is complete. To this end, it includes several features to make your preparation more efficient.

Overview

Each chapter begins with a bulleted overview listing the topics covered in the chapter. This allows you to target the areas in which you are most interested.

Summing It Up

Each chapter ends with a point-by-point summary that reviews the most important items in the chapter. The summaries offer a convenient way to review key points.

SPECIAL ADVERTISING SECTION

At end of the book, don't miss the special section of ads placed by Peterson's preferred clients. Their financial support helps make it possible for Peterson's Publishing to continue to provide you with the highest-quality test-prep, educational exploration, and career-preparation resources you need to succeed on your educational journey.

YOU ARE WELL ON YOUR WAY TO SUCCESS

You have made the decision to become a dental hygienist and have taken a very important step in that direction. Master the Physician Assistant National Exam will help you score high and prepare you for everything you need to know on the day of the exam and beyond it. Good luck!

FIND US ON FACEBOOK®

Join the career conversation on Facebook® at www.facebook.com/careerresource and receive additional test-prep tips and advice. Peterson's resources are available to help you do your best on these important exams—and others in your future.

Peterson's publishes a full line of books—career preparation, test prep, education exploration, and financial aid. Peterson's publications can be found at high school guidance offices, college libraries and career center, and your local bookstore and library. Peterson's books are now also available as eBooks.

We welcome any comments or suggestions you may have about this publication. Your feedback will help us make educational dreams possible for you—and others like you.

PART I

PHYSICIAN ASSISTANT BASICS

CHAPTER 1

What Physician Assistants Do

OVERVIEW

- **What is a physician assistant?**
- **Responsibilities of a physician assistant**
- **How do physicians and physician assistants differ?**
- **History of the National Commission on Certification of Physician Assistants (NCCPA)**
- **Traits and skills of a physician assistant**
- **Where physician assistants work**
- **Tools and technology used by physician assistants**
- **Necessary education and experience**
- **Competencies required of a physician assistant**
- **Required *Code of Conduct* and penalties**
- **The PANCE and the PANRE**
- **Salary and benefits**
- **Advancement opportunities**
- **Related occupations**
- **For more information**
- **Summing it up**

WHAT IS A PHYSICIAN ASSISTANT?

Physician assistants, commonly called PAs in the medical field, are health-care professionals who work under the supervision of licensed physicians and surgeons. PAs are important members of the health-care team, which also consists of physicians, nurses, and medical assistants. PAs work with other health-care professionals to provide patients with quality care. After completing specific medical training, PAs may perform many of the same tasks as physicians. A PA might take medical histories, examine and diagnose patients, write prescriptions, order laboratory tests and X-rays, perform minor procedures, and offer follow-up care.

For many patients, PAs are the medical professional whom they see most frequently. Patients who make same-day appointments for minor illnesses are often referred to PAs since the physicians' schedules may be booked far in advance. Thus, PAs often become the first line of care offered to these patients. It is often the PA who must decide if a patient's illness is minor or requires more investigation. Some PAs also act as surgical assistants who routinely provide pre-operative and post-operative care and assist during surgeries. In rural or low-income areas, PAs may actually act as the sole medical provider at a medical practice in which a physician only sees patients in the office one or two days a week. PAs may also perform home-care or nursing-home visits to care for patients who are unable to leave their homes. In these situations, PAs report back to their supervising physician, as required by law, regarding each patient.

PAs work in many different medical fields. They are widely employed in medical practices ranging from dermatology, pediatrics, family practice, and obstetrics and gynecology. They may also provide first-line medical care in hospitals. Since PAs are hired to perform specific functions within a medical practice, their job description varies according to the type of practice. This flexibility in job function gives PAs one of the broadest and most interesting careers in the medical arena.

As you can see by looking at these job postings from www.paworld.net, PAs work in a variety of medical settings and may have wide-ranging responsibilities:

> We are seeking a **Physician Assistant** for a rural health position in western Illinois. Will consider experienced providers only. Schedule will be M–F, 7:30 a.m.–5:30 p.m. No weekends, no call. May work 4–9s. Anticipated patient volume will be 22–26 ppd. Salary will be $80–95k (with incentives) plus a comprehensive benefit package including 4 wks vacation, malpractice, health insurance, retirement and one wk paid CME. Relocation assistance and separate sign-on bonus.

> We are seeking a **Physician Assistant** for a general surgery position in Arizona. Will consider an experienced provider or strong new graduate. Duties will be multispecialty—Orthopedics, OB/GYN, Urology and other General Surgery. Schedule will be M–F, 7 a.m.–3:30 p.m. Periodic weekend call. Salary will be $90–150k+ with potential incentives. Comprehensive benefit package includes 3 wks paid time off, malpractice, health insurance, retirement and 1 wk paid CME. Relocation assistance and separate sign-on bonus.

RESPONSIBILITIES OF A PHYSICIAN ASSISTANT

Most PAs have the following responsibilities:

- See patients by appointment as part of a medical practice
- Record patients' medical histories
- Examine and treat patients
- Order laboratory tests, as needed
- Order X-rays, sonograms, Magnetic Resonance Imaging (MRI), and CT scans, as needed
- Diagnose and treat patient illnesses
- Perform minor procedures such as casting, splinting, and suturing
- Record notes regarding patients' diagnoses and treatments
- Write prescriptions
- Order medical supplies
- Supervise medical assistants and technicians
- Record notes regarding a patient's illness or progress
- Provide counseling or therapy
- Provide care to home-bound or nursing-home patients
- Provide pre-operative or post-operative care
- Assist during surgical procedures

- Frequently consult with supervising physician regarding patient care
- Research current medical information to improve knowledge base

HOW DO PHYSICIANS AND PHYSICIAN ASSISTANTS DIFFER?

While physicians and PAs perform many of the same duties, PAs have certain limitations. Physicians make decisions unilaterally and without consultation. PAs, on the other hand, must provide medical care under the supervision and guidance of a physician. While PAs may perform a broad range of duties, their assignments may not fall outside the supervising physician's expertise or exceed the training that the PA has received in a specific area. For example, a PA focusing on low-risk prenatal care in an obstetrics/gynecology practice would not be able to treat a patient's gastroenterological issues. For diagnosis and treatment, the patient must be referred to a more experienced physician with a broader range of knowledge encompassing the digestive system.

PAs frequently handle a practice's routine medical cases and refer the more challenging cases to their supervising physicians. While a PA can typically handle about 80 percent of the same medical cases that a physician can handle, some complicated medical issues such as cancer or uncommon diagnoses must be referred to the supervising doctor.

Both PAs and physicians undergo medical training. PA programs last approximately 2 years, while physicians' education lasts much longer. After completing an undergraduate degree, physicians attend medical school for 4 years to earn the designation of Medical Doctor (MD). Physicians must then complete up to 7 years of graduate medical education, including a hospital residency, in which the doctors train in a specific field. At this point, a doctor may become board certified in a chosen specialty. While PAs possess a broad base of medical knowledge, they do not receive the same amount of specialized, hands-on medical training as physicians do.

Interestingly, PAs possess more flexibility regarding an area of medical concentration than is granted to physicians. If physicians choose to change their area of specialization, they must return to school and reenter a residency program for training. For example, if after practicing obstetrics and gynecology for several years, a physician decides to work as a pathologist, he or she must reenroll full time (most likely leaving the obstetrics/gynecology practice) in a pathology residency to train for the new area of expertise. When a PA decides to change specialties, he or she simply finds a new job in a different medical specialty; no additional education is required.

Physicians also typically earn more money than PAs, even though they may work similar hours side-by-side in a medical practice. Likewise, some patients prefer to see a physician as opposed to a PA, even though the PA may be more experienced.

Both physicians and PAs may perform the following duties:

- Provide well- and sick-care to patients as part of a medical practice
- Record patients' medical histories and notes regarding treatment
- Examine and treat patients
- Write prescriptions
- Order laboratory tests, X-rays, MRIs, and CT scans
- Provide diagnostic and follow-up care to patients
- Remain up-to-date on medical care and advances in their areas of expertise

Only physicians may perform these duties:

- Supervise physician assistants (PAs)
- Bear the ultimate responsibility for providing and coordinating a patient's medical care
- Determine the guidelines and scope of each medical professional in a medical office or setting
- Perform surgeries and in-office procedures
- Undergo in-depth training specific to a medical specialty
- Act as partners in their medical practices
- Work in administrative or research capacities

What Is a Medical Assistant?

Physician assistants should not be confused with medical assistants, who commonly work in medical practices. While PAs diagnose and treat patients as doctors would, medical assistants perform basic administrative and clinical tasks such as handling medical records, answering phones, checking patients' vital signs, recording patients' medical histories, administering injections, drawing blood, and scheduling patient tests and procedures.

Medical assistants typically attend a 2-year community college program to earn an associate degree, whereas a physician assistant's 2-year program is more akin to medical school. This extra training is reflected in the salary difference between the two positions. Medical assistants earn an average of $25,000 per year, while physician assistants earn approximately $75,000 per year.

HISTORY OF THE NATIONAL COMMISSION ON CERTIFICATION OF PHYSICIAN ASSISTANTS (NCCPA)

Physicians have historically trained medical assistants to provide mid-level care while under their supervision. In the 1940s, a physician named Amos Johnson hired and trained Henry "Buddy" Treadwell to act in the capacity of a PA in Dr. Johnson's rural-based general practice in Garland, North Carolina. At the same time, Dr. Johnson actively discussed the idea of PAs with another physician, Dr. Eugene Stead, and with general medicine residents at Duke University's School of Medicine. In response to a lack of available civilian doctors for the general population during World War II, Dr. Stead then developed a 3-year fast-track training program for medical students. Once they completed this program, they were allowed to run the Emory University and Grady Hospitals in Atlanta, Georgia, on a short-term basis.

While doctors came to depend upon mid-level providers, they called for more rigorous training, as well as formal recognition and certification of PAs. In a 1961 issue of the *Journal of the American Medical Association*, a physician named Dr. Charles Hudson asserted that former military corpsmen should be allowed to act as "mid-level" providers when they returned home from active duty. Also in 1961, Surgeon General William Stewart created the MEDEX (Medicine Ex-tension) model, which allowed students and graduates to provide medical care in rural, medically underserved communities. Later, in 1965, three former Navy corpsmen enrolled in the country's first formalized PA training program at Duke University. Upon their graduation in 1967, Victor H. Germino, Kenneth F. Ferrell, and Richard J. Scheele became the United States' first formally trained PAs who were charged to operate in the arena between a nurse and a doctor. Their graduation date, October 6, was later designated as "National PA Day" by the American Academy of Physician Assistants (AAPA).

Throughout the 1970s, the PA profession became more formalized. Duke University hosted a series of conferences designed to further develop and standardize PA educational programs, study and promote the concept of PAs, and develop legislation to govern the profession. In 1970, the American Medical Association (AMA) officially recognized the profession of PA, and the American Registry of Physician Associates (ARPA) formed in North Carolina to certify graduates of approved medical programs or others who could demonstrate the knowledge and skills required of PAs. At the same time, the AMA began developing and codifying specific national guidelines for PAs. In 1972, the National Board of Medical Examiners created a nationally standardized certification examination for the graduates of accredited PA programs. In 1975, the National Commission on Certification of Physician Assistants (NCCPA) incorporated and began sponsoring the national certifying exam, which grew to later include clinical skills problems. Through the NCCPA, PAs received the first time-limited certificates.

In the 1980s, PAs heightened their status within the medical community and cemented their role as medical providers. A 1981 study by the Kaiser-Permanente Health Services Research Center, now the Center for Health Research, titled *Staffing Primary Care in 1990: Physician Replacement and Costs Savings,* concluded that PAs based in an HMO can adequately provide 79 percent of the care traditionally performed by primary care physicians at 50 percent of the cost. To standardize the quality of care provided by PAs, the NCCPA redesigned the Physician Assistant National Certifying Examination (PANCE) to encompass a general knowledge component, an extended core component in surgery or primary care, and a clinical skills problems component (CSPs). In 1988, the first edition of the *Journal of the American Academy of Physician Assistants* (*JAAPA*) was published.

As the PA profession continued to mature, its membership grew and became an integrated part of mainstream medical care. By 1997, about 28,000 PAs actively practiced medicine in the United States, its territories, and the District of Columbia, though they were only authorized to write prescriptions in 40 states. The NCCPA also redesigned the PANCE by eliminating the clinical skills problems and the extended core component. PAs with a surgical concentration could now take a stand-alone certifying surgery examination. In 1998, the NCCPA began requiring PAs to pass the Physician Assistant National Recertifying Examination (PANRE) within two attempts to maintain their certification as a PA.

The PA profession boomed and gained full legal status across the United States in 2000 when Mississippi became the final state to grant PAs legal status and medical privileges. As of 2002, 45,000 PAs actively worked across the United States, and a survey of PAs revealed a 90-percent job satisfaction rate. In 2010, 75,000 PAs practiced in all areas of the medical and surgical professions.

The great majority of physicians and patients report satisfaction with PAs, according to the 2005 survey of health-care employers who employ PAs (www.nccpa.net):

Statement Regarding Physician Assistants	Percentage of Physicians Agreeing with Statement
PAs have helped increase the number of patients seen by medical providers.	94%
Using PAs has shortened the amount of time that patients must wait for appointments.	92%
Using PAs allows patients more time to ask questions during office visits.	91%

TRAITS AND SKILLS OF A PHYSICIAN ASSISTANT

While PAs work in different types of medical practices and in hospitals, they must all possess a battery of physical, emotional, personality, and technical traits to succeed as a PA.

Physical Characteristics

PAs must possess the physical stamina to work a flexible schedule that may include nights and weekends. A typical workweek might involve 60–70 hours of work when a PA is on call. These long hours require PAs to stay healthy. A strong immune system is important, as PAs are often exposed to the viruses and diseases constantly present in a medical practice. Good eyesight and coordination are also essential traits, since PAs must often perform medical procedures that require them to see details at close range while executing quick, coordinated movements, such as when suturing or examining a squirming child.

Emotional Characteristics

Since medical providers largely depend on their patients to provide personal health information, PAs must be active and attentive listeners. This often requires patience, since some patients may have difficulty communicating or may have a limited proficiency in English. Regardless of a patient's cultural, socioeconomic, physical, or mental status, a PA must be willing and able to treat all individuals with respect and empathy—without becoming emotionally attached. Since PAs work as part of a health-care team, they must be true team players. They must get along with a variety of employees—ranging from medical assistants to supervising physicians—and have great respect for their colleagues.

Personality Traits

As is true of many health-care professionals, PAs must be able to think critically while quickly sorting through a patient's symptoms to accurately diagnose and prescribe treatment. In addition to possessing analytical problem-solving skills, PAs must be accurate and detail-oriented professionals who work well under pressure-filled, possibly life-threatening, situations. They must also be reliable, flexible, and cooperative to help ensure that the health-care team is providing the best possible service to patients at all times.

Technical Skills

PAs must possess excellent technical skills. While PAs are required to use the practice's computer system with ease, they must also operate a wide variety of high-tech medical instruments and machines. Since many medical offices only maintain electronic records, medical professionals must possess the skills to access, amend, and add to the electronically stored information. They must also use the available resources to help maintain a wide range of medical information and to stay up-to-date on current medical research.

WHERE PHYSICIAN ASSISTANTS WORK

As of 2010, about 75,000 PAs worked in the U.S. medical industry in areas ranging from general practice to surgical care. PAs serve patients in rural areas, inner-cities, medical practices, hospitals, nonprofit clinics, HMO outpatient care centers, and the military.

Fifty-three percent of the PAs in the United States work in doctors' offices, providing primary care in family medicine, internal medicine, pediatrics, and obstetrics and gynecology. Some specialize in dermatology, radiology, otolaryngology, psychiatry, or pathology. Twenty-four percent of PAs provide care in surgical subspecialties and hospitals. The remaining 23 percent serve in HMO outpatient care centers, colleges, universities, and the federal government. PAs typically work for an employer, as opposed to being self-employed. Some PAs work part time in hospitals or clinics.

TOOLS AND TECHNOLOGY USED BY PHYSICIAN ASSISTANTS

As you know, PAs must be comfortable utilizing technology, as well as a wide variety of medical tools and devices. Since PAs work across the entire medical spectrum, the tools and technology they employ varies by assignment. The most commonly used tools are the following:

- Stethoscopes to listen to sounds related to the heart and lungs
- Hypodermic needles, including intramuscular subcutaneous needles, to administer injections and IVs
- Ophthalmoscopes to examine the interior of the eye
- Otoscopes to examine the external canal and tympanic membrane of the ear
- Spinal trays or needles, such as bone marrow biopsy and lumbar puncture equipment
- Surgical clamps, such as bull dog nose clamps and vascular straight aortic clamps
- Forceps, such as artery and mosquito artery forceps, to seize or hold objects
- Vacuum blood collection tubes or containers, such as evacuated blood collection or vacutainer tubes
- Suture kits to suture or stitch skin wounds
- Oxygen, respiratory, and cardio-pulmonary equipment

PAs commonly use the following types of technology:

- Laptop computers to access and add to patient data. Many medical offices have now replaced paper-and-pencil medical charts with electronic data that is accessed via laptop computer when a provider sees a patient.
- Internet browser software to research medical data.
- Medical software that provides and stores patient charts and data.
- Spreadsheet software to access patient records.
- Word-processing software to write notes regarding patients.
- E-mail and personal digital assistants (PDAs) to communicate with co-workers and the supervising physician.
- Electrocardiographs to detect heart disease.
- X-ray equipment to view bones.

NECESSARY EDUCATION AND EXPERIENCE

While PA candidates may take different paths toward becoming a physician assistant, all PAs must graduate from an accredited physician assistant training program and pass the Physician Assistant National Certifying Exam (PANCE). Though 76 percent of students entering PA programs hold bachelor's degrees, some students may possess associate degrees and may have previously worked as emergency medical technicians (EMTs), military medics, and paramedics. As PAs become more widely utilized across the medical spectrum, the competition to gain admission to PA programs increases. One hundred forty accredited PA programs exist across the United States. Most of these programs are affiliated with accredited 2- and 4-year medical colleges or universities or schools of allied health. Depending on the academic program, it is possible to earn an associate, a baccalaureate, or a master's degree in a PA program. Regardless of the degree obtained, all candidates are held to the same medical standards, must pass the same initial certifying exam, will take at least 100 hours of continuing medical education every 2 years, and must sit for the same recertifying exam by the end of the sixth year of certification.

For candidates with undergraduate degrees, a major in a hard science with course work in anatomy, biology, chemistry, college math, computer science, English, nutrition, organic chemistry, physiology, psychology, social science, and statistics is recommended. As admission to PA programs becomes more competitive, preference is often given to candidates possessing multiple years of clinical experience as a nurse, a paramedic, or an emergency medical technician.

A typical PA education program lasts approximately 24 to 27 months. While most programs are full-time, some allow students to attend part-time if they are changing careers. The first 9 to 12 months of training consists mainly of classroom work, which is followed by 9 to 15 months of supervised clinical rotations in a hospital or medical office setting. A conventional PA program would encompass the following classroom and clinical work:

1st Year of Study	2nd Year of Study
Classroom Studies	Clinical Rotations
Anatomy	Family Medicine
Physiology	Internal Medicine
Pharmacology	Emergency Medicine
Microbiology	Pediatrics
Biochemistry	Geriatric Medicine
Pathology	Obstetrics/Gynecology
Clinical Lab	Surgery
Health Promotion	Orthopedics
Clinical Medicine	Psychiatry
Medical Ethics	Radiology

After graduating from an accredited PA program, PA candidates must sit for and pass the Physician Assistant National Certifying Exam (PANCE), as well as take at least 100 hours of continued medical education every 2 years. PAs must then take a recertification test every 6 years to maintain their national certification.

COMPETENCIES REQUIRED OF A PHYSICIAN ASSISTANT

In 2003, the American Academy of Physician Assistants (AAPA), the Accreditation Review Commission on Education for the Physician Assistant, Inc. (ARC-PA), the National Commission on Certification of Physician Assistants (NCCPA), and the Physician Assistant Education Association (PAEA) combined their efforts to outline six key competencies that are to be incorporated into the practice, training, continuing education, and evaluation of PAs.

As presented on the NCCPA Web site (www.nccpa.net), PA competencies include the following.

Medical Knowledge

PAs are expected to understand the risk factors, symptoms, appropriate treatments, and possible preventions for a wide range of medical conditions. Additionally, PAs should be able to select and interpret diagnostic and lab tests while also managing chronic, general medical, and general surgical conditions.

Interpersonal and Communication Skills

As you learned earlier, PAs are expected to effectively listen to and ethically respond to patients' concerns. PAs must also work effectively with other health-care professionals and accurately document medical information for therapeutic, legal, and financial purposes.

Patient Care

When interacting with patients, PAs must demonstrate caring and respectful behavior while performing medical procedures, counseling, or educating individuals. PAs must also gather essential and accurate information and consider the patients' preferences when carrying out patient management plans.

Professionalism

PAs are expected to adhere to legal and regulatory requirements involving medications, prescriptions, and the PA–physician supervisory relationship. PAs must also commit themselves to ongoing professional development, as well as maintain standards of patient confidentiality and informed consent.

Practice-Based Learning and Improvement

PAs are expected to analytically integrate the most recent scientific research with a patient's symptoms to formulate a treatment plan in concert with other members of the health-care delivery team. PAs must also utilize available technology to manage information, access online medical information, and support self-education.

Systems-Based Practice

PAs must commit to practicing cost-effective health care without compromising the quality of care. This includes working with a team of health-care professionals to improve the delivery of health-care services. At the same time, PAs must understand and work within the funding sources and payment systems that provide coverage for patient care.

REQUIRED *CODE OF CONDUCT* AND PENALTIES

Once PAs become licensed and obtain the designation of PA-C (Physician Assistant-Certified), they are required to meet the standards of knowledge and care outlined by the National Commission on Certification of Physical Assistants (NCCPA). Additionally, PAs are expected to adhere to standards of ethical practice and professionalism.

The NCCPA *Code of Conduct*

The NCCPA's *Code of Conduct* for Certified and Certifying Physician Assistants (www.nccpa.net) sets the professional and ethical standards PAs are required to adhere to while working as medical professionals. According to the NCCPA, certified PAs must not engage in the following behaviors:

- Cheating or other dishonest behavior that violates exam security (including unauthorized reproducing, distributing, displaying, discussing, sharing, or otherwise misusing test questions or any part of test questions) before, during, or after an NCCPA examination

- Submitting a document with misstatements or omitted facts to the NCCPA in order to obtain eligibility, certification, or recertification (or to help others do so)

- Manufacturing, modifying, reproducing, distributing, or using a fraudulent certificate (one not authorized by the NCCPA)

- Representing oneself as a Physician Assistant-Certified (PA-C) designee unless one holds current NCCPA certification

- Failing to inform the NCCPA when one knows of or has evidence of cheating on or misuse of questions from an NCCPA examination, fraudulent use of an NCCPA card, certificate or other document or misrepresentation of NCCPA certification status by a PA or any other individual

Certified or certifying PAs must comply with any laws, regulations, or standards that apply to the state, medical setting, and jurisdiction in which they practice medicine. The following standards of conduct must be followed by PAs:

- Respect appropriate professional boundaries in regards to their interactions with patients

- Avoid behaviors that might threaten the health, well-being, or safety of patients, aside from reasonable risks taken to assist the patient while delivering health care

- Recognize and understand professional and personal limitations

- Refrain from practicing medicine under impairment from substance abuse, cognitive deficiency, or mental illness

- Demonstrate and maintain the ability to engage in the practice of medicine within their chosen areas of practice safely and competently

Source: *National Commission on Certification of Physician Assistants*

Submitting a Complaint Against a Certified Physician Assistant

Maintaining your certification as a PA depends upon your continued demonstration of medical competence and ethical behavior in regard to patient care. Any formal complaint regarding a certified PA must be submitted to the NCCPA in writing and signed by the complainant. The complaint should include all relevant details regarding the allegations against the PA. All written complaints must include the following statement:

I authorize NCCPA to release this complaint and all other supporting material I have provided or may provide in the future to the subject of the complaint, members of NCCPA's Board of Directors, attorneys and others as deemed appropriate by NCCPA or as required by law.

—*National Commission on Certification of Physician Assistants (www.nccpa.net)*

Upon receiving a written complaint, the NCCPA will acknowledge its receipt and notify the PA involved within 30 days. The PA may then respond to the complaint in writing, and/or request a phone interview or a personal conversation with the NCCPA Review Panel. The PA will then be notified of the Review Panel's decision within 14 days. A PA who wishes to appeal the Review Board's decision has 30 days to do so. The NCCPA has the sole discretion to determine if a claim warrants investigation. The NCCPA may instead turn the complaint over to additional licensing boards or legal authorities. An NCCPA investigation may or may not be made public.

Penalties for Violating the Physician Assistant Code of Conduct

PAs who violate the NCCPA *Code of Conduct* can have their certification denied or revoked. As stated by the NCCPA, the penalties for violating the ethical standards expected of a certified PA are as follows:

- Giving or receiving assistance during the NCCPA certifying examination
- Removing test materials from the testing site with the intent of reproducing or redistributing them
- Submitting inaccurate information to the NCCPA
- Submitting or assisting another person in submitting fraudulent information regarding one's education or certification

Several circumstances result in automatic revocation of a PA's license. A PA who is declared mentally incompetent by a court of law can no longer work as a PA. Likewise, a PA who pleads no contest to a felony crime that involves the practice of medicine will automatically lose his or her license. Finally, if a PA whose license is revoked by the federal government for any reason will automatically lose the right to practice as a PA.

The following actions by a PA may lead to revocation of the individual's certification, a letter of censure, or any other actions deemed appropriate by the NCCPA:

- Conviction of or pleading no contest to a felony
- Revocation of one's credentials to practice medicine on a military base or in a military setting
- Evidence of medical incompetence or unprofessional or unethical conduct
- Violating the NCCPA *Code of Conduct*
- Not reporting legal, regulatory, or credentialing actions to the NCCPA in a timely manner

If a PA's certification is revoked for a specific time period, he or she may reapply to become a certified PA once the time period expires.

THE PANCE AND THE PANRE

The Physician Assistant National Certifying Exam (PANCE)

After graduating from a certified physician assistant program, you must pass the Physician Assistant National Certifying Exam (PANCE) before you can earn the designation of PA-C (Physician Assistant-Certified). The PANCE is a multiple-choice exam designed to assess the minimum competencies necessary to become an entry-level PA. The exam consists of 360 questions broken into six 60-minute blocks of time for a total of 6 hours.

The PANCE focuses on knowledge from seven core areas:

1. **History Taking and Performing Physical Examinations** (16 percent of the PANCE): Questions in this area assess a PA's ability to evaluate a patient's symptoms or clinical results, assess a patient's risk factors due to family history and lifestyle, and demonstrate techniques of performing physical examinations.
2. **Using Laboratory and Diagnostic Studies** (14 percent of the PANCE): These questions address a PA's knowledge of diagnostic and lab tests, costs and benefits of diagnostic tests and procedures, and the use of normal and abnormal lab test results.
3. **Formulating the Most Likely Diagnosis** (18 percent of the PANCE): Questions in this area focus on a PA's ability to interpret a patient's history, the findings of a physical exam, and the results of laboratory tests to arrive at an accurate diagnosis.
4. **Clinical Intervention** (14 percent of the PANCE): These questions examine a PA's knowledge of procedures, non-pharmaceutical therapies, what constitutes an emergency, surgical principles, wound healing, and indications for hospital admission.
5. **Clinical Therapeutics** (18 percent of the PANCE): Test items of this type focus on the properties, side effects, contraindications, and dosage of drugs.
6. **Health Maintenance** (10 percent of the PANCE): Test questions in this area address immunizations, epidemiology, risk factors for conditions, and patient education for preventable conditions and lifestyle changes.
7. **Applying Scientific Concepts** (10 percent of the PANCE): These questions examine pathology, anatomy, physiology, sexuality, and microbiology.

The Physician Assistant National Recertifying Exam (PANRE)

After becoming initially certified, a PA must complete 100 hours of classroom education each year and must pass a recertification exam between years 5 and 6 to maintain an active PA certification. After this time, a PA must be recertified. Recertification is obtained when a PA takes and passes the Physician Assistant National Recertifying Examination (PANRE).

The PANRE consists of 300 timed, multiple-choice questions administered in a traditional, proctored test-taking setting. PAs may not use any books or reference materials while taking the test.

In the past, PAs who had accrued and documented 100 points through educational or experiential activities were eligible to take a test called Pathway II. This was an at-home exam in which PAs were given 6 weeks to answer 300 multiple-choice questions, using books or other reference materials. Beginning in 2011, however, the Pathway II will no longer be given.

SALARY AND BENEFITS

The job outlook for a PA is very good. The demand for PAs, especially in rural and inner-city areas, is projected to grow 39 percent between 2008 and 2018. New PAs will be needed to replace retiring PAs working in primary care medical practices, clinics, hospitals, and medical centers.

According to the U.S. Bureau of Labor Statistics, the 2008 median annual wage for PAs was $81,230, with the middle 50 percent of PAs earning between $68,210 and $97,070. The lowest 10 percent earned less than $51,360, and the highest 10 percent earned more than $110,240.

The median wage for PAs varies based on the work setting:

- **General medical and surgical hospitals:** $84,550
- **Outpatient care centers:** $84,390
- **Physicians' offices:** $80,440
- **Government setting:** $78,200
- **College and university clinics:** $74,200

The American Academy of Physician Assistants' 2008 Census reported the median income for PAs in full-time clinical practice as $85,710. While salary varies by specialty, practice setting, and geographical area, first-year PAs earn approximately $74,470.

Benefits vary depending on where a PA works, but many employers pay the professional liability insurance, registration fees with the Drug Enforcement Administration (DEA), state licensing fees, and credentialing fees for PAs. Many also provide PAs with more common benefits, such as health insurance, a retirement plan, and paid vacation and sick time.

ADVANCEMENT OPPORTUNITIES

PAs may gain additional responsibilities and earn a higher salary by attaining additional education in a specialty. Postgraduate educational programs for certified PAs are available in areas such as internal medicine, rural primary care, emergency medicine, surgery, pediatrics, neonatology, and occupational medicine. Regardless of the educational level attained, a PA must always work under the supervision of a physician.

RELATED OCCUPATIONS

Those with similar educational backgrounds and health-care experience may seek other jobs related to the PA profession:

- **Audiologists:** Audiologists work with people who have hearing problems and other ear-related issues. Audiologists test patients' hearing, diagnose and formulate plans to assist patients with hearing loss, and fit patients for hearing aids and other auditory equipment. Audiologists work in doctors' offices, schools, and private practices.

- **Occupational therapists:** Occupational therapists help to improve patients' ability to perform daily tasks in their living and working environments. Occupational therapists typically work with individuals whose health has been compromised due to an illness, a developmental delay, an injury, or a mental impairment. Occupational therapists work in hospitals, nursing-care facilities, medical offices, and educational settings.

- **Physical therapists:** Physical therapists work to rehabilitate or improve patients' ability to move and function in their daily lives. Physical therapists tend to people who have suffered an injury or have a physical disability. Physical therapists work in private practice, physicians' offices, and hospitals.

- **Registered nurses (RNs):** Registered nurses treat and provide emotional support to patients. They act as first-line medical personnel who record patients' histories and symptoms, perform diagnostic tests, administer medication, and explain follow-up treatment. Nurses work in private medical practices, hospitals, and public health services.

- **Speech-language pathologists:** Speech-language pathologists help to improve patients' ability to speak. They work with people who have difficulty speaking due to developmental delays, learning disabilities, or mental or physical disabilities. Speech-language pathologists work in schools, hospitals, private medical practices, and nursing-care centers.

FOR MORE INFORMATION

For more information regarding a career as a PA, contact the following organizations:

- American Academy of Physician Assistants (www.aapa.org)
- Accreditation Review Commission on Education for the Physician Assistants, Inc. (www.arc-pa.org)
- Physician Assistant Education Association (www.paeaonline.org)
- National Commission on Certification of Physician Assistants (www.nccpa.net)
- Physician Assistant History Center (http://pahx.org)

SUMMING IT UP

- Physician assistants (PAs) act as medical professionals under the supervision of certified surgeons and physicians. After receiving specific medical training, PAs can perform many of the same tasks as physicians. These tasks include taking medical histories, examining and diagnosing patients, writing prescriptions, ordering laboratory tests and X-rays, performing minor procedures, and providing follow-up care.

- While physicians and PAs perform many of the same functions, physicians can make decisions unilaterally and without consultation, whereas physician assistants must provide medical care under the supervision and guidance of a physician. PA training programs last approximately two years, while physicians must additionally partake in several years of internship or residency in their chosen medical fields.

- The PA profession officially began in 1965, when three former Navy corpsmen enrolled in the country's first formalized physician assistant training program at Duke University in Durham, North Carolina. In the 1970s, the American Medical Association (AMA) officially recognized the profession of physician assistant, and physician assistants received the first time-limited certificates through the National Commission on Certification of Physician Assistants (NCCPA). As of 2010, 75,000 PAs practice in the United States with full legal status in all areas of the medical and surgical professions.

- Physician assistants must be able to work long hours on their feet while performing a variety of tasks. They must be able to closely listen to and observe a patient's history and symptoms to analytically reach an accurate diagnosis. PAs must be willing to continuously educate themselves so they can stay abreast of current medical knowledge.

- PAs typically work in medical practices providing primary care, but also work in subspecialty practices, HMOs, outpatient care centers, clinics, and the military.

- PAs must be comfortable utilizing technology to research and access patient records, as well as a wide variety of medical tools and devices to examine and treat patients.

- PAs must adhere to the *Code of Conduct* outlined by the National Commission on Certification of Physical Assistants (NCCPA). Penalties for non-adherence include censure; denial or revocation of a PA's eligibility, certification, recertification, or proficiency recognition; or revocation of a PA's certification.

- To become a physician assistant, one must attend an accredited PA training program. A typical PA education program lasts approximately 24 to 27 months, with the first year consisting mainly of classroom education and the second year as clinical rotations. After graduating from an accredited PA program, PA candidates must sit for and pass the Physician Assistant National Certifying Exam (PANCE), as well as take at least 100 hours of classroom education every two years and retake the recertification test every six years to maintain their national certification.

- The American Academy of Physician Assistants (AAPA), Accreditation Review Commission on Education for the Physician Assistant, Inc. (ARC-PA), National Commission on Certification of Physician Assistants (NCC-PA), and Physician Assistant Education Association (PAEA) have defined and delineated the six key competencies of Medical Knowledge, Interpersonal and Communication Skills, Patient Care, Professionalism, Practice-Based Learning and Improvement, and Systems-Based Practice that are to be incorporated into the practice, training, continuing education, and evaluation of PAs.

- After graduating from a certified physician or surgeon assistant program, an individual must pass the PANCE before gaining the designation of PA-C (Physician Assistant-Certified). A certified physician assistant must pass a recertification exam between years five and six of certification. To do so, a PA may elect to take the Physician Assistant National Recertifying Examination (PANRE). The former Pathway II examination (an at-home recertification exam) is no longer given.

- The demand for physician assistants is expected to grow in coming years. PAs do have the opportunity to gain additional responsibilities and earn a higher salary by attaining additional education in a specialty.

- Audiologists, occupational therapists, physical therapists, registered nurses, and speech-language pathologists possess similar educational backgrounds, health-care experience, and levels of responsibility as physician assistants.

CHAPTER 2

Becoming a Physician Assistant

OVERVIEW

- Step 1: Complete an accredited formal education program
- Step 2: Register for the Physician Assistant National Certifying Exam (PANCE)
- Step 3: Prepare for the written exam
- Step 4: Take the written exam
- Step 5: Find and apply for physician assistant jobs
- Step 6: Receive a job offer
- Step 7: Explore opportunities for advancement
- Summing it up

STEP 1: COMPLETE AN ACCREDITED FORMAL EDUCATION PROGRAM

To qualify for the Physician Assistant National Certifying Exam (PANCE), you must first complete a physician assistant (PA) education program accredited by the Accreditation Review Commission on Education for the Physician Assistant (ARC-PA). This organization sets quality standards for and evaluates PA education programs to ensure that standards are met and maintained.

Accredited Physician Assistant Programs

Most accredited PA education programs are affiliated with 2- and 4-year medical colleges, universities, or schools of allied health. Many programs offer students the chance to pursue an associate, bachelor's, or master's degree. Though a non-accredited program may teach you the same information about diagnosing and treating medical problems, completion of such a program will not qualify you to take the PANCE. In addition, individuals who have earned a medical degree in a country other than the United States must complete an accredited PA education program in the United States to be eligible to take the PANCE.

Though PA programs have become increasingly competitive as the medical field expands, these programs usually consist of students from a variety of academic and professional backgrounds. A typical candidate for a PA program possesses college credit and approximately 4 years of experience in the health-care field. Many applicants are nurses, emergency medical technicians (EMTs), and paramedics. Though some candidates entering PA education programs have undergraduate degrees, this is not a prerequisite for program admission.

Exceptions

According to the National Commission on Certification of Physician Assistants (NCCPA), in addition to candidates who have recently graduated from an accredited PA program, individuals who have met one of the following requirements are also eligible to take the PANCE:

- Those who completed a PA program or a surgeon assistant program between July 1, 1994, and December 31, 2000, that was accredited by the Commission on Accreditation of Allied Health Education Programs (CAAHEP)
- Those who completed a PA program or a surgeon assistant program between January 1, 1986, and June 30, 1994, that was accredited by the American Medical Association (AMA) Committee on Allied Health Education and Accreditation
- Those who completed either a program to educate and train assistants to the primary care physician or a surgeon assistant program between January 1, 1977, and December 31, 1985, that was accredited by the American Medical Association (AMA) Committee on Allied Health Education and Accreditation
- Those who completed a program to educate and train assistants to the primary care physician or a surgeon assistant program before December 31, 1976, that was accredited by the American Medical Association (AMA) Council on Medical Education
- Those who have been awarded unrestricted eligibility and have previously taken the initial certification examination administered by the NCCPA

STEP 2: REGISTER FOR THE PHYSICIAN ASSISTANT NATIONAL CERTIFYING EXAM (PANCE)

Eligibility

To obtain the designation of PA-C (Physician Assistant-Certified), you must first pass the Physician Assistant National Certifying Exam (PANCE) within 180 days of graduating from an accredited PA education program. The computer-based exam is offered at more than 200 Pearson Vue testing centers throughout the United States. You can find where the center nearest you is located by visiting the National Commission on Certification of Physician Assistants (NCCPA) testing section of the Pearson Vue Web site (www.pearsonvue.com/nccpa/). Though the NCCPA once offered an at-home alternative to the PANCE called Pathway II, this exam is no longer a certification option.

About 4 months before graduation, your PA education program should provide eligibility information to the NCCPA. After you graduate, you are eligible to take the PANCE.

Registration

PA-C candidates can register for the PANCE right on the NCCPA Web site (https://www.nccpa.net/PA/login.aspx). To do so, first create a record with the NCCPA, using your birth date and Social Security number or NCCPA identification (ID) number to log into the system. You also have to pay the $425 exam fee, which you can do online using a credit card.

If you have a documented disability that limits your ability to see, hear, walk, speak, breathe, read, concentrate, communicate, or perform other essential activities, you may request special testing accommodations under the Americans with Disabilities Act (ADA).

The NCCPA Web site provides a Special Testing Accommodations Request form, which you fill out and mail or fax to the NCCPA when you register. You also need to send a signed, typed statement describing your condition in detail, as well as a statement from a qualified medical professional. The NCCPA will review these documents and decide what special testing accommodations (e.g., an individual testing room, a reader, extended testing time, etc.) it will provide under the circumstances.

Once you register for the exam, you must take the exam within a 180-day timeframe. After you register, you will receive a confirmation e-mail containing directions on how to access, download, and print the permit required for admission to the Pearson Vue testing center. Your permit will be available until your examination window has expired.

Restrictions

Individuals may take the PANCE up to six times within a 6-year period. If a candidate does not pass the exam within the 6 years or within six attempts, he or she will lose eligibility to take the exam. Candidates may take the PANCE only once within a 90-day period or three times in a calendar year, and applicants may only register for one exam window at a time.

STEP 3: PREPARE FOR THE WRITTEN EXAM

The PANCE is a computer-based, multiple-choice test consisting of 360 questions focusing on medical and surgical knowledge. All questions address either medical disorders and diseases or the skills and knowledge that a PA must have when confronted with those disorders and diseases.

The test items are developed by committees consisting of PAs and physicians. Each committee member independently writes a set of questions, referencing a current medical textbook (not journal articles) in each question. After being reviewed by medical editors and content experts, questions are selected for pre-testing. Each PANCE test contains both scored and unscored items.

According to the National Commission on Certification of Physician Assistants Web site (www.nccpa.net), the PANCE questions address each organ system in the following percentages:

Organ System	Percent of Exam Content
Cardiovascular	16%
Pulmonary	12%
Endocrine	6%
Eyes, Ears, Nose, and Throat (EENT)	9%

Gastrointestinal/Nutritional	10%
Genitourinary	6%
Musculoskeletal	10%
Reproductive	8%
Neurologic System	6%
Psychiatry/Behavioral	6%
Dermatologic	5%
Hematologic	3%
Infectious Diseases	3%
TOTAL	**100%**

From: The National Commission on Certification of Physician Assistants (NCCPA)
(www.nccpa.net/ExamsContentBPOrgans.aspx)

Since the PANCE focuses on critical thinking across the spectrum of medicine, PA-C candidates must have a comprehensive review plan to adequately prepare for the exam. First, allocate study time appropriately according to study area. Since nearly half of the test items address the cardiovascular, pulmonary, gastrointestinal/nutritional, and musculoskeletal systems, test-takers should spend about half of their time studying these areas. When studying each organ system, be sure to address the following five subtopics: embryology, gross anatomy, physiology, pathology, and pharmacology.

Instead of focusing on individual organ systems, some PA education programs use a problem-based or integrated curriculum. Students in these programs may want to organize their studying based on the following categories: behavioral sciences, physiology, immunology, genetics, anatomy, pathology, pharmacology, microbiology, and biochemistry.

While each student must develop his or her own way of preparing for the PANCE, you can use several tried-and-true study methods to help you achieve a high score on the PANCE:

- **Form a study group.** Group learning allows each member to benefit from the knowledge of others in the group. Together, you can decide which study methods work best for the specific people involved. Your group may prefer to review a specific organ system each time you meet. Your group might also choose to assign a specific system for each group member to research and develop questions to help the other group members retain the information. Study groups work well for students who learn best through speaking and conversation; however, make sure you are doing more studying than socializing. Otherwise, you are not really helping each other become certified PAs.

- **Create note cards.** Some students find that studying with note cards helps them remember information before a test. Creating note cards encourages you to separate large amounts of information into individual, concise thoughts that are easier to absorb and remember. For instance, you might create a note card for each individual disease or disorder that might appear on the PANCE. Note cards are also an effective way to study on your own, without the support of a group. This method works well for students who remember facts by writing or typing them.

- **Review all notes and textbooks.** Review the material in your course textbooks and read through your notes to refresh your memory of the information you learned in your PA program. You might find that making outlines helps you organize the information so that it makes more sense to you and is easier to remember.

- **Use pictures and diagrams.** Drawing and labeling organ systems, creating diagrams of processes, and color-coding material frequently helps learners store and recall information. This practice is most effective for visual learners, who often summon information they have studied by picturing their study tools, such as diagrams or color-coded notes.

- **Practice, practice, practice.** Be sure to review test questions similar to those on the PANCE and take PANCE practice tests. You will find a diagnostic test and two full-length practice tests in this book. When taking these tests, you should try to simulate the actual test-taking situation by eliminating distractions and tracking the amount of time it takes you to complete a full-length test. If you find that you are exceeding the 360 total minutes you are allotted for the official test, brainstorm methods for improving your time, such as spending less time on questions you do not know and dedicating more study time to the difficult topics you encounter during the practice tests. The more you practice before taking the PANCE, the less anxiety you will experience on test day.

- **Allow plenty of time to study.** The PANCE is designed to test the knowledge a PA-C candidate has gained during a 2-year PA education program. You will need plenty of time to review all you have learned and to practice answering PANCE-style questions. Start studying for the exam several months before you intend to take it. Keep in mind that engaging in frequent, short study sessions over a long period of time is generally more effective than cramming all the information into a few intense study sessions over a short period of time.

- **Take care of yourself.** Getting adequate sleep, staying hydrated, and eating well are all great practices to help ensure that you are in the best frame of mind to take the PANCE.

Test Day Tips

Taking a test can be a stressful experience. When the time comes to take the PANCE, make sure you are prepared, focused, and feeling great. This section of the chapter provides you with suggestions to help you do your best on test day.

- **Get at least 8 hours of sleep the night before the test.** Sleep refreshes the body and allows you to think clearly. Do not take sleep-inducing medications the night before the test, as they may cause you to feel groggy instead of alert the next day.

- **Eat well.** Be sure to eat a healthy meal that will keep you full during the test so you are not distracted by hunger. Some foods, however, are heavy or filled with sugar. Avoid carbohydrate-loaded foods such as pasta and potatoes, and instead opt for fresh fruits and veggies, eggs, and fish.

- **Avoid drinking caffeinated beverages or energy drinks that may overly excite you, making it difficult to concentrate.** Also stay away from alcohol the night before the test. Alcohol causes dehydration. Staying hydrated with water or fruit juice will help you feel great on test day.

- **Stop studying.** Holding back from studying may seem counterproductive, but any information that you try to pack into your brain the night before the test will be quickly forgotten before it becomes a part of your long-term memory. Instead of cramming for the test the night before, try to find a relaxing activity such as reading a book or seeing a movie.

- **Gather the items that you will need for the test.** To avoid a chaotic rush the morning of the test, gather what you need ahead of time. Remember to bring two forms of ID to the testing center. One of the two IDs must contain a permanently affixed photo with your name and signature. The other should show your printed name and signature. Candidates will not be admitted to the test if the names on both forms of ID do not match the candidate's name as it is registered with NCCPA.

STEP 4: TAKE THE WRITTEN EXAM

Test-takers may not bring any personal belongings into the room in which they will test. This includes items such as purses and handbags, hats, backpacks, books, notes, study materials, calculators, watches of any kind, electronic paging devices, recording or filming devices, radios, cellular phones, or food and beverages. Candidates will be given a location in which to store personal items and may access them at "scheduled" breaks. During an "unscheduled" break, candidates may not access any personal items other than medication, food, or drink. To avoid any appearance of cheating, it is probably best not to take any study-related materials into or access any medically related Web sites or information while at the test center.

The Test-Taking Experience

Upon arrival at the Pearson VUE test center, the staff will teach you how to use the computer equipment and will allow you to complete a short tutorial before taking the test.

The 6-hour PANCE exam includes 360 multiple-choice questions administered in six sections, or blocks, of 60 questions. Test-takers are allotted with 60 minutes to complete each block. The 5-hour PANRE (the recertification exam) includes 300 multiple-choice questions administered in five blocks of 60 questions with 60 minutes to complete each block.

Each PANCE test-taker will receive 45 minutes of scheduled break time throughout the testing day. Though test-takers are responsible for monitoring their own break time, the testing facility times breaks using a digital finger/palm scan. Test-takers must use the scanner each time they enter or leave the room. If a test-taker exceeds the 45-minute total, the additional break time is deducted from her or his exam time.

At the end of each block, a message will appear recommending a "scheduled" break. Though you may not think you need a break, it is a good idea to rest your mind and prepare for what is to come.

If you take a break before completing a block of questions, this is considered an "unscheduled" break. Unscheduled break time is deducted from the hour allotted to complete a block of questions, so it is best not to take unscheduled breaks unless they are absolutely necessary.

Test-Taking Tips

Test-taking can be a stressful experience. To reduce your test-taking anxiety and help yourself concentrate to achieve a better score, keep in mind the following tips:

- **Do not panic.** You have learned and studied the test material for 2 years and have most likely studied several weeks or months for the PANCE. You are prepared to score high on the exam, so instead of worrying, focus on the content and feel confident about your chances for success.

- **Read each question carefully.** Be sure to understand exactly what each question is asking. Some questions will be more complicated than others. Regardless, make sure you fully comprehend each question before you answer it.

- **Anticipate the answer.** Before answering the question, analyze the clues and decide what the answer may be. Then look at the choices to see if your preliminary answer is listed.

- **Read all the answer choices and think before answering the question.** If one of the choices matches your anticipated answer, mark it. If you are unsure of the answer, eliminate possible choices using logic and general knowledge. Then choose an answer from the remaining possibilities.

- **Visualize the answer.** When confronted with a situational question, visualize the patient in the situation. Thinking about the patient in a real-life scenario may make the test question seem more real and the correct answer to it more logical.

- **Do not get confused.** Test writers sometimes include distracting answers or answers containing bias. Analyze each answer choice individually, looking for distracters or bias that might mask the correct answer.

- **Look for the general over the exceptional.** The PANCE tends to focus on general concepts rather than on atypical medical conditions that would rarely be seen by a PA. When in doubt, look for the common answer over the rare occurrence.

- **Notice patterns.** In graphs and tables, look for trends and patterns. In all questions, be alert for relationships between the question choices. Try to link the questions to previously learned information.

- **Anticipate the intent of the question.** When in doubt, think about what the question is intended to gauge. Which skill is being tested? Is the question trying to determine if you can recognize the general symptoms of an illness or is it asking you to diagnose a less-common disease?

- **Block out any previous negative test-taking experience.** If you have ever had a tough time with a standardized test in the past, try not to bring that negative experience into the testing room with you. Remember, the PANCE is not designed to torment and trick the test-taker! The aim of the PANCE is to ensure the skill level and knowledge of PAs.

Once you have mastered the PANCE, you are ready to start looking for employment as a PA!

STEP 5: FIND AND APPLY FOR PHYSICIAN ASSISTANT JOBS

During the last semester of a PA education program, you should begin searching for permanent employment. A thorough job search takes several months. Give yourself a jump start on the process by applying for jobs before graduation. If a prospective employer shows interest or offers you a job, as long as you pass the PANCE when you graduate, you will be able to begin work.

Creating a Credential File and Resume

Before applying for professional jobs, assemble a file documenting your education and professional experiences. Gather and maintain the following documents in both paper and electronic format, if possible:

- Educational transcripts
- Any type of verifications of applicable experiences such as internships, jobs, or volunteer work in the medical field
- Letters of recommendation from people who have supervised you in school or at work
- A list of references and their contact information (phone numbers, physical addresses, and e-mail addresses)
- Medical certifications such as life-support training, EMT certifications, nursing certifications, etc.
- Cover letter
- Resume

Bring these documents to interviews, or mail copies to prospective employers. The more prepared you are, the more you will impress them, which will increase your chances of getting the job.

Writing a Resume

Your resume represents you when you cannot represent yourself in person. Your resume should accurately convey your professional experience, education, and drive to succeed in your field. It should also be well-written and well-organized to help you stand out among a sea of prospective PAs.

Before creating a resume, look at a variety of other resumes and notice how they are organized. Consider the information you will include on your resume, and decide on a format that best showcases your specific job qualifications and professional attributes. If you think you need help putting your resume together, go to your college's or university's career center and ask for assistance. The job search professionals who work there most likely will have helpful information to share with you.

When you are ready to assemble your information, start by creating a list of educational, job, and life experiences to include on your resume. Though your resume should be a unique representation of you, the following points are important to keep in mind as you organize your information and decide what to include:

- Organize your information under headings such as Educational Experience, Work Experience, Research Experience, and Publications.

- Account for gaps in time. If you worked for several years between completing your undergraduate degree and entering a PA education program, account for that time by detailing the work and volunteer experiences you took on during the transition.

- Explain how each educational, job, or volunteer experience prepared you to be a PA. Use dynamic language and details in your descriptions—there is nothing interesting about a dry list of activities that do not provide details or explanation.

- Include only specific information that is relevant to your future job as a PA. Do not include hobbies or lengthy details about jobs that have no relation to your field or future duties.

- Include a summary statement containing key words pertaining to the job. Many potential employers place resumes in a database. Then, when they need to fill a certain position, they search the database using key words that describe the ideal candidate and his or her skills. Adding these key words to your resume will help ensure that your resume is retrieved and read by potential employers. To find the right key words, read several job postings and note the specific language that employers use to describe a qualified potential employee.

- Carefully proofread the resume and ask several others to proofread it as well. Mistakes on a resume show a lack of attention to detail and poor dedication to professional excellence.

Locating Potential Jobs

Before you begin applying for jobs, consider the following:

- **Medical field:** Do you want to work in primary care or in a specialization?

- **Medical setting:** Do you want to work in a hospital or a private practice?

- **Location:** Do you want to work in a rural or an urban area?

- **Licensing requirements:** If you are considering relocating to another state, research any specific licensing requirements in that state.

The following are some good places to look for work:

- **PA Job Link** (http://www.healthecareers.com/aapa/): According to the American Academy of Physician Assistants (AAPA), PA Job Link connects 70,000 PAs with prospective employers. In addition to job postings, the site also features interview tips, a resume builder, and newsletters.

- **Career center at your college or university:** Be sure to utilize any job-search resources offered by the career center at your college or university. The trained job counselors can help candidates locate and apply for jobs, create a resume, and brush up on interviewing techniques.

- **Medical Workers.com** (www.medicalworkers.com/physician-assistant-jobs.aspx): This site contains job listings for PAs, nurses, pharmacists, and physicians.

- **PA World** (https://www.paworld.net/jobs/): This site contains job listings for PAs and nurse practitioners.

Interviewing for Positions

Preparation is the key to acing an interview. Keep these tips in mind:

- Research the practice or hospital where you are interviewing. Know enough about the practice or hospital to ask specific questions about it. This shows the interviewer that you care about the organization.

- Practice potential questions and answers. Anticipate what interviewers will ask and craft possible answers ahead of time. You can start by researching interview questions online and composing possible answers to these questions. Then ask a friend or colleague to conduct a mock interview. Remember that the best interviews become conversations between the interviewer and job candidate rather than an awkward series of questions and answers. Also keep in mind that initial interviews are not the time to ask about benefits, on-call rotations, or salary; these topics should only be approached by the interviewer, if at all.

- Print several copies of your resume. Take at least two copies to the interview.

- Prepare a professional outfit to wear to job interviews.

- Practice relaxation techniques. The more relaxed you are, the better you will be able to sell yourself to a potential employer. Staying relaxed also allows you to pay attention to what an interviewer is telling you about the job, so that you can decide if it is the right fit for you.

STEP 6: RECEIVE A JOB OFFER

Compensation plans for PAs vary with each medical practice and setting. You will probably learn the details of a potential employer's compensation plans once you receive a job offer. While many job offers are delivered orally, either in person or over the phone, it is a good idea to get the details of the offer in writing as well. This not only protects you legally by spelling out the terms of the agreement, it also allows you to review the specific details several times before accepting or declining the offer.

Before accepting a job offer, be sure to come to an agreement and understand each of the following aspects of the employment package:

- The start date of employment
- Details about training or introductory programs for new employees
- Termination provisions and legitimate reasons for dismissal
- Frequency of formal job performance reviews (and what criteria will be used to evaluate PAs)
- Payment of bonuses and the guidelines for receiving them
- Vacation time and sick days
- Procedures for interacting with, seeking advice from, and having paperwork signed by the supervising physician
- Working times (including on-call rotation), location of work, and specific duties within the practice
- Specifics of malpractice insurance and who will pay for it
- Credentials and hospital privileges, if any, that the PA must possess

- How compensation will be determined (i.e., salary, hourly, percentage of fees billed or collected, or salary plus bonus based on productivity)

- Coverage of miscellaneous fees such as professional, licensure, and hospital medical staff fees; cost of books and professional journals; and Drug Enforcement Administration (DEA) registration fees

- Specifics regarding health insurance, sick leave, disability, life insurance, and retirement plan

- Non-compete clause, if applicable

STEP 7: EXPLORE OPPORTUNITIES FOR ADVANCEMENT

After gaining the certification of PA-C, PAs may choose to continue their education by enrolling in a clinical post-graduate program. The 12- to 24-month programs focus on specific medical or surgical specialties. As of 2011, four accredited clinical postgraduate PA education programs exist in the United States:

1. Mayo Clinic in Arizona: Postgraduate PA Hospital Internal Medicine Residency
2. Arrowhead Orthopedics in California: Postgraduate PA Orthopedics Residency
3. Johns Hopkins Hospital Department of Surgery in Maryland: Postgraduate PA Surgical Residency
4. Duke University Medical Center in North Carolina: Postgraduate PA Surgical Residency

In addition to seeking further education, PAs may choose to pursue a buy-in arrangement with a medical practice. Doing so first involves valuing the practice's assets and its physical site. Any agreement should explicitly detail the cost of the buy-in and the terms of payment, how long it will take to become a full partner, the expectations of each business partner, and to what extent each co-owner will be involved in the practice's business decisions.

SUMMING IT UP

- Before you can become a physician assistant (PA), you must complete a program that is accredited by the Accreditation Review Commission on Education for the Physician Assistant (ARC-PA) and pass the Physician Assistant National Certifying Exam (PANCE).

- The PANCE is a computer-based, multiple-choice test containing 360 questions about medical and surgical knowledge. All questions address either medical disorders and diseases or the skills and knowledge that a PA must have when confronted with these disorders and diseases.

- You will be given 6 hours to complete the task. You will also have a 45-minute break during the test.

- Before you begin looking for work as a PA, you should prepare a resume and a cover letter and gather the following supplies: educational transcripts, verifications of experiences such as internships, letters of recommendation from past employers and educators, a list of references and their contact information, and medical certifications, if applicable.

- While there are many different styles of resumes, you should choose one that best conveys your education and experience.

- You can pursue many different avenues when looking for work. One good choice is the PA Job Link (http://www.healthecareers.com/aapa/).

- Preparation is the key to succeeding on a job interview. Get ready ahead of time, and learn as much about the organization as you can.

- Before accepting a job offer, be sure that you understand all aspects of the employment package, including working time, vacation and sick leave, and who will pay for malpractice insurance.

PART II

Diagnosing Strengths and Weaknesses

ANSWER SHEET PRACTICE TEST 1: DIAGNOSTIC

1. Ⓐ Ⓑ Ⓒ Ⓓ Ⓔ	37. Ⓐ Ⓑ Ⓒ Ⓓ Ⓔ	73. Ⓐ Ⓑ Ⓒ Ⓓ Ⓔ	109. Ⓐ Ⓑ Ⓒ Ⓓ Ⓔ	145. Ⓐ Ⓑ Ⓒ Ⓓ Ⓔ
2. Ⓐ Ⓑ Ⓒ Ⓓ Ⓔ	38. Ⓐ Ⓑ Ⓒ Ⓓ Ⓔ	74. Ⓐ Ⓑ Ⓒ Ⓓ Ⓔ	110. Ⓐ Ⓑ Ⓒ Ⓓ Ⓔ	146. Ⓐ Ⓑ Ⓒ Ⓓ Ⓔ
3. Ⓐ Ⓑ Ⓒ Ⓓ Ⓔ	39. Ⓐ Ⓑ Ⓒ Ⓓ Ⓔ	75. Ⓐ Ⓑ Ⓒ Ⓓ Ⓔ	111. Ⓐ Ⓑ Ⓒ Ⓓ Ⓔ	147. Ⓐ Ⓑ Ⓒ Ⓓ Ⓔ
4. Ⓐ Ⓑ Ⓒ Ⓓ Ⓔ	40. Ⓐ Ⓑ Ⓒ Ⓓ Ⓔ	76. Ⓐ Ⓑ Ⓒ Ⓓ Ⓔ	112. Ⓐ Ⓑ Ⓒ Ⓓ Ⓔ	148. Ⓐ Ⓑ Ⓒ Ⓓ Ⓔ
5. Ⓐ Ⓑ Ⓒ Ⓓ Ⓔ	41. Ⓐ Ⓑ Ⓒ Ⓓ Ⓔ	77. Ⓐ Ⓑ Ⓒ Ⓓ Ⓔ	113. Ⓐ Ⓑ Ⓒ Ⓓ Ⓔ	149. Ⓐ Ⓑ Ⓒ Ⓓ Ⓔ
6. Ⓐ Ⓑ Ⓒ Ⓓ Ⓔ	42. Ⓐ Ⓑ Ⓒ Ⓓ Ⓔ	78. Ⓐ Ⓑ Ⓒ Ⓓ Ⓔ	114. Ⓐ Ⓑ Ⓒ Ⓓ Ⓔ	150. Ⓐ Ⓑ Ⓒ Ⓓ Ⓔ
7. Ⓐ Ⓑ Ⓒ Ⓓ Ⓔ	43. Ⓐ Ⓑ Ⓒ Ⓓ Ⓔ	79. Ⓐ Ⓑ Ⓒ Ⓓ Ⓔ	115. Ⓐ Ⓑ Ⓒ Ⓓ Ⓔ	151. Ⓐ Ⓑ Ⓒ Ⓓ Ⓔ
8. Ⓐ Ⓑ Ⓒ Ⓓ Ⓔ	44. Ⓐ Ⓑ Ⓒ Ⓓ Ⓔ	80. Ⓐ Ⓑ Ⓒ Ⓓ Ⓔ	116. Ⓐ Ⓑ Ⓒ Ⓓ Ⓔ	152. Ⓐ Ⓑ Ⓒ Ⓓ Ⓔ
9. Ⓐ Ⓑ Ⓒ Ⓓ Ⓔ	45. Ⓐ Ⓑ Ⓒ Ⓓ Ⓔ	81. Ⓐ Ⓑ Ⓒ Ⓓ Ⓔ	117. Ⓐ Ⓑ Ⓒ Ⓓ Ⓔ	153. Ⓐ Ⓑ Ⓒ Ⓓ Ⓔ
10. Ⓐ Ⓑ Ⓒ Ⓓ Ⓔ	46. Ⓐ Ⓑ Ⓒ Ⓓ Ⓔ	82. Ⓐ Ⓑ Ⓒ Ⓓ Ⓔ	118. Ⓐ Ⓑ Ⓒ Ⓓ Ⓔ	154. Ⓐ Ⓑ Ⓒ Ⓓ Ⓔ
11. Ⓐ Ⓑ Ⓒ Ⓓ Ⓔ	47. Ⓐ Ⓑ Ⓒ Ⓓ Ⓔ	83. Ⓐ Ⓑ Ⓒ Ⓓ Ⓔ	119. Ⓐ Ⓑ Ⓒ Ⓓ Ⓔ	155. Ⓐ Ⓑ Ⓒ Ⓓ Ⓔ
12. Ⓐ Ⓑ Ⓒ Ⓓ Ⓔ	48. Ⓐ Ⓑ Ⓒ Ⓓ Ⓔ	84. Ⓐ Ⓑ Ⓒ Ⓓ Ⓔ	120. Ⓐ Ⓑ Ⓒ Ⓓ Ⓔ	156. Ⓐ Ⓑ Ⓒ Ⓓ Ⓔ
13. Ⓐ Ⓑ Ⓒ Ⓓ Ⓔ	49. Ⓐ Ⓑ Ⓒ Ⓓ Ⓔ	85. Ⓐ Ⓑ Ⓒ Ⓓ Ⓔ	121. Ⓐ Ⓑ Ⓒ Ⓓ Ⓔ	157. Ⓐ Ⓑ Ⓒ Ⓓ Ⓔ
14. Ⓐ Ⓑ Ⓒ Ⓓ Ⓔ	50. Ⓐ Ⓑ Ⓒ Ⓓ Ⓔ	86. Ⓐ Ⓑ Ⓒ Ⓓ Ⓔ	122. Ⓐ Ⓑ Ⓒ Ⓓ Ⓔ	158. Ⓐ Ⓑ Ⓒ Ⓓ Ⓔ
15. Ⓐ Ⓑ Ⓒ Ⓓ Ⓔ	51. Ⓐ Ⓑ Ⓒ Ⓓ Ⓔ	87. Ⓐ Ⓑ Ⓒ Ⓓ Ⓔ	123. Ⓐ Ⓑ Ⓒ Ⓓ Ⓔ	159. Ⓐ Ⓑ Ⓒ Ⓓ Ⓔ
16. Ⓐ Ⓑ Ⓒ Ⓓ Ⓔ	52. Ⓐ Ⓑ Ⓒ Ⓓ Ⓔ	88. Ⓐ Ⓑ Ⓒ Ⓓ Ⓔ	124. Ⓐ Ⓑ Ⓒ Ⓓ Ⓔ	160. Ⓐ Ⓑ Ⓒ Ⓓ Ⓔ
17. Ⓐ Ⓑ Ⓒ Ⓓ Ⓔ	53. Ⓐ Ⓑ Ⓒ Ⓓ Ⓔ	89. Ⓐ Ⓑ Ⓒ Ⓓ Ⓔ	125. Ⓐ Ⓑ Ⓒ Ⓓ Ⓔ	161. Ⓐ Ⓑ Ⓒ Ⓓ Ⓔ
18. Ⓐ Ⓑ Ⓒ Ⓓ Ⓔ	54. Ⓐ Ⓑ Ⓒ Ⓓ Ⓔ	90. Ⓐ Ⓑ Ⓒ Ⓓ Ⓔ	126. Ⓐ Ⓑ Ⓒ Ⓓ Ⓔ	162. Ⓐ Ⓑ Ⓒ Ⓓ Ⓔ
19. Ⓐ Ⓑ Ⓒ Ⓓ Ⓔ	55. Ⓐ Ⓑ Ⓒ Ⓓ Ⓔ	91. Ⓐ Ⓑ Ⓒ Ⓓ Ⓔ	127. Ⓐ Ⓑ Ⓒ Ⓓ Ⓔ	163. Ⓐ Ⓑ Ⓒ Ⓓ Ⓔ
20. Ⓐ Ⓑ Ⓒ Ⓓ Ⓔ	56. Ⓐ Ⓑ Ⓒ Ⓓ Ⓔ	92. Ⓐ Ⓑ Ⓒ Ⓓ Ⓔ	128. Ⓐ Ⓑ Ⓒ Ⓓ Ⓔ	164. Ⓐ Ⓑ Ⓒ Ⓓ Ⓔ
21. Ⓐ Ⓑ Ⓒ Ⓓ Ⓔ	57. Ⓐ Ⓑ Ⓒ Ⓓ Ⓔ	93. Ⓐ Ⓑ Ⓒ Ⓓ Ⓔ	129. Ⓐ Ⓑ Ⓒ Ⓓ Ⓔ	165. Ⓐ Ⓑ Ⓒ Ⓓ Ⓔ
22. Ⓐ Ⓑ Ⓒ Ⓓ Ⓔ	58. Ⓐ Ⓑ Ⓒ Ⓓ Ⓔ	94. Ⓐ Ⓑ Ⓒ Ⓓ Ⓔ	130. Ⓐ Ⓑ Ⓒ Ⓓ Ⓔ	166. Ⓐ Ⓑ Ⓒ Ⓓ Ⓔ
23. Ⓐ Ⓑ Ⓒ Ⓓ Ⓔ	59. Ⓐ Ⓑ Ⓒ Ⓓ Ⓔ	95. Ⓐ Ⓑ Ⓒ Ⓓ Ⓔ	131. Ⓐ Ⓑ Ⓒ Ⓓ Ⓔ	167. Ⓐ Ⓑ Ⓒ Ⓓ Ⓔ
24. Ⓐ Ⓑ Ⓒ Ⓓ Ⓔ	60. Ⓐ Ⓑ Ⓒ Ⓓ Ⓔ	96. Ⓐ Ⓑ Ⓒ Ⓓ Ⓔ	132. Ⓐ Ⓑ Ⓒ Ⓓ Ⓔ	168. Ⓐ Ⓑ Ⓒ Ⓓ Ⓔ
25. Ⓐ Ⓑ Ⓒ Ⓓ Ⓔ	61. Ⓐ Ⓑ Ⓒ Ⓓ Ⓔ	97. Ⓐ Ⓑ Ⓒ Ⓓ Ⓔ	133. Ⓐ Ⓑ Ⓒ Ⓓ Ⓔ	169. Ⓐ Ⓑ Ⓒ Ⓓ Ⓔ
26. Ⓐ Ⓑ Ⓒ Ⓓ Ⓔ	62. Ⓐ Ⓑ Ⓒ Ⓓ Ⓔ	98. Ⓐ Ⓑ Ⓒ Ⓓ Ⓔ	134. Ⓐ Ⓑ Ⓒ Ⓓ Ⓔ	170. Ⓐ Ⓑ Ⓒ Ⓓ Ⓔ
27. Ⓐ Ⓑ Ⓒ Ⓓ Ⓔ	63. Ⓐ Ⓑ Ⓒ Ⓓ Ⓔ	99. Ⓐ Ⓑ Ⓒ Ⓓ Ⓔ	135. Ⓐ Ⓑ Ⓒ Ⓓ Ⓔ	171. Ⓐ Ⓑ Ⓒ Ⓓ Ⓔ
28. Ⓐ Ⓑ Ⓒ Ⓓ Ⓔ	64. Ⓐ Ⓑ Ⓒ Ⓓ Ⓔ	100. Ⓐ Ⓑ Ⓒ Ⓓ Ⓔ	136. Ⓐ Ⓑ Ⓒ Ⓓ Ⓔ	172. Ⓐ Ⓑ Ⓒ Ⓓ Ⓔ
29. Ⓐ Ⓑ Ⓒ Ⓓ Ⓔ	65. Ⓐ Ⓑ Ⓒ Ⓓ Ⓔ	101. Ⓐ Ⓑ Ⓒ Ⓓ Ⓔ	137. Ⓐ Ⓑ Ⓒ Ⓓ Ⓔ	173. Ⓐ Ⓑ Ⓒ Ⓓ Ⓔ
30. Ⓐ Ⓑ Ⓒ Ⓓ Ⓔ	66. Ⓐ Ⓑ Ⓒ Ⓓ Ⓔ	102. Ⓐ Ⓑ Ⓒ Ⓓ Ⓔ	138. Ⓐ Ⓑ Ⓒ Ⓓ Ⓔ	174. Ⓐ Ⓑ Ⓒ Ⓓ Ⓔ
31. Ⓐ Ⓑ Ⓒ Ⓓ Ⓔ	67. Ⓐ Ⓑ Ⓒ Ⓓ Ⓔ	103. Ⓐ Ⓑ Ⓒ Ⓓ Ⓔ	139. Ⓐ Ⓑ Ⓒ Ⓓ Ⓔ	175. Ⓐ Ⓑ Ⓒ Ⓓ Ⓔ
32. Ⓐ Ⓑ Ⓒ Ⓓ Ⓔ	68. Ⓐ Ⓑ Ⓒ Ⓓ Ⓔ	104. Ⓐ Ⓑ Ⓒ Ⓓ Ⓔ	140. Ⓐ Ⓑ Ⓒ Ⓓ Ⓔ	176. Ⓐ Ⓑ Ⓒ Ⓓ Ⓔ
33. Ⓐ Ⓑ Ⓒ Ⓓ Ⓔ	69. Ⓐ Ⓑ Ⓒ Ⓓ Ⓔ	105. Ⓐ Ⓑ Ⓒ Ⓓ Ⓔ	141. Ⓐ Ⓑ Ⓒ Ⓓ Ⓔ	177. Ⓐ Ⓑ Ⓒ Ⓓ Ⓔ
34. Ⓐ Ⓑ Ⓒ Ⓓ Ⓔ	70. Ⓐ Ⓑ Ⓒ Ⓓ Ⓔ	106. Ⓐ Ⓑ Ⓒ Ⓓ Ⓔ	142. Ⓐ Ⓑ Ⓒ Ⓓ Ⓔ	178. Ⓐ Ⓑ Ⓒ Ⓓ Ⓔ
35. Ⓐ Ⓑ Ⓒ Ⓓ Ⓔ	71. Ⓐ Ⓑ Ⓒ Ⓓ Ⓔ	107. Ⓐ Ⓑ Ⓒ Ⓓ Ⓔ	143. Ⓐ Ⓑ Ⓒ Ⓓ Ⓔ	179. Ⓐ Ⓑ Ⓒ Ⓓ Ⓔ
36. Ⓐ Ⓑ Ⓒ Ⓓ Ⓔ	72. Ⓐ Ⓑ Ⓒ Ⓓ Ⓔ	108. Ⓐ Ⓑ Ⓒ Ⓓ Ⓔ	144. Ⓐ Ⓑ Ⓒ Ⓓ Ⓔ	180. Ⓐ Ⓑ Ⓒ Ⓓ Ⓔ

CHAPTER 3

Practice Test 1: Diagnostic

Directions: Choose the option that best answers the questions.

1. A 10-year-old girl is brought into the clinic by her parents. She has been suffering from diarrhea and excessive flatulence after certain meals that include foods like breads, pastas, cereals, etc. Her parents also report that she has begun to show signs of weight loss and her abdomen is slightly distended. Her stool is free of blood, she does not report any abdominal pain, and does not have a fever. Which diagnosis is the most likely to be correct given her symptoms?
   (A) Malabsorption
   (B) Volvulus
   (C) Celiac disease (celiac sprue)
   (D) Irritable bowel syndrome
   (E) Crohn's disease

2. An elderly male patient arrives in the emergency room and is believed to be suffering from congestive heart failure. You must determine whether the patient's heart failure is occurring predominantly on the left or right side of his heart. Which of the following symptoms would indicate right-sided failure?
   (A) Exertional dyspnea
   (B) Distended neck veins
   (C) Gallops
   (D) Non-productive cough
   (E) Orthopnea

3. A 47-year-old non-smoking male patient who was recently treated for a lung infection complains of difficulty breathing and a persistent cough that is frequently accompanied by odorous mucus. The patient's physical examination also reveals clubbing and localized chest crackles. He shows no signs of asthenia or hepatomegaly. Which of the following diagnoses is most likely to be correct?
   (A) Cystic fibrosis
   (B) Chronic obstructive pulmonary disease (COPD)

   (C) Asthma
   (D) Bronchogenic carcinoma
   (E) Bronchiectasis

4. A young female patient is believed to be suffering from pharyngitis and is exhibiting a tender anterior cervical adenopathy, a 100.2°F fever, pharyngotonsillar exudates, and a persistent cough. How many of the four Centor criteria is the patient presenting?
   (A) One
   (B) Two
   (C) Three
   (D) Four
   (E) None

5. An 18-year-old man is suffering from mumps and what appears to be a urinary tract infection. He has unilateral testicular swelling and a slight fever. A urinalysis study shows pyuria and bacteriuria accompanied by bacterial infection. Which of the following diagnoses is most likely to be accurate?
   (A) Prostatitis
   (B) Cystitis
   (C) Orchitis
   (D) Epididymitis
   (E) Pyelonephritis

6. A 40-year-old male is suffering from an anorectal abscess causing anal swelling, erythema, and difficulty with defecation. Which of the following treatments would be most appropriate in this case?
   (A) High fiber diet and increased fluids
   (B) Use of bulking agents and increased fluids
   (C) Surgical drainage and antibiotics
   (D) Surgical drainage and cleansing
   (E) Saline enema

7. A 38-year-old woman has come to the clinic complaining for the first time of sudden, severe stomach pain. She believes she has an ulcer. The examination shows no signs of any type of ulcer and she appears to be in good physical health. She is known to be an honest and upstanding individual and she has a history of anxiety and depression. From which of the following somatoform disorders is the patient most likely suffering?
   (A) Factitious disorder
   (B) Hypochondriasis
   (C) Pain disorder
   (D) Malingering
   (E) Conversion disorder

8. A 33-year-old male patient who is known to be a frequent runner arrives with severe pain in the area of his right ankle The patient reported that he was in the middle of a low-stress run when he began to feel the pain developing. The pain is located on the right posterior calf, 2 cm above the insertion of the Achilles tendon. Which of the following diagnoses is most likely to be correct?
   (A) Achilles tendonitis
   (B) Cruciate ligament injury
   (C) Ankle sprain/strain
   (D) Osgood-Schlatter disease
   (E) Meniscal injury

9. A male automobile accident victim arrives in the emergency room complaining of severe arm pain. The patient's left upper arm is significantly swollen and slightly deformed. He is not holding the arm to his chest and does not appear to have any injuries to his arm ligaments or rotor cuff. Which of the following diagnoses is most likely to be correct?
   (A) Fractured clavicle
   (B) Acromioclavicular separation
   (C) Humeral head fracture
   (D) Humeral shaft fracture
   (E) Supracondylar humerus fracture

10. A 63-year-old female patient with a history of kidney problems arrives at the clinic with new complaints. You diagnose her with early stage nephrotic syndrome. Which of the following treatments should be administered first?
   (A) Chlorothiazide
   (B) Warfarin
   (C) Captopril
   (D) NSAIDs
   (E) Rosuvastatin

11. An elderly female patient suffering from dysrhythmia arrives in the emergency room. She has a history of kidney problems and her laboratory findings indicate her serum potassium level is 6.5 mEq/L, her serum calcium level is 9 mg/dl, and her phosphate serum level is 1 mg/dL. Which of the following diagnoses is the most likely cause of her distress?
   (A) Hypokalemia
   (B) Hyperkalemia
   (C) Hypercalcemia
   (D) Hypocalcemia
   (E) Hyperphosphatemia

12. A 27-year-old female patient has been consistently suffering for some time from a severe mucus-producing cough, weakness, sinus pain, diarrhea, and abdominal pain. She has also been struggling with infertility issues. Her examination reveals clubbing and apical crackles. There is no reported bronchial damage. Which of the following diagnoses is most likely to be correct?
   (A) Chronic obstructive pulmonary disease (COPD)
   (B) Cystic fibrosis
   (C) Bronchiectasis
   (D) Asthma
   (E) Pleural effusion

13. A 48-year-old male patient has severe arthritic knee pain and shows signs of mucocutaneous lesions. He is sexually active and has been previously treated for chlamydial urethritis. His laboratory results return positive for HLA-B27. Of the following diagnoses, which is most likely to be correct?
   (A) Infectious arthritis
   (B) Psoriatic arthritis
   (C) Rheumatoid arthritis
   (D) Osteoarthritis
   (E) Reactive arthritis (Reiter syndrome)

14. An infant has received immunization with PRP-OMP for Haemophilus influenza type b at two and four months. Which of the following would be an appropriate age for the third dose?
   (A) 12 months
   (B) 10 months
   (C) 9 months
   (D) 8 months
   (E) 6 months

15. A 65-year-old female patient is being examined during the summer for a skin condition. Her right exterior forearm exhibits thick, solid, firm plaques and no scaling. She also has a few small lesions and reports a strong desire to scratch the affected area. Lichenification indicates that she has been scratching the area frequently. She has been treated for Atropic dermatitis in the past. Which of the following diagnoses is most likely to be correct?
    (A) Stasis dermatitis
    (B) Lichen simplex chronicus
    (C) Perioral dermatitis
    (D) Nummular dermatitis
    (E) Seborrheic dermatitis

16. Which of the following is the predominant presenting feature of acute thrombocytopenia?
    (A) Development of petechiae on the skin and mucus membranes
    (B) Development of petechiae, purpura, and hemorrhagic bullae on the skin and mucus membranes
    (C) Splenomegaly
    (D) Menorrhagia
    (E) Epistaxis

17. You are treating a 12-year-old male patient with peritonsillar cellulitis and abscess. You've administered the basic treatment, but you think he might require a tonsillectomy. Which of the following conditions would be an absolute indication for tonsillectomy?
    (A) Recurrent streptococcal infection
    (B) Chronic tonsillitis
    (C) Recurrent abscess
    (D) Deviation of the soft palate and uvula
    (E) Persistent marked asymmetry of tonsils

18. A 4-year-old male patient is brought to the clinic presenting with facial redness and a pink, lacy, macular rash on his torso. You suspect he is suffering from erythema infectiosum. Which of the following would be the cause of this condition?
    (A) Coxsackievirus
    (B) Human herpes virus
    (C) Rotavirus
    (D) Human parvovirus B19
    (E) Rubella virus

19. Which of the following individuals would be most likely to be at risk of á-Thalassemia?
    (A) A 35-year-old Italian man
    (B) A 41-year-old Chinese woman
    (C) A 24-year-old Greek man
    (D) A 53-year-old German man
    (E) A 30-year-old Tunisian woman

20. A 55-year-old female patient presents at the clinic with fever, cough, shortness of breath, and persistent hiccups. She also reports sharp chest pain that worsens when she coughs. You suspect she may be suffering from a pleural effusion and diagnostic testing reveals that the patient has an infection within the pleural space. Based on this information, from which type of pleural effusion is the patient suffering?
    (A) Exudate
    (B) Transudate
    (C) Empyema
    (D) Hemothorax
    (E) Pneumothorax

21. A 23-year-old female patient presents at the clinic with back and flank pain, persistent headache, hematuria, and renal colic. Her physical examination reveals palpable kidneys that feel tender. You suspect she may be suffering from polycystic kidney disease. Which of the following tests would you most likely use as your primary means of confirming your diagnosis?
    (A) CT scan
    (B) Excretory infusion urography
    (C) Ultrasonography
    (D) Urinalysis
    (E) Plain-film radiography

22. A 43-year old woman arrives at the clinic presenting with irritative voiding symptoms and hematuria. You suspect she may have a urinary tract infection and laboratory testing confirms a diagnosis of cystitis. Which of the following would most likely be considered the primary form of treatment for this condition?
    (A) Trimethoprim
    (B) Fluoroquinolone
    (C) Sulfamethoxazole
    (D) Hot sitz bath
    (E) Phenazopyridine

23. A 58-year-old male patient with a history of cirrhosis arrives in the emergency room after he starts vomiting blood. The patient also reports lightheadedness, excessive thirst, and reduced urination. You diagnose him with esophageal varices. Which of the following would be the most likely form of treatment for this condition?
    (A) Balloon tamponade
    (B) Endoscopic injection therapy
    (C) Transjugular intrahepatic portosystemic shunt (TIPS)
    (D) Liver transplant
    (E) Variceal litigation

24. A 15-year-old male patient arrives with an apparent infection in his left leg. The affected area is swollen, warm, and painful. Some parts of the skin have become darkened and have developed blisters and bullae with clear, yellowish fluid. Which of the following diagnoses is most likely to be correct?
    (A) Erysipelas
    (B) Impetigo
    (C) Necrotizing fasciitis
    (D) Cellulitis
    (E) Seborrheic dermatitis

25. A 41-year-old male patient arrives in the emergency room complaining of chest discomfort. He has a history of pericardial disorders. Which of the following sets of symptoms would indicate that he is suffering from cardiac tamponade?
    (A) Pleuritic substernal radiating chest pain and a friction rub
    (B) Slowly progressive dyspnea, fatigue, and weakness with edema, heptomegaly, and ascites
    (C) Chest pain with cough and dyspnea
    (D) Cough, fever, back and flank pain, and GI complaints
    (E) Tachycardia, tachypnea, narrow pulse pressure, and pulsus paradoxus

26. A 63-year-old female patient who has just had a hip replacement is started on Coumadin therapy and fitted with graduated compression stockings. You also prescribe pneumatic compression therapy. What condition arc these measures primarily aimed at preventing?
    (A) Pulmonary embolism
    (B) Thrombophlebitis
    (C) Chronic venous insufficiency

    (D) Deep vein thrombosis
    (E) Peripheral arterial disease

27. A 17-year-old male patient presents with a high fever, persistent headache, vomiting, and a stiff neck. He has also developed a petechial rash. You diagnose him with bacterial meningitis. Based on the patient's symptoms, which of the following pathogens is most likely to be the cause of the patient's condition?
    (A) *Streptococcus pneumoniae*
    (B) *Neisseria meningitidis*
    (C) *Haemophilus influenzae*
    (D) *Listeria monocytogenes*
    (E) *Escherichia coli*

28. A 52-year-old female patient is seen at the clinic complaining of chronic dry eye and dry mouth. She does not present any other symptoms and appears otherwise healthy. Which of the following diagnoses is most likely to be correct?
    (A) Lupus
    (B) Scleroderma
    (C) Sjögren's syndrome
    (D) Polyarteritis nodosa
    (E) Polymyositis

29. A 13-year-old female patient presents at the clinic with bilateral erythema of the conjucntiva, watery discharge, and ipsilateral tender preauricular lymphadenopathy. A day earlier, she had been swimming in a public pool. Based on this information, which of the following diagnoses is most likely to be correct?
    (A) Pterygium
    (B) Bacterial conjunctivitis
    (C) Pinguecula
    (D) Viral conjunctivitis
    (E) Orbital cellulitis

30. A 59-year-old male patient arrives at the clinic complaining of abdominal pain. Physical examination shows a herniation of the stomach through the diaphragm. He had no previous abdominal surgeries. Based on these findings, from which type of hernia is the patient suffering?
    (A) Umbilical hernia
    (B) Hiatal hernia
    (C) Incisional hernia
    (D) Inguinal hernia
    (E) Ventral hernia

31. A 42-year-old female patient is suffering from an apparent infection that is causing a fever, sore throat, and a general feeling of malaise. Her examination reveals a tenacious gray membrane covering her tonsils and pharynx. The membrane is not affecting her ability to breath. Based on this information, she is diagnosed with diphtheria. What is the first and most important form of treatment for this condition?
    (A) Removal of the membrane
    (B) Penicillin
    (C) Treatment of contacts with erythromycin
    (D) Horse serum
    (E) Immediate isolation

32. A 63-year-old male patient presents at the clinic with abdominal pain, frequent and painful urination, and hematuria. You suspect he may have bladder cancer. Which of the following diagnostic tests would be most likely to confirm this diagnosis?
    (A) Urine cytology
    (B) Biopsy
    (C) CT scan
    (D) MRI
    (E) Cystoscopy

33. A 57-year-old female patient who recently quit smoking presents at the clinic with bloody, pus-filled diarrhea, abdominal cramping, and tenesmus. Examination reveals continuous inflammation of the colon. Based on this information, which of the following diagnoses is most likely to be correct?
    (A) Crohn's disease
    (B) Irritable bowel syndrome
    (C) Toxic megacolon
    (D) Ulcerative colitis
    (E) Ischemic bowel disease

34. A 64-year-old male patient with a history of cardiac problems presents at the clinic with fatigue, dyspnea, and decreased exercise intolerance. You believe he may be suffering from a valvular disorder. Which of the following symptoms would exclusively suggest an aortic, rather than mitral, disorder?
    (A) Impeded blood flow between the left atrium and ventricle
    (B) Backflow and volume overload of left atrium

    (C) Bicuspid valve regurgitation
    (D) Pain radiating to left axilla
    (E) Volume overloading of the left ventricle

35. A 5-year-old male patient is brought to the clinic by his parents. They report that he appears to have suffered a growth stunt, noting that his younger sister has started to outgrow him. You suspect he may be suffering from growth hormone deficiency and diagnostic testing confirms your diagnosis. Which of the following treatment options would be appropriate for this condition?
    (A) Hydrocortisone
    (B) Somatropin
    (C) Desmopressin
    (D) Levoxyl
    (E) Prednisone

36. A 39-year-old female patient presents at the clinic with pelvic pain, excessively long menstrual periods, and urinary difficulty. An ultrasound reveals the presence of uterine fibroids. Which of the following treatment options would be the least likely for the patient's condition?
    (A) Leuprolide
    (B) Danazol
    (C) Hysterectomy
    (D) NSAIDs
    (E) Progestin-releasing intrauterine device (IUD)

37. A 73-year-old female patient presents at the clinic with nervous tingling, poor coordination, edema, weakness, and cardiac dysfunction. You believe she may be suffering from a nutritional deficiency. Which of the following vitamins is the patient most likely lacking?
    (A) Vitamin A
    (B) Biotin
    (C) Riboflavin
    (D) Folate
    (E) Thiamin

38. A newborn male patient suddenly shows signs of a congenital heart defect. The baby has become cyanotic and presents with shock, respiratory distress, and apparent heart failure. From which of the following congenital heart defects is the patient most likely suffering?
(A) Transposition of the great vessels
(B) Pulmonary atresia
(C) Hypoplastic left heart syndrome
(D) Atrial septal defect
(E) Tetralogy of Fallot

39. A 32-year-old female patient arrives at the clinic presenting with pain and swelling around the base of her right thumb. She has difficulty moving the thumb and experiences increased pain when she does. You diagnose her with de Quervain's disease. Which of the following treatment options would be least likely for the patient's condition?
(A) NSAIDs
(B) Thumb spica splint
(C) Physical therapy
(D) Surgical intervention
(E) Injection of steroids

40. A 71-year-old male patient who is currently hospitalized after a hip replacement begins to show signs of sepsis. Which of the following symptoms would indicate a severe case of sepsis?
(A) 102.5°F fever
(B) Heart rate of 97 BPM
(C) Patches of mottled skin
(D) Breathing rate of 25 breaths per minute
(E) Confirmed infection

41. A 35-year-old male patient presents at the clinic with painful fluid-filled blisters on the palms of his hands and fissures. He reports that his palms are extremely itchy. Which of the following diagnoses is most likely to be correct?
(A) Psoriasis
(B) Dyshidrosis
(C) Lichen planus
(D) Molluscum contagiosum
(E) Pityriasis rosea

42. A 59-year-old male patient presents at the clinic with fatigue, weight loss, salt craving, hypoglycemia, and hyperpigmentation. After laboratory testing, you diagnose him with Addison's disease. Which of the following treatment options would

most likely be the patient's primary form of treatment?
(A) Injected corticosteroids
(B) Dehydroepiandrosterone
(C) IV saline
(D) Oral corticosteroids
(E) IV glucose

43. You are treating a 78-year-old female patient for thyroiditis and you need to determine the specific form of the disease she is suffering from. Which of the following symptoms would indicate a diagnosis of Hashimoto's thyroiditis?
(A) Fluctuant neck mass
(B) Dysphagia
(C) Glandular atrophy
(D) Low-grade fever
(E) Difficulty swallowing

44. A 77-year-old male patient presents at the clinic with a painful, itchy red rash on the right side of his chest that is beginning to form blisters. He also reports headache, overall achiness, and fatigue. Which of the following diagnoses is most likely to be correct?
(A) Seborrheic dermatitis
(B) Shingles
(C) Stasis dermatitis
(D) Perioral dermatitis
(E) Neurodermatitis

45. A 58-year-old female patient presents at the clinic with a painful left index finger tip. The nail appears brittle and crumbly and is slightly separated from the nail bed. It is also dull and discolored. The surrounding tissue does not appear to be affected. Which of the following diagnoses is most likely to be correct?
(A) Felon
(B) Onycholysis
(C) Paronychia
(D) Leukonychia
(E) Onychomycosis

46. Which of the following is the most common cause of appendicitis?
(A) Cytomegalovirus
(B) Fecalith
(C) Histoplasma
(D) Collagen vascular disease
(E) Inflammatory bowel disease

47. You are treating a 68-year-old male patient with Parkinson's disease. Which of the following medications would you prescribe to specifically treat the tremor associated with this condition?
  (A) Tolcapone
  (B) Selegiline
  (C) Pramipexole
  (D) Levodopa
  (E) Benztropine

48. A diabetic 68-year-old female patient arrives at the clinic complaining of an ocular problem. Her examination reveals macular edema, exudates, and ischemia. You diagnose her with diabetic retinopathy. From which type of diabetic retinopathy is she suffering?
  (A) Nonproliferative retinopathy
  (B) Background retinopathy
  (C) Maculopathy
  (D) Proliferative retinopathy
  (E) Maculopathy *and* proliferative retinopathy

49. A 40-year-old female patient arrives at the clinic complaining of fatigue, malaise, and sudden weight loss. She presents with jaundice and pruritis. Examination shows hepatomegaly and splenomegaly. Based on the patient's condition, which of the following diagnoses is most likely to be correct?
  (A) Primary sclerosing cholangitis
  (B) Acute cholangitis
  (C) Cirrhosis
  (D) Acute cholecystitis
  (E) Choledocholithiasis

50. A 62-year-old male patient presents at the clinic with urinary difficulties. He reports increased frequency, hesitancy and straining, post-void dribbling, and nocturia. Examination shows an enlarged prostate free of any lesions. Based on the patient's symptoms, which of the following diagnoses is most likely to be correct?
  (A) Prostate cancer
  (B) Benign prostatic hyperplasia
  (C) Prostatitis
  (D) Cystitis
  (E) Pyelonephiritis

51. A 30-year-old male patient who smokes is suffering from abdominal cramping, bloody diarrhea, and a slight fever. Examination reveals areas of bowel inflammation, particularly around the terminal ileum and right colon. Based on this information, which of the following diagnoses is most likely to be correct?
  (A) Ulcerative colitis
  (B) Irritable bowel syndrome
  (C) Celiac disease (celiac sprue)
  (D) Crohn's disease (regional enteritis)
  (E) Volvulus

52. Which of the following symptoms would a patient experiencing metabolic acidosis be most likely to present?
  (A) Lethargy
  (B) Shock
  (C) Confusion
  (D) Ventricular arrhythmia
  (E) Hyperventilation

53. Which of the following toxidromes would most likely be treated with gastric lavage?
  (A) Organophosphate
  (B) Caustic
  (C) Acetaminophen
  (D) Hydrocarbon
  (E) Iron

54. A 40-year-old woman who recently moved to the United States from Kenya comes to the office with hemoptysis, fatigue, fever, and night sweats. You suspect *Mycobacterium tuberculosis* (TB). She reports receiving many vaccines as a child. It is highly likely that she received the bacilli Calmette-Guerin (BCG) vaccine against TB, but she is not sure whether she received that particular vaccine. Which test yields the quickest results for diagnosing TB in this patient?
  (A) A TB skin test (Mantoux)
  (B) A chest X-ray
  (C) Interferon-Gamma Release Assay blood test
  (D) Sputum specimen for acid-fast bacilli (AFB) and mycobacterial cultures
  (E) Computerized axial tomography (CAT) of the chest

55. A 38-year-old male patient is complaining of mild chest pain. He has recently experienced severe vomiting due to excessive alcohol consumption. Examination reveals a Mallory-Weiss tear in his esophagus. Which of the following treatments would likely be the most appropriate?
   (A) Release; no treatment necessary
   (B) Injection of epinephrine
   (C) Thermal coagulation
   (D) Surgical repair
   (E) Hospital admittance for observation

56. A 58-year-old male patient arrives in the emergency room with chest pain and an apparent arrhythmia. His examination reveals ventricular tachycardia with symptomatic ventricular premature beats. He has not yet shown any signs of ventricular fibrillation and you want to prevent any such occurrence. Which of the following treatments would be most appropriate for the patient's current condition?
   (A) Lidocaine
   (B) Propafenone
   (C) Quinidine
   (D) Sotalol
   (E) Adenosine

57. A 63-year-old male patient arrives at the clinic complaining of pain in his left foot. The skin on that foot appears slightly inflamed. Laboratory tests reveal an elevated erythrocyte sedimentation rate and a normal rheumatoid factor. No bacterial infection is found. Radiography shows a "Pencil in Cup" deformity of the proximal phalanx. Based on this information, which of the following diagnoses is most likely to be correct?
   (A) Rheumatoid arthritis
   (B) Osteoarthritis
   (C) Septic arthritis
   (D) Reactive arthritis
   (E) Psoriatic arthritis

58. A 48-year-old female patient comes to the clinic complaining of a skin problem that is affecting her neck and face. Parts of the skin in those regions have become thickened and hard. She also shows slight signs of this condition around the distal region of her elbows. Further testing does not reveal any internal abnormalities. Which of the following diagnoses is most likely to be correct?
   (A) Fibromyalgia
   (B) Diffuse scleroderma

   (C) Limited scleroderma
   (D) Polymyositis
   (E) Sjögren's syndrome

59. A 37-year-old male construction worker is brought to the emergency room after a falling tool struck him in the head. He exhibits some symptoms that suggest brain trauma, likely a concussion. Which of the following symptoms would more likely indicate a different diagnosis?
   (A) Tinnitus
   (B) Slurred speech
   (C) Nausea and vomiting
   (D) Elevated blood pressure
   (E) Dizziness

60. A 47-year-old female patient arrives at the clinic complaining of severe left hip pain. The joint is warm, swollen, tender, and has limited range of movement. You diagnose her with septic arthritis. Diagnostic testing reveals that *Staphylococcus aureus* is the infecting pathogen. Based on this information, which of the following clinical interventions would be most necessary?
   (A) Osteotomy
   (B) Arthrotomy
   (C) Arthrocentesis
   (D) Full joint replacement
   (E) Arthrodesis

61. A 39-year-old female patient who suffered serious injuries in an automobile accident is on a ventilator with endotracheal intubation in the intensive care unit. After two days, she begins to show signs of illness and you diagnose her with hospital-acquired pneumonia. Based on her condition, which of the following pathogens is most likely to have caused the patient's pneumonia?
   (A) *Escherichia coli*
   (B) *Staphylococcus aureus*
   (C) *Klebsiella* sp.
   (D) *Pseudomonas aeruginosa*
   (E) *Enterobacter* sp.

62. A mother brings her 2½-year-old son to the clinic because he has swollen salivary glands, a fever, and aching muscles and joints. When asked if her son had received his routine childhood vaccines, she said no. The mother said she is against vaccines because she believes they cause autism. She believes childhood infections are "a normal part of

growing up," and that vaccines are unnecessary. The patient's current condition is most likely a result of having missed which vaccination?
(A) DPT (diphtheria, pertussis, and tetanus)
(B) Hepatitis B
(C) Poliovirus
(D) MMR (measles, mumps, and rubella)
(E) Influenza

63. A 28-year-old football player arrives in the emergency room with a forearm fracture. An X-ray reveals a fracture that runs diagonally across the bone. Which type of fracture has the patient endured?
(A) Transverse
(B) Spiral
(C) Oblique
(D) Comminuted
(E) Segmental

64. A 60-year-old male patient arrives in the emergency room complaining of respiratory difficulty. He presents with insidious dry cough, exertion dyspnea, fatigue, and malaise. Which of the following diagnoses is most likely to be correct?
(A) Sarcoidosis
(B) Idiopathic fibrosing interstitial pneumonia
(C) Silicosis
(D) Acute respiratory distress syndrome
(E) Hyaline membrane disease

65. A 74-year-old female patient is seen at the clinic complaining of visual distortions, decreased brightness of colors, and blurriness in her left eye. Examination reveals retinal mottling, serous leaks, and hemorrhages. Which of the following diagnoses is most likely to be correct?
(A) Retinopathy
(B) Retinal detachment
(C) Central retinal artery occlusion
(D) Central retinal vein occlusion
(E) Macular degeneration

66. A baker's yeast allergy would be a contraindication for immunization with which of the following vaccines?
(A) Influenza vaccine
(B) Varicella vaccine
(C) MMR vaccine
(D) DTP vaccine
(E) Hepatitis B vaccine

67. Which of the following most accurately describes a Torsades de pointes ventricular arrhythmia?
(A) Arrhythmia resulting in syncope, a 0.6-second QT interval, and possible sudden death
(B) Genetic disorder especially common among Asians and males
(C) Cessation of all cardiac pumping
(D) QRS complex twisted around the baseline and a continuously changing axis
(E) Three or more consecutive ventricular premature beats

68. A 34-year-old female comes to the office complaining of nausea and occasional vomiting after taking the antidepressant sertraline, 50 mg daily. She is taking sertraline for depression. She asks if there is another medication you could give her that won't cause nausea. What medication should you prescribe as a substitute for this patient?
(A) A serotonin and norepinephrine reuptake inhibitor (SNRI) such as venlafaxine
(B) An atypical antidepressant such as bupropion
(C) A tricyclic antidepressant such as amitriptyline
(D) Another selective serotonin reuptake inhibitor (SSRI) such as fluoxetine
(E) A monoamine oxidase inhibitor (MAOI) such as phenelzine

69. A 44-year-old male presents at the clinic with an itchy, burning annular patch on his abdomen. The patch is covered with fine scaling. Which of the following diagnoses is most likely to be correct?
(A) Tinea corporis
(B) Tinea cruris
(C) Tinea unguium
(D) Tinea capitis
(E) Tinea barbae

70. Which of the following symptoms would suggest a B6 pyridoxine deficiency?
(A) Dermatitis
(B) Flaky skin
(C) Oral inflammation
(D) Bleeding gums
(E) Nervous tingling

71. A 65-year-old male patient arrives at the clinic complaining of gastrointestinal discomfort. Which of the following symptoms would be most likely to indicate that the patient is suffering from ulcerative colitis?
    (A) Fistulas
    (B) Left side pain
    (C) Bloody, pus-filled diarrhea
    (D) Weight loss
    (E) Malaise

72. A 45-year-old businessman comes to the clinic for his routine physical. He states that he is traveling to India in six weeks and asks you if he needs a hepatitis A vaccination. What do you tell him?
    (A) That the hepatitis A vaccination is not one of the vaccines needed when traveling to India
    (B) That the hepatitis A vaccination is only required for people with weakened immune systems
    (C) That the hepatitis A vaccination is not needed when traveling to India because it is not an area of high prevalence
    (D) That the hepatitis A vaccination is recommended by the Centers for Disease Control and Prevention because India is a country of high prevalence of antibody to hepatitis A virus
    (E) That the hepatitis A vaccination is only recommended for people older than 65 years of age

73. A pregnant 26-year-old patient in her 16th week presents at the clinic with vaginal bleeding and severe cramping. Upon examination, you find that no membranes have been ruptured, but her cervix is dilated. Which form of spontaneous abortion is she most likely experiencing?
    (A) Missed abortion
    (B) Threatened abortion
    (C) Complete abortion
    (D) Incomplete abortion
    (E) Inevitable abortion

74. A 28-year-old pregnant woman in her 21st week presents at the clinic with high blood pressure and severe headaches. A urinalysis reveals an unusually high proteinuria level. You diagnose her with preeclampsia. Which of the following symptoms would indicate that her condition has progressed on to eclampsia?
    (A) Severe epigastric pain
    (B) Blurred vision
    (C) Significantly reduced urination rate
    (D) Seizures
    (E) Vaginal discharge

75. A 64-year-old male patient arrives at the clinic complaining of frequent upper abdominal pain, indigestion, weight loss, and oily, odorous stools. He says he has had these symptoms on and off for years. You diagnose him with chronic pancreatitis. Which of the following is most likely to be the cause of this condition?
    (A) Cholelithiasis
    (B) Alcohol abuse
    (C) Peptic ulcer disease
    (D) Hyperparathyroidism
    (E) Hyperlipidemia

76. A 58-year-old male patient is brought to the clinic by his wife, who reports recent changes in mental status. The patient presents with intellectual decline, changes in personality, slowed mental activity, and expressive aphasia. You believe he may have a brain tumor. Based on the patient's symptoms, what part of his brain has most likely been affected?
    (A) Frontal lobe
    (B) Temporal lobe
    (C) Parietal lobe
    (D) Occipital lobe
    (E) Brain stem or cerebellum

77. A 47-year-old male patient with a history of alcohol abuse presents at the clinic with a fever, cough, breathlessness, shaking chills, and fatigue. You diagnose him with pneumonia. Which of the following organisms is the most likely cause of his condition?
    (A) *Haemophilus pneumoniae*
    (B) *Mycoplasma pneumoniae*
    (C) *Streptococcus pneumoniae*
    (D) *Klebsiella pneumoniae*
    (E) *Legionella pneumonia*

78. Which of the following dermatological terms refers to pinpoint bleeding after the removal of a scale?
    (A) Darier's sign
    (B) Auspitz's sign

(C) Nikolsky's sign

(D) Koebner's phenomenon

(E) Courvoisier's sign

79. A 50-year-old male patient is seen at the clinic complaining of suprapubic pain and irritative voiding problems. His urinalysis study reveals pyuria, bacteriuria, and hematuria. A urine culture shows infection with *Escherichia coli*. Based on this information, which of the following diagnoses is most likely to be correct?
(A) Pyelonephritis
(B) Cystitis
(C) Prostatitis
(D) Orchitis
(E) Epididymitis

80. A 12-year-old female patient who has suffered a brief seizure has arrived in the emergency room. She is short of breath and experiencing muscle cramping and numbness in her hands and feet. Her examination reveals crackles, bradycardia, and a third heart sound. You notice that she exhibits a carpel tunnel spasm after a blood pressure cuff has been left on her arm for several minutes. Based on this information, which of the following diagnoses is most likely to be correct?
(A) Hypocalcemia
(B) Hypercalcemia
(C) Hypermagnesemia
(D) Hypokalemia
(E) Hypomagnesemia

81. A 23-year-old female patient thought to be suffering from a personality disorder is brought to the clinic. She experiences frequent mood swings and severe bouts of seemingly uncontrollable anger. She has great difficulty with being alone, but cannot maintain normal relationships. She also shows signs of self-mutilation. From what type of personality disorder is the patient most likely suffering?
(A) Schizotypal
(B) Borderline
(C) Histronic
(D) Antisocial
(E) Paranoid

82. A 34-year-old female patient presents at the clinic complaining of abdominal discomfort and excessively heavy and painful periods. An ultrasound reveals significant endometrial growth around the ovaries, fallopian tubes, and pelvic tissue, as well as cysts and scar tissue. You diagnose her with endometriosis. Which of the following treatment options would least likely be appropriate based on the patient's condition?
(A) Hormonal contraceptives
(B) Danazol
(C) Medroxyprogesterone
(D) Expectant management
(E) Hysterectomy

83. A 57-year-old female patient arrives at the clinic complaining of vertigo-related symptoms such as dizziness, hearing loss, nausea, vomiting, and tinnitus. After her examination, she is determined to be suffering from Meniere's disease. Based on this information, what form of vertigo is she experiencing?
(A) True vertigo
(B) Peripheral vertigo
(C) Central vertigo
(D) Labyrinthitis
(E) Otitis externa

84. A diabetic 56-year-old male patient arrives at the hospital with apparent muscular weakness on the left side of his face. He reports waking up in the morning with a pronounced pain in his left ear and then discovered that he was unable to move any part of the left side of his face. His general health is otherwise normal and unremarkable. Based on this information, which of the following diagnoses is most likely to be correct?
(A) Cerebral palsy
(B) Bell's palsy
(C) Stroke
(D) Diabetic peripheral neuropathy
(E) Guillain-Barre syndrome

85. A 16-year-old girl is brought to the clinic by her mother. She complains of throat pain and difficulty swallowing. She has low-grade fever and swollen and tender lymph nodes in the neck. You suspect streptococcal laryngitis. Which of the following diagnostic tests can be used to accurately confirm this diagnosis in as little time as possible?
(A) Rapid antigen test
(B) Culture
(C) Rapid DNA test
(D) Blood culture
(E) Viral blood assay

86. A 75-year-old female patient is brought to the clinic by her daughter, who believes she may be suffering from a degenerative mental disorder. Although she has a strong memory and awareness, the patient exhibits frequent bouts of extreme euphoria, apathy, and disinhibition. She also frequently displays several primitive reflexes like the palmomental reflex and the palmar grasp. She has no history of strokes. Based on her condition, what is the patient's most likely diagnosis?
    (A) Alzheimer's disease
    (B) Vascular dementia
    (C) Parkinson's disease
    (D) Frontotemporal dementia
    (E) Pseudodementia

87. A 53-year-old patient is brought to the emergency room after an abrupt and severe illness has lasted for several hours. He is experiencing abdominal pain, diarrhea, and tenesmus. He has a 102.3°F fever and his stool contains some blood and mucus and his abdomen is tender to the touch. His blood culture does not show any sign of *Salmonella entrica*. Which of the following diagnoses is most likely to be correct?
    (A) Diphtheria
    (B) Gastroenteritis
    (C) Shigellosis
    (D) Bacteremia
    (E) Pertussis

88. A 16-year-old girl comes to the clinic asking for the "cancer vaccine." After questioning her further, you determine she is requesting the vaccine called Gardisil. Before you give her the vaccine, what do you tell the patient that Gardisil protects against?
    (A) Breast cancer
    (B) Most strains of genital human papilloma-virus (HPV)
    (C) HIV
    (D) Syphilis
    (E) Ovarian cancer

89. A 58-year-old male is seen at the clinic and complains of back and leg pain. He reports a burning back pain that spreads down his legs as he walks. He also reports that he can frequently alleviate the pain by leaning forward. He displays a normal posture. Radiographic imaging tests reveal soft-tissue and thecal narrowing. Based on this information, which of the following diagnoses is most likely to be correct?
    (A) Spinal stenosis
    (B) Ankylosing spondylitis (AS)
    (C) Cauda equina syndrome
    (D) Kyphosis
    (E) Scoliosis

90. A 68-year-old male patient who was recently treated for pneumonia comes to the clinic complaining of a sudden loss of hearing in his right ear. He also presents with pain and pressure. No fluid is found in the ear. Based on his symptoms, what type of hearing loss is he most likely suffering from?
    (A) Otis externa
    (B) Meniere's disease
    (C) Otis media
    (D) Presbycusis
    (E) Otosclerosis

91. A 60-year-old male patient arrives at the clinic complaining of pain in his left big toe. The affected appendage appears red and swollen around the joint and is extremely sensitive to pressure. The patient says that the pain started very suddenly overnight. His health is otherwise unremarkable. Of the following diagnoses, which is the most likely to be correct?
    (A) Calcium pyrophosphate dehydrate disease
    (B) Gout
    (C) Polymyositis
    (D) Psoriatic arthritis
    (E) Reactive arthritis

92. A 16-year-old female softball pitcher comes to the clinic complaining of pain and tenderness on the inside of her right elbow. She is a right-handed pitcher and reports increased pain that radiates down her forearm when she attempts to throw a ball. She has not fallen or suffered any direct trauma to the site recently. Based on this information, which of the following diagnoses is most likely to be correct?
    (A) Lateral epicondylitis
    (B) Medial epicondylitis
    (C) Olecranon bursitis
    (D) Radial head fracture
    (E) Scaphoid fracture

93. A 35-year-old male patient arrives at the clinic complaining of severe pain on the left side of his scrotum. Examination reveals swelling and a fluidic buildup primarily around the left testicle. There are no signs of extraordinary scrotal masses. Based on this information, which of the following diagnoses is most likely to be correct?
    (A) Hydrocele
    (B) Spermatocele
    (C) Varicocele
    (D) Phimosis
    (E) Testicular torsion

94. A 20-year-old female college student walks into the clinic complaining of vaginal itching, a thin white discharge, and a fishy vaginal odor. She also reports burning on urination. She is sexually active with more than one sexual partner, and is not consistent in using condoms. She also douches regularly. Microscopic examination of her vaginal fluid shows clue cells, a pH of >4.5, and a fishy odor after addition of 10% KOH (i.e., the whiff test). What is the most likely cause of her vaginitis?
    (A) Bacterial vaginosis
    (B) Chlamydia
    (C) Gonorrhea
    (D) Syphilis
    (E) Candidiasis

95. A 25-year-old female presents with pale skin, fatigue, and numbness in her hands and feet. She reports that she exercises three times a week and eats a healthy vegan diet, though she does not take vitamin supplements. You suspect that her diet is depriving her of essential nutrients, which is causing mild megaloblastic anemia and possible nerve damage. Which nutrient is most likely missing from this patient's diet?
    (A) Vitamin E
    (B) Vitamin K
    (C) Vitamin B6
    (D) Vitamin B12
    (E) Vitamin C

96. Which of the following women would be most at risk for developing uterine fibroids?
    (A) A 32-year-old white woman with familial history
    (B) A 25-year-old black woman without familial history

(C) A 15-year old Asian woman on birth-control pill
(D) A 28-year-old pregnant black woman
(E) A 40-year-old white woman without familial history

97. A 19-year-old female presents with a complaint of an itchy rash on the skin between her fingers. She reports that the itching is intense at night and that she is often awakened by her dorm roommate, who tells her that she is scratching her hands in her sleep. Upon examination of the rash, red bumps, small blisters, and thin red lines are discovered. Laboratory results reveal the presence of *Sarcoptes scabiei* and mite eggs. Which of the following treatments would be most appropriate for this patient's condition?
    (A) 5% permethrin cream, applied from the chin to the feet
    (B) Salicylic acid plasters, applied at night and removed in the morning
    (C) Ketoconazole, ingested in tablet form
    (D) 1% lindane lotion, applied to the affected area
    (E) 1% gentian violet, applied to the affected area

98. Which of the following individuals would be most likely to develop berryliosis?
    (A) A demolition crewmember
    (B) A quarry worker
    (C) A construction worker
    (D) A tool and die manufacturer
    (E) A coal miner

99. A 42-year-old female presents with a persistent bladder infection, which has been treated with fluoroquinolone for 5 days. The patient's original irritative voiding symptoms are currently accompanied by fever, flank pain, and vomiting. Urinalysis shows hematuria and WBC casts. What additional findings would you expect to see in this patient?
    (A) Androgen excess
    (B) High concentrations of protein in the urine
    (C) Elevated serum chloride levels in the blood
    (D) Heavy growth of *Escherichia coli* in the urine
    (E) Low red blood cell count indicating anemia

100. Which of the following is the most likely cause of a combination of dysmenorrhea, dyspareunia, dyschezia, and pelvic pain?
(A) Uterine prolapse
(B) Leiomyomata
(C) Endometriosis
(D) Ovarian cysts
(E) Premenstrual syndrome

101. Which eye condition is characterized by the presence of profuse purulent discharge and a decrease in visual clarity?
(A) Bacterial conjunctivitis
(B) Pinguecula
(C) Pterygium
(D) Blepharitis
(E) Macular degeneration

102. A complete blood count (CBC) for a 27-year-old female suffering from fatigue and headaches resulting from microcytic anemia reveals a mean corpuscular volume (MCV) of less than 80 fL. The woman has no family history of thalassemia. Which of the following is most likely the cause of her anemia?
(A) G6PD deficiency
(B) Vitamin B12 deficiency
(C) Folic acid deficiency
(D) Iron deficiency
(E) Platelet deficiency

103. Which of the following immunizations could cause an anaphylactic reaction in an infant with an egg allergy?
(A) Measles, mumps, and rubella (MMR) vaccine
(B) Hepatitis B vaccine
(C) Varicella vaccine
(D) Diphtheria, tetanus, and pertussis (DTaP) vaccine
(E) Influenza vaccine

104. A 45-year-old male with hypertension undergoes a series of laboratory tests including a lipid profile. The lipid profile is most important to determining which of the following?
(A) Presence of hypoglycemia
(B) Risk of atherosclerosis
(C) Decreased hemoglobin levels
(D) Occurrence of intracranial hemorrhage
(E) Presence of pulmonary edema

105. A 16-year-old boy presents with a cough, which began as a dry cough about a month ago and has progressed to a productive cough with hemoptysis. The boy has lost weight, complains of chest pain and night sweats, and has a fever. After diagnosis, the boy received a 2-month pharmaceutical regimen including a combination of isoniazid, rifampin, pyrazinamide, and ethambutol. This combination of drugs is used to treat which of the following pulmonary conditions?
(A) Tuberculosis
(B) Pneumonia
(C) Acute bronchitis
(D) COPD
(E) Cystic fibrosis

106. Which of the following individuals is most at-risk for developing multiple myeloma?
(A) A 35-year-old white male
(B) A 62-year-old black female
(C) A 65-year-old black male
(D) A 70-year-old white male
(E) An obese 60-year-old white male

107. Which of the following results of a spirometry test on a 9-year-old child is indicative of moderate persistent asthma?
(A) FEV1 > 80 percent predicted; FEV1/FVC > 85 percent
(B) FEV1 > 80 percent predicted; FEV1/FVC > 80 percent
(C) FEV1 = 60–80 percent predicted; FEV1/FVC = 75–80 percent
(D) FEV1 = 40–60 percent predicted; FEV1/FVC = 65–70 percent
(E) FEV1 <60 percent predicted; FEV1/FVC < 75 percent

108. Which of the following is the most common etiology of mesothelioma?
(A) Exposure to radon gas
(B) Exposure to tobacco smoke
(C) Exposure to coal dust
(D) Exposure to asbestos
(E) Exposure to carbon monoxide

109. A 12-year-old girl has been diagnosed with type 1 diabetes mellitus. To maintain her health, the girl will have to make certain lifestyle modifications. Which of the following recommendations should be made in regard to eating a well-balanced diet?

(A) Caloric intake should break down as follows: 10–35 percent carbohydrates, 45–65 percent protein, 25–35 percent fat, with less than 7 percent saturated fat.

(B) Caloric intake should break down as follows: 25–35 percent carbohydrates, 10–35 percent protein, 45–65 percent fat, with less than 20 percent saturated fat.

(C) Caloric intake should break down as follows: 45–65 percent carbohydrates, 25–40 percent protein, 5–10 percent fat, with less than 18 percent saturated fat.

(D) Caloric intake should break down as follows: 20–30 percent carbohydrates, 40–70 percent protein, 15–25 percent fat, with less than 7 percent saturated fat.

(E) Caloric intake should break down as follows: 45–65 percent carbohydrates, 10–35 percent protein, 25–35 percent fat, with less than 7 percent saturated fat.

110. An 18-year-old male awoke early and experienced intermittent periumbilical pain throughout the morning. By evening, the pain had become constant and is centered toward the right lower quadrant of the patient's abdomen. Movement increases the pain. The patient also feels nauseated and has a low-grade fever. The diagnosis is appendicitis. Which of the following is the recommended treatment for appendicitis?
(A) Administration of broad-spectrum antibiotics
(B) Surgical removal via appendectomy
(C) Laparoscopic biopsy
(D) Administration of NSAIDS
(E) Administration of diuretics

111. A 58-year-old obese woman with type 2 diabetes and hypercholesterolemia comes to your office with dyspnea, nausea, and pain in her neck and jaw. Her blood pressure is 170/90 and her pulse is 100. Which of the following is the most likely diagnosis?
(A) Gastroesophageal reflux disease
(B) An abscessed molar
(C) Myocardial infarction
(D) Acute gastritis
(E) Acute cholelithiasis

112. A 30-year-old woman comes to the office complaining of abdominal bloating and pain. She also complains of chronic diarrhea with pale, foul-smelling, oily stool and weight loss (5 pounds in 2 months). She reports fatigue, numbness and tingling in the hands and feet, and feeling "down in the dumps." She also has a "really itchy rash" on her hands, which appears as small red dots with blisters. What is the most likely diagnosis?
(A) Mercury poisoning
(B) Inflammatory bowel disease
(C) Giardia
(D) Irritable bowel syndrome
(E) Celiac disease

113. A 19-year-old woman comes to the clinic complaining of localized, dull pain along the 2nd distal metatarsal area of the right foot. She states the pain happened spontaneously during running and was not related to any type of specific injury or trauma. The upper portion of the foot is slightly edematous, and when the 2nd metatarsal area is palpated, the patient complains of pain. She has difficulty lifting her toes on the affected foot. The patient is limping slightly. She states she has run track for 4 years, and is on the women's track team in college. Recently the patient has stepped up her training to prepare for a major track event. An X-ray of her foot shows no obvious fracture. What is her most likely diagnosis?
(A) Osteoarthritis
(B) Fractured ankle
(C) Stress fractured
(D) Bunion
(E) Gout

114. A 2-year-old boy is brought into the clinic by his mother. He is crying and his right nostril is bleeding slightly. The mother states the boy was playing quietly by himself in the playroom when he suddenly began to cry. She investigated, and stated she found him holding his nose, screaming, "Ow!" She noticed blood and mucus coming from his nostril. When the mother asked what had happened, the boy would not answer her. What procedure would you be most likely to perform based on your observations?
    (A) A nasal X-ray
    (B) Magnetic resonance imaging (MRI) of the head
    (C) Rhinoscopy
    (D) Nasal irrigation
    (E) Laryngoscope

115. A 42-year-old woman comes to the office with pain, slight redness, and edema in the right calf. She had been placed on oral contraceptives for the first time 5 weeks previously by her gynecologist in order to provide contraception and to help regulate her menstrual cycle. The only other medication she is taking is 20 mg atorvastatin (Lipitor) daily for hypercholesterolemia. The patient said she noticed the calf pain three days previously, and thought she had pulled a muscle. The pain intensified, and by the third day, she noticed her lower leg appeared swollen and red. She also reported throbbing pain in her leg when standing. What do you suspect is causing the symptoms in her leg?
    (A) Osteomyelitis
    (B) Contact dermatitis
    (C) Lymphadema
    (D) Fracture
    (E) Deep vein thrombosis

116. You are concerned that a 50-year-old male patient with obesity, high blood pressure, and hypercholesterolemia is at risk of type 2 diabetes. You screen him using the HbA1c (A1C) test. According to the American Diabetes Association (ADA), at what A1C level should you diagnose your patient with diabetes?
    (A) ≥ 6.5%
    (B) ≥ 7.0%
    (C) ≥ 7.5%
    (D) ≥ 8.0%
    (E) ≥ 6.0%

117. A 21-year-old male patient comes to the office complaining of a "funny-looking penis." He appears very distressed. He says his penis is "bent down" when it is erect. The patient also says his "peehole" is located in the wrong place. He says he has to sit on the toilet to urinate to prevent urine from spraying in different directions. He says he is too embarrassed to have sexual intercourse. He has heard there is a type of surgery to correct his condition, but usually it is done on babies. After examining the patient, what do you tell him his condition is called?
    (A) Ambiguous genitals
    (B) Pseudohermaphroditism
    (C) Epispadias
    (D) Balanitis
    (E) Hypospadias

118. A 70-year-old female patient comes to the office complaining of abdominal pain. She states she has had heartburn for several weeks, but it is usually relieved with chewable antacid tablets. The pain appears to be worse when she is hungry or at night. When asked about the color of her stools, the patient said sometimes they are "dark." She denies any frank blood in her stools. She has had no vomiting, but some nausea. She also complains of fatigue. Her medications are lisinopril for high blood pressure and Cosopt eye drops for glaucoma. She has osteoarthritis, for which she takes over-the-counter naproxen. When asked how much naproxen she takes, the patient states she takes "two or three every few hours when the pain is bad." She doesn't know the dosage she is taking. She states she has had more pain than usual in the last few weeks. What diagnosis do you suspect in this patient?
    (A) Cholelithiasis
    (B) Peptic ulcer disease
    (C) Gastroesophageal reflux disease
    (D) Cirrhosis
    (E) Crohn's disease

119. An 18-year-old male is brought into the office by his mother. She states she is concerned, because for the last few months he has exhibited "strange" behavior, which seems to be worsening. Although she states he has always been a bit "different"— occasionally talking gibberish to himself and wearing outlandish clothes—she said the unusual

behaviors are becoming worse. He is seeing things such as bats flying in the house. He seems to think the programs on TV are real, and he talks about the characters as if he knows them. He becomes withdrawn at times, but can also become agitated for no apparent reason, shouting obscenities and throwing things. The patient sometimes refuses to bathe or brush his teeth. What is the most likely diagnosis in this patient?

(A) Attention deficit disorder
(B) Bipolar disorder
(C) Generalized anxiety disorder
(D) Major depression
(E) Schizophrenia

120. A 32-year-old woman comes to the clinic with burning on urination, hematuria, and low-grade fever (100 degrees F). She has just returned from a weekend vacation with her husband, and she reports they had frequent sexual intercourse. She has pain when palpated in the lower abdomen, just above the pubic bone. What is the most likely diagnosis?

(A) Pyelonephritis
(B) A sexually transmitted disease such as chlamydia
(C) Cystitis
(D) Interstitial cystitis
(E) Vulvovaginitis

121. A 58-year-old man and his wife come to the clinic. He complains of skin flushing, dizziness, itching, nausea, and vomiting. He is tachycardic (120 bpm). His blood pressure is 150/102. An EKG shows regular heart rhythm with no missing QRS complexes. He has been prescribed niacin (vitamin B3) for hypercholesterolemia and hypertriglyceridemia. The patient is unsure of his dose, but he takes 4 tablets twice daily. The patient recently changed the type of over-the-counter niacin he was using from tablets to capsules, because the capsules are less expensive. His wife thinks the patient has been taking 1,000-mg tablets. This would make his current dose 8,000 mg daily, or 8 grams. Niacin capsules are available in 250–500 mg doses. If the patient was previously taking four 250-mg capsules twice daily, he was taking 2,000 mg, or 2 grams daily. If the capsules he previously took were 500 mg, he was taking 4,000 mg daily,

or 4 grams. What do you suspect is this patient's diagnosis?

(A) Niacin overdose
(B) Severe infection
(C) Hyperthyroidism
(D) Electrolyte imbalance
(E) Ventricular tachycardia

122. A 17-year-old high school student comes to the office with what he says is a spider bite on top of his foot, which he has had for five days. There is a red, swollen, painful abscess on the top of his right foot. It is about 2 cm in diameter. The patient said he thinks he got the spider bite from walking barefoot in the school locker room after a wrestling match. He said the pustule will not go away, and it seems to be getting bigger and redder every day. You lance the abscess and biopsy it. What do you suspect is the cause of the boy's condition?

(A) Brown recluse spider bite
(B) Foliculitis
(C) Poison ivy
(D) Ringworm
(E) Methicilin-resistant *Staphylococcus aureus* skin infection

123. A 78-year-old woman is brought to the clinic by her daughter with shortness of breath, fatigue, edema of the lower extremities, irregular heartbeat, and productive cough. The patient appears sleepy and has difficulty staying awake. The daughter states her mother's symptoms started about two weeks ago and have worsened over time. She also says that her mother has not been to a clinician in two years because "she hates hospitals." The patient is on no medications and states that she has no known history of heart disease. However, she sometimes has chest pain that radiates down her left arm, which lasts for several minutes. Her blood pressure is 160/90, and her pulse is 100 and irregular. Her respirations are 28 and labored. She is producing white sputum when coughing. Rales are heard bilaterally in both lung bases. What is the most likely diagnosis?

(A) Pulmonary embolism
(B) Pneumonia
(C) Bronchitis
(D) Congestive heart failure
(E) Chronic obstructive pulmonary disease

124. A 38-year-old woman comes to the office with red to brownish-gray colored patches on her inner elbows. She reports severe itching, especially at night. There are small, raised bumps that leak fluid and crust over when scratched. Her skin also appears scaly and cracked as well as raw from scratching. What is the most likely diagnosis?
(A) Poison ivy
(B) Measles
(C) Scabies
(D) Psoriasis
(E) Eczema

125. A 25-year-old woman comes to the office complaining of severe headaches. She said they started several months ago, and have been increasing in frequency to about once every two weeks. The pain is isolated to the left side of her head, and she says it is an intense, throbbing pain. She is experiencing nausea, vomiting, and sensitivity to light and loud noises. She denies any head injury. What is the most likely diagnosis?
(A) Subdural hematoma
(B) Sinus headache
(C) Migraine
(D) Brain tumor
(E) Transient ischemic attack (TIA)

126. A 72-year-old man is brought into the clinic by ambulance. He is obese and has hypertension and hypercholesterolemia. His blood pressure is 180/100. He fell in the bathroom, and could not get up. He has weakness of the left arm and leg, left facial drooping, confusion, difficulty speaking, and numbness in the left arm. What is the most likely diagnosis?
(A) Transient ischemic attack (TIA)
(B) Syncope
(C) Left-sided cerebrovascular accident (CVA)
(D) Guillain-Barré syndrome
(E) Right-sided cerebrovascular accident (CVA)

127. A 37-year-old female comes to the clinic with spotty vaginal bleeding, breast tenderness, mild cramping and worsening pain in the lower right abdomen, and nausea. She also complains of lightheadedness. She is slightly hypotensive, with a blood pressure of 100/60. When asked about menstruation, the patient states she is about a week past due for her period. The patient states she is sexually active. When asked about contraception, the patient states she is not on any form of birth control, and that her partner does not use condoms. What test would you most likely perform first on this patient?
(A) Pregnancy test
(B) White blood cell (WBC) count blood test
(C) Colonoscopy
(D) Endometrial biopsy
(E) Culture for *Chlamydia trachomatis*

128. A 55-year-old male comes to the clinic with chest pain, dyspnea, and diaphoresis. He is a smoker, has hypertension, hypercholesterolemia, and a strong family history for cardiac disease. What is the first test you would order to detect possible acute myocardial infarction (MI)?
(A) Creatine kinase (CK) blood enzyme level
(B) Echocardiogram
(C) Electrocardiogram (EKG)
(D) Cardiac catheterization
(E) Chest X-ray

129. An 80-year-old male comes to the office complaining of a frequent need to urinate, especially at night. He also complains of difficulty starting urination and holding back urine flow. He also reports occasional burning on urination, hematuria, and pain in his lower back, hips, and upper thighs. A digital rectal exam of the prostate shows it to be enlarged, hard, and lumpy. The patient's prostate-specific antigen (PSA) result is 9.0 ng/mL. What test would you most likely order next?
(A) Ultrasound with biopsy
(B) Ultrasound without biopsy
(C) Cystoscopy
(D) Bone scan
(E) Computerized tomography (CT) of the pelvis

130. A 40-year-old female comes to the office complaining of swelling at the base of her neck, rapid heartbeat, increased appetite, sudden weight loss, nervousness, tremor, irregular menstruation, and insomnia. Her resting pulse is 102. She has had one period in the last three months and has lost 10 pounds. She states she is only sleeping about three hours a night. What is the most likely diagnosis?
(A) Generalized anxiety disorder (GAD)
(B) Paroxysmal supraventricular tachycardia
(C) Cardiomyopathy
(D) Too much caffeine consumption
(E) Hyperthyroidism

131. A 20-year-old woman is brought into the clinic by her mother, who is asking for an antidepressant for her daughter. The daughter is crying and refuses to answer questions. Her mother says she is "very depressed" and "doing scary things." When asked to explain specifics of her daughter's behavior, the mother states that her daughter frequents bars and picks up men for sex. She is also drinking heavily. The daughter recently wrecked a car belonging to her father. When confronted about the accident, the daughter became very angry and screamed at her father. At other times, her daughter is withdrawn and doesn't want to talk to anyone. She is unable to hold down a job or keep friends. She does not like being alone. In the past, she has cut herself with razor blades, making small incisions on her arms and legs. She has also expressed thoughts of suicide. Although she has seen a psychiatrist, the daughter will not take her medications as prescribed. What is the most likely diagnosis?
   (A) Major depression
   (B) Bipolar disorder
   (C) Schizophrenia
   (D) Borderline personality disorder (BPD)
   (E) Post-traumatic stress disorder (PTSD)

132. A 46-year-old woman comes to the office complaining of syncope, especially when standing up from a sitting position. The previous week, she was placed on 2 mg of the alpha blocker prazosin twice daily for Raynaud's disease by her physician. Her other medications are 20 mg of atorvastatin daily and 60 mg of raloxiphene daily. What is likely to be causing the patient's syncope?
   (A) Prazosin
   (B) Possible transcient ischemic attack (TIA)
   (C) Panic disorder
   (D) Heart arrhythmia
   (E) Seizure

133. A 32-year-old obese woman comes to the office complaining of hirsuitism of the face, alopecia, irregular menstruation, acne, and inability to conceive. She has not had a period in four months, and thought she was pregnant several times. She has hirsuitism of the upper lip and cheeks. Alopecia is in a male pattern. Acne consists of red papules, mainly on the forehead and cheeks. What is the most likely diagnosis?
   (A) Endometriosis
   (B) Polycystic ovary syndrome (PCOS)
   (C) Early menopause
   (D) Alopecia areata
   (E) Telogen effluvium

134. An African-American mother brings her 3-month-old infant to the clinic. The baby has edema of the hands and feet, jaundice, and cries often, sometimes loudly, as if he is in pain. He has only gained 4 ounces from his birth weight. His temperature is 101.4 degrees F. What condition does this infant likely have?
   (A) Sickle cell anemia
   (B) Hepatitis
   (C) Failure to thrive
   (D) Pneumonia
   (E) Malaria

135. A 51-year-old man comes to the office for his annual physical. The patient's only complaint is arthritic-type pain in his left knee. What routine procedure would you order to test for possible cardiovascular disease?
   (A) Exercise stress test
   (B) Cardiac catheterization
   (C) Creatine kinase (CK) blood enzyme level
   (D) Electrocardiogram (EKG)
   (E) Echocardiogram

136. A 25-year-old healthy married woman comes to the office for a routine Pap smear and pelvic exam. Her last Pap smear was a year ago, and it was normal. Prior to that, she had yearly Pap smears starting at age 18, and all were normal. The patient asks you if she can have Pap smears less frequently. Based on her history and recommendations from organizations such as the American College of Obstetricians and Gynecologists (ACOG), what time interval would you advise for this patient?
   (A) Yearly
   (B) Every two years
   (C) Every three years
   (D) Every five years
   (E) Only if she has symptoms of human papillomavirus (HPV)

137. A 65-year-old woman comes to the clinic with a 101°F fever, diarrhea of three days' duration, and abdominal cramps. The patient takes simvastatin, 20 mg daily; metoprolol, 50 mg daily; and a daily aspirin. What is the most likely diagnosis?
(A) A foodborne illness such as salmonella
(B) Ulcerative colitis
(C) Intolerance to foods such as lactose or gluten
(D) Drug adverse effect
(E) Clostridium difficile

138. A 44-year-old slightly overweight man comes to the office complaining of numbness of the skin on his arms, back, and buttocks; tremors in his hands; double vision; and cognitive problems, such as short-term memory loss. The patient reports no other medical problems and states he is "usually healthy as a horse." During the interview, you learn the patient has been dieting for three months, and eats a lot of fish and salads. When questioned further, the patient states that he eats some type of fish daily, including salmon, tuna, and swordfish, and some freshwater fish such as mackerel. Based on this information, what is the most likely diagnosis?
(A) Diabetes
(B) Malnutrition
(C) Mercury poisoning
(D) Hypothyroidism
(E) Dementia

139. A 10-year-old boy is brought to the clinic by his mother after sustaining a head injury during soccer practice. He was shoved by another player, fell, and hit his head on the ground. He has dizziness and a headache. He had ringing in the ears for a few minutes after it happened and felt dazed afterward, but did not lose consciousness. Initial neurologic exam checking vision, coordination, hearing, reflexes, memory, and concentration are normal. The patient has some difficulty with balance. You suspect a mild concussion. What test should you order first?
(A) Computerized tomography (CT) scan of the head
(B) Magnetic resonance imaging (MRI) of the head

(C) Electroencephalogram (EEG)
(D) Insertion of an intracranial pressure (ICP) probe
(E) Fluoroscopy

140. A 22-year-old woman is brought to the clinic by her husband. She has vaginal bleeding, pain and cramping in the lower abdomen, and is passing tissue from her vagina. She says she is 14 weeks' pregnant. After performing a pelvic exam and ordering a human chorionic gonadotropin (HCG) level and a pelvic ultrasound, your diagnosis is spontaneous abortion. You explain both medical and surgical treatment options to the patient. She chooses surgery. What type of surgery will you prescribe for her?
(A) Colposcopy
(B) Hysteroscopy
(C) Cryosurgery
(D) Pelvic laparoscopy
(E) Suction dilation and curettage (D&C)

141. On a June afternoon, a 65-year-old man comes to the office for an annual physical exam. He states he does not remember the last time he had a vaccination, but it was probably when he was a child. The only surgery he has ever had was an appendectomy as a child. What type of vaccination should he receive?
(A) Seasonal influenza
(B) Meningococcal polysaccharide or conjugate
(C) Pneumococcal pneumonia
(D) *Haemophilus influenzae* type b (Hib) conjugate vaccine
(E) Human papillomavirus (Gardisil)

142. A 62-year-old female comes to the office complaining of cough and shortness of breath. She states she has had a cold and cannot seem to recover from it. She is wheezing. She says she has smoked two packs of cigarettes a day for more than 40 years. She has pursed lips while breathing and a barrel chest. There are decreased bilateral breath sounds with wheezes and crackles. Lung function testing (spirometry) shows that the forced vital capacity (FVC) is reduced. The amount of air exhaled during the initial 1 second (FEV1) is reduced, and it is decreased to a greater degree than the entire FVC. Chest X-ray shows hyperinflated lungs with flattened diaphragm, hyperlucent lungs, and enlargement of the central pulmonary artery.

Based on this information, from what condition is the patient most likely suffering?
(A) Chronic bronchitis
(B) Chronic obstructive pulmonary disease (COPD)
(C) Gastroesophageal reflux disease (GERD)
(D) Transudative pleural effusion
(E) Pneumothorax

143. A 53-year-old female comes to the office complaining of vaginal dryness, itchiness, and irritation. She also states that sexual intercourse is painful. She says she previously enjoyed intercourse with her husband, and would like to have pleasurable sex with him again. The patient is postmenopausal and has vaginal atrophy. She was previously given topical estrogen vaginal creams, but she did not like the "messiness" of them. What alternative treatment would you suggest to help relieve her vaginal atrophy?
(A) Oral estrogen and progesterone
(B) An estrogen vaginal ring
(C) Over-the-counter vaginal lubrication products
(D) Estrogen vaginal suppositories
(E) Abstinence from sexual intercourse

144. A 24-year-old male comes to the office complaining of pain in the cheekbones, upper teeth, and under the eyes. The pain worsens when the patient is upright and improves when he is reclining. He also complains of halitosis. He has clear nasal discharge, and a fever of 100.5°F. What is the most likely diagnosis?
(A) Abscessed upper tooth
(B) Migraine headache
(C) Maxillary sinusitis
(D) Sphenoid sinusitis
(E) Labyrinthitis

145. An obese 40-year-old male comes to the office complaining of heartburn. He also states that he experiences dysphagia when eating certain foods, such as bread and meat. He also has a chronic dry cough, sometimes with wheezing. What is the most likely diagnosis?
(A) Congestive heart failure
(B) Chronic bronchitis
(C) Peptic ulcer disease
(D) Asthma
(E) Gastroesophageal reflux disease (GERD)

146. A 30-year-old female comes to the office complaining of fever, chills, nausea and vomiting, back and flank pain, frequent urination, pain on urination, and hematuria. You suspect pyelonephritis. Urinalysis shows bacterial infection with the type of bacteria commonly found in 90 percent of urinary tract infections. Which bacteria is that?
(A) Escherichia coli
(B) Staphylococcus saprophyticus
(C) Klebsiella
(D) Proteus mirabilis
(E) Mycoplasma hominis

147. A 53-year-old male comes to the clinic with chest pain, diaphoresis, nausea, lightheadedness, and shortness of breath. An electrocardiogram confirms the patient is having an acute myocardial infarction (MI). What medication should you administer to the patient immediately?
(A) Tissue plasminogen activator, or tPA
(B) Streptokinase
(C) Morphine
(D) Beta blockers
(E) Aspirin

148. A 46-year-old female comes to the office complaining of fatigue, dizziness, cognitive problems, and cold hands and feet. Her skin is pale. Her vital signs are normal, except that she is slightly tachycardic with a pulse of 100. On further questioning, she tells you she has been having heavy menstrual bleeding for the past six months, possibly related to perimenopause. You suspect she has iron-deficiency anemia. Which of the following most likely reflects her hematocrit and hemoglobin values?
(A) Hematocrit 25 percent; hemoglobin 8 grams per deciliter
(B) Hematocrit 36 percent; hemoglobin 12 grams per deciliter
(C) Hematocrit 43 percent; hemoglobin 15 grams per deciliter
(D) Hematocrit 50 percent; hemoglobin 20 grams per deciliter
(E) Hematocrit 55 percent; hemoglobin 25 grams per deciliter

149. A 12-year-old boy comes to the clinic with his mother. He complains of left ear pain and itching. Upon examination, you find a small amount of yellow drainage from the ear canal. His temperature is 98.4°F. He says he swims every day because he is on the swim team. What is this patient's most likely diagnosis?

(A) Otitis media

(B) Otitis externa

(C) Temporomandibular joint (TMJ) syndrome

(D) Labyrinthitis

(E) Ceruminosis

150. A 67-year-old woman comes to the clinic with a slight nosebleed, which ceases with the application of pressure and an ice pack. Her vital signs are normal, and her blood pressure is 120/84. She is taking warfarin based on International Normalizing Ratio (INR) results for treatment of atrial fibrillation. (Her usual dose is 5 mg daily.) When asked about her other medications, the patient states that she takes omeprazole, 20 mg daily, for gastroestophageal reflux disease (GERD), and amiodarone for atrial fibrillation. She also states she just started taking ginkgo biloba about two weeks ago to improve her memory. The patient's INR is 3.8. Just prior to taking ginkgo, it was 2.4, according to her medical records, and it had stayed between 2 and 3 for more than a year. The patient does not know the dose of ginkgo she is taking, but she said she followed the label's instructions. She is taking one tablet in the morning and one at night. What would you tell this patient regarding taking the gingko supplement?

(A) To keep taking gingko, but to decrease her daily warfarin dose to 2.5 mg.

(B) To keep taking gingko, but to take only one tablet daily instead of two a day.

(C) To stop taking gingko altogether, not take warfarin the following day, and to have a repeat INR done the next day.

(D) To stop taking gingko altogether, and to have another INR done in two weeks.

(E) To stop taking gingko altogether, and to have another INR done in a month.

151. A 24-year-old pregnant patient at 34 weeks' gestation comes to the office complaining of headaches, blurred vision, nausea and vomiting, and swelling in her feet and hands. She has gained 5 pounds since her last appointment a week ago. On physical examination, there is tenderness in the upper right abdomen. Her blood pressure is 140/92. Urinalysis indicates proteinuria. What is the most likely diagnosis?

(A) Gestational hypertension

(B) Urinary tract infection (UTI)

(C) Cirrhosis of the liver

(D) Preeclampsia

(E) Eclampsia

152. A 51-year-old male comes to the office for a physical exam. He asks you whether he needs a colonoscopy, and how often he should have one. He states that he has no first-degree relatives with colon cancer or other risk factors. His overall health is good. What do you tell him?

(A) He needs his first colonoscopy now because he is age 50 or older, and if his colonoscopy is normal, he doesn't need another for 1 year.

(B) He needs his first colonoscopy now because he is age 50 or older, and if his colonoscopy is normal, he doesn't need another for 5 years.

(C) He needs his first colonoscopy now because he is age 50 or older, and if his colonoscopy is normal, he doesn't need another for 10 years.

(D) He needs his first colonoscopy now because he is age 50 or older, and if his colonoscopy is normal, he doesn't need another for 20 years.

(E) He doesn't need his first colonoscopy until age 60, and if it is normal, he does not need another one.

153. A 39-year-old female comes to the office complaining of pain in the heel of her right foot. She is overweight (170 pounds) and has recently taken up walking for exercise. She has started walking a mile a day on relatively flat, paved terrain. She limps slightly when she walks, and the pain is worst when she first gets out of bed. She states there has been no specific injury to her foot. Pain is temporarily relieved by ibuprofen and ice packs, but as soon as she starts using her foot again, the pain returns. What is the most likely diagnosis?

(A) Bone bruise

(B) Gout

(C) Osteomyelitis
(D) Plantar fasciitis
(E) Peripheral neuropathy

154. A 9-month-old infant accidentally ingests an unknown quantity of digitalis. The infant has congenital heart disease, characterized by ventricular septal defect, patent foramen ovale, and patent ductus arteriosus. Cardiac evaluation shows tachycardia (152 beats/minute) and a pansystolic murmur. The abdomen is distended but nontender. The remainder of the examination is unremarkable. Serum electrolytes reveal a potassium level of 5.7 mEq/L. An electrocardiogram (EKG) demonstrates a complete atrioventricular dissociation, with a good ventricular rhythm. The most important non-cardiac manifestation of toxicity in this infant is:
(A) Fever
(B) Dizziness
(C) Vomiting
(D) Visual disturbances
(E) Confusion

155. A 10-year-old boy, the star goalie for the Salt Lake City Little League soccer team, had a sore throat about two weeks ago but did not tell anyone because he was afraid he would miss the play-offs. Since several children have been diagnosed with rheumatic fever in the area, his mother is worried that he may be at risk as well. You tell her that several criteria must be met to make the diagnosis but that the most common finding is:
(A) Carditis
(B) Arthralgia
(C) Erythema marginatum
(D) Chorea
(E) Fever

156. Which of the following manifestations of acute rheumatic fever is NOT relieved by salicylate or steroid therapy?
(A) Carditis
(B) Abdominal pain
(C) Arthritis
(D) Chorea
(E) Fever

157. The parents of a 2-month-old boy are concerned about his risk of coronary artery disease because of the recent death of his 40-year-old maternal uncle from a myocardial infarction. In managing this situation, you would do which of the following?
(A) Screen the parents for total cholesterol.
(B) Counsel the parents regarding appropriate dietary practices for a 2-month-old infant and test him for total cholesterol at 6 months of age.
(C) Initiate lipid-lowering agents.
(D) Recommend yearly EKGs for the patient.
(E) Have a screen for cholesterol of the infant.

158. For the past year, a 12-year-old boy has had recurrent episodes of swelling of his hands and feet, which has been getting worse recently. These episodes occur following exercise and emotional stress, last for two to three days, and resolve spontaneously. The last episode was accompanied by abdominal pain, vomiting, and diarrhea. The results of a routine laboratory workup are normal. An older sister and a maternal uncle have had similar episodes but were not told a diagnosis. The most compatible diagnosis is:
(A) Systemic lupus erythematosus
(B) Focal glomerulosclerosis
(C) Congenital nephrotic syndrome
(D) Hereditary angioedema
(E) Nephritis

159. During a regular checkup on an 8-year-old child, you note a loud first heart sound with a fixed and widely split second heart sound at the upper left sternal border that does not change with respirations. The patient is otherwise active and healthy. The mostly likely heart lesion to explain these findings is:
(A) Atrial septal defect
(B) Ventricular septal defect
(C) Isolated tricuspid regurgitation
(D) Tetralogy of Fallot
(E) Mitral valve prolapse

160. A 2-year-old boy is brought into the emergency nursing clinic with a complaint of fever for 6 days and development of a limp. On examination, he is found to have an erythematous macular exanthem over his body, ocular conjunctivitis, dry and cracked lips, a red throat, and cervical lymphadenopathy. There is a grade II/VI systolic ejection murmur at the lower left sternal border. A white blood cell count and differential show predominant neutrophils with increased platelets on smear. What is the most likely diagnosis?
    (A) Scarlet fever
    (B) Rheumatic fever
    (C) Kawasaki disease
    (D) Juvenile rheumatoid arthritis
    (E) Beri Beri

161. What would be the next steps in the management of the child in the preceding question?
    (A) Intramuscular or oral penicillin, outpatient follow-up
    (B) Pooled immunoglobulin (IVIG) and high-dose aspirin, inpatient admission
    (C) Nonsteroidal anti-inflammatory medication, outpatient follow-up
    (D) Blood cultures, intravenous vancomycin, inpatient admission
    (E) Outpatient followup

162. A newborn infant has mild cyanosis, diaphoresis, poor peripheral pulses, hepatomegaly, and cardiomegaly. Respiratory rate is 60 breaths per min, and heart rate is 250 beats per min. The child most likely has congestive heart failure caused by:
    (A) A large atrial septal defect and valvular pulmonic stenosis
    (B) A ventricular septal defect and transposition of the great vessels
    (C) Total anomalous pulmonary venous return
    (D) Paroxysmal atrial tachycardia
    (E) Patent ductous artriosus

163. A 2-year-old child with minimal cyanosis has an S3 and S4 (a quadruple rhythm), a systolic murmur in the pulmonic area, and a mid-diastolic murmur along the lower left sternal border. An electrocardiogram shows right atrial hypertrophy and a ventricular block pattern in the right chest leads. What is the most likely diagnosis?
    (A) Tricuspid regurgitation and pulmonic stenosis

(B) Pulmonic stenosis and a ventricular septal defect (tetralogy of Fallot)
(C) An atrioventricular canal
(D) Ebstein's anomaly
(E) Ventricular septal defect

164. A 4-year-old girl is brought to the nursing clinic. Her father reports that she suddenly became pale and stopped running while he had been playfully chasing her. After 30 min, she was no longer pale and wanted to resume the game. She has never had a previous episode or ever been cyanotic. Her physical examination was normal, as were her chest X-ray and echocardiogram. An electrocardiogram showed the pattern seen here, which indicates:

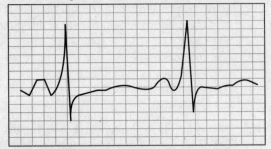

(A) Paroxysmal ventricular tachycardia
(B) Paroxysmal supraventricular tachycardia
(C) Wolff-Parkinson-White syndrome
(D) Excessive stress during play
(E) Asthma

165. A child has a history of spiking fevers, which have been as high as 40°C (104°F). She has spindle-shaped swelling of finger joints and complains of upper sternal pain. What is the most likely diagnosis?
    (A) Rheumatic fever
    (B) Juvenile rheumatoid arthritis
    (C) Toxic synovitis
    (D) Septic arthritis
    (E) Osteoarthritis

166. A cyanotic newborn is suspected of having congenital heart disease. The EKG shows left axis deviation and left ventricular hypertrophy (LVH). What is the most likely diagnosis?
    (A) Transposition of the great arteries
    (B) Truncus arteriosus
    (C) Tricuspid atresia
    (D) Tetralogy of Fallot
    (E) Patent ductus arteriosus

167. A 3-day-old infant with a single second heart sound has had progressively deepening cyanosis since birth but no respiratory distress. Chest radiography demonstrates no cardiomegaly and normal pulmonary vasculature. An electrocardiogram shows an axis of 120° and right ventricular prominence. Which congenital cardiac malformation is most likely responsible for the cyanosis?
    (A) Tetralogy of Fallot
    (B) Transposition of the great vessels
    (C) Tricuspid atresia
    (D) Pulmonary atresia with intact ventricular septum
    (E) Patent ductous arteriosus

168. During a physical examination for participation in a sport, a 16-year-old girl is noted to have a late apical systolic murmur, which is preceded by a click. The rest of the cardiac examination is normal. She states that her mother also has some type of heart "murmur" but knows nothing else about it. What is the most likely diagnosis?
    (A) Atrial septal defect
    (B) Aortic stenosis
    (C) Tricuspid regurgitation
    (D) Mitral valve prolapse
    (E) Ventricular septal defect

169. Which of the following medications commonly prescribed for AD/HD is a non-stimulant drug?
    (A) Atomoxetine
    (B) Buproprion
    (C) Levoamphetamine
    (D) Lisdexamfetamine dimesylate
    (E) Methylphenidate

170. Leber's hereditary optic neuropathy (LHON) is a genetic disease that causes degeneration of the optic nerve, leading to blindness. The disorder is caused by a mutation in the genome of the mitochondria. LHON can therefore be passed from:
    (A) Fathers to sons only
    (B) Mothers to daughters only
    (C) Mothers to sons or daughters
    (D) A parent who shows symptoms of the disorder only
    (E) A parent who is a carrier but shows no symptoms of LOIIN

171. Which of the following infectious diseases causes gastrointestinal symptoms, such as upset stomach, diarrhea, and nausea, which may progress to myalgia, fever, weakness, splinter hemorrhaging of the nails, and circumorbital edema, and is most commonly transmitted by eating undercooked pork?
    (A) Entamoebiasis caused by *Entamoeba histolytica*
    (B) Gatroenteritis caused by *Campylobacter jejuni*
    (C) Giardiasis caused by *Giardia lamblia*
    (D) Hemorrhagic diarrhea caused by *Escherichia coli*
    (E) Trichinosis caused by *Trichinella spiralis*

172. Blood pressure is gauged as the pressure exerted by blood as it moves through the brachial artery of the upper arm. The difference between the systolic and the diastolic pressure is known as the:
    (A) Arterial compliance
    (B) Cardiac output
    (C) Mean arterial pressure
    (D) Pulse pressure
    (E) Stroke volume

173. In order to diagnose AD/HD in an adult, the symptoms of the disorder must:
    (A) Appear for the first time in adulthood
    (B) Be present between the ages of 18 and 30
    (C) Have appeared before the age of 7
    (D) Include hyperactivity
    (E) Not include hyperactivity

174. Which of the following describes painful, recurring lesions on the oral mucosa that appear yellow or white with an erythematous border?
    (A) Acute herpetic gingivostomatitis
    (B) Aphthous ulcers
    (C) Oral candidiasis
    (D) Oral herpes simplex
    (E) Oral leukoplakia

175. During pregnancy, Braxton Hicks contractions:
(A) Are often mild or painless, and do not signal labor
(B) Are often mild or painless, and signal the onset of labor
(C) Become longer, more intense, and more frequent, but do not signal labor
(D) Become longer, more intense, and more frequent, signaling labor
(E) Occur both throughout pregnancy and during labor

176. Oral rehydration salts (ORS), used to prevent dehydration in patients experiencing diarrhea, include sugar and salt in specific proportions because:
(A) Glucose is required for the transport of sodium through the intestinal lumen
(B) Levels of ATP must be restored quickly in patients experiencing diarrhea
(C) Patients experiencing severe diarrhea tend to suffer from hypernatremia
(D) Sodium is required for the transport of glucose through the intestinal lumen
(E) The contents of the intestinal lumen must be hyper-osmotic to blood

177. Genital herpes is caused by the herpes simplex virus type 1 or type 2, and causes outbreaks of painful, red blisters on the genitals. Transmission of genital herpes:
(A) Cannot be spread to the eyes, lips, or areas other than the genitals
(B) Cannot occur unless one partner has a visible sore
(C) Is more common from female to male than from male to female
(D) Is more common from male to female than from female to male
(E) Is not affected by taking medications such as acyclovir

178. An aromatase inhibitor is prescribed to post-menopausal women with breast cancer tumors that are:
(A) Estrogen receptor (ER) positive
(B) Hormone receptor (HR) negative
(C) Invasive
(D) Non-invasive
(E) Progesterone receptor (PR) positive

179. Hypothyroidism is indicated by clinical findings of:
(A) Low TSH level, high T3 level, and high T4 level
(B) Low TSH level, high T3 level, and low T4 level
(C) Low TSH level, low T3 level, and low T4 level
(D) High TSH level, high T3 level, and high T4 level
(E) High TSH level, low T3 level, and low T4 level

180. In most medical settings, the standard vital signs include:
(A) Body temperature, blood pressure, height, and weight
(B) Body temperature, blood pressure, pulse, and pupil dilation
(C) Body temperature, blood pressure, pulse, and respiratory rate
(D) Blood pressure, height, respiratory rate, and weight
(E) Blood pressure, pulse, pupil dilation, respiratory rate, and weight

ANSWER KEY AND EXPLANATIONS

1. C	37. E	73. E	109. E	145. E
2. B	38. C	74. D	110. B	146. A
3. E	39. D	75. B	111. C	147. E
4. B	40. C	76. A	112. E	148. A
5. C	41. B	77. D	113. C	149. B
6. D	42. D	78. B	114. C	150. C
7. B	43. C	79. B	115. E	151. D
8. A	44. B	80. A	116. A	152. C
9. D	45. E	81. B	117. E	153. D
10. C	46. B	82. D	118. B	154. C
11. B	47. E	83. B	119. E	155. B
12. B	48. C	84. B	120. C	156. D
13. E	49. A	85. A	121. A	157. A
14. A	50. B	86. D	122. E	158. D
15. B	51. D	87. C	123. D	159. A
16. B	52. E	88. B	124. E	160. C
17. E	53. E	89. A	125. C	161. B
18. D	54. B	90. C	126. E	162. D
19. B	55. A	91. B	127. A	163. D
20. C	56. A	92. B	128. C	164. C
21. C	57. E	93. E	129. A	165. B
22. B	58. C	94. A	130. E	166. C
23. E	59. D	95. D	131. D	167. B
24. C	60. B	96. B	132. A	168. D
25. E	61. D	97. A	133. B	169. A
26. D	62. D	98. D	134. A	170. C
27. B	63. C	99. D	135. D	171. E
28. C	64. B	100. C	136. B	172. A
29. D	65. E	101. A	137. A	173. C
30. B	66. E	102. D	138. C	174. B
31. D	67. D	103. E	139. A	175. A
32. E	68. D	104. B	140. E	176. D
33. D	69. A	105. A	141. C	177. D
34. E	70. B	106. C	142. B	178. A
35. B	71. C	107. C	143. B	179. A
36. D	72. D	108. D	144. C	180. C

1. **The correct answer is (C).** The proximity of the patient's symptoms to her meals indicates an issue directly related to those meals and would suggest a clinical reaction, in this case, to glutens. Although celiac disease (celiac sprue) is a genetic condition, its presentation may occur at any time, especially in mild cases. The lack of physical discomfort and clean stool are also indicators of celiac disease.

2. **The correct answer is (B).** Distended neck veins are a symptom exclusively associated with right-sided failure. Exertional dyspnea, gallops, non-productive cough, and orthopnea are all symptoms associated only with left-sided failure.

3. **The correct answer is (E).** The key factor that would indicate this diagnosis is the patient's history of lung infection. Bronchiectasis occurs because of bronchial damage caused by previous infection. Odorous sputum may also be unique to bronchiectasis.

4. **The correct answer is (B).** A tender anterior cervical adenopathy and pharyngotonsillar exudates are two of the Centor criteria. The 100.2°F fever is just under the prescribed temperature of 100.4°F and, thus, does not meet the Centor criteria. The final component of the criteria would be the absence of a cough, which eliminates that symptom.

5. **The correct answer is (C).** The patient's symptoms are common to orchitis and this condition is frequently connected to post pubertal males suffering from mumps.

6. **The correct answer is (D).** Surgical drainage and cleansing would be the most appropriate treatment in this scenario. A high fiber diet and increased fluids, choice A, is a treatment option in the event of Stage I or II internal hemorrhoids. Bulking agents and increased fluids, choice B, would be prescribed for the treatment of anal fissures. Choice C, surgical drainage and antibiotics, would be appropriate in cases of Pilonidal disease. Finally, a saline enema, choice E, would be used to treat impacted fecal matter.

7. **The correct answer is (B).** The patient is most likely suffering from hypochondriasis. The patient genuinely believes she is suffering from a physical condition and her psychiatric history denotes a probable cause.

8. **The correct answer is (A).** Achilles tendonitis is a degenerative condition that is caused by overuse and, sometimes, poor stretching and training. Since the patient is a frequent runner and the pain is located in the proper location for Achilles tendonitis, this is the appropriate diagnosis.

9. **The correct answer is (D).** The most likely diagnosis is humeral shaft fracture. This is indicated by the fact that the injury was sustained due to an automobile accident, the presence of swelling and deformity, the position in which the patient is holding the arm, and the lack of other indicative injuries.

10. **The correct answer is (C).** Captopril, which is an ACE inhibitor, should be administered first. ACE inhibitors are commonly used to treat nephrotic syndrome in its early stages.

11. **The correct answer is (B).** Hyperkalemia refers to an elevated potassium level, which can cause dysrhythmia or cardiac arrest and is commonly associated with kidney failure.

12. **The correct answer is (B).** The patient's symptoms and her history with infertility should indicate that the correct answer is cystic fibrosis. Most patients suffering from this condition are under 30 years of age and present with a history of infertility, chronic lung disease, or pancreatitis.

13. **The correct answer is (E).** Reactive arthritis (Reiter syndrome) is commonly seen as a sequelae to sexually transmitted diseases like chlamydial urethritis and others. The presence of mucocutaneous lesions and HLA-B27 are also common indicators of this condition.

14. **The correct answer is (A).** When PRP-OMP is administered for Haemophilus influenza type b immunization at two and four months, a third dose at six months is not required. Rather, the third dose may be administered between 12-18 months.

15. **The correct answer is (B).** The patient's plaques, lesions, lack of scaling, and habit of scratching the affected area all suggest Lichen simplex chronicus, which is a long-term manifestation of atopic dermatitis.

16. **The correct answer is (B).** The predominant presenting feature of acute thrombocytopenia is

the development of petechiae, purpura, and hemor-rhagic bullae on the skin and mucus membranes. This dermatologic presentation is most commonly associated with acute cases of thrombocytopenia.

17. **The correct answer is (E).** Persistent marked asymmetry of tonsils is an absolute indication for tonsillectomy in this case.

18. **The correct answer is (D).** Erythema infectiosum is caused by human parvovirus B19. This condition is also known as fifth disease or slapped cheek.

19. **The correct answer is (B).** A 41-year-old Chinese woman would be most at risk because á-Thalassemia is most common among people of Chinese and southeast Asian descent.

20. **The correct answer is (C).** Empyema is the only type of pleural effusion connected with infection within the pleural space.

21. **The correct answer is (C).** Ultrasonography is the method of choice for diagnosis of polycystic kidney disease. This type of imaging scan can easily reveal the presence of the fluid-filled renal cysts that characterize polycystic kidney disease.

22. **The correct answer is (B).** The most common primary form of treatment for cystitis is a fluoro-quinolone regimen lasting three to five days.

23. **The correct answer is (E).** Variceal litigation, in which an endoscope is used to snare the varices with an elastic band, is the safest means of treating esophageal varices and the most effective in pre-venting future episodes.

24. **The correct answer is (C).** Necrotizing fasciitis is the correct answer in this scenario. The patient is suffering from a bacterial infection and his symptoms indicate flesh-eating bacteria.

25. **The correct answer is (E).** Tachycardia, tachypnea, narrow pulse pressure, and pulsus paradoxus are the classic presenting symptoms of cardiac tamponade.

26. **The correct answer is (D).** The measures men-tioned in the question are all primarily aimed at preventing deep vein thrombosis, which is the formation of a blood clot, most often in the legs. Such blood clots can lead to other, more serious conditions.

27. **The correct answer is (B).** The most likely cause of the patient's condition is *Neisseria meningitidis*, which is the only pathogen among the options that would result in a petechial rash.

28. **The correct answer is (C).** Sjögren's syndrome is an autoimmune disorder that causes the destruction of salivary and lacrimal glands. The patient's symptoms are consistent with the normal clinical presentation of Sjögren's syndrome.

29. **The correct answer is (D).** The patient is presenting the classic symptoms of viral conjunctivitis, also known as "pink eye. " She likely contracted this viral infection while swimming in the public pool.

30. **The correct answer is (B).** The patient is suffering from a hiatal hernia. Also known as diaphragmatic hernia, this form of hernia occurs when part of the stomach protrudes through the diaphragm by way of the esophageal hiatus.

31. **The correct answer is (D).** Horse serum is the correct form of treatment. Administration of a horse serum antitoxin is immediately required in all cases of this condition.

32. **The correct answer is (E).** Cystoscopy would be the best means of confirming the suspected diag-nosis. This procedure has an almost 100% accuracy rate and is the definitive means for diagnosing bladder cancer.

33. **The correct answer is (D).** The patient is exhibiting common signs of ulcerative colitis. In addition, recent smoking cessation is likely to cause a flare-up of this condition.

34. **The correct answer is (E).** Volume overloading of the left ventricle occurs exclusively with aortic insufficiency.

35. **The correct answer is (B).** Treatment with soma-tropin, which is also known as growth hormone, would make up for the pituitary gland's dimin-ished natural production of growth hormone and encourage normal growth.

36. **The correct answer is (D).** Although NSAIDs are commonly used to treat patients suffering from heavy vaginal bleeding, they are ineffective for treating bleeding caused by uterine fibroids.

37. **The correct answer is (E).** The patient is lacking thiamin, which is commonly found in pork, grains, dried beans, and peas. A thiamin deficiency would cause the type of symptoms the patient is experiencing.

38. **The correct answer is (C).** Hypoplastic left heart syndrome is a cyanotic defect that is more common in males and would present with symptoms like those the patient is exhibiting.

39. **The correct answer is (D).** Surgery is only required in severe cases when the patient does not respond to basic treatments.

40. **The correct answer is (C).** Mottled skin is an indicator of severe sepsis. Other possible indicators include significant drop in urination, sudden mental abnormalities, lowered platelet count, difficulty breathing, or irregular heart activity.

41. **The correct answer is (B).** Dyshidrosis, which occurs most frequently in patients under 40 years of age, presents with the symptoms the patient is experiencing.

42. **The correct answer is (D).** Oral corticosteroids will act as replacements for hormones that the patient's body is failing to produce.

43. **The correct answer is (C).** Glandular atrophy is common in elderly female patients with Hashimoto's thyroiditis.

44. **The correct answer is (B).** Shingles often presents with a rash, such as the patient is exhibiting, that often forms a band that wraps from the breastbone to the spine on one side of the chest.

45. **The correct answer is (E).** The most likely diagnosis would be onychomycosis, which is a fungal infection of the nail.

46. **The correct answer is (B).** A fecalith is a hardened, stone-like mass of fecal matter that can cause an obstruction. If a fecalith obstructs the appendix, appendicitis ensues. This is the most frequent cause of appendicitis.

47. **The correct answer is (E).** The anticholinergic drug benztropine is typically prescribed to patients with Parkinson's disease for the specific purpose of controlling the tremor that often accompanies the condition.

48. **The correct answer is (C).** The patient is suffering from maculopathy, which results in symptoms involving the macula.

49. **The correct answer is (A).** The patient is exhibiting classic signs of primary sclerosing cholangitis, which results in a chronic thickening of the bile duct walls.

50. **The correct answer is (B).** In patients with benign prostatic hyperplasia, natural enlargement of the prostate causes the prostatic urethra to compress, which results in obstructive urinary symptoms.

51. **The correct answer is (D).** Although Crohn's disease (regional enteritis) presents similarly to ulcerative colitis, skip areas are common and the entire region is not always affected.

52. **The correct answer is (E).** Hyperventilation is the most common, and often the first, sign of metabolic acidosis. This symptom is a result of pulmonary compensation.

53. **The correct answer is (E).** Iron toxidromes frequently require gastric lavage, which is a form of gastric emptying, among other treatments.

54. **The correct answer is (B).** A chest X-ray test would allow the clinician to determine as quickly as possible whether active tuberculosis pneumonia is present.

55. **The correct answer is (A).** The patient can be released without treatment, as most instances of Mallory-Weiss tears will heal without any treatment.

56. **The correct answer is (A).** Lidocaine is used to treat the type of ventricular tachycardia from which the patient is suffering. Mexiletine can also be administered in this situation.

57. **The correct answer is (E).** Psoriatic arthritis is an inflammatory arthritis accompanied by skin involvement. When affecting the foot, "Pencil in Cup" deformities of the proximal phalanx are common.

58. **The correct answer is (C).** Limited scleroderma, which presents with a deposition of collagen, affects only the skin and is commonly associated with the face, neck, and distal elbows and knees.

59. **The correct answer is (D).** Elevated blood pressure is not a common sign of concussion and may indicate a cerebral aneurysm, which can also be caused by head trauma in some cases.

60. **The correct answer is (B).** Arthrotomy, which involves surgically opening the joint for drainage and debridement of the infection, is usually required with hip joint infections. The only exception to this is if the infecting pathogen is *Neisseria gonorrhoeae*.

61. **The correct answer is (D).** *Pseudomonas aeruginosa* is the most common hospital-acquired pneumonia-causing pathogen for patients in the intensive care unit. Patients who are artificially ventilated through endotracheal intubation are at particularly high risk of developing hospital-acquired pneumonia.

62. **The correct answer is (D).** Since the patient presents with the classic symptoms of mumps, including swollen salivary glands, his condition is most likely a result of having missed the MMR, or the measles, mumps, rubella vaccine.

63. **The correct answer is (C).** The patient has suffered an oblique fracture. These fractures are identified by a slanted fracture line.

64. **The correct answer is (B).** The patient is suffering from idiopathic fibrosing interstitial pneumonia. This diagnosis could be easily confirmed with diagnostic imaging.

65. **The correct answer is (E).** Macular degeneration is frequently associated with aging and presents with symptoms like those the patient is experiencing.

66. **The correct answer is (E).** Administration of the hepatitis B vaccine is contraindicated for patients with baker's yeast allergies.

67. **The correct answer is (D).** A Torsades de pointes ventricular arrhythmia is most accurately described as a QRS complex twisted around the baseline and a continuously changing axis. This condition can occur spontaneously, with certain conditions, or after the administration of QT prolonging medications.

68. **The correct answer is (D).** You should prescribe another SSRI, such as fluoxetine. Since this class of antidepressant appears to be effective against the patient's depression, it is prudent to stay within this class of drugs and prescribe another SSRI that may be less likely to cause nausea.

69. **The correct answer is (A).** The most likely diagnosis is tinea corporis, which is a fungal infection of the trunk. It is also commonly known as ringworm.

70. **The correct answer is (B).** Patients suffering from B6 pyridoxine deficiency commonly present with flaky skin, headache, anemia, seizures, and sore tongue.

71. **The correct answer is (C).** Bloody, pus-filled diarrhea is the most prominent indicator of ulcerative colitis.

72. **The correct answer is (D).** You should tell the patient that the hepatitis A vaccination is recommended by the Centers for Disease Control and Prevention (CDC) because India is considered a country of high prevalence of antibody to hepatitis A virus.

73. **The correct answer is (E).** In inevitable abortion, bleeding and cramping accompany the dilation of the cervix and possible rupture of membranes. No passage of the products of conception has yet occurred.

74. **The correct answer is (D).** Eclampsia is clinically recognized when a patient presenting the signs and symptoms of preeclampsia experiences a seizure.

75. **The correct answer is (B).** Alcohol abuse is the cause of chronic pancreatitis in up to 90% of cases.

76. **The correct answer is (A).** Intracranial tumors located in the frontal lobe frequently present with the symptoms the patient is experiencing.

77. **The correct answer is (D).** *Klebsiella pneumoniae* is the most common cause of pneumonia among patients with a history of alcohol abuse.

78. **The correct answer is (B).** Auspitz's sign is a dermatological sign that refers to pinpoint bleeding following the removal of a scale.

79. **The correct answer is (B).** The patient is presenting the classic symptoms of cystitis and his urinalysis and urine culture confirm the diagnosis.

80. **The correct answer is (A).** Hypocalcemia is an abnormally low level of serum calcium and will yield symptoms like those the patient is presenting. The patient's carpel tunnel spasm is known as

Trousseau's sign and is a classic neurological indicator of this condition.

81. **The correct answer is (B).** Patients with borderline personality disorder suffer from mood swings, abandonment issues, anger management problems, psychotic episodes, and other behavioral difficulties. Self-mutilation and suicide attempts are also common with this disorder. In addition, borderline personality disorder is more common in females than males.

82. **The correct answer is (D).** In this scenario, the patient is suffering from a severe case of endometriosis and requires proactive treatment, so expectant management would not be appropriate.

83. **The correct answer is (B).** Peripheral vertigo is associated with conditions like Meniere's disease, vestibular neuronitis, or obstructing anatomic abnormalities. It is also commonly associated with the symptoms the patient is suffering from.

84. **The correct answer is (B).** Bell's palsy is an abrupt loss of strength in the facial muscles on one side of the face. It is commonly preceded by a noticeable pain in the ear on the same side as the affected facial muscles.

85. **The correct answer is (A).** A rapid antigen test can detect streptococcal bacteria in minutes by detecting antigens in a throat specimen.

86. **The correct answer is (D).** Frontotemporal dementia, which presents secondary to degeneration of the frontal lobe, is characterized by the types of physical and behavior symptoms the patient is displaying.

87. **The correct answer is (C).** Shigellosis is a bacterial infection that causes an abrupt onset of gastrointestinal symptom such as the patient is experiencing.

88. **The correct answer is (B).** Gardisil protects against approximately 70% of the known strains of HPV. It is recommended for females aged 11 to 26, ideally before they become sexually active.

89. **The correct answer is (A).** Spinal stenosis is a nerve compression that can be caused by a narrowing of the spinal canal or neural foramina. Back and leg pain that can be relieved by leaning forward is common to this condition.

90. **The correct answer is (C).** Otis media is due to an infection and is commonly caused by Streptococcus pneumonia, which could likely still be in the patient's system after his bout with pneumonia.

91. **The correct answer is (B).** Gout is a common form of arthritis that most frequently presents in the joint of the big toe and causes pain, swelling, and redness. The affected area is generally very sensitive to pressure. Chronic cases may present with tophi formations.

92. **The correct answer is (B).** Medial epicondylitis, also known as "golfer's elbow" or "baseball elbow", causes pain and tenderness specifically on the inside of the elbow. The pain may radiate down the forearm and, sometimes, into one or more fingers. Numbness or tingling may also occur.

93. **The correct answer is (E).** Testicular torsion occurs when the testis becomes twisted on its spermatic cord.

94. **The correct answer is (A).** The most likely cause of the patient's vaginitis is bacterial vaginosis (BV), which is a polymicrobial clinical syndrome resulting from replacement of the normal *Lactobacillus* species in the vagina with high concentrations of anaerobic bacteria such as *Mycoplasma hominis*.

95. **The correct answer is (D).** Vitamin B12 is naturally found in animal products such as fish, beef, poultry, eggs, milk, and milk products. Since these foods are not part of a vegan diet, vegans who do not take Vitamin B12 supplements put themselves at risk for developing megaloblastic anemia and nerve damage.

96. **The correct answer is (B).** Black women are more likely to develop uterine fibroids than any other women, regardless of any other circumstances.

97. **The correct answer is (A).** The best course of treatment for the patient's condition would be a 5% permethrin cream, applied from the chin to the feet. Permethrin is considered a safe treatment, unlike other medications used to treat scabies. In most cases, one application of permethrin cream kills scabies mites, though the itching may persist for several weeks after mites have died.

98. **The correct answer is (D).** A tool and die manufacturer would be most at risk for developing berryliosis, which is caused by the inhalation of beryllium, a metal element.

99. **The correct answer is (D).** The patient in this scenario is suffering from pyelonephritis, or a kidney infection. In this case, the patient was previously diagnosed with cystitis, or a bladder infection, which was apparently caused by *Escherichia coli* bacteria. Though the patient was treated for the original infection with 5 days of fluoroquinolone, she did not respond to the antibiotic, and developed pyelonephritis as a complication of the cystitis. *Escherichia coli* is the most common cause of bladder and kidney infection.

100. **The correct answer is (C).** All of the answer choices are reproductive disorders, but only endometriosis, a condition in which endometrial-like cells grow outside the uterine cavity, results in a combination of pelvic pain, dysmenorrhea (severe uterine pain during menstruation), dyspareunia (pain during intercourse), and dyschezia (trouble passing bowel movements).

101. **The correct answer is (A).** Bacterial conjunctivitis is a bacterial infection of the conjunctiva, the clear membrane that lines the sclera (white part of the eye) and the insides of the eyelids. Symptoms of bacterial conjunctivitis include the eyes feeling "glued shut" upon awakening, purulent discharge (pus), and somewhat blurry vision.

102. **The correct answer is (D).** The typical causes of microcytic anemias resulting in MCVs of less than 00 fL are iron deficiency and thalassemia, a hereditary blood disorder that results in the production of an abnormal form of hemoglobin, the protein in red blood cells responsible for transporting oxygen throughout the body. Because the woman has no family history of thalassemia, iron deficiency is the most likely cause.

103. **The correct answer is (E).** The influenza vaccine has been known to cause anaphylactic reactions in children with egg allergies. Some children are allergic to the neomycin and streptomycin in MMR vaccines. Children with baker's yeast allergies should not receive the hepatitis B vaccine. The varicella vaccine can affect children with gelatin allergies. The DTaP vaccine usually does not cause an allergic reaction.

104. **The correct answer is (B).** Hypertension increases a patient's risk for developing other forms of cardiovascular disease including atherosclerosis, which is a build-up of cholesterol and lipids on artery walls. A lipid profile measures total cholesterol, high-density lipoprotein (HDL) cholesterol, low-density lipoprotein (LDL) cholesterol, and triglycerides. It is important for determining the risk of atherosclerosis.

105. **The correct answer is (A).** The patient shows classic symptoms of tuberculosis (TB) infection. The 2-month combination of isoniazid, rifampin, pyrazinamide, and ethambutol is recommended to treat active TB. Additional drug therapy may be necessary following completion of the first round.

106. **The correct answer is (C).** A 65-year-old black male is the most at risk because multiple myeloma is more common in the elderly, effects blacks more than whites, and effects more men than women.

107. **The correct answer is (C).** A forced expiratory volume in 1 second (FEV1) equal to 60–80 percent predicted in combination with a forced expiratory volume in 1 second to forced vital capacity ratio (FEV1/FVC) equal to 75–80 percent is indicative of moderate persistent asthma.

108. **The correct answer is (D).** Mesothelioma is a rare form of cancer that develops from the mesothelium, a protective membrane that covers many of the body's organs. Mesothelioma usually develops as a result of exposure to asbestos, any of several minerals formerly used in insulation and other construction materials. Asbestos has since been banned.

109. **The correct answer is (E).** The recommended caloric intake for a patient with type 1 diabetes mellitus is 45–65 percent carbohydrates, 10–35 percent protein, 25–35 percent fat, with less than 7 percent saturated fat. In addition, the patient should limit cholesterol intake to fewer than 33 mg/day.

110. **The correct answer is (B).** The treatment for appendicitis is surgical removal via appendectomy. If perforation or peritonitis are suspected, broad-spectrum antibiotics should be administered pre- and post-operatively.

111. **The correct answer is (C).** This patient exhibits signs of myocardial infarction (MI) that are more typical in women than men. These signs may not appear to be cardiac in nature. Women may have symptoms such as discomfort in the upper body, including the arms, back, neck, jaw, or stomach. They may also have classic signs of an MI, such as pain in the center of the chest, diaphoresis, and lightheadedness.

112. **The correct answer is (E).** The patient is exhibiting signs of celiac disease, which is also referred to as "gluten intolerance" or "celiac sprue." It is a multi-systemic disorder and not just an intestinal disease. When people with celiac disease eat foods containing gluten, their immune system responds by damaging or destroying villi. These are tiny, fingerlike protrusions that line the small intestine. Villi normally allow nutrients from food to be absorbed through the walls of the small intestine into the bloodstream. Without healthy villi, a person becomes malnourished, no matter how much food he or she eats. (Malnutrition explains the patient's low ferritin level.) The itchy rash that can occur in patients with celiac disease is called dermatitis herpetiformis. This condition is unique to patients with celiac disease.

113. **The correct answer is (C).** The most likely diagnosis is a stress fracture. This patient exhibits pain and edema in the 2nd metatarsal region of her right foot. Metatarsal fractures comprise about one-fourth of stress fractures, and are most likely in the distal 2nd and 3rd metatarsals. Stress fractures are more likely to occur when athletes step up their training. X-rays do not always detect a stress fracture as soon as the injury occurs. In about half of cases, evidence of a stress fracture is apparent on X-ray in two to 10 weeks as the bone attempts to heal. A stress fracture is more likely to be detected on a bone scan or magnetic resonance imaging (MRI).

114. **The correct answer is (C).** Rhinoscopy (also called nasoscopy) would be the most appropriate procedure because it allows the provider to view the nasal cavity for the source of the injury. It is not uncommon for a child of this age to thrust an object up his nose and injure the nasal membrane. Or, he may have fallen and hit his nose on a hard surface.

115. **The correct answer is (E).** Deep vein thrombosis (DVT) occurs when a thrombus forms in one or more of the deep veins of the body, usually in the legs. DVT is serious because the thrombus may travel to the lungs, causing pulmonary embolism. Oral contraceptives are considered a risk factor for DVT, particularly in women who are obese, smoke, or who have hypercoagulability conditions such as Factor V Leiden.

116. **The correct answer is (A).** Although the American Diabetes Association formerly considered an A1C of 7% the cut-off level for diagnosing diabetes, the organization dropped that number to >6.5% when it determined that patients with an A1C of >6.5% were at decreased risk of diabetes complications such as retinopathy.

117. **The correct answer is (E).** Hypospadias is the medical term for a birth defect that causes the urethra to open on the underside of the penis. A defect called "chordee," taken from the French word "cordee," for its corded appearance, often accompanies hypospadias. This causes the penis to bend downward when erect. The meatus may be located anywhere along the shaft of the penis, from just below the glans to the scrotum, although in most cases the meatus is close to the glans. Surgery entails widening the meatus, correcting chordee, and reconstructing the part of the urethra that is missing. Most surgeons prefer to do a hyperspadias repair on children who are between 1 to 3 years of age, but it can be done on adults as well.

118. **The correct answer is (B).** The patient is most likely suffering from peptic ulcer disease. She is unsure whether she is taking 250 or 500 mg tablets and states that she takes two to three tablets every few hours. That means the dosage could be anywhere from 2,000 to 4,000 mg a day, if she takes the medication every three hours around the clock. The usual dosage of naproxen is 250-500 mg twice daily, or 500-1,000 mg. She may be exceeding the normal dose by as much as four times. Naproxen and other non-steroidal anti-inflammatory drugs (NSAIDs) such as ibuprofen are known to increase the risk of peptic ulcer disease, particularly in the elderly.

119. **The correct answer is (E).** Symptoms of schizophrenia may present at a young age in children,

before psychosis occurs, but the condition itself most often presents as adult-onset schizophrenia starting at age 18. There are two types of symptoms in schizophrenia—positive and negative. Positive symptoms include psychotic behaviors such as hallucinations, delusions, and thought disorders. Negative symptoms include "flat" affect (speaking in a monotone voice), lack of pleasure in everyday life, and lack of ability to begin and sustain everyday activities.

120. **The correct answer is (C).** The patient is most likely suffering from cystitis, which is also called a bladder infection or urinary tract infection. Frequent sexual intercourse may increase the risk of cystitis because it introduces bacteria, most often *Escherichia coli*, into the urethra.

121. **The correct answer is (A).** The patient is most likely experiencing a niacin overdose. The recommended daily dose of niacin is not to exceed 6 grams, or 6,000 mg daily. The patient is not certain of his dose, but it is likely he has increased his dose significantly by changing brands of niacin. In fact, it is possible he has been taking as much as 8,000 mg daily, or 8 grams.

122. **The correct answer is (E).** The patient's condition was most likely caused by a methicillin-resistant *Staphylococcus aureus* skin infection. The patient may have indeed acquired MRSA in the school locker room, as this is a common source of community-acquired MRSA. A skin infection with MRSA almost always causes a red pustule that grows rapidly and, without prompt treatment, may turn into a deep abscess that spreads the infection to the organs, bloodstream, bones, and joints.

123. **The correct answer is (D).** The patient is exhibiting classic signs of congestive heart failure (CHF), including lower extremity edema, productive cough with white sputum, chest congestion, tachycardia with irregular pulse, hypertension, shortness of breath, and fatigue.

124. **The correct answer is (E).** The patient is most likely suffering from eczema, which is also called atopic dermatitis. This patient exhibits classic signs of eczema, such as itching at night, scaly and cracked skin, and small raised bumps that leak and then crust over.

125. **The correct answer is (C).** The patient is exhibiting the classic signs of a migraine, including throbbing pain in one side of the head, light and sound sensitivity, and nausea and vomiting.

126. **The correct answer is (E).** The patient is exhibiting the classic symptoms of a right-sided cerebrovascular accident (CVA), including left-sided weakness and numbness and difficulty speaking. His earlier fall probably occurred due to the weakness of his left side.

127. **The correct answer is (A).** You would most likely begin with a pregnancy test. This patient exhibits the classic signs of ectopic pregnancy, including non-menstrual vaginal bleeding, pain in the lower abdomen, and not using contraception. Her period is a week late, indicating possible pregnancy. She also has breast tenderness, which is an additional sign of pregnancy. Hypotension and lightheadedness (or fainting) may occur as the condition worsens. The patient is also older than 35, which further increases her risk of ectopic pregnancy.

128. **The correct answer is (C).** An electrocardiogram (EKG) can detect a previous or current MI. This test is often performed immediately on a patient with symptoms of a myocardial infarction (MI).

129. **The correct answer is (A).** The next test for this patient should be an ultrasound with biopsy. The patient exhibits typical symptoms of prostate cancer, including problems with urination, and a hard, lumpy prostate on digital rectal exam. His PSA also is elevated at 9.0. The patient's symptoms could also indicate benign prostatic hypertrophy (BPH). However, because of the irregular size of the prostate and the patient's complaint of bone pain, a rectal ultrasound with biopsy is indicated to obtain samples of prostate cells for the presence of cancer.

130. **The correct answer is (E).** The patient's symptoms, coupled with swelling at the base of her neck, strongly indicate hyperthyroidism. Blood tests of thyroxine and thyroid-stimulating hormone (TSH) levels would confirm the diagnosis.

131. **The correct answer is (D).** The patient is most likely experiencing borderline personality disorder (BPD). The major symptoms of BPD include impulsive and risky behavior, inability to

maintain friendships, strong emotions, that often change, intense and short incidents of anxiety or depression, severe anger that may escalate into physical confrontations, inability to control emotions or impulses, suicidal behavior, and fear of being alone. The patient exhibits all of these behaviors.

132. **The correct answer is (A).** The patient's condition is most likely being caused by the prazosin. One of the side effects of alpha blockers like prazosin is orthostatic hypotension, which causes a drop in blood pressure when standing after sitting.

133. **The correct answer is (B).** Polycystic ovary syndrome (PCOS) is the most common hormonal disorder among reproductive-age women. The condition is named for the enlarged, cystic ovaries that commonly appear in most women with PCOS. In these patients, the pituitary gland often secretes high levels of luteinizing hormone, and in response, the ovaries may make excess androgens. This process affects the menstrual cycle, and may cause infertility, excess body hair, and acne. It also contributes to obesity and alopecia in a male pattern on the top and crown of the head.

134. **The correct answer is (A).** Sickle cell anemia occurs primarily in African-Americans. Pain is caused when sickle-cell red blood cells prevent the flow of blood through tiny blood vessels to the torso and extremities. Edema is caused by blockage of blood flow in the hands and feet from sickle-shaped red blood cells. Jaundice occurs because the liver is unable to break down sickle-shaped red blood cells. Infection is caused by damage to the spleen by sickle-shaped red blood cells. Low weight is caused by lack of oxygen and nutrients in normal red blood cells needed for normal growth.

135. **The correct answer is (D).** An electrocardiogram (EKG) would best be used to test the patient for possible cardiovascular disease. This test is performed to detect heart damage from a myocardial infarction (MI) or other conditions, heart arrhythmia, and the size of the heart (to detect congestive heart failure, for example).

136. **The correct answer is (B).** Since the patient has no history of abnormal Pap smear results, you should recommend that she should undergo future Pap smears at least once every two years.

137. **The correct answer is (A).** The patient is most likely suffering from a foodborne illness, such as salmonella. The patient exhibits the classic signs of a foodborne gastrointestinal infection.

138. **The correct answer is (C).** The patient presents with some of the classic neurologic signs of organic mercury poisoning, except for seizures. One of the most common causes of mercury poisoning is the ingestion of large amounts of fish containing mercury.

139. **The correct answer is (A).** You should immediately order a computerized tomography (CT) scan of the patient's head. This procedure would indicate whether there is bleeding inside the patient's skull, such as a subdural hematoma.

140. **The correct answer is (E).** You should prescribe suction dilation and curettage (D&C). This procedure uses cervical dilation to use suction or a curette to remove tissue from inside the uterus.

141. **The correct answer is (C).** The patient should receive the pneumococcal pneumonia vaccine. This vaccine is recommended for all patients aged 65 or older. It is also recommended for particularly high-risk patients, such as those with HIV, asplenia, or chronic alcoholism.

142. **The correct answer is (B).** The patient is most likely suffering from chronic obstructive pulmonary disease (COPD). The patient exhibits the classic signs of this condition, including cough, dyspnea, wheezing, and a long history of smoking. Her pursed lips while breathing, barrel chest, and reduced forced vital capacity and FEV1 on spirometry testing also indicate a diagnosis of COPD.

143. **The correct answer is (B).** The best alternative treatment for this patient would be an estrogen vaginal ring. This is an estrodiol-containing flexible ring that is inserted into the vagina every three months. It may be removed for sexual intercourse. It rests behind the pubic bone in the upper vagina, much like a diaphragm without the dome. It contains no cream or gel, so it is not messy. It works topically on vaginal tissue. The ring releases about 7.5 mcg of estradiol every 24 hours. It improves symptoms of vaginal atrophy comparatively to estradial creams and other topical formulations and has low systemic absorption.

144. **The correct answer is (C).** The patient is most likely suffering from maxillary sinusitis. The patient's areas of pain correspond with the maxillary sinuses, which are behind the cheekbones. Pain worsens when the patient is upright because pressure increases in the maxillary sinuses when he is upright, and lessens when reclining. He also has other symptoms of sinusitis, such as fever, nasal drainage, and halitosis.

145. **The correct answer is (E).** The most likely diagnosis is gastroesophageal reflux disease (GERD). The patient's symptoms—heartburn, dysphagia, coughing, and wheezing—are related to acid reflux.

146. **The correct answer is (A).** The patient's infection was most likely caused by *Escherichia coli*. This bacterium is responsible for most cases of pyelonephritis, especially in young women.

147. **The correct answer is (E).** Aspirin decreases blood clotting, thus helping maintain blood flow through the affected coronary artery or arteries. It is usually given immediately when acute MI is suspected.

148. **The correct answer is (A).** The most likely findings are hematocrit 25 percent and hemoglobin 8 grams per deciliter. These findings are consistent with lab values found in a person with anemia. Normal values are 32-43 percent for hematocrit and 11-15 grams per deciliter for hemoglobin. A hematocrit result of 25 percent and a hemoglobin result of 8 grams per deciliter are well below normal range.

149. **The correct answer is (B).** The patient is most likely suffering from otitis externa, also known as "swimmer's ear." Pain and itching are common symptoms with otitis externa, as is drainage, although it is not always present. Otitis externa usually does not cause fever, and is common in swimmers.

150. **The correct answer is (C).** You should instruct the patient to stop taking gingko altogether, not take warfarin the following day, and to have a repeat INR done the next day. This is the correct course of action because the gingko may be increasing the patient's bleeding time, which means that it should be stopped. She also needs a repeat INR the next day with warfarin dosage adjustments based on INR results.

151. **The correct answer is (D).** The most likely diagnosis is preeclampsia. This is a condition that occurs after 20 weeks of pregnancy. It causes high blood pressure and proteinuria as well as edema of the extremities, headache, and visual problems. It may only cause slight increases in blood pressure. If left untreated, however, it can lead to serious complications for mother and baby.

152. **The correct answer is (C).** The patient needs his first colonoscopy now and, if it is normal, he doesn't need another one for 10 years. This recommendation comes from the American Cancer Society (ACS), the American Gastroenterological Association (AGA), and the American College of Gastroenterologists (ACG).

153. **The correct answer is (D).** The most likely diagnosis is plantar fasciitis, or heel spur. This condition is more common in overweight or obese people. It also can be aggravated by exercise that involves weight-bearing. Plantar fasciitis causes inflammation of the plantar fascia, which is the thick band of tissue that spans the bottom of the foot from the heel to the toes.

154. **The correct answer is (C).** The most important non-cardiac manifestation of digitalis toxicity in this case is vomiting. Most manifestations of intoxication with digitalis in infants occur during or shortly after the loading phase with digoxin.

155. **The correct answer is (B).** The most common finding is arthralgia. It is often difficult to establish a diagnosis of rheumatic fever because there is no single clinical manifestation or laboratory test that is confirmatory. The importance of doing so relates to the need to treat the acute problems promptly and effectively, as well as to the importance of instituting long-term antibiotic prophylaxis to prevent recurrences. To assist in diagnosis, the American Heart Association identified a set of major and minor standards relating to the manifestations of the disease, called the Jones criteria (modified), and recommends that these criteria be applied in the diagnosis of every patient with possible rheumatic fever. The major criteria are carditis, arthritis, erythema marginatum, chorea, and subcutaneous nodules. The minor criteria are arthralgia (joint pain with no objective findings), fever or history of rheumatic fever, increased

erythrocyte sedimentation rate (ESR), positive C-reactive protein, increased WBC and anemia, and prolonged PR and QT intervals on EKG.

156. The correct answer is (D). Chorea cannot be relieved with salicylate or steroid therapy. Neither salicylates nor corticosteroids have a therapeutic effect on chorea, but barbiturates and chlorpromazine may be helpful.

157. The correct answer is (A). You should screen the parents for total cholesterol. Identification of those with a genetic predisposition to hypercholesterolemia and of the factors that increase the risk of the condition is recommended so that dietary and other measures to reduce serum lipids can be introduced if indicated. Children with a first- or second-degree relative with early onset of coronary heart disease should be evaluated early in life, but only after two years of age. Other known risk factors include obesity, diabetes, hypertension, and smoking.

158. The correct answer is (D). Hereditary angioedema, transmitted as an autosomal dominant trait, is due to inadequate function (due to either deficient quantity or quality) of an inhibitor of the first step in the complement cascade, which results in the excessive production of a vasoactive kinin. In addition to otherwise asymptomatic subcutaneous edema, edema can occur in the gastrointestinal tract and produce the symptoms mentioned in the question. Laryngeal edema with airway obstruction can also occur.

159. The correct answer is (A). Most commonly, children with an atrial septal defect (ASD) are asymptomatic, with the lesion found during a routine examination. In older children, exercise intolerance can be noted if the lesion is of significant size. On examination, the pulses are normal, a right ventricular systolic lift at the left sternal border is palpable, and a fixed splitting of the second heart sound is audible.

160. The correct answer is (C). Many conditions can be associated with prolonged fever, a limp caused by arthralgia, exanthem, adenopathy, and pharyngitis. Conjunctivitis, however, is suggestive of Kawasaki disease. An increase in platelets within the patient's constellation of symptoms is also suggestive of Kawasaki disease.

161. The correct answer is (B). Initial treatment is typically IVIG and high-dose aspirin. The child should defervesce shortly after the infusion. Aspirin is typically kept at a higher dose until the platelet count begins to decrease, and then is continued at a lower dose for several weeks.

162. The correct answer is (D). Congestive heart failure from any cause can result in mild cyanosis, even in the absence of a right-to left shunt, and in poor peripheral pulses when cardiac output is low. Congestive heart failure from many causes can be associated with a rapid pulse rate (up to 200 beats per min). A pulse rate greater than 250 beats per min, however, should suggest the presence of a tachyarrhythmia.

163. The correct answer is (D). A quadruple rhythm associated with the murmur of tricuspid regurgitation and a mid-diastolic murmur at the lower left sternum suggests the diagnosis of Ebstein anomaly (downward displacement of the tricuspid valve). The presence of right atrial hypertrophy and right ventricular conduction defects confirms the diagnosis.

164. The correct answer is (C). The child described in the question has no cyanosis or murmur, no cardiac or pulmonary vascular abnormalities by chest X-ray, and no evidence of structural anomalies by echocardiogram. As a result, she is unlikely to have an underlying gross anatomic defect. The electrocardiographic pattern in the figure shows the configuration of preexcitation, the pattern seen in the Wolff-Parkinson-White syndrome (WPW). These patients have an aberrant atrioventricular conduction pathway, which causes the early ventricular depolarization appearing on the electrocardiogram as a shortened PR interval. The initial slow ventricular depolarization wave is referred to as the delta wave. Seventy percent of patients with WPW have single or repeated episodes of paroxysmal supraventricular tachycardia, which can cause the symptoms described in the question. The preexcitation electrocardiographic pattern and WPW can occur in Ebstein malformation, but this is unlikely in the absence of cyanosis and with a normal echocardiogram.

165. The correct answer is (B). Juvenile rheumatoid arthritis (JRA) frequently causes spindle-shaped swelling of finger joints and can involve unusual joints such as the sternoclavicular joint. Presentation of JRA occurs as either polyarthritis (5 or more joints, systemic symptoms not so severe or persistent), pauciarticular (4 or fewer joints, lower extremity joints, extra-articular disease unusual), or systemic disease (severe constitutional disease, systemic symptoms prior to arthritis, rheumatoid rash, high spiking fevers, variable joints).

166. **The correct answer is (C).** Tricuspid atresia has a hypoplastic right ventricle and, therefore, the EKG shows left axis deviation and left ventricular hypertrophy.

167. **The correct answer is (B).** Transposition of the great vessels with an intact ventricular septum presents with early cyanosis, a normal sized heart (classic "egg on a string" radiographic pattern in one-third of cases), normal or slightly increased pulmonary vascular markings, and an electrocardiogram showing right axis deviation and right ventricular hypertrophy.

168. **The correct answer is (D).** Mitral valve prolapse occurs with the billowing into the atria of one or both mitral valve leaflets at the end of systole. It is a congenital abnormality that frequently manifests only during adolescence or later. It is more common in girls than in boys and seems to be inherited in an autosomal dominant fashion. On clinical examination, an apical murmur is noted late in systole, which can be preceded by a click. The diagnosis is confirmed with an echocardiogram that shows prolapse of the mitral leaflets during mid- to late systole. The EKG and chest X-ray are usually normal. Beta blockers and digitalis are unlikely to be required, but penicillin prophylaxis for dental procedures for patients with mitral valve prolapse, who have had a transplant or artificial valves, is indicated.

169. **The correct answer is (A).** Atomoxetine, sold under the brand name Strattera, is a selective norepinephrine reutake inhibitor (SNRI). Unlike other methyphenidate- and amphetamine-derived medications for AD/HD, it has little potential for abuse. Buproprion is a stimulant anti-depressant.

170. **The correct answer is (C).** Because the mutation causing LHON occurs in the mitochondria of the cell, and mitochondria are inherited only from mothers, LOHN can be passed from mothers to children of either sex. Only egg cells, not sperm cells, contributed mitochondria to the embryo.

171. **The correct answer is (E).** Trichinosis, caused by the roundworm *Trichinella spiralis* or other *Trichinella* species, is transitted via undercooked pork or wild game. *Trichinella* cysts in the ingested meat break open in the intestine, producing roundworms that result in the initial gastrointestinal symptoms. The roundworms eventually migrate through the intestinal wall, affecting other organ systems. Trichinosis is rare in the United States.

172. **The correct answer is (A).** The difference between systolic and diastolic pressure is the pulse pressure. Low arterial compliance results in greater pulse pressures, as the brachial artery is less able to absorb the force generated by the systolic blood surge.

173. **The correct answer is (C).** In order to diagnose AD/HD in an adult, the symptoms of the disorder must have been present during childhood, normally by the age of seven. Adult-onset AD/HD does not exist.

174. **The correct answer is (B).** Aphthous ulcers, commonly known as canker sores, are small, yellow, or white lesions with an inflamed red border that occur on the oral mucosa. The exact cause of aphthous ulcers is unknown, but they can be triggered by certain foods, vitamin deficiencies, mechanical trauma, or use of toothpastes containing sodium lauryl sulfate.

175. **The correct answer is (A).** Braxton Hicks contractions are painless or mild, brief contractions that may occur at any point after the sixth week of pregnancy. These contractions do not signal the onset of labor, and can be distinguished from true labor contractions in that they do not become steadily longer, more intense, or more frequent.

176. **The correct answer is (D).** Oral rehydration salts contain salt and sugar in specific proportions in order to allow salt to re-enter the epithelial cells that line the intestinal lumen. Sodium ions enter these cells via a sodium-glucose transport protein channel, which is activated by glucose. The intake of sodium results in the reabsorption of water from the lumen, leading to rehydration.

177. **The correct answer is (D).** Transmission of genital herpes is more common from males to females. Genital herpes is more common in women than in men, can occur even when no sores are visible, can spread to other areas (such as the lips or eyes), and can be prevented to some degree by taking anti-herpes medications such as acyclovir.

178. **The correct answer is (A).** Aromatase is an enzyme that converts androgens to estrogens. An aromatase inhibitor can decrease the amount of estrogen present in a postmenopausal woman, thereby reducing the growth of ER positive tumors. (It does not affect estrogen produced by other means, and therefore will not have an effect in premenopausal women.)

179. **The correct answer is (A).** Hypothyroidism is a deficiency in the amounts of thyroxine (T4) and triiodothyronine (T3) hormones produced by the thyroid gland. It is clinically indicated by lower-than-normal values of these hormones along with higher-than-normal levels of thyroid stimulating hormone (TSH). TSH is produced by the pituitary in response to low levels of circulating T3 and T4.

180. **The correct answer is (C).** The standard vital signs in most medical settings include body temperature, blood pressure, pulse (or heart rate), and respiratory rate. Vital signs assess basic body functions and are a key component of physical evaluation of patients.

PART III

Overview of Question Types

CHAPTER 4

Using Laboratory and Diagnostic Studies Questions

OVERVIEW
- **Preparing for using laboratory and diagnostic studies questions**
- **Tips for answering using laboratory and diagnostic studies questions**
- **Practice questions**
- **Answers and explanations**
- **Summing it up**

PREPARING FOR USING LABORATORY AND DIAGNOSTIC STUDIES QUESTIONS

The first type of question you will find on the PANCE are those that refer to laboratory and diagnostic studies. These questions are designed to test your knowledge of the various laboratory and diagnostic procedures used in the medical field and your ability to use them properly. This group of questions makes up 14 percent of the exam, or about 50 items.

The using laboratory and diagnostic studies domain of the PANCE may include questions based on a variety of topics, such as:

- types of laboratory and diagnostic procedures;
- indications and contraindications for procedures;
- relevant procedures for selected conditions;
- safe and appropriate use of diagnostic equipment;
- collection, interpretation, and use of normal and abnormal diagnostic data;
- risks associated with laboratory and diagnostic procedures;
- cost effectiveness of selected procedures; and
- patient education regarding laboratory and diagnostic procedures.

Diagnosis is a critical element in the treatment of disease and injury. Developing an accurate, detailed picture of the patient's condition is crucial for developing and implementing the safest and most effective treatment possible. Often visual observation and verbal communication alone are not enough to establish a definitive diagnosis. In such cases, physician's assistants need to rely upon laboratory work and other forms of diagnostic testing in order to fully analyze the patient's condition and articulate a proper diagnosis. As a result, it is very important for physician's assistants to have a strong understanding of the types of laboratory and other diagnostic tests used on a regular basis.

When preparing for the using laboratory and diagnostic studies questions you will encounter on the PANCE, you should be familiar with all of the different laboratory tests and diagnostic procedures you will have at your disposal as a physician's assistant. Be sure that you understand what information these tests and procedures are designed to provide, which types of diagnostic procedures are most appropriate for use with a given condition, and how to use diagnostic equipment properly. You should also be familiar with the potential risks associated with these procedures and know when you should or should not use a particular procedure.

The PANCE may also contain questions that pertain to your ability to effectively communicate with your patients about the laboratory tests and diagnostic studies they are to undergo. Such questions will likely involve discussing specific instructions for a given procedure, explaining how a procedure works, obtaining the patient's consent, and more.

The multiple-choice questions on the PANCE will require you to choose the correct answer from a field of five potential choices.

TIPS FOR ANSWERING USING LABORATORY AND DIAGNOSTIC STUDIES QUESTIONS

When you are taking the PANCE, you may find it helpful to remember these hints:

1. Remember the purposes of common laboratory and diagnostic procedures. The most important parts of these questions are the laboratory and diagnostic procedures themselves. Understanding what these procedures are designed to do and how they work is critically important. When you are asked to choose the most appropriate procedure to use in a given situation, quickly scan the answer choices and eliminate any procedures that would not help you arrive at a diagnosis.

2. The patient's condition should dictate which procedure you use. Though there are many different types of laboratory and diagnostic procedures that can help you to formulate an accurate diagnosis, the choice of which procedure to use is not meant to be made randomly. When you are faced with a question that asks you to choose the most appropriate procedure for a particular patient, be sure to read carefully and pay close attention to all of the information it gives you about the patient's condition. This information should guide you toward the correct answer.

3. Remember when you should or should not use a certain procedure. Again, as you read the question, pay close attention to details about the patient's condition. In most cases, the patient's signs and symptoms will be an important factor in choosing the most appropriate procedure. Look for any signs or symptoms that indicate or contraindicate a certain procedure and make sure that you choose the safest and most effective procedure for the patient at hand.

Common Laboratory and Diagnostic Studies:

Blood tests	Electrocardiography
Auscultation	MRI
X-rays	Ultrasound
CT scan	Urinalysis
Echocardiography	

PRACTICE QUESTIONS

1. A 13-year-old male presents with complaints of dizziness, shortness of breath, headaches, nosebleeds, and chest pain. You suspect this is due to the congenital heart defect coarctation of the aorta. Which of the following imaging modalities would you suggest to confirm this diagnosis?
    (A) Echocardiogram
    (B) Myocardial perfusion imaging
    (C) Chest X-ray
    (D) Magnetic resonance angiography
    (E) MUGA scan

2. A 45-year-old African-American male with a history of uncontrolled hypertension presents with sudden, intense, stabbing pain in the back. Blood pressure is 220/110 mmHg, electrocardiogram is normal, troponin levels are normal, d-dimer is normal. Which diagnostic procedure would you perform immediately?
    (A) CT scan of the chest to rule out pulmonary embolism
    (B) Lung V/Q scan to rule out pulmonary embolism
    (C) Echocardiogram to rule out pericarditis
    (D) Myocardial perfusion imaging to rule out cardiac ischemia
    (E) CT scan to rule out aortic dissection

3. A potassium hydroxide (KOH) smear would be a useful tool to confirm the diagnosis of which of the following dermatologic conditions?
    (A) Onychomycosis
    (B) Alopecia
    (C) Rosacea
    (D) Dyshidrosis
    (E) Psoriasis

4. A hydrogen breath test is the easiest and most reliable method to diagnose which of the following disorders?
    (A) Lactose intolerance
    (B) Celiac disease
    (C) *H. Pylori* infection
    (D) Irritable bowel syndrome
    (E) Gastritis

5. In order to accurately diagnose the condition of pertussis, which of the following specimens must be analyzed by a laboratory?
    (A) Blood
    (B) Saliva
    (C) Stool
    (D) Urine
    (E) Mucous

ANSWERS AND EXPLANATIONS

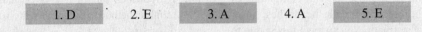

1. D   2. E   3. A   4. A   5. E

1. **The correct answer is (D).** Coarctation of the aorta can be accurately diagnosed with magnetic resonance angiography. Echocardiograms may not be conclusive for teenagers and adults. In adults with untreated coarctation, blood often reaches the lower body through collaterals, e.g., internal thoracic arteries via the subclavian arteries. Those can be seen on MR or CT angiography.

2. **The correct answer is (E).** Aortic dissection is a tear or partial tear in the aorta which is the largest blood vessel in the body. This condition is most common in individuals with uncontrolled hypertension and presents as a sudden, intense, stabbing pain in the back. This is an extremely emergent condition; therefore, if aortic dissection is suspected, a CT scan is recommended immediately in order to confirm or nullify the diagnosis.

3. **The correct answer is (A).** Onychomycosis is a fungal infection of the nails of the fingers or toes. A KOH preparation would be a useful tool to confirm the diagnosis of this disorder. A KOH preparation is used to confirm the presence of fungi.

4. **The correct answer is (A).** The hydrogen breath test is the most convenient and reliable test for lactase deficiency and lactose intolerance. For the breath test, pure lactose, usually 25 grams (the equivalent of 16 oz of milk) is ingested with water after an overnight fast. In persons who are lactose intolerant, the lactose that is not digested and absorbed in the small intestine reaches the colon where the bacteria split the lactose into glucose and galactose and produce hydrogen (and/or methane) gas.

5. **The correct answer is (E).** In order for pertussis to be accurately diagnosed, a sample of mucous obtained from nasal passages must be collected and sent to a laboratory for analysis.

SUMMING IT UP

- Using laboratory and diagnostic studies questions will require an understanding of laboratory and diagnostic procedures; the indications and contraindications for these procedures; relevant procedures for selected conditions; safe and appropriate use of diagnostic equipment; the collection, interpretation, and use of normal and abnormal diagnostic data; the risks associated with specific procedures; the cost effectiveness of diagnostic procedures; and patient education regarding laboratory and diagnostic procedures.

- When studying for these questions, pay close attention to what each procedure is used for, how it works, what kind of data it should yield, the potential risks associated with it, and more. You will need to have a very strong understanding of the various diagnostic procedures you would be likely to use as a physician's assistant.

- Pay close attention to the details. Many of these questions will provide you with specific information about the patient's condition. Be sure to read this information carefully and pay attention to the specific details related to the patient's presentation. You will need to know as much about the patient's condition as possible before you choose a course of action, so make sure to carefully take all of the patient's signs and symptoms into consideration.

- When you prepare for questions related to patient education regarding laboratory and diagnostic procedures, make sure that you understand the procedures involved well enough to be able to properly inform your patient about the procedure you want to perform, how it works, what it is designed to do, the possible risks, the potential benefits, and so on. Be sure that you are able to explain this information in a clear and concise manner that the patient can easily understand.

CHAPTER 5

History Taking and Performing Physical Examinations Questions

OVERVIEW
- Preparing for history taking and performing physical examinations questions
- Tips for answering history taking and performing physical examinations questions
- Practice questions
- Answers and explanations
- Summing it up

PREPARING FOR HISTORY TAKING AND PERFORMING PHYSICAL EXAMINATIONS QUESTIONS

History taking and performing physical examinations questions are a second type of question on the PANCE. The questions pertaining to history taking and performing physical examinations will test your knowledge of a variety of issues related to interviewing and examining patients and reviewing their medical histories. This group of questions makes up 16 percent of the exam, or about 58 items.

The history taking and performing physical examinations domain of the PANCE may include questions based on a variety of topics, such as:

- conducting thorough interviews;
- recognizing relevant historical data;
- performing thorough physical examinations;
- relating presenting complaints with medical history;
- recognizing relevant physical examination findings;
- associating historical data with selected conditions;
- recognizing risk factors for selected conditions;
- recognizing common signs and symptoms of selected conditions;

- techniques for performing physical examinations;
- conducting an appropriate physical exam directed toward a specific condition; and
- making a differential diagnosis based on presenting symptoms or exam findings.

Taking patient histories and performing physical examinations are among the most important parts of providing quality medical care. The information you gather from medical histories and physical examinations plays a crucial role in formulating an accurate diagnosis and choosing the most appropriate course of treatment. With this in mind, it is very important for physician's assistants to be adequately skilled in this domain.

History taking and performing physical examinations questions are designed to test your understanding of concepts like conducting interviews, identifying relevant historical and physical examination data, performing comprehensive physical examinations, and correlating patient complaints with historical information.

Some of the specific topics that are covered in this domain include historical information related to specific medical conditions, risk factors for specific conditions, typical signs and symptoms of specific conditions, examination techniques, typical examination findings related to specific conditions, appropriate physical examinations directed to specific conditions, and differential diagnoses related to presenting symptoms or physical observations.

When you prepare for the history taking and performing physical examinations domain, you should be sure that you have a firm understanding of the appropriate techniques for researching and utilizing patient medical histories and conducting thorough, focused physical examinations.

The multiple-choice questions on the PANCE will require you to choose the correct answer from a field of five potential choices.

TIPS FOR ANSWERING HISTORY TAKING AND PERFORMING PHYSICAL EXAMINATIONS QUESTIONS

When you are taking the PANCE, you may find it helpful to remember these hints:

1. Pay close attention to details. History taking and performing physical examinations questions will provide you with important details that you will need to recognize and take into consideration before choosing the correct answer. Be sure to pay special attention to key details, such as signs, symptoms, complaints, findings, and so on.

2. Remember that your ultimate goal is diagnosis. Although the questions in this domain focus primarily on the methods and techniques for gathering information about your patients, it is important to remember that your goal in this process is to arrive at a diagnosis of the patient's condition. As you answer history taking and performing physical examinations questions, it may be helpful to keep this goal in mind.

PRACTICE QUESTIONS

1. A 48-year-old female presents with dizziness, hearing loss, and drainage of the left ear. Examination of the ear revealed a type of skin cyst in the middle ear. Based on this examination, which of the following is the proper diagnosis?
   (A) Acoustic neuroma
   (B) Hemangioma
   (C) Hematoma
   (D) Cholesteatoma
   (E) Tympanic membrane perforation

2. A 29-year-old female presents with complaints of abnormal tastes, difficulty opening her mouth, dry mouth, and facial pain while eating. Physical examination revealed swelling in front of the ears and below the jaw. Based on the patient's history and physical examination, which of the following is the most appropriate diagnosis?
   (A) Parotitis
   (B) Laryngitis
   (C) Epiglottitis
   (D) Pharyngitis
   (E) Oral candidiasis

3. A 40-year-old woman presents with a persistent lump on her wrist. Which of the following is the most appropriate diagnosis?
   (A) Carpal tunnel
   (B) Rheumatoid arthritis
   (C) Ganglion cyst
   (D) Osteoarthritis
   (E) Hematoma

4. A 24-year-old female presents with painful redness, swelling, and pus-filled blisters around the cuticles of the fingernails. Which of the following would be the most appropriate diagnosis?
   (A) Onychomycosis
   (B) Paronychia
   (C) Dermatitis
   (D) Erisypelas
   (E) Impetigo

5. A 28-year-old male presents with several painful open sores on the inside of the mouth and upper throat. Which of the following is the most appropriate diagnosis?
   (A) Oral candidiasis
   (B) Oral leukoplakia
   (C) Aphthous ulcers
   (D) Oral herpes simplex
   (E) Peritonsillar abscess

ANSWERS AND EXPLANATIONS

1. D	2. A	3. C	4. B	5. C

1. **The correct answer is (D).** Cholesteatoma is a type of skin cyst located in the middle ear that is primarily caused by recurrent ear infections. Poor function in the eustachian tube leads to negative pressure in the middle ear. This pulls a part of the eardrum into the middle ear, creating a pocket or cyst that fills with old skin cells and other waste material.

2. **The correct answer is (A).** Parotitis is defined as inflammation of the parotid glands, which are the largest of the salivary glands. Parotitis can manifest with abnormal tastes or foul tastes, difficulty opening the mouth, dry mouth, mouth or facial pain while eating, redness on the affected side of the face or neck, and swelling in the front of the ears or behind the jaw.

3. **The correct answer is (C).** A ganglion cyst is a swelling that often occurs at the joints or tendons of the hand or foot. These are most commonly found on the dorsum of the wrist and on the fingers. Ganglion cysts are commonly referred to as bible cysts or bible bumps.

4. **The correct answer is (B).** Paronychia is a skin infection that occurs around the nails. This disorder is most commonly associated with a painful, red, swollen area around the nail, often at the cuticle or at the site of a hangnail or other injury. Pus-filled blisters may also be associated with this condition.

5. **The correct answer is (C).** Aphthous ulcers are also known as canker sores. These ulcers are several painful open sores on the inside of the mouth and upper throat characterized by a break in the mucous membranes.

SUMMING IT UP

- History taking and performing physical examinations questions are intended to evaluate your ability to conduct thorough, focused interviews; recognize important and relevant historical information; perform comprehensive physical examinations; recognize signs, symptoms, and risk factors for selected conditions; and use the data gathered to arrive at a diagnosis.

- To prepare for questions related to this domain, be sure to review the recommended techniques for reviewing and applying historical information, conducting appropriate patient interviews, and performing adequate physical examinations.

- When answering history taking and performing physical examinations questions, be sure to pay attention to the details presented in each question and remember that your overall goal in taking patient histories and performing physical examinations is to arrive at an accurate diagnosis of the patient's medical condition.

CHAPTER 6

Formulating the Most Likely Diagnosis Questions

OVERVIEW
- Preparing for formulating the most likely diagnosis questions
- Tips for answering formulating the most likely diagnosis questions
- Practice questions
- Answers and explanations
- Summing it up

PREPARING FOR FORMULATING THE MOST LIKELY DIAGNOSIS QUESTIONS

Formulating the most likely diagnosis questions are another set of questions on the PANCE. The questions pertaining to formulating the most likely diagnosis are designed to test your ability to correctly diagnose a patient based on history, observations, and laboratory and diagnostic studies. This group of questions makes up 18 percent of the exam, or about 65 items.

The formulating the most likely diagnosis domain of the PANCE may include questions based on a variety of topics, such as:

- identifying the most likely diagnosis based on available information;
- recognizing the significance of medical history, physical findings, and the results of laboratory and diagnostic studies as they relate to making a diagnosis;
- formulating differential diagnoses; and
- correlating both normal and abnormal diagnostic data.

Formulating the most likely diagnosis is, perhaps, the most important part of a physician's assistant's responsibilities. The course of treatment for any patient begins with, and is primarily dictated by, the diagnosis of his or her condition. As a result, being able to make an accurate diagnosis through the use of all available information is a critical skill set for a prospective physician's assistant.

Formulating the most likely diagnosis questions will require you to demonstrate your ability to determine the correct diagnosis based on history, observations, and laboratory and diagnostic studies; correlate normal and abnormal diagnostic data; and formulate differential diagnoses.

Most of these questions will, as the name of the domain implies, ask you to identify the correct diagnosis of a given patient's condition. In order to do this, you will have to rely on information you are given about the patient in the question. This information may be related to the patient's medical history, the physical findings you observe during the examination, and/or the results of various laboratory or diagnostic tests. Some of these questions may also require you to arrive at your conclusion by making a differential diagnosis, which means making a diagnosis through a process of elimination.

When you are studying for formulating the most likely diagnosis questions, you should be sure that you are familiar with the signs and symptoms of common conditions and the appropriate methods of diagnosis. You should make certain that you understand the importance of medical history, physical findings, and diagnostic testing results and how to properly use this information to make an accurate diagnosis.

For those questions that ask you to make a differential diagnosis, you should be sure that you have a firm understanding of the process involved in making such a diagnosis.

The multiple-choice questions on the PANCE will require you to choose the correct answer from a field of five potential choices.

TIPS FOR ANSWERING FORMULATING THE MOST LIKELY DIAGNOSIS QUESTIONS

When you are taking the PANCE, you may find it helpful to remember these hints:

1. Pay close attention to the patient's signs and symptoms. In many cases, the specific signs and symptoms your patient exhibits will be the most important factor in your diagnosis. Be sure to take note of the patient's clinical presentation and keep this information in mind as you consider the possible diagnoses.

2. Take everything into consideration. Though the patient's clinical presentation may be the most important factor to consider, remember to use all the information you have at your disposal. All the data you are given is important and will play an important role in determining the correct diagnosis. Pay attention to all of the details in each question.

3. Be efficient. The PANCE is a closely timed examination, so you only have a short amount of time to spend on each question. Though you will want to read carefully and pay close attention to the details, you will need to do so quickly. Try scanning the question and eliminating any obviously incorrect answer choices. This can help you to focus your concentration on the important elements of the question and arrive at an answer more quickly.

PRACTICE QUESTIONS

1. A 24-year-old male presents after a motor vehicle accident with blood accumulation filling over 1/2 of the space of the anterior chamber of the right eye. Which of the following is the most accurate diagnosis?
   (A) Hordeolum
   (B) Orbital cellulitis
   (C) Hyphema
   (D) Nystagmus
   (E) Pterygium

2. A 52-year-old postmenopausal woman presents with unwanted urine leakage when coughing or sneezing as well as incomplete emptying of the bladder. Which of the following is the most appropriate diagnosis?
   (A) Vaginitis
   (B) Cystitis
   (C) Cystocele
   (D) Rectocele
   (E) Vaginal Prolapse

3. A 60-year-old female, with a previous history of hysterectomy, presents with vaginal pressure, painful intercourse, constipation, and intermittent vaginal bleeding. Which of the following is the most appropriate diagnosis?
   (A) Vaginitis
   (B) Cystitis
   (C) Cystocele
   (D) Rectocele
   (E) Vaginal prolapse

4. An 8-year-old boy presents with involuntary, excessive eye blinking, facial grimacing, and shoulder shrugging. In addition, he also has been noticed muttering inappropriate words and repeating words or phrases he hears from other people. Which of the following is the most appropriate diagnosis?
   (A) Huntingdon's disease
   (B) Parkinson's disease
   (C) Guillan-Barre syndrome
   (D) Attention deficit disorder
   (E) Tourette syndrome

5. A 32-year-old 'woman, who has never been pregnant, presents with inappropriate and spontaneous flow of milk from her breasts. Which of the following is the most appropriate diagnosis?
   (A) Mastitis
   (B) Galactorrhea
   (C) Gynecomastia
   (D) Fibrocytic disease
   (E) Breast abscess

ANSWERS AND EXPLANATIONS

| 1. C | 2. C | 3. D | 4. E | 5. B |

1. **The correct answer is (C).** Hyphema, by definition, is blood accumulation in the front part of the eye. This disorder is most often caused by trauma to the eye; however, hyphema can also be caused by cancer of the eye, blood vessel abnormalities of the eye, and inflammation of the iris.

2. **The correct answer is (C).** A cystocele, otherwise known as a fallen bladder, occurs when the wall between a woman's bladder and her vagina weakens and allows the bladder to droop into the vagina. This condition may cause unwanted urine leakage when coughing, sneezing, or laughing as well as incomplete emptying of the bladder.

3. **The correct answer is (D).** A rectocele is a tear in the rectovaginal septum. The two causes of this disorder are childbirth and hysterectomy. Individuals with a rectocele may experience vaginal pressure, painful intercourse, constipation, intermittent vaginal bleeding, difficulty passing stools, incomplete emptying of the colon, and a feeling of something "falling" from the vagina.

4. **The correct answer is (E).** Tourette syndrome is a neurological disorder characterized by repetitive, stereotyped, involuntary movements and vocalizations called tics. Individuals with this disorder can experience excessive eye blinking, facial grimacing, and shoulder shrugging. In addition, this disorder may result in muttering inappropriate or curse words and repeating words or phrases heard from other people.

5. **The correct answer is (B).** Galactorrhea is defined as the inappropriate and spontaneous flow of milk from the breasts that is not associated with pregnancy, childbirth, and nursing. This condition will affect 20-25% of the female population at one time or another and, although rare, can also occur in males.

SUMMING IT UP

- Formulating the most likely diagnosis questions will require an understanding of the importance of patient medical history, physical findings, and the results of laboratory and diagnostic studies to the formation of a diagnosis, and the methods involved in forming a differential diagnosis.

- When you are studying for formulating the most likely diagnosis questions, be sure to familiarize yourself with the various signs and symptoms of common medical conditions. You should also make sure that you know how to use other information, such as medical history and data obtained from diagnostic testing, to establish a diagnosis.

- Pay attention to the details in each question. Since your diagnosis is entirely based on the information provided to you in the question, it is critically important that you pay close attention to this data. These details will offer you important clues that can steer you toward the correct answer. Take everything into consideration and make your choice carefully.

CHAPTER 7

Health Maintenance Questions

OVERVIEW

- Preparing for health maintenance questions
- Tips for answering health maintenance questions
- Practice questions
- Answers and explanations
- Summing it up

PREPARING FOR HEALTH MAINTENANCE QUESTIONS

Health maintenance questions are a fourth subgroup of questions on the PANCE. The questions pertaining to health maintenance will test your knowledge of a wide variety of topics related to disease prevention and the overall maintenance of good health. This group of questions makes up 10 percent of the exam, or about 36 items.

The health maintenance domain of the PANCE may include questions based on a variety of topics, such as:

- adapting various health maintenance techniques to a patient's specific needs;
- communicating effectively with patients about health maintenance;
- using counseling, patient education techniques, and informational databases;
- epidemiology of given conditions;
- prevention and early detection of given conditions;
- the relative value of routine screening tests;
- patient education regarding preventable diseases or lifestyle changes;
- healthy lifestyles;
- communicable disease prevention;
- immunization schedules and recommendations;
- the risks and benefits associated with immunization;
- growth and development;
- sexuality;
- risks associated with environmental or occupational exposure;

- the effects of stress;
- the psychological impact of disease or injury;
- aging;
- indications of abuse or neglect; and
- barriers to proper care.

The practice of medicine isn't just about diagnosing and treating diseases, it's also about preventing disease. As a physician's assistant, you must be familiar with the common methods of disease prevention, the risk factors associated with various diseases, the impact of a patient's daily life on his or her health, and the many ways to promote long-term good health.

Health maintenance questions are designed to test your ability to adapt various health maintenance techniques to a patient's specific needs, communicate effectively with patients about health maintenance; and use counseling, patient education techniques, and informational databases to facilitate health maintenance.

The multiple-choice questions on the PANCE will require you to choose the correct answer from a field of five potential choices.

TIPS FOR ANSWERING HEALTH MAINTENANCE QUESTIONS

When you are taking the PANCE, you may find it helpful to remember these hints:

1. Remember what you have learned. The health maintenance domain covers a broad range of topics, many of which are closely tied to other domains. Referencing the information you have used to study for other portions of the PANCE may be helpful when answering health maintenance questions.

2. Think critically. Some of these questions may ask you to choose the best course of action in a given situation. When you encounter such a question, read the scenario carefully, examine your options, and quickly think about the pros and cons of each before you make a selection.

3. Pay close attention to details. As with any questions on the PANCE, make sure you pay attention to all of the details provided and take them all into consideration before proceeding. You will need to know as much about the scenario in each question as possible in order to choose the correct answer.

PRACTICE QUESTIONS

1. Hypertriglyceridemia can effectively be managed with daily consumption of which of the following vitamins?
   (A) Niacin
   (B) Vitamin C
   (C) Vitamin D
   (D) Riboflavin
   (E) Thiamine

2. Individuals who suffer from phenylketonuria should avoid a diet rich in which of the following substances?
   (A) Sugar
   (B) Fat
   (C) Salt
   (D) Protein
   (E) Carbohydrates

3. Fecal impaction may result from overuse of which of the following over-the-counter medications?
   (A) Antacids
   (B) Fever reducers
   (C) NSAIDS
   (D) Laxatives
   (E) Cough suppressants

4. Methimazole is commonly prescribed for maintenance treatment of which of the following disorders?
   (A) Hyperparathyroidism
   (B) Hypoparathyroidism
   (C) Hyperthyroidism
   (D) Hypothyroidism
   (E) Subacute thyroiditis

5. Individuals who suffer from gout should adhere to a diet consisting of low quantities of which of the following substances?
   (A) Folic acid
   (B) Citric acid
   (C) Uric acid
   (D) Omega-3 fatty acids
   (E) Omega-6 fatty acids

ANSWERS AND EXPLANATIONS

| 1. A | 2. D | 3. A | 4. C | 5. C |

1. **The correct answer is (A).** The B-complex vitamin, niacin, has been proven clinically effective for treatment of hypertriglyceridemia. Administration of at least 1.5 grams/day can reduce triglyceride levels by up to 50%.

2. **The correct answer is (D).** Individuals with phenylketonuria should avoid foods rich in phenylalanine, which is contained primarily in protein rich foods such as fish, chicken, milk, cheese, and eggs.

3. **The correct answer is (A).** Overuse of antacids, particularly antacids that contain aluminum, can result in constipation that progresses to the point of fecal impaction. Other medications that may cause fecal impaction include calcium channel blockers, antidepressants, and tranquilizers.

4. **The correct answer is (C).** Methimazole, more commonly referred to as Tapazole, is used to treat hyperthyroidism, a condition that occurs when the thyroid gland produces too much thyroid hormone.

5. **The correct answer is (C).** Gout occurs when high levels of uric acid in the blood cause crystals to form and accumulate around a joint. A diet with reduced amounts of red meat, dairy products, alcohol, and sugar should reduce the amount of uric acid and assist in relieving gout symptoms.

SUMMING IT UP

- The health maintenance questions on the PANCE are designed to test your abilities in regards to adapting various health maintenance techniques to a patient's specific needs; communicating effectively with patients about health maintenance; and using counseling, patient education techniques, and informational databases to facilitate health maintenance.

- The topics covered in this domain include the epidemiology of given conditions, prevention and early detection of given conditions, the relative value of routine screening tests, patient education regarding preventable diseases or lifestyle changes, healthy lifestyles, communicable disease prevention, immunization schedules and recommendations, the risks and benefits associated with immunization, growth and development, sexuality, risks associated with environmental or occupational exposure, the effects of stress, the psychological impact of disease or injury, aging, indications of abuse or neglect, and barriers to proper care.

CHAPTER 8

Clinical Intervention Questions

OVERVIEW
- Preparing for clinical intervention questions
- Tips for answering clinical intervention questions
- Practice questions
- Answers and explanations
- Summing it up

PREPARING FOR CLINICAL INTERVENTION QUESTIONS

Clinical intervention questions are a fifth type of question you will encounter on the PANCE. The questions pertaining to clinical intervention will test your knowledge of a wide variety of issues related to the overall process of care. This group of questions makes up 14 percent of the exam, or about 50 items.

The clinical intervention domain of the PANCE may include questions based on a variety of topics, such as:

- the formation and implementation of treatment plans;
- your ability to demonstrate expertise in performing various procedures;
- using effective methods of communication and counseling techniques;
- encouraging patient participation in and adherence to treatment plans;
- treating selected medical conditions;
- the indications, contraindications, benefits, risks, potential complications, and techniques for certain procedures;
- standard precautions;
- special isolation procedures;
- sterilization techniques;
- monitoring therapeutic regimes;
- recognizing medical emergencies;
- hospital admissions and discharges;
- community resources;
- patient education;

- working with other medical professionals;
- end-of-life concerns; and
- the potential benefits and risks of alternative medicine.

Clinical intervention is a very broad topic that covers a large portion of the regular responsibilities of a physician's assistant. Having a firm understanding of various clinical intervention techniques and procedures is essential for the physician's assistant.

Clinical intervention questions on the PANCE are designed to test your skills as they relate to concepts like the formation and implementation of treatment plans, your ability to demonstrate expertise in performing various procedures, using effective methods of communication and counseling techniques, and encouraging patient participation in and adherence to treatment plans.

When you prepare for clinical intervention questions, you should focus on building a firm understanding of the fundamental principles underlying the basic process of care. Reviewing the concepts and topics mentioned above will go a long way toward ensuring that you are ready for both the clinical intervention domain and the rest of the PANCE.

The multiple-choice questions on the PANCE will require you to choose the correct answer from a field of five possible choices.

TIPS FOR ANSWERING CLINICAL INTERVENTION QUESTIONS

When you are taking the PANCE, you may find it helpful to remember these hints:

1. Use what you already know. Since clinical intervention questions are frequently related to topics covered in other domains, use what you have learned while studying for these other domains to help you choose the correct answer. Being well prepared for the other parts of the PANCE will be very helpful when it comes to answering clinical intervention questions.

2. Pay close attention to the details. As with many questions on the PANCE, the details included in clinical intervention questions are critically important. Be sure to take all the details into consideration before making a choice. Ignoring or overlooking details may lead you to an incorrect solution.

3. Be efficient. The PANCE is a closely timed examination, so you only have a short amount of time to spend on each question. Though you will want to read carefully and pay close attention to the details, you will need to do so quickly. Try scanning the question and eliminating any obviously incorrect answer choices. This can help you to focus your concentration on the important elements of the question and arrive at an answer more quickly.

PRACTICE QUESTIONS

1. An 80-year-old female presents with sick sinus syndrome. Which of the following procedures are required to treat this condition?
   (A) Cardiac catheterization
   (B) Coronary artery bypass graft
   (C) Cardiac ablation
   (D) Pacemaker insertion
   (E) Coronary stenting

2. Which of the following is the proper intervention when individuals with thrombotic thrombocyto-penic purpura are unresponsive to treatments?
   (A) Plasmapheresis
   (B) Splenectomy
   (C) Intravenous anticoagulants
   (D) Intravenous antibiotics
   (E) High-dose corticosteroids

3. Orchiopexy is the surgical procedure performed in order to correct which of the following disorders?
   (A) Testicular torsion
   (B) Epididymitis
   (C) Hydrocele
   (D) Cryptorchidism
   (E) Orchitis

4. Which of the following types of medications is an appropriate intervention for a seizure lasting longer than 30 minutes?
   (A) Benzodiazapenes
   (B) Imidazopyridines
   (C) Pyrazalopyridines
   (D) Cyclopyrrolones
   (E) b-Carbolones

5. Intravenous Amphotericin B combined with oral flucytosin has been proven to be an effective treatment for which of the following infectious diseases?
   (A) Malaria
   (B) Cryptoccosis
   (C) Shigellosis
   (D) Salmonellosis
   (E) Botulism

ANSWERS AND EXPLANATIONS

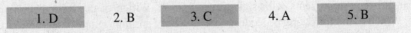

1. D   2. B   3. C   4. A   5. B

1. **The correct answer is (D).** Sick sinus syndrome is a disorder characterized by malfunction of the sinus node, the heart's primary pacemaker. This disorder can cause abnormal and dangerously slow heart rates. It is primarily treated by the placement of a pacemaker.

2. **The correct answer is (B).** Thrombotic thrombocytopenic purpura is a blood disorder that causes blood clots to form in small blood vessels around the body, and leads to a low platelet count. Individuals who are unresponsive to treatments or have several recurrences should undergo a splenectomy to correct this disorder.

3. **The correct answer is (C).** Cryptorchidism is a disorder of an undescended testicle. Ochiopexy is performed to move an undescended testicle into the scrotum and permanently fix it there.

4. **The correct answer is (A).** Seizures that last for longer than 30 minutes are characteristic of the disorder of status epilecicus. Randomized controlled trials show that benzodiazepines, particularly diazepam and lorazepam, should be the initial drug therapy in patients with status epilepticus.

5. **The correct answer is (B).** Cryptococcosis is a potentially fatal fungal disease that is particularly damaging to individuals with weakened immune systems such as HIV patients. Intravenous Amphotericin B combined with oral flucytosin has been proven to be an effective treatment for this disorder and this medical intervention does not further weaken the immune system.

SUMMING IT UP

- The clinical intervention domain is designed to test your knowledge of a wide variety of issues related to the overall process of care.

- Clinical intervention questions will be based on a broad range of topics, including the formation and implementation of treatment plans; your ability to demonstrate expertise in performing various procedures; using effective methods of communication and counseling techniques, including encouraging patient participation in and adherence to treatment plans; managing and treating selected medical conditions and monitoring therapeutic regimens; the indications, contraindications, benefits, risks, potential complications, and techniques for certain procedures; standard precautions as well as special isolation measures and sterilization techniques; recognizing medical emergencies; hospital admissions and discharges; community resources; patient education; working with other medical professionals; end-of-life concerns; and the potential benefits and risks of alternative medicine.

- Many of these questions are related to other PANCE domains, so a firm understanding of the other topics covered on the test will likely improve your performance on this section.

CHAPTER 9

Pharmaceutical Therapeutics Questions

OVERVIEW
- Preparing for pharmaceutical therapeutics questions
- Tips for answering pharmaceutical therapeutics questions
- Practice questions
- Answers and explanations
- Summing it up

PREPARING FOR PHARMACEUTICAL THERAPEUTICS QUESTIONS

Pharmaceutical therapeutics questions are a sixth category of question on the PANCE. The questions pertaining to pharmaceutical therapeutics are designed to test your knowledge of the vast array of drugs administered by physician's assistants and your ability to use them properly. This group of questions makes up 18 percent of the exam, or about 65 items.

The pharmaceutical therapeutics domain of the PANCE is comprised of questions based on many different topics, including:

- choosing the best pharmacologic treatment for a specific condition;
- mechanism of action;
- indications and contraindications for use;
- possible side effects;
- potential adverse reactions;
- monitoring and follow-up of pharmacologic regimens;
- risks related to drug interactions;
- clinical presentation and treatment of drug interactions;
- drug toxicity;
- cross reactivity;
- methods used to reduce medication errors; and
- recognizing and treating allergic reactions.

Pharmaceutical therapeutics, which refers to the prescription and administration of drugs to treat a specific medical condition, is a very important part of the job of a physician's assistant. In most cases, physician's assistants are authorized to prescribe, dispense, and administer a wide variety of drugs. As such, it is extremely important that any current or prospective physician's assistant has a firm understanding of the many different types of drugs he or she will encounter in the course of practice.

Pharmaceutical therapeutics questions on the PANCE will ask about choosing the most appropriate pharmaceutical treatment for a given condition; monitoring and adjusting pharmacological regimens as needed; and recognizing, evaluating, and properly reporting adverse reactions.

Some questions may require you to recognize the mechanism of action of a particular drug, the indications and contraindications for its use, the possible side effects, potential adverse reactions, the risks for and presentation and treatment of drug interactions, drug toxicity, the cross reactivity of similar drugs, and the methods used to reduce medication errors.

When you prepare for pharmaceutical therapeutics questions, you should be sure that you are thoroughly familiar with the wide variety of drugs commonly used by physician's assistants, as well as their indications and contra-indications, any possible side effects they may have, and their potential for cross reactivity with other similar medications.

The PANCE also includes questions that are designed to test your ability to monitor and evaluate a patient's pharmacological regimen. These questions will require you to have a strong understanding of potential drug interactions and how to recognize and treat any complications that may arise from such interactions. You will also need to demonstrate your ability to recognize and treat allergic reactions.

The multiple-choice questions on the PANCE will require you to choose the correct answer from a field of five choices.

TIPS FOR ANSWERING PHARMACEUTICAL THERAPEUTICS QUESTIONS

When you are taking the PANCE, you may find it helpful to remember these hints:

1. The right drug for one patient may not be the right drug for all patients. Every patient is different. The effect a certain drug has on one patient may be significantly different from the effect it has on another. When you are asked to choose the most appropriate drug to administer to a given patient, be sure to pay close attention to the specific information you are given about that patient's condition and history. Though there are general guidelines for prescribing and administering drugs that you should routinely follow, you must be sure to adjust your approach based on the particular circumstances of the given situation.

2. Many drugs have multiple applications. Many of the drugs you will need to be familiar with can be used in more than one way. Remember that a certain drug may have alternative uses beyond its main purpose. When you are considering which medication you should prescribe, keep these additional uses in mind.

3. Remember when a drug should or should not be used. Remembering to consider the indications and contraindications for using a particular drug is critically important. When you are faced with choosing the best drug to use, remember to pay close attention to the specifics of the patient's condition and his or her presenting signs and symptoms. The patient's signs and symptoms may indicate or contraindicate the use of a certain medication. Be sure that the drug you choose is appropriate for the patient at hand.

4. Be sure you're familiar with the following drug classifications:

Analgesics and anti-inflammatory drugs

Anesthetics

Antidotes and reversal agents

Antimicrobials

Antiparasitic drugs

Cardiovascular drugs

Chemotherapeutic and immunological drugs

Gastrointestinal drugs

Hormones and other endocrine drugs

Respiratory drugs

Topical drugs

PRACTICE QUESTIONS

1. Which of the following is an appropriate treatment for oral candidiasis?
   (A) Cipro
   (B) Nystatin
   (C) Ampicillin
   (D) Levaquin
   (E) Zithromax

2. Which of the following anti-inflammatory medications is commonly used in conjunction with ibuprofen for treatment of acute pericarditis?
   (A) Colchicine
   (B) Naproxen
   (C) Azapropazone
   (D) Etodolac
   (E) Meloxicam

3. Helminth infections are most effectively treated by which of the following medications?
   (A) Combantrin
   (B) Mebendazole
   (C) Abamectin
   (D) Ivermectin
   (E) Thiabendazole

4. The dermatologic condition of alopecia is commonly treated by which of the following medications?
   (A) Erythromycin
   (B) Clindamycin
   (C) Minoxidil
   (D) Accutane
   (E) Tretinoin

5. Birth-control pills can prevent the occurrence of which of the following disorders?
   (A) Cystocele
   (B) Rectocele
   (C) Ovarian tumors
   (D) Ovarian cysts
   (E) Cervical tumors

ANSWERS AND EXPLANATIONS

1. B	2. A	3. A	4. C	5. D

1. **The correct answer is (B).** Oral candidiasis is an infection of the mucous membranes of the mouth that is caused by yeast fungi. Nystatin is an antifungal medication that is useful for treatment of this disorder. The other four medications on the list are antibacterial medications.

2. **The correct answer is (A).** Colchicine is an older and well-established anti-inflammatory drug that can help control the inflammation and prevent pericarditis from recurring weeks or even months later.

3. **The correct answer is (A).** Helminth infections are caused by a parasitic worm that infests the body. Combantrin is the drug of choice for treating this type of infection due to the fact that it paralyzes the worms preventing them from attaching to the walls of the intestines.

4. **The correct answer is (C).** Alopecia is the disorder of thinning hair or hair loss either in a pattern or in spots. Minoxidil, commonly known as Rogaine, is the most effective medication to stop hair loss and promote hair growth.

5. **The correct answer is (D).** Birth-control pills may be very effective in preventing further occurrences of ovarian cysts. In addition, birth-control pills can also greatly reduce the risk of developing ovarian cancer.

SUMMING IT UP

- Pharmaceutical therapeutics questions will require you to demonstrate your ability to choose the most appropriate pharmaceutical treatment for a given condition; monitor and adjust pharmacological regimens as needed; and recognize, evaluate, and properly report adverse reactions.

- When preparing for pharmaceutical therapeutics questions, you will need to be sure that you are keenly familiar with the various drugs used in the field of medicine. Remember to pay close attention to the mechanism of action, indications and contraindications for use, side effects, potential adverse reactions, drug interactions, drug toxicity, and cross reactivity. You should also be sure that you are able to recognize and treat any potential reactions or interactions and are familiar with the methods for reducing medication errors.

- Read the details of the questions carefully. The information the questions will provide you concerning the patient's condition, especially his or her signs and symptoms, will play a crucial role in determining the best course of action. Pay close attention to these details and remember to keep the indications, contraindications, and alternative uses of the drugs you are considering in mind.

CHAPTER 10

Applying Basic Science Concepts Questions

OVERVIEW
- Preparing for applying basic science concepts questions
- Tips for answering applying basic science concepts questions
- Practice questions
- Answers and explanations
- Summing it up

PREPARING FOR APPLYING BASIC SCIENCE CONCEPTS QUESTIONS

Applying basic science concepts questions are a final type of question on the PANCE. The questions pertaining to applying basic science concepts will test your knowledge of the basic scientific principles related to human health and the diagnosis of medical conditions. This group of questions makes up 10 percent of the exam, or about 36 items.

The applying basic science concepts domain of the PANCE may include questions based on a variety of topics, such as:

- anatomy, physiology, pathophysiology, microbiology, and biochemistry;
- the pathological process of disease;
- identifying normal and abnormal anatomy and physiology;
- relating pathophysiologic principles to selected disease processes;
- relating abnormal physical examination findings to selected disease processes; and
- relating abnormal diagnostic testing results to selected disease processes.

The practice of medicine is based on the fundamental principles of a wide array of sciences, including biology, chemistry, physiology, anatomy, and others. For physician's assistants, or any medical professionals, having a solid understanding of the basic science behind medicine is critically important. The ability to appropriately and accurately examine, diagnose, and treat patients is founded on a strong scientific understanding of the human body, health, and disease.

The applying basic science concepts questions will require you to have a basic understanding of the various sciences related to the practice of medicine. Most notably, you will need to be familiar with basic principles of human anatomy and physiology, pathophysiology, microbiology, and biochemistry.

Applying basic science concepts questions are designed to test your ability to identify normal and abnormal anatomy and physiology, and relate pathophysiologic principles, abnormal physical examination findings, and abnormal diagnostic testing results to selected disease processes.

One of the most important concepts to review in preparation for applying basic science concepts questions is the pathological process of disease. The pathological process of a given disease includes its cause (often called its etiology), its mechanism of development (or pathogenesis), the changes it causes, and the effects it eventually has on a patient. Many of the questions in this domain will be focused on or related to pathological processes in some way.

When you study for the applying basic science concepts domain, be sure to familiarize yourself with the basic principles of the important sciences associated with the practice of medicine. You should also be sure to develop a broad understanding of the pathological process of disease, both as a concept and as it applies to various common medical conditions.

The multiple-choice questions on the PANCE will require you to choose the correct answer from a field of five potential choices.

TIPS FOR ANSWERING APPLYING BASIC SCIENCE CONCEPTS QUESTIONS

When you are taking the PANCE, you may find it helpful to remember these hints:

1. Remember what you have learned. This portion of the PANCE is primarily based on hard science, so you will likely have to rely on the specific information you have studied in order to arrive at the correct answer. However, since the concepts covered in this domain ultimately inform every aspect of the practice of medicine, it may also be helpful to keep the information you have learned while studying for other domains in mind as well.

2. Pay close attention to details. As with all of the other domains on the PANCE, it is very important to pay close attention to the details included in the applying basic science concepts questions. Make sure you understand exactly what the question is asking and remember to take all the provided details into consideration.

PRACTICE QUESTIONS

1. Exanthems are defined as a widespread rash caused by a virus or bacteria that normally occur in children. Which of the following types of exanthem is caused by a bacterium?
   (A) Measles
   (B) Mumps
   (C) Erythema infectosium
   (D) Scarlet fever
   (E) Roseola infantum

2. Condyloma acuminatum is a dermatologic disorder caused by which of the following viruses?
   (A) HIV virus
   (B) Human papilloma virus
   (C) Human parainfluenza virus
   (D) Varicella zoster virus
   (E) Parvovirus

3. Which of the following refers to an abnormal or difficult pregnancy or childbirth that is often assisted by forceps, ventouse, or caesarian section?
   (A) Dystocia
   (B) Ectopic pregnancy
   (C) Abruptio placentae
   (D) Spontaneous abortion
   (E) Placenta previa

4. Which of the following types of bacteria is the most common cause of bullous impetigo?
   (A) *Staphylococcus epidermis*
   (B) *Staphylococcus folliculitis*
   (C) *Staphylococcus saprophyticus*
   (D) *Staphylococcus aureus*
   (E) *Staphylococcus hominus*

5. Individuals who are diagnosed with G6PD deficiency are susceptible to which of the following types of anemia?
   (A) Iron-deficiency anemia
   (B) Pernicious anemia
   (C) Hemolytic anemia
   (D) Sickle cell anemia
   (E) Folate-deficiency anemia

ANSWERS AND EXPLANATIONS

1. D	2. B	3. D	4. D	5. C

1. **The correct answer is (D).** Scarlet fever is a form of exanthem that is caused by the *Streptococcus pyogenes* bacteria. Measles, mumps, erythema infectosium, and roseola infantum are all exanthems that are caused by viruses.

2. **The correct answer is (B).** Condyloma acuminatum, commonly known as genital warts, is a dermatologic disorder caused by the human papilloma virus.

3. **The correct answer is (D).** Dystocia is defined as abnormal or difficult pregnancy or childbirth. Approximately one out of every five childbirths involves dystocia. Dystocia is caused by incoordinate uterine activity, abnormal fetal lie, or presentation. These childbirths are assisted by forceps, ventouse, or caesarian section.

4. **The correct answer is (D).** Impetigo is a contagious skin infection that usually produces blisters or sores on the face, neck, hands, and diaper area and is one of the most common skin infections among children. Bullous impetigo, the form that produces large blisters, is most commonly caused by the *Staphylococcus aureus* bacteria.

5. **The correct answer is (C).** G6PD deficiency is an inherited condition in which the body doesn't have enough of the enzyme glucose-6-phosphate dehydrogenase, or G6PD, which helps red blood cells function normally. This deficiency can cause hemolytic anemia.

SUMMING IT UP

- The applying basic science concepts questions on the PANCE focus on the basic scientific principles associated with the practice of medicine. Some of the sciences that will be involved in these questions include human anatomy and physiology, pathophysiology, microbiology, and biochemistry.

- The applying basic science concepts questions are designed to test your ability to identify normal and abnormal anatomy and physiology, and relate pathophysiologic principles, abnormal physical examination findings, and abnormal diagnostic testing results to selected disease processes.

PART IV

Two Practice Tests

1. Ⓐ Ⓑ Ⓒ Ⓓ Ⓔ
2. Ⓐ Ⓑ Ⓒ Ⓓ Ⓔ
3. Ⓐ Ⓑ Ⓒ Ⓓ Ⓔ
4. Ⓐ Ⓑ Ⓒ Ⓓ Ⓔ
5. Ⓐ Ⓑ Ⓒ Ⓓ Ⓔ
6. Ⓐ Ⓑ Ⓒ Ⓓ Ⓔ
7. Ⓐ Ⓑ Ⓒ Ⓓ Ⓔ
8. Ⓐ Ⓑ Ⓒ Ⓓ Ⓔ
9. Ⓐ Ⓑ Ⓒ Ⓓ Ⓔ
10. Ⓐ Ⓑ Ⓒ Ⓓ Ⓔ
11. Ⓐ Ⓑ Ⓒ Ⓓ Ⓔ
12. Ⓐ Ⓑ Ⓒ Ⓓ Ⓔ
13. Ⓐ Ⓑ Ⓒ Ⓓ Ⓔ
14. Ⓐ Ⓑ Ⓒ Ⓓ Ⓔ
15. Ⓐ Ⓑ Ⓒ Ⓓ Ⓔ
16. Ⓐ Ⓑ Ⓒ Ⓓ Ⓔ
17. Ⓐ Ⓑ Ⓒ Ⓓ Ⓔ
18. Ⓐ Ⓑ Ⓒ Ⓓ Ⓔ
19. Ⓐ Ⓑ Ⓒ Ⓓ Ⓔ
20. Ⓐ Ⓑ Ⓒ Ⓓ Ⓔ
21. Ⓐ Ⓑ Ⓒ Ⓓ Ⓔ
22. Ⓐ Ⓑ Ⓒ Ⓓ Ⓔ
23. Ⓐ Ⓑ Ⓒ Ⓓ Ⓔ
24. Ⓐ Ⓑ Ⓒ Ⓓ Ⓔ
25. Ⓐ Ⓑ Ⓒ Ⓓ Ⓔ
26. Ⓐ Ⓑ Ⓒ Ⓓ Ⓔ
27. Ⓐ Ⓑ Ⓒ Ⓓ Ⓔ
28. Ⓐ Ⓑ Ⓒ Ⓓ Ⓔ
29. Ⓐ Ⓑ Ⓒ Ⓓ Ⓔ
30. Ⓐ Ⓑ Ⓒ Ⓓ Ⓔ
31. Ⓐ Ⓑ Ⓒ Ⓓ Ⓔ
32. Ⓐ Ⓑ Ⓒ Ⓓ Ⓔ
33. Ⓐ Ⓑ Ⓒ Ⓓ Ⓔ
34. Ⓐ Ⓑ Ⓒ Ⓓ Ⓔ
35. Ⓐ Ⓑ Ⓒ Ⓓ Ⓔ
36. Ⓐ Ⓑ Ⓒ Ⓓ Ⓔ

37. Ⓐ Ⓑ Ⓒ Ⓓ Ⓔ
38. Ⓐ Ⓑ Ⓒ Ⓓ Ⓔ
39. Ⓐ Ⓑ Ⓒ Ⓓ Ⓔ
40. Ⓐ Ⓑ Ⓒ Ⓓ Ⓔ
41. Ⓐ Ⓑ Ⓒ Ⓓ Ⓔ
42. Ⓐ Ⓑ Ⓒ Ⓓ Ⓔ
43. Ⓐ Ⓑ Ⓒ Ⓓ Ⓔ
44. Ⓐ Ⓑ Ⓒ Ⓓ Ⓔ
45. Ⓐ Ⓑ Ⓒ Ⓓ Ⓔ
46. Ⓐ Ⓑ Ⓒ Ⓓ Ⓔ
47. Ⓐ Ⓑ Ⓒ Ⓓ Ⓔ
48. Ⓐ Ⓑ Ⓒ Ⓓ Ⓔ
49. Ⓐ Ⓑ Ⓒ Ⓓ Ⓔ
50. Ⓐ Ⓑ Ⓒ Ⓓ Ⓔ
51. Ⓐ Ⓑ Ⓒ Ⓓ Ⓔ
52. Ⓐ Ⓑ Ⓒ Ⓓ Ⓔ
53. Ⓐ Ⓑ Ⓒ Ⓓ Ⓔ
54. Ⓐ Ⓑ Ⓒ Ⓓ Ⓔ
55. Ⓐ Ⓑ Ⓒ Ⓓ Ⓔ
56. Ⓐ Ⓑ Ⓒ Ⓓ Ⓔ
57. Ⓐ Ⓑ Ⓒ Ⓓ Ⓔ
58. Ⓐ Ⓑ Ⓒ Ⓓ Ⓔ
59. Ⓐ Ⓑ Ⓒ Ⓓ Ⓔ
60. Ⓐ Ⓑ Ⓒ Ⓓ Ⓔ
61. Ⓐ Ⓑ Ⓒ Ⓓ Ⓔ
62. Ⓐ Ⓑ Ⓒ Ⓓ Ⓔ
63. Ⓐ Ⓑ Ⓒ Ⓓ Ⓔ
64. Ⓐ Ⓑ Ⓒ Ⓓ Ⓔ
65. Ⓐ Ⓑ Ⓒ Ⓓ Ⓔ
66. Ⓐ Ⓑ Ⓒ Ⓓ Ⓔ
67. Ⓐ Ⓑ Ⓒ Ⓓ Ⓔ
68. Ⓐ Ⓑ Ⓒ Ⓓ Ⓔ
69. Ⓐ Ⓑ Ⓒ Ⓓ Ⓔ
70. Ⓐ Ⓑ Ⓒ Ⓓ Ⓔ
71. Ⓐ Ⓑ Ⓒ Ⓓ Ⓔ
72. Ⓐ Ⓑ Ⓒ Ⓓ Ⓔ

73. Ⓐ Ⓑ Ⓒ Ⓓ Ⓔ
74. Ⓐ Ⓑ Ⓒ Ⓓ Ⓔ
75. Ⓐ Ⓑ Ⓒ Ⓓ Ⓔ
76. Ⓐ Ⓑ Ⓒ Ⓓ Ⓔ
77. Ⓐ Ⓑ Ⓒ Ⓓ Ⓔ
78. Ⓐ Ⓑ Ⓒ Ⓓ Ⓔ
79. Ⓐ Ⓑ Ⓒ Ⓓ Ⓔ
80. Ⓐ Ⓑ Ⓒ Ⓓ Ⓔ
81. Ⓐ Ⓑ Ⓒ Ⓓ Ⓔ
82. Ⓐ Ⓑ Ⓒ Ⓓ Ⓔ
83. Ⓐ Ⓑ Ⓒ Ⓓ Ⓔ
84. Ⓐ Ⓑ Ⓒ Ⓓ Ⓔ
85. Ⓐ Ⓑ Ⓒ Ⓓ Ⓔ
86. Ⓐ Ⓑ Ⓒ Ⓓ Ⓔ
87. Ⓐ Ⓑ Ⓒ Ⓓ Ⓔ
88. Ⓐ Ⓑ Ⓒ Ⓓ Ⓔ
89. Ⓐ Ⓑ Ⓒ Ⓓ Ⓔ
90. Ⓐ Ⓑ Ⓒ Ⓓ Ⓔ
91. Ⓐ Ⓑ Ⓒ Ⓓ Ⓔ
92. Ⓐ Ⓑ Ⓒ Ⓓ Ⓔ
93. Ⓐ Ⓑ Ⓒ Ⓓ Ⓔ
94. Ⓐ Ⓑ Ⓒ Ⓓ Ⓔ
95. Ⓐ Ⓑ Ⓒ Ⓓ Ⓔ
96. Ⓐ Ⓑ Ⓒ Ⓓ Ⓔ
97. Ⓐ Ⓑ Ⓒ Ⓓ Ⓔ
98. Ⓐ Ⓑ Ⓒ Ⓓ Ⓔ
99. Ⓐ Ⓑ Ⓒ Ⓓ Ⓔ
100. Ⓐ Ⓑ Ⓒ Ⓓ Ⓔ
101. Ⓐ Ⓑ Ⓒ Ⓓ Ⓔ
102. Ⓐ Ⓑ Ⓒ Ⓓ Ⓔ
103. Ⓐ Ⓑ Ⓒ Ⓓ Ⓔ
104. Ⓐ Ⓑ Ⓒ Ⓓ Ⓔ
105. Ⓐ Ⓑ Ⓒ Ⓓ Ⓔ
106. Ⓐ Ⓑ Ⓒ Ⓓ Ⓔ
107. Ⓐ Ⓑ Ⓒ Ⓓ Ⓔ
108. Ⓐ Ⓑ Ⓒ Ⓓ Ⓔ

109. Ⓐ Ⓑ Ⓒ Ⓓ Ⓔ
110. Ⓐ Ⓑ Ⓒ Ⓓ Ⓔ
111. Ⓐ Ⓑ Ⓒ Ⓓ Ⓔ
112. Ⓐ Ⓑ Ⓒ Ⓓ Ⓔ
113. Ⓐ Ⓑ Ⓒ Ⓓ Ⓔ
114. Ⓐ Ⓑ Ⓒ Ⓓ Ⓔ
115. Ⓐ Ⓑ Ⓒ Ⓓ Ⓔ
116. Ⓐ Ⓑ Ⓒ Ⓓ Ⓔ
117. Ⓐ Ⓑ Ⓒ Ⓓ Ⓔ
118. Ⓐ Ⓑ Ⓒ Ⓓ Ⓔ
119. Ⓐ Ⓑ Ⓒ Ⓓ Ⓔ
120. Ⓐ Ⓑ Ⓒ Ⓓ Ⓔ
121. Ⓐ Ⓑ Ⓒ Ⓓ Ⓔ
122. Ⓐ Ⓑ Ⓒ Ⓓ Ⓔ
123. Ⓐ Ⓑ Ⓒ Ⓓ Ⓔ
124. Ⓐ Ⓑ Ⓒ Ⓓ Ⓔ
125. Ⓐ Ⓑ Ⓒ Ⓓ Ⓔ
126. Ⓐ Ⓑ Ⓒ Ⓓ Ⓔ
127. Ⓐ Ⓑ Ⓒ Ⓓ Ⓔ
128. Ⓐ Ⓑ Ⓒ Ⓓ Ⓔ
129. Ⓐ Ⓑ Ⓒ Ⓓ Ⓔ
130. Ⓐ Ⓑ Ⓒ Ⓓ Ⓔ
131. Ⓐ Ⓑ Ⓒ Ⓓ Ⓔ
132. Ⓐ Ⓑ Ⓒ Ⓓ Ⓔ
133. Ⓐ Ⓑ Ⓒ Ⓓ Ⓔ
134. Ⓐ Ⓑ Ⓒ Ⓓ Ⓔ
135. Ⓐ Ⓑ Ⓒ Ⓓ Ⓔ
136. Ⓐ Ⓑ Ⓒ Ⓓ Ⓔ
137. Ⓐ Ⓑ Ⓒ Ⓓ Ⓔ
138. Ⓐ Ⓑ Ⓒ Ⓓ Ⓔ
139. Ⓐ Ⓑ Ⓒ Ⓓ Ⓔ
140. Ⓐ Ⓑ Ⓒ Ⓓ Ⓔ
141. Ⓐ Ⓑ Ⓒ Ⓓ Ⓔ
142. Ⓐ Ⓑ Ⓒ Ⓓ Ⓔ
143. Ⓐ Ⓑ Ⓒ Ⓓ Ⓔ
144. Ⓐ Ⓑ Ⓒ Ⓓ Ⓔ

145. Ⓐ Ⓑ Ⓒ Ⓓ Ⓔ
146. Ⓐ Ⓑ Ⓒ Ⓓ Ⓔ
147. Ⓐ Ⓑ Ⓒ Ⓓ Ⓔ
148. Ⓐ Ⓑ Ⓒ Ⓓ Ⓔ
149. Ⓐ Ⓑ Ⓒ Ⓓ Ⓔ
150. Ⓐ Ⓑ Ⓒ Ⓓ Ⓔ
151. Ⓐ Ⓑ Ⓒ Ⓓ Ⓔ
152. Ⓐ Ⓑ Ⓒ Ⓓ Ⓔ
153. Ⓐ Ⓑ Ⓒ Ⓓ Ⓔ
154. Ⓐ Ⓑ Ⓒ Ⓓ Ⓔ
155. Ⓐ Ⓑ Ⓒ Ⓓ Ⓔ
156. Ⓐ Ⓑ Ⓒ Ⓓ Ⓔ
157. Ⓐ Ⓑ Ⓒ Ⓓ Ⓔ
158. Ⓐ Ⓑ Ⓒ Ⓓ Ⓔ
159. Ⓐ Ⓑ Ⓒ Ⓓ Ⓔ
160. Ⓐ Ⓑ Ⓒ Ⓓ Ⓔ
161. Ⓐ Ⓑ Ⓒ Ⓓ Ⓔ
162. Ⓐ Ⓑ Ⓒ Ⓓ Ⓔ
163. Ⓐ Ⓑ Ⓒ Ⓓ Ⓔ
164. Ⓐ Ⓑ Ⓒ Ⓓ Ⓔ
165. Ⓐ Ⓑ Ⓒ Ⓓ Ⓔ
166. Ⓐ Ⓑ Ⓒ Ⓓ Ⓔ
167. Ⓐ Ⓑ Ⓒ Ⓓ Ⓔ
168. Ⓐ Ⓑ Ⓒ Ⓓ Ⓔ
169. Ⓐ Ⓑ Ⓒ Ⓓ Ⓔ
170. Ⓐ Ⓑ Ⓒ Ⓓ Ⓔ
171. Ⓐ Ⓑ Ⓒ Ⓓ Ⓔ
172. Ⓐ Ⓑ Ⓒ Ⓓ Ⓔ
173. Ⓐ Ⓑ Ⓒ Ⓓ Ⓔ
174. Ⓐ Ⓑ Ⓒ Ⓓ Ⓔ
175. Ⓐ Ⓑ Ⓒ Ⓓ Ⓔ
176. Ⓐ Ⓑ Ⓒ Ⓓ Ⓔ
177. Ⓐ Ⓑ Ⓒ Ⓓ Ⓔ
178. Ⓐ Ⓑ Ⓒ Ⓓ Ⓔ
179. Ⓐ Ⓑ Ⓒ Ⓓ Ⓔ
180. Ⓐ Ⓑ Ⓒ Ⓓ Ⓔ

181. Ⓐ Ⓑ Ⓒ Ⓓ Ⓔ 217. Ⓐ Ⓑ Ⓒ Ⓓ Ⓔ 253. Ⓐ Ⓑ Ⓒ Ⓓ Ⓔ 289. Ⓐ Ⓑ Ⓒ Ⓓ Ⓔ 325. Ⓐ Ⓑ Ⓒ Ⓓ Ⓔ
182. Ⓐ Ⓑ Ⓒ Ⓓ Ⓔ 218. Ⓐ Ⓑ Ⓒ Ⓓ Ⓔ 254. Ⓐ Ⓑ Ⓒ Ⓓ Ⓔ 290. Ⓐ Ⓑ Ⓒ Ⓓ Ⓔ 326. Ⓐ Ⓑ Ⓒ Ⓓ Ⓔ
183. Ⓐ Ⓑ Ⓒ Ⓓ Ⓔ 219. Ⓐ Ⓑ Ⓒ Ⓓ Ⓔ 255. Ⓐ Ⓑ Ⓒ Ⓓ Ⓔ 291. Ⓐ Ⓑ Ⓒ Ⓓ Ⓔ 327. Ⓐ Ⓑ Ⓒ Ⓓ Ⓔ
184. Ⓐ Ⓑ Ⓒ Ⓓ Ⓔ 220. Ⓐ Ⓑ Ⓒ Ⓓ Ⓔ 256. Ⓐ Ⓑ Ⓒ Ⓓ Ⓔ 292. Ⓐ Ⓑ Ⓒ Ⓓ Ⓔ 328. Ⓐ Ⓑ Ⓒ Ⓓ Ⓔ
185. Ⓐ Ⓑ Ⓒ Ⓓ Ⓔ 221. Ⓐ Ⓑ Ⓒ Ⓓ Ⓔ 257. Ⓐ Ⓑ Ⓒ Ⓓ Ⓔ 293. Ⓐ Ⓑ Ⓒ Ⓓ Ⓔ 329. Ⓐ Ⓑ Ⓒ Ⓓ Ⓔ
186. Ⓐ Ⓑ Ⓒ Ⓓ Ⓔ 222. Ⓐ Ⓑ Ⓒ Ⓓ Ⓔ 258. Ⓐ Ⓑ Ⓒ Ⓓ Ⓔ 294. Ⓐ Ⓑ Ⓒ Ⓓ Ⓔ 330. Ⓐ Ⓑ Ⓒ Ⓓ Ⓔ
187. Ⓐ Ⓑ Ⓒ Ⓓ Ⓔ 223. Ⓐ Ⓑ Ⓒ Ⓓ Ⓔ 259. Ⓐ Ⓑ Ⓒ Ⓓ Ⓔ 295. Ⓐ Ⓑ Ⓒ Ⓓ Ⓔ 331. Ⓐ Ⓑ Ⓒ Ⓓ Ⓔ
188. Ⓐ Ⓑ Ⓒ Ⓓ Ⓔ 224. Ⓐ Ⓑ Ⓒ Ⓓ Ⓔ 260. Ⓐ Ⓑ Ⓒ Ⓓ Ⓔ 296. Ⓐ Ⓑ Ⓒ Ⓓ Ⓔ 332. Ⓐ Ⓑ Ⓒ Ⓓ Ⓔ
189. Ⓐ Ⓑ Ⓒ Ⓓ Ⓔ 225. Ⓐ Ⓑ Ⓒ Ⓓ Ⓔ 261. Ⓐ Ⓑ Ⓒ Ⓓ Ⓔ 297. Ⓐ Ⓑ Ⓒ Ⓓ Ⓔ 333. Ⓐ Ⓑ Ⓒ Ⓓ Ⓔ
190. Ⓐ Ⓑ Ⓒ Ⓓ Ⓔ 226. Ⓐ Ⓑ Ⓒ Ⓓ Ⓔ 262. Ⓐ Ⓑ Ⓒ Ⓓ Ⓔ 298. Ⓐ Ⓑ Ⓒ Ⓓ Ⓔ 334. Ⓐ Ⓑ Ⓒ Ⓓ Ⓔ
191. Ⓐ Ⓑ Ⓒ Ⓓ Ⓔ 227. Ⓐ Ⓑ Ⓒ Ⓓ Ⓔ 263. Ⓐ Ⓑ Ⓒ Ⓓ Ⓔ 299. Ⓐ Ⓑ Ⓒ Ⓓ Ⓔ 335. Ⓐ Ⓑ Ⓒ Ⓓ Ⓔ
192. Ⓐ Ⓑ Ⓒ Ⓓ Ⓔ 228. Ⓐ Ⓑ Ⓒ Ⓓ Ⓔ 264. Ⓐ Ⓑ Ⓒ Ⓓ Ⓔ 300. Ⓐ Ⓑ Ⓒ Ⓓ Ⓔ 336. Ⓐ Ⓑ Ⓒ Ⓓ Ⓔ
193. Ⓐ Ⓑ Ⓒ Ⓓ Ⓔ 229. Ⓐ Ⓑ Ⓒ Ⓓ Ⓔ 265. Ⓐ Ⓑ Ⓒ Ⓓ Ⓔ 301. Ⓐ Ⓑ Ⓒ Ⓓ Ⓔ 337. Ⓐ Ⓑ Ⓒ Ⓓ Ⓔ
194. Ⓐ Ⓑ Ⓒ Ⓓ Ⓔ 230. Ⓐ Ⓑ Ⓒ Ⓓ Ⓔ 266. Ⓐ Ⓑ Ⓒ Ⓓ Ⓔ 302. Ⓐ Ⓑ Ⓒ Ⓓ Ⓔ 338. Ⓐ Ⓑ Ⓒ Ⓓ Ⓔ
195. Ⓐ Ⓑ Ⓒ Ⓓ Ⓔ 231. Ⓐ Ⓑ Ⓒ Ⓓ Ⓔ 267. Ⓐ Ⓑ Ⓒ Ⓓ Ⓔ 303. Ⓐ Ⓑ Ⓒ Ⓓ Ⓔ 339. Ⓐ Ⓑ Ⓒ Ⓓ Ⓔ
196. Ⓐ Ⓑ Ⓒ Ⓓ Ⓔ 232. Ⓐ Ⓑ Ⓒ Ⓓ Ⓔ 268. Ⓐ Ⓑ Ⓒ Ⓓ Ⓔ 304. Ⓐ Ⓑ Ⓒ Ⓓ Ⓔ 340. Ⓐ Ⓑ Ⓒ Ⓓ Ⓔ
197. Ⓐ Ⓑ Ⓒ Ⓓ Ⓔ 233. Ⓐ Ⓑ Ⓒ Ⓓ Ⓔ 269. Ⓐ Ⓑ Ⓒ Ⓓ Ⓔ 305. Ⓐ Ⓑ Ⓒ Ⓓ Ⓔ 341. Ⓐ Ⓑ Ⓒ Ⓓ Ⓔ
198. Ⓐ Ⓑ Ⓒ Ⓓ Ⓔ 234. Ⓐ Ⓑ Ⓒ Ⓓ Ⓔ 270. Ⓐ Ⓑ Ⓒ Ⓓ Ⓔ 306. Ⓐ Ⓑ Ⓒ Ⓓ Ⓔ 342. Ⓐ Ⓑ Ⓒ Ⓓ Ⓔ
199. Ⓐ Ⓑ Ⓒ Ⓓ Ⓔ 235. Ⓐ Ⓑ Ⓒ Ⓓ Ⓔ 271. Ⓐ Ⓑ Ⓒ Ⓓ Ⓔ 307. Ⓐ Ⓑ Ⓒ Ⓓ Ⓔ 343. Ⓐ Ⓑ Ⓒ Ⓓ Ⓔ
200. Ⓐ Ⓑ Ⓒ Ⓓ Ⓔ 236. Ⓐ Ⓑ Ⓒ Ⓓ Ⓔ 272. Ⓐ Ⓑ Ⓒ Ⓓ Ⓔ 308. Ⓐ Ⓑ Ⓒ Ⓓ Ⓔ 344. Ⓐ Ⓑ Ⓒ Ⓓ Ⓔ
201. Ⓐ Ⓑ Ⓒ Ⓓ Ⓔ 237. Ⓐ Ⓑ Ⓒ Ⓓ Ⓔ 273. Ⓐ Ⓑ Ⓒ Ⓓ Ⓔ 309. Ⓐ Ⓑ Ⓒ Ⓓ Ⓔ 345. Ⓐ Ⓑ Ⓒ Ⓓ Ⓔ
202. Ⓐ Ⓑ Ⓒ Ⓓ Ⓔ 238. Ⓐ Ⓑ Ⓒ Ⓓ Ⓔ 274. Ⓐ Ⓑ Ⓒ Ⓓ Ⓔ 310. Ⓐ Ⓑ Ⓒ Ⓓ Ⓔ 346. Ⓐ Ⓑ Ⓒ Ⓓ Ⓔ
203. Ⓐ Ⓑ Ⓒ Ⓓ Ⓔ 239. Ⓐ Ⓑ Ⓒ Ⓓ Ⓔ 275. Ⓐ Ⓑ Ⓒ Ⓓ Ⓔ 311. Ⓐ Ⓑ Ⓒ Ⓓ Ⓔ 347. Ⓐ Ⓑ Ⓒ Ⓓ Ⓔ
204. Ⓐ Ⓑ Ⓒ Ⓓ Ⓔ 240. Ⓐ Ⓑ Ⓒ Ⓓ Ⓔ 276. Ⓐ Ⓑ Ⓒ Ⓓ Ⓔ 312. Ⓐ Ⓑ Ⓒ Ⓓ Ⓔ 348. Ⓐ Ⓑ Ⓒ Ⓓ Ⓔ
205. Ⓐ Ⓑ Ⓒ Ⓓ Ⓔ 241. Ⓐ Ⓑ Ⓒ Ⓓ Ⓔ 277. Ⓐ Ⓑ Ⓒ Ⓓ Ⓔ 313. Ⓐ Ⓑ Ⓒ Ⓓ Ⓔ 349. Ⓐ Ⓑ Ⓒ Ⓓ Ⓔ
206. Ⓐ Ⓑ Ⓒ Ⓓ Ⓔ 242. Ⓐ Ⓑ Ⓒ Ⓓ Ⓔ 278. Ⓐ Ⓑ Ⓒ Ⓓ Ⓔ 314. Ⓐ Ⓑ Ⓒ Ⓓ Ⓔ 350. Ⓐ Ⓑ Ⓒ Ⓓ Ⓔ
207. Ⓐ Ⓑ Ⓒ Ⓓ Ⓔ 243. Ⓐ Ⓑ Ⓒ Ⓓ Ⓔ 279. Ⓐ Ⓑ Ⓒ Ⓓ Ⓔ 315. Ⓐ Ⓑ Ⓒ Ⓓ Ⓔ 351. Ⓐ Ⓑ Ⓒ Ⓓ Ⓔ
208. Ⓐ Ⓑ Ⓒ Ⓓ Ⓔ 244. Ⓐ Ⓑ Ⓒ Ⓓ Ⓔ 280. Ⓐ Ⓑ Ⓒ Ⓓ Ⓔ 316. Ⓐ Ⓑ Ⓒ Ⓓ Ⓔ 352. Ⓐ Ⓑ Ⓒ Ⓓ Ⓔ
209. Ⓐ Ⓑ Ⓒ Ⓓ Ⓔ 245. Ⓐ Ⓑ Ⓒ Ⓓ Ⓔ 281. Ⓐ Ⓑ Ⓒ Ⓓ Ⓔ 317. Ⓐ Ⓑ Ⓒ Ⓓ Ⓔ 353. Ⓐ Ⓑ Ⓒ Ⓓ Ⓔ
210. Ⓐ Ⓑ Ⓒ Ⓓ Ⓔ 246. Ⓐ Ⓑ Ⓒ Ⓓ Ⓔ 282. Ⓐ Ⓑ Ⓒ Ⓓ Ⓔ 318. Ⓐ Ⓑ Ⓒ Ⓓ Ⓔ 354. Ⓐ Ⓑ Ⓒ Ⓓ Ⓔ
211. Ⓐ Ⓑ Ⓒ Ⓓ Ⓔ 247. Ⓐ Ⓑ Ⓒ Ⓓ Ⓔ 283. Ⓐ Ⓑ Ⓒ Ⓓ Ⓔ 319. Ⓐ Ⓑ Ⓒ Ⓓ Ⓔ 355. Ⓐ Ⓑ Ⓒ Ⓓ Ⓔ
212. Ⓐ Ⓑ Ⓒ Ⓓ Ⓔ 248. Ⓐ Ⓑ Ⓒ Ⓓ Ⓔ 284. Ⓐ Ⓑ Ⓒ Ⓓ Ⓔ 320. Ⓐ Ⓑ Ⓒ Ⓓ Ⓔ 356. Ⓐ Ⓑ Ⓒ Ⓓ Ⓔ
213. Ⓐ Ⓑ Ⓒ Ⓓ Ⓔ 249. Ⓐ Ⓑ Ⓒ Ⓓ Ⓔ 285. Ⓐ Ⓑ Ⓒ Ⓓ Ⓔ 321. Ⓐ Ⓑ Ⓒ Ⓓ Ⓔ 357. Ⓐ Ⓑ Ⓒ Ⓓ Ⓔ
214. Ⓐ Ⓑ Ⓒ Ⓓ Ⓔ 250. Ⓐ Ⓑ Ⓒ Ⓓ Ⓔ 286. Ⓐ Ⓑ Ⓒ Ⓓ Ⓔ 322. Ⓐ Ⓑ Ⓒ Ⓓ Ⓔ 358. Ⓐ Ⓑ Ⓒ Ⓓ Ⓔ
215. Ⓐ Ⓑ Ⓒ Ⓓ Ⓔ 251. Ⓐ Ⓑ Ⓒ Ⓓ Ⓔ 287. Ⓐ Ⓑ Ⓒ Ⓓ Ⓔ 323. Ⓐ Ⓑ Ⓒ Ⓓ Ⓔ 359. Ⓐ Ⓑ Ⓒ Ⓓ Ⓔ
216. Ⓐ Ⓑ Ⓒ Ⓓ Ⓔ 252. Ⓐ Ⓑ Ⓒ Ⓓ Ⓔ 288. Ⓐ Ⓑ Ⓒ Ⓓ Ⓔ 324. Ⓐ Ⓑ Ⓒ Ⓓ Ⓔ 360. Ⓐ Ⓑ Ⓒ Ⓓ Ⓔ

Practice Test 2

1. A 62-year-old white female presents with sudden onset of crushing sub-sternal chest pain, shortness of breath, and hemoptysis. She underwent left hip arthroplasty two weeks ago. Electrocardiogram reveals sinus tachycardia at a rate of 115 beats per minute with no ST segment abnormality. Pulse oximetry reveals a level of 89% on room air. Laboratory findings include:

Troponin level	> 0.1
D-dimer level	2.60
Blood Urea Nitrogen	38
Serum Creatinine	2.2
GFR	52

Which diagnostic study would you perform next and why?
(A) Myocardial perfusion scan to rule out acute myocardial infarction
(B) CT scan with contrast of the abdomen to rule out aortic dissection
(C) CT scan with contrast of the chest to rule out pulmonary embolism
(D) Lung ventilation and perfusion scan to rule out pulmonary embolism
(E) Echocardiogram to evaluate cardiac function

2. A 44-year-old female presents with pain in the inner ear as a result of an airplane flight. She states she flies on a regular basis for her job. You diagnose this patient with barotraumas. Which of the following practices would you advise this patient to perform during an airplane flight?
(A) Place head between her legs prior to takeoff
(B) Place seat in supine position prior to takeoff
(C) Yawn or swallow when she feels pressure begin to increase
(D) Take diuretics the day prior to eliminate mucosal edema
(E) Take medication for motion sickness before takeoff

3. A 55-year-old obese African-American male presents with sudden onset of chest tightness radiating to his back and left arm, along with nausea. Chest X-ray was normal, and electrocardiogram reveals normal sinus rhythm with ST segment elevation. Troponin level was 0.4. D-dimer level was 0.24. Pulse oximetry was normal at 100% on room air. Blood pressure was 160/80. Patient was administered nitroglycerin with no resolution of chest pain. Which diagnostic study would you perform and why?
(A) Echocardiogram to evaluate cardiac function
(B) Myocardial perfusion scan to evaluate for myocardial infarction
(C) CT scan with contrast of the chest to rule out pulmonary embolism
(D) Coronary angiography to evaluate for myocardial infarction
(E) Treadmill test to detect reduced blood supply to the heart

4. A 44-year-old female presents with a history of weakness, fatigue, low blood pressure, and abnormal skin color. Thyroid hormone levels are within normal limits. Chest X-ray is normal. CT scan and ultrasound exams of the abdomen both reveal abnormalities to the adrenal glands. Which is the appropriate diagnosis?
(A) Addison's disease
(B) Grave's disease
(C) Wilson's disease
(D) Pheochromocytoma
(E) Hypothyroidism

5. The X-ray image known as a Water's view is useful in diagnosing which of the following conditions?
   (A) Blowout fracture of the orbital floor
   (B) Sinusitis
   (C) Mastoiditis
   (D) Rhinitis
   (E) Deviated nasal septum

6. Which of the following malignant disorders is a malignancy of plasma cells?
   (A) Multiple myeloma
   (B) Chronic lymphocytic anemia
   (C) Hodgkin's lymphoma
   (D) Acute myologenous leukemia
   (E) Non-Hodgkin's lymphoma

7. A 36-year-old male presents with severe chemical burns of the eyes. Which of the following treatments would you perform immediately?
   (A) Apply topical antibiotic cream to the eyelids.
   (B) Place antibiotic drops in the eyes.
   (C) Irrigate eyes with normal saline solution.
   (D) Apply ice packs to the eyes.
   (E) Test acuity of vision.

8. A 27-year-old Asian male presents to the emergency room in an unresponsive state. Blood pressure is reduced at 80/50 mmHg. Auscultation of the chest reveals a rapid, irregular heart rhythm. The patient's electrocardiogram is illustrated below. Based on the patient's ancestry and clinical presentation, this patient suffers from which of the following disorders?

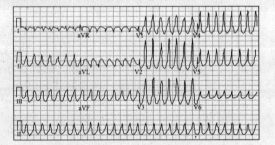

   (A) Wolff-Parkinson-White syndrome
   (B) Sick sinus syndrome
   (C) Brugada syndrome
   (D) Hypoplastic left heart syndrome
   (E) Long Q-T syndrome

9. A 22-year-old female presents to the emergency room with chest trauma, chest pain, and shortness of breath. The examination and chest X-ray reveal a tension pneumothorax. Due to the emergent nature of the situation, what is the first priority of treatment?
   (A) Insert chest tube
   (B) Insert large bore needle in the chest
   (C) Perform thoracentesis
   (D) Perform high-resolution CT scan
   (E) Tracheotomy

10. A 68-year-old obese Caucasian female presents with skin irritation of the lower legs. The skin of the lower legs appears purplish-red in color. Upon examination, the patient is noticed to have varicose veins in the lower legs. What is the appropriate diagnosis from this examination?
    (A) Contact eczema
    (B) Seborrheic eczema
    (C) Stasis dermatitis
    (D) Neurodermatitis
    (E) Atopic dermatitis

11. A 42-year-old female presents with increasing frequency and urgency of urination. She complains of intermittent hematuria. Urinalysis reveals bacteriemia and hematuria. Physical exam reveals suprapubic tenderness. Your diagnosis for this female is cystitis. Which of the following medications would you suggest to treat this condition?
    (A) ACE inhibitors
    (B) Ceftriaxone
    (C) Fluoroquinolone
    (D) Doxycycline
    (E) Amoxicillin

12. A 16-year-old female presents with irrational preoccupation with her appearance. She has a history of several visits to a plastic surgeon. Your clinical diagnosis is body dysmorphic disorder. Which of the following medications would you prescribe to treat this psychological disorder?
    (A) Neuroleptic medications
    (B) Antipsychotic medications
    (C) Serotonin-modulating medications
    (D) Tricyclic antidepressant medications
    (E) Monoamine oxidase inhibitor medications

13. Which of the following classes of anti-diabetes medications acts by delaying carbohydrate absorption from the intestine, thus lowering glucose levels in the bloodstream?
(A) Sulfonylureas
(B) Thiazolidinediones
(C) Statins
(D) Alpha-glucosidase inhibitors
(E) Biguanides

14. Which of the following medications is indicated for long-term maintenance therapy of cardiogenic transient ischemic attacks?
(A) Ticlopidine
(B) Sulfinpyrazone
(C) Dipyridamole
(D) Warfarin
(E) Heparin

15. A 17-year-old male presents with dizziness and nausea without loss of consciousness. The patient had been active all day at a wrestling tournament. No chest X-ray abnormalities, CT scan abnormalities, or bloodwork abnormalities were detected. Which is the most appropriate diagnosis?
(A) Vasovagal reaction
(B) Adrenal insufficiency
(C) Orthostatic hypotension
(D) Micturition syncope
(E) Inebriation

16. An elderly, gravely ill, 88-year-old woman with a history of sepsis presents in the intensive care unit with rapid onset of profound dyspnea. Physical examination reveals tachypnea, frothy pink sputum, diffuse crackles, and cyanosis. Chest X-ray reveals peripheral infiltrates with air bronchograms. Based on the patient's presentation, history, and test results, which of the following is the most accurate diagnosis?
(A) Cystic fibrosis
(B) Adult respiratory distress syndrome
(C) Septic shock
(D) Acute respiratory failure
(E) Pulmonary embolism

17. An 80-year-old male with a history of coronary-bypass graft surgery presents with abdominal pain that occurs within 30 minutes after eating. The pain only subsides after the patient lies down. Abdominal X-ray reveals colonic dilatation. Abdominal angiography was positive for chronic mesenteric ischemia. Which of the following procedures would you perform in order to correct this disorder?
(A) Endoscopic decompression
(B) Colonoscopy
(C) Barium enema
(D) Colostomy
(E) Surgical revascularization

18. A healthy 28-year-old male presents with severe itching on the palms of the hands and the soles of the feet. Upon examination, the patient exhibits a very deep, blistering "tapioca pudding" rash on these areas. What is the appropriate diagnosis from this examination?
(A) Dyshidrotic eczema
(B) Contact eczema
(C) Seborrheic eczema
(D) Stasis dermatitis
(E) Neurodermatitis

19. A 37-year-old male construction worker presents with penetrating trauma to the left eye. Which of the following is the correct course of treatment?
(A) Surgically remove the object, place eye patch over the eye, prescribe eye drops, and send home.
(B) Do not remove object, place patch over the eye, and send patient home and follow up with an opthalmologist.
(C) Do not remove object and arrange for patient to be transported to nearest emergency room for consult with an opthalmologist.
(D) Surgically remove the object, place patch over the eye, and send patient home and follow up with an opthalmologist.
(E) Surgically remove the object, place patch over the eye, and arrange for patient to be transported to nearest emergency room for consult with an opthalmologist.

20. An otherwise healthy 22-year-old male presents with episodes of heart palpitations, dizziness, and shortness of breath. The patient's electrocardiogram is shown below. Based on the findings, this patient suffers from which of the following disorders?

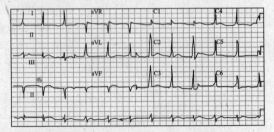

(A) Wolff-Parkinson-White syndrome
(B) Sick sinus syndrome
(C) Brugada syndrome
(D) Hypoplastic left heart syndrome
(E) Long Q-T Syndrome

21. A 66-year-old female who has recently undergone radiation therapy for breast cancer presents with shortness of breath and reduced exercise capacity. Auscultation of the chest reveals right-sided rales. Chest X-ray shows mildly enlarged cardiac silhouette. Echocardiogram reveals mildly reduced left ventricular function. Based on the patient's presentation, physical examination, and test results, which of the following is the most appropriate diagnosis?

(A) Dilated cardiomyopathy
(B) Hypertrophic cardiomyopathy
(C) Restrictive cardiomyopathy
(D) Congestive heart failure
(E) Pulmonary hypertension

22. Which of the following anti-seizure medications is used primarily when patients are unresponsive to other anti-seizure medications?

(A) Valproic acid
(B) Phenytoin
(C) Felbamate
(D) Gabapentin
(E) Clonazepam

23. A 65-year-old African-American male presents with a recent diagnosis of chronic kidney disease. Which of the following medications would you prescribe for treatment of chronic kidney disease?

(A) ACE inhibitors
(B) Diuretics
(C) Calcium channel blockers
(D) Alpha-adrenergic antagonists
(E) Beta-adrenergic antagonists

24. A 16-year-old male presents with pain in his hand following a fight. Physical examination reveals puncture wounds over the fourth and fifth metacarpal phalangeal joints. X-ray reveals fractures on the metacarpal necks of these fingers. Based on the patient's presentation, physical examination, and test results, which of the following is the most appropriate diagnosis?

(A) Scaphoid fracture
(B) Rolando fracture
(C) Bennet's fracture
(D) Boxer's fracture
(E) Smith's fracture

25. A 55-year-old male presents with headache, dizziness, weakness, fatigue, and blurred vision. Physical examination reveals systolic hypertension, engorged retinal veins, and splenomegaly. Bloodwork reveals hematocrit of 57%, elevated red cell mass, neutrophilic leukocytosis, increased basophils and eosinophils, and increased numbers of large, bizarre platelets. Based on the patient's presentation, physical examination, and lab results, which of the following is the most appropriate diagnosis?

(A) Thrombocytopenia
(B) Hemolytic anemia
(C) Polycythemia vera
(D) Leukemia
(E) Sickle cell anemia

26. An 18-year-old male sustains a boxer's fracture with puncture wounds. Due to the puncture wounds, what additional treatment is necessary other than splinting the affected fingers?

(A) Anti-inflammatories
(B) Corticosteroids
(C) Antibiotics
(D) Opiate pain medication
(E) Suturing the wound

27. A 17-year-old female presents with blindness, inability to speak, and numbness in the extremities. She expresses little or no concern about the symptoms she is experiencing. Full workup, including bloodwork and radiographic study, fail to find any clinical explanation for the symptoms. Based on the patient's presentation and workup,

which of the following is the most appropriate diagnosis?
(A) Somatization disorder
(B) Body dysmorphic disorder
(C) Conversion disorder
(D) Factitious disorder
(E) Ganser syndrome

28. An 86-year-old-female presents with a history of dizziness and loss of consciousness during urination. All lab values are within normal limits; chest X-ray is normal; and CT scans of chest, abdomen, and pelvis are all within normal limits. Which of the following is the best diagnosis?
(A) Orthostatic hypotension
(B) Micturition syncope
(C) Septicemia
(D) Vasovagal reaction
(E) Labyrinthitis

29. Centor Criteria were established in order to quickly diagnose the presence of streptococcal pharyngitis in adult patients who presented to an urban emergency room complaining of a sore throat. Which of the following accurately describe Centor Criteria indicating streptococcal infection?
(A) Lack of fever, tender anterior cervical adenopathy, lack of cough, and pharyngotonsillar exudates
(B) Fever of greater than 100.4°F, tender anterior cervical adenopathy, lack of cough, and pharyngotonsillar exudates
(C) Fever of greater than 100.4°F, tender anterior cervical adenopathy, productive cough, and pharyngotonsillar exudates
(D) Lack of fever, tender anterior cervical adenopathy, productive cough, and pharyngotonsillar exudates
(E) Fever greater than 100.4°F, dry non-productive cough, sinus pain, and pharyngotonsillar exudates

30. An obese 25-year-old male presents with a painful, fluctuant eruption on the sacrococcygeal cleft. The eruption is diagnosed as a pilonidal cyst. Which of the following is the proper treatment for a pilonidal cyst?
(A) Topical antibiotics
(B) Warm compresses
(C) Topical anti-inflammatories
(D) Surgical drainage
(E) Corticosteroids

31. Which of the following medical signs is an indication of acute appendicitis wherein pressure on the left lower quadrant of the abdomen causes pain in the right lower quadrant of the abdomen?
(A) Levine's sign
(B) Rovsing's sign
(C) Psoas sign
(D) Obturator sign
(E) McBurney's sign

32. A 46-year-old, otherwise healthy, male presents with recurrent chest pain that occurs through the night, at rest. Chest X-ray was within normal limits. EKG was within normal limits. Auscultation of the chest reveals no abnormalities. Cardiac stress testing was performed, but was uneventful and the patient remained asymptomatic throughout the exam. Based on the patient's presentation, physical exam, and test results, which of the following is the most likely diagnosis?
(A) Stable angina
(B) Unstable angina
(C) Prinzmetal's angina
(D) Ischemic heart disease
(E) Congestive heart failure

33. A 42-year-old female presents in November stating she has been lethargic and depressed and has experienced lack of interest in any activities for the past 3 to 4 weeks. She states this happens to her every year around this time of year. Based on the patient's history and presentation, which of the following is the most accurate diagnosis?
(A) Melancholia
(B) Seasonal affective disorder
(C) Atypical depression
(D) Catatonic depression
(E) Major depressive disorder

34. A 14-year-old athletic male presents with hip and thigh pain and a noticeable painful limp. X-rays reveal posterior and medial displacement of the epiphysis. Based on the patient's presentation and test results, which of the following is the most appropriate diagnosis?
(A) Aseptic necrosis
(B) Slipped capital femoral epiphysis
(C) Osgood-Schlatter disease
(D) Acute hip dislocation
(E) Hip dysplasia

35. A 35-year-old male presents prior to going on a cruise vacation. He states he suffers from terrible motion sickness and vertigo. Which of the following treatment options would you prescribe to lessen his symptoms while on vacation?
(A) Scopolamine
(B) Meclizine
(C) Dimenhydrinate
(D) Diazepam
(E) Droperidol

36. A 53-year-old female presents to the emergency room with numbness and tingling in the extremities and weakness. The patient's electrocardiogram is shown below. Which of the following electrolyte disorders can be diagnosed from this electrocardiogram?

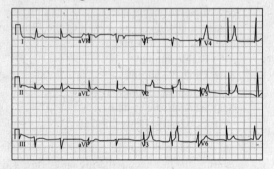

(A) Hypercalcemia
(B) Hyperkalemia
(C) Hypernatremia
(D) Hypermagnesemia
(D) Hypochloremia

37. A 48-year-old male presents with productive cough, shortness of breath, fever, sore throat, headache, and body aches. Auscultation of the chest reveals expiratory rhonchi and wheezes. Chest X-ray was performed and was negative. Based on patient symptoms and physical examination, which of the following is the proper diagnosis?
(A) Acute bronchitis
(B) Acute epiglottitis
(C) Tuberculosis
(D) Pneumonia
(E) Pulmonary edema

38. A 46-year-old female presents with foul smelling, purulent sputum, hemoptysis, and chronic cough. She has had recurrent bouts of pneumonia. Auscultation of the chest reveals localized chest crackles and clubbing. High-resolution CT scan reveals dilated, tortuous airways. Based on the patient's presentation, history, and test results, which of the following is the most accurate diagnosis?
(A) Asthma
(B) Bronchiectasis
(C) COPD
(D) Cystic fibrosis
(E) Tuberculosis

39. A 48-year-old male presents with throbbing pain to the groin, hip, and buttocks that is relieved with rest. You suspect aseptic necrosis of the hip. Which diagnostic procedure would you obtain to confirm this diagnosis?
(A) X-ray of the hips
(B) Nuclear medicine bone scan
(C) CT scan of the hips
(D) MRI of the hips
(E) Biopsy of the hip joint

40. Which of the following radiologic imaging modalities is required to differentiate between ischemic and hemorrhagic strokes?
(A) CT scan
(B) Angiogram
(C) Ultrasound
(D) MRI
(E) PET scan

41. A 70-year-old male presents with chest pain and shortness of breath. Physical examination and auscultation reveal low-intensity pulse in the carotid arteries. Chest X-ray shows fluid in the lungs. Echocardiogram reveals a calcified, poorly functioning aortic valve. Which of the following is the correct diagnosis?
(A) Pericarditis
(B) Aortic stenosis
(C) Mitral valve prolapse
(D) Carotid stenosis
(E) Pulmonary embolism

42. A 26-year-old male presents with spontaneous, acute chest pain and shortness of breath. Auscultation of the chest reveals diminished breath sounds on the right side. Chest X-ray reveals the accumulation of air in the pleural space without mediastinal shift. Based on the patient's

presentation, history, and test results, which of the following is the most accurate diagnosis?
(A) Pulmonary embolism
(B) Pleural effusion
(C) Pulmonary hypertension
(D) Pneumothorax
(E) Pulmonary edema

43. A 52-year-old female presents with generalized weakness, body aches, nausea, loss of appetite, and increased thirst. Bloodwork reveals an elevated blood calcium level. Based on this information, what would be the most appropriate initial diagnosis?
(A) Diabetes mellitus
(B) Hypothyroidism
(C) Hyperthyroidism
(D) Hyperparathyroidism
(E) Addison's disease

44. A 54-year-old African-American female presented with dizziness and nausea when transitioning from a sitting to a standing position. You have diagnosed her with orthostatic hypotension. What course of treatment would you suggest to this patient?
(A) Change diet to include more water, caffeinated beverages, and salt
(B) Change diet to include less water, caffeine, and salt
(C) Prescribe beta blockers
(D) Prescribe ACE inhibitors
(E) Recommend an exercise regimen

45. A 28-year-old male presents with bright red, raspberry-like nodules on the forearm after removal of a cast to heal a fracture of the ulna. You diagnose these nodules as pyogenic granulomas. Which of the following treatment options would you suggest for treatment of this disorder?
(A) Topical steroids
(B) Cauterization with silver nitrate
(C) Cryosurgery
(D) Excision
(E) Injection of vasoconstricting agents

46. A 22-year-old female who is undergoing treatment for an inner ear infection presents with increased fever along with pain and redness around the outside of the ear. Based on the patient's history and presentation, which of the following is the most likely diagnosis?
(A) Labyrinthitis
(B) Otitis externa
(C) Otitis media
(D) Mastoiditis
(E) Tympanic membrane rupture

47. A 68-year-old female presents to the emergency room with classic chest pain lasting for 30 minutes. Patient does not complain of pain radiating to other parts of the body and blood pressure is slightly elevated at 140/90 mmHg. Electrocardiogram performed in the emergency room reveals S-T segment elevation (see illustration).

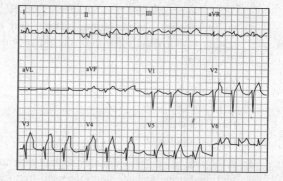

Based on the patient's symptoms and electrocardiographic findings, which of the following is the most accurate diagnosis?
(A) Left-sided congestive heart failure
(B) Right-sided congestive heart failure
(C) Cardiomyopathy
(D) Ischemic heart disease
(E) Acute myocardial infarction

48. Which of the following diabetes medications acts to increase insulin secretion, has very few drug interactions, and can cause weight gain?
(A) Metformin
(B) Glyburide
(C) Miglitol
(D) Exenatide
(E) Rosilitazone

49. A 44-year-old male presents with a long history of heartburn, chest pain, and regurgitation. His symptoms are relieved with the administration of antacids. Electrocardiogram shows normal sinus rhythm with no S-T segment abnormalities. Based on the patient's presentation and physical examination, which of the following is the most appropriate diagnosis?
   (A) Reflex esophagitis
   (B) Gastroesophageal reflux disease
   (C) Esophageal dysmotility
   (D) Esophageal neoplasm
   (E) Barrett's esophagus

50. A 58-year-old male presents with progressive shortness of breath and excessive cough with sputum production. Auscultation of the chest reveals decreased breath sounds, early inspiratory crackles, and prolonged expiration. Chest X-ray reveals hyperinflation and flat diaphragm. Based on the patient's presentation, history, and test results, which of the following is the most accurate diagnosis?
   (A) Asthma
   (B) Bronchiectasis
   (C) COPD
   (D) Cystic fibrosis
   (E) Tuberculosis

51. A 68-year-old diabetic female presents with unintentional urine leakage and increased frequency and urgency of urination. This is a classic case of urinary incontinence. Which of the following medications would you prescribe in order to treat this disorder?
   (A) ACE inhibitors
   (B) Tolterodine
   (C) Fluoroquinolone
   (D) Doxycycline
   (E) Vasodilators

52. A 20-year-old female with a history of systemic lupus erythematosus presents with petechiae on the skin and mucous membranes. She also complains of abnormal bleeding in the gums. Bloodwork reveals a decreased platelet count of 44,000 platelets/mcL. You diagnose this patient with thrombocytopenia. Which of the following medications would you prescribe for treatment of this disorder?
   (A) Erythropoietin
   (B) Folic acid

   (C) Prednisone
   (D) Vitamin B12
   (E) Vitamin D

53. An X-ray of a patient's hands reveals a lesion on the proximal phalanx of the ring finger. The lesion has a lobular morphology and punctate calcifications are noted. Further analysis revealed that the lesion is composed of hyaline cartilage. This common primary bone neoplasm of the hand is known as:
   (A) Ewing's sarcoma
   (B) Lipoma
   (C) Enchondroma
   (D) Multiple myeloma
   (E) Unicameral bone cyst

54. A 37-year-old HIV-positive female presents with fever, tachypnea, and nonproductive cough. Chest X-ray reveals perihilar infiltrates, but no pleural effusions. Bloodwork reveals lymphopenia and a CD4 count of 122 cells/mL. Based on the patient's presentation and test results, which of the following is the most appropriate diagnosis?
   (A) Nosocomial pneumonia
   (B) Pneumocystis pneumonia
   (C) Cryptogenic organizing pneumonitis
   (D) Tuberculosis
   (E) Eosinophilic pneumonia

55. A 44-year-old obese female with a history of hypertension and diabetes presents with inappropriate uterine bleeding. Endometrial biopsy confirms the diagnosis of endometrial cancer. Which of the following is the appropriate treatment for endometrial cancer?
   (A) Total hysterectomy
   (B) Radiation therapy
   (C) High-dose progestins
   (D) Cryosurgery
   (E) Endometrial ablation

56. A 46-year-old white male presents with dizziness, chest pressure, shortness of breath, and heart palpitations that have occurred over several weeks. EKG is normal with no S-T segment abnormalities. Cholesterol is borderline elevated at 210. Troponin levels are normal at 0.2 ng/mL. D-dimer level is normal at 0.37. Which diagnostic test would you suggest and why?
   (A) CT scan of the chest to rule out pulmonary embolism

(B) Myocardial perfusion imaging to rule out cardiac ischemia

(C) Cardiac catheterization to rule out cardiac ischemia

(D) Echocardiogram to rule out cardiac valve abnormalities

(E) Cardiac stress test to rule out cardiac ischemia

57. Which of the following preventative measures would you advise an individual with pediculosis who is concerned with transmission to others?
(A) Wash hair several times daily.
(B) Shower thoroughly several times daily.
(C) Avoid close personal contact.
(D) Avoid sharing contact items.
(E) Use a disinfecting agent on contact items.

58. A 25-year-old male undergoing treatment for an inner ear infection presents with additional symptoms, resulting in a diagnosis of mastoiditis. Treatment with IV antibiotics has proven ineffective. Which course of treatment would you prescribe for further treatment of this condition?
(A) Biopsy of affected ear
(B) Antibiotic therapy combined with corticosteroids
(C) Antibiotic therapy combined with anti-inflammatory agents
(D) Additional broad-spectrum antibiotics
(E) Mastoidectomy

59. A 60-year-old male presents with episodes of heart palpitations and shortness of breath. Auscultation of the chest reveals a regular heart rhythm. The electrocardiogram reveals a cardiac arrhythmia.

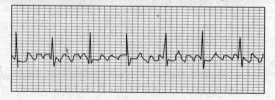

Which cardiac arrhythmia is denoted on the patient's electrocardiogram?
(A) Atrial tachycardia
(B) Atrial flutter
(C) Atrial fibrillation
(D) Sinus tachycardia
(E) Normal sinus rhythm with occasional premature atrial contractions

60. Which of the following anti-diabetic medications act to reduce hepatic glucose production and can reduce glucose levels without risk of hypoglycemia?
(A) Metformin
(B) Glyburide
(C) Miglitol
(D) Exenatide
(E) Rosilitazone

61. Which of the following diagnostic studies is the most useful in evaluating pulmonary arterial pressure in patients with pulmonary hypertension?
(A) Electrocardiogram
(B) Pulmonary function test
(C) Echocardiogram
(D) Cardiac catheterization
(E) Angiogram

62. A 9-year-old female presents with cough, excess sputum, sinus pain, nasal discharge, diarrhea, and abdominal pain. Physical examination reveals clubbing and apical crackles. Thin-section CT reveals bronchiectasis. Chest X-ray reveals hyperinflation and mucous plugging. Based on the patient's presentation, history, and test results, which of the following is the most accurate diagnosis?
(A) Asthma
(B) Bronchiectasis
(C) COPD
(D) Cystic fibrosis
(E) Tuberculosis

63. A 42-year-old male presents with diarrhea, abdominal cramps, tenesmus, fever, chills, and headache. Stools are mixed with blood and mucous. Physical examination reveals a tender abdomen. Stool examination is positive for white blood cells and red blood cells. Sigmoidoscopy reveals inflamed, engorged mucosa. Based on the patient's presentation, physical examination, and test results, which of the following is the most appropriate diagnosis?
(A) Salmonellosis
(B) Shigellosis
(C) Diptheria
(D) Botulism
(E) Trichinosis

64. A radiograph that reveals a "pencil in cup" deformity of the phalangeal joints is commonly associated with which musculoskeletal disorder?
    (A) Septic arthritis
    (B) Rheumatoid arthritis
    (C) Psoriatic arthritis
    (D) Reactive arthritis
    (E) Gout

65. Which of the following types of bacteria is most likely to colonize the lungs and cause pneumonia in a patient with a history of alcohol abuse?
    (A) *Legionella pneumoniae*
    (B) *Klebsiella pneumoniae*
    (C) *Mycoplasma pneumoniae*
    (D) *Chlamydia pneumoniae*
    (E) *Streptococcus pneumoniae*

66. Which of the following disorders is characterized by the extension of the endometrial glands into the uterine musculature?
    (A) Endometriosis
    (B) Adenomyosis
    (C) Leiomyomata
    (D) Prolapse
    (E) Endometrial hyperplasia

67. A healthy 40-year-old male presents for routine, annual checkup. The patient does not complain of any symptoms. Electrocardiogram and blood pressure are normal. Auscultation of the heart reveals a "swishing" sound. Which diagnostic procedure would you order to evaluate the "swishing" sound?
    (A) 24-hour holter monitor to rule out cardiac arrhythmia
    (B) Cardiac stress test to assess for ischemia
    (C) Echocardiogram to assess valvular function
    (D) Cardiac catheterization to assess for ischemia
    (E) Myocardial perfusion imaging to rule out cardiac ischemia

68. Which of the following preventative measures would you recommend to the staff of a nursing home to avoid the occurrence of decubitus ulcers?
    (A) Bathe patients regularly.
    (B) Change bed linens regularly.
    (C) Reposition patients regularly.
    (D) Massage patients regularly.
    (E) Examine all areas of patients regularly.

69. A 10-year-old female presents with eyelid edema, exopthalmos, conjunctivitis, and purulent discharge from both eyes. Physical examination reveals fever, decreased range of motion of the eye muscles, and sluggish pupillary response. CT scan reveals broad infiltration of the orbital soft tissue. Based on the patient's presentation, physical examination, and test results, which of the following is the most likely diagnosis?
    (A) Angle closure glaucoma
    (B) Orbital cellulitis
    (C) Dacryostenosis
    (D) Viral conjunctivitis
    (E) Bacterial conjunctivitis

70. A 2-year-old female presents with a barking, seal-like cough, hoarseness, and a low-grade fever. Chest X-ray of this child shows a "steeple sign" at the midline. Based on the symptoms and the X-ray interpretation, which of the following is the most appropriate diagnosis?
    (A) Croup
    (B) Epiglottitis
    (C) Acute bronchiolitis
    (D) Acute bronchitis
    (E) Pneumonia

71. Which of the following types of stroke is associated with evidence of brain stem dysfunction such as coma, drop attacks, vertigo, nausea, vomiting, and ataxia?
    (A) Strokes involving anterior circulation
    (B) Strokes involving posterior circulation
    (C) Transient ischemic attacks
    (D) Hemorrhagic strokes
    (E) Silent strokes

72. A 40-year-old pregnant female with a history of successful previous childbirths and cigarette smoking presents in her 18th week of gestation with painless vaginal bleeding. Based on the patient's presentation and medical history, which of the following is the most appropriate diagnosis?
    (A) Ectopic pregnancy
    (B) Miscarriage
    (C) Abruptio placentae
    (D) Placenta previa
    (E) Preeclampsia

73. Patients who are treated with monoamine oxidase inhibitors (MAOIs) are advised to stay away

from foods that contain which of the following compounds?

(A) Glutamine
(B) Tyramine
(C) Quercetin
(D) Arginine
(E) Histamine

74. A 50-year-old active African-American male presents with chest discomfort that only occurs under resting conditions. Electrocardiogram and subsequent cardiac stress testing are both within normal limits. You diagnose this patient with Prinzmetal's angina. Which of the following would be the proper course of therapy for this patient?

(A) Nitrates
(B) Diuretics
(C) Beta-adrenergic antagonists
(D) ACE Inhibitors
(E) Corticosteroids

75. A 32-year-old male presents with severe sore throat, pain when swallowing and opening mouth widely, and muffled voice. Physical examination reveals deviation of the soft palate and uvula. Based on the patient's symptoms and physical examination, which of the following is the most appropriate diagnosis?

(A) Streptococcal pharyngitis
(B) Viral pharyngitis
(C) Tonsillitis
(D) Peritonsillar cellulitis
(E) Sinusitis

76. A 61-year-old female presents with bleeding from the gums, epistaxis, menorrhagia, lethargy, and shortness of breath. Lab work reveals decreased white cells, decreased red cells, and 22% blasts. Urinalysis reveals hyperuricemia. Based on the patient's presentation and lab results, which of the following is the most likely diagnosis?

(A) Polycythemia vera
(B) Thrombocytopenia
(C) Acute lymphocytic leukemia
(D) Acute myologenous leukemia
(E) Hodgkin's lymphoma

77. A 15-year-old female patient states during a routine physical examination that she has been experiencing pain in the left, anterior side of her chest. The pain is sharp, comes on suddenly, and resolves completely after 10 to 30 seconds. It does not radiate, and is not accompanied by tachycardia, vertigo, syncope, or other symptoms. The patient states that she remains still and takes shallow breaths until the pain resolves. Based on the patient's symptoms, the most likely diagnosis is

(A) Costochondritis
(B) Gastroesophageal reflux
(C) Pericarditis
(D) Pleurisy
(E) Precordial catch syndrome

78. A 17-year-old male presents with restlessness, muscles spasms, excitability, and bizarre behavior. Physical examination reveals excessively thick saliva. Patient also states he experiences pain when drinking water. Based on patient's history, presentation, and physical examination, which of the following is the most appropriate diagnosis?

(A) Tetanus
(B) Shigellosis
(C) Diptheria
(D) Botulism
(E) Rabies

79. A 68-year-old male presents with shortness of breath, retrosternal chest pain, weakness, fatigue, ascites, and cyanosis. Physical examination reveals narrow splitting and accentuation of the second heart sound and a systolic ejection click. Chest X-ray reveals enlarged pulmonary arteries. Based on the patient's presentation, physical examination, and test results, which of the following is the most appropriate diagnosis?

(A) Pneumonia
(B) Pulmonary hypertension
(C) Bronchitis
(D) Pleural effusion
(E) Pulmonary embolism

80. A 24-year-old female presents with sudden-onset shortness of breath and dizziness. An electrocardiogram reveals the following rhythm.

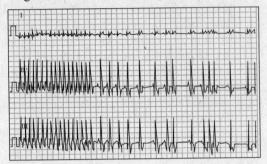

Which of the following describes this cardiac arrhythmia?
(A) Atrial fibrillation
(B) Ventricular tachycardia
(C) Atrial flutter
(D) Supraventricular tachycardia
(E) Bradychardia

81. A 40-year-old man presents with acute pain and swelling in the right eyelid. Examination of the right eyelid reveals a palpable, indurate area with a central area of purulence and surrounding redness. Which of the following is the proper diagnosis based on this information?
(A) Blepharitis
(B) Hordeolum
(C) Chalazion
(D) Dacrycystostenosis
(E) Corneal abrasion

82. A 68-year-old African-American female presents with generalized weakness and fatigue, persistent low-grade fever, and shortness of breath. Lab work and radiographic exams lead to a diagnosis of sarcoidois. Which of the following is the proper course of treatment for this disorder?
(A) Treat with corticosteroids
(B) Treat with antibiotics
(C) Treat with diuretics
(D) Treat with anti-inflammatories
(E) Treat with anti-immunoglobulin

83. A 35-year-old male presents with a history of abdominal pain, heartburn, bloating, and nausea. Treatments for peptic ulcer disease have provided no relief of symptoms. Bloodwork reveals a fasting gastrin level of 268 pg/mL, which is indicative of hypergastrinemia. Endoscopy reveals a gastrinoma in the duodenum. Based on the patient's presentation and test results, which of the following is the most appropriate diagnosis?
(A) Zollinger-Ellison syndrome
(B) Gastric adenocarcinoma
(C) Carcinoid stomach tumor
(D) Gastric lymphoma
(E) Barrett's esophagus

84. A 12-month-old infant presents with skull deformity and rib-breastbone joint enlargement. The child had development issues including delays in sitting, walking, and crawling. Bloodwork showed decreased calcium and vitamin D. X-ray reveals flattened skull, bowing of long bones, and dorsal kyphosis. Based on the patient's presentation, history, and test results, which of the following is the correct diagnosis?
(A) Osteomalacia
(B) Rickets
(C) Paget's disease
(D) Osteoporosis
(E) Fibrous dysplasia

85. A 38-year-old male presents with cough, purulent sputum, shortness of breath, fever, and sweats. Auscultation of the chest reveals altered breath sounds and crackles. Cultures of respiratory secretion were positive for Streptococcus pneumonia. Chest X-ray of the patient reveals lobar infiltrates, air bronchograms, and pleural effusions. Based on the patient's presentation, physical examination, and test results, which of the following is the most appropriate diagnosis?
(A) Nosocomial pneumonia
(B) Pneumocystis pneumonia
(C) Community-acquired pneumonia
(D) Ventilator-associated pneumonia
(E) Tuberculosis

86. Which of the following medications is used to reduce the damage caused by a stroke?
(A) Heparin
(B) Warfarin
(C) Alteplase
(D) Reteplase
(E) Prednisone

87. Which of the following signs refers to the event of minor trauma precipitating new lesions at the site of the trauma?
    (A) Darier's sign
    (B) Auspitz's sign
    (C) Crowe sign
    (D) Nikolsky's sign
    (E) Koebner's phenomenon

88. A 15-year-old female, whom you have been treating for an adjustment disorder, presents with complaints of anxiety, insomnia, and depression. Which of the following types of therapy would you suggest to treat these specific symptoms?
    (A) Pharmacotherapy
    (B) Group therapy
    (C) Psychotherapy
    (D) Electroconvulsive therapy
    (E) Cognitive-behavioral therapy

89. A 33-year-old male presents with low-grade fever, anorexia, and malaise. He complains of back pain in the morning that lasts for more than 30 minutes. He states that long periods of inactivity make his pain worse and that his pain is relieved with exercise. Bloodwork is positive for HLA-B27 and lateral spine X-rays have a "bamboo" appearance of the vertebral spine and sacroiliac region. Which of the following is the most appropriate diagnosis?
    (A) Spinal stenosis
    (B) Ankylosing spondylitis
    (C) Cauda equina syndrome
    (D) Kyphosis
    (E) Lordosis

90. A 52-year-old obese Caucasian female presents with uncontrolled hypertension and intermittent chest pain. You suggest a cardiac stress test to evaluate her symptoms. The electrocardiogram prior to stress testing was within normal limits. During the stress test, the patient develops chest pain and S-T segment depression (see EKG below).

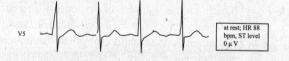

at rest; HR 88 bpm, ST level 0 μV

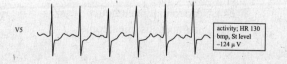

activity; HR 130 bmp, St level −124 μV

Based on the patient's symptoms and electrocardiographic findings, which of the following is the most accurate diagnosis?
    (A) Left-sided congestive heart failure
    (B) Right-sided congestive heart failure
    (C) Cardiomyopathy
    (D) Ischemic heart disease
    (E) Acute myocardial infarction

91. A 44-year-old male presents with itchy eyelids, burning eyes, and light sensitivity. Physical examination reveals red eyelid margins, swollen eyelids, and frothy tears. What would be the most appropriate diagnosis based on this examination?
    (A) Blepharitis
    (B) Cataracts
    (C) Chalazion
    (D) Glaucoma
    (E) Hordeola

92. A 37-year-old pregnant female, in week 30 of gestation, presents with seizure activity secondary to eclampsia. What course of treatment would you suggest to treat this condition?
    (A) Delivery
    (B) Diuretics
    (C) Intravenous hydralazine
    (D) Intravenous magnesium sulfate
    (E) Perform cervical cerclage

93. A healthy 38-year-old male presents for his yearly physical examination. Auscultation of the chest reveals a pancystolic murmur, decreased S2 sound, and prolonged apical impulse with radiation to the left axilla. Chest X-ray reveals atrial enlargement. Based on the presentation and physical examination, which of the following is the proper diagnosis?
    (A) Aortic regurgitation
    (B) Aortic stenosis
    (C) Mitral regurgitation
    (D) Mitral stenosis
    (E) Tricuspid regurgitation

f www.facebook.com/CareerResource   123

94. Which of the following areas of an electrocardiogram represent the inferior wall of the heart muscle?

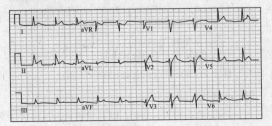

(A) Leads II, III, and aVF
(B) Leads V1 and V2
(C) Leads V1, V2, and V3
(D) Leads V1, V2, and VF
(E) Leads V4, V5, and V6

95. Stroke therapy with recombinant tissue plasminogen activator is most effective when administered within how many hours after the initial onset of symptoms?

(A) 3 hours
(B) 6 hours
(C) 12 hours
(D) 24 hours
(E) 48 hours

96. Which of the following treatments is recommended for protection of areas of depigmented skin due to vitiligo?

(A) Bleaching agents
(B) Sunscreens
(C) Topical antibiotics
(D) Topical corticosteroids
(E) Topical insecticides

97. A 9-year-old female who was recently treated for influenza presents with vomiting, lethargy, jaundice, altered mental status, and seizures. Bloodwork reveals increased liver enzymes, hypoglycemia, increased ammonia levels, and prolonged prothrombin time. Based on the patient's presentation and lab results, which of the following is the most likely diagnosis?

(A) Influenza
(B) Lyme disease
(C) Rabies
(D) Reye's syndrome
(E) Varicella zoster

98. Which of the following interventions is commonly used to promote ovulation in anovulatory women?

(A) Clomiphene citrate
(B) Ethynodiol diacetate
(C) Ethinyl estradiol
(D) Progestin
(E) Topical 5-flurouracil

99. An 18-year-old male has presented with neurological symptoms that were not able to be explained clinically. You have diagnosed this patient with conversion disorder. What form of treatment is most appropriate for conversion disorder?

(A) Antipyschotic drugs
(B) Serotonin-modulating drugs
(C) Psychotherapy
(D) Tricyclic antidepressants
(E) Monoamine oxidase inhibitors

100. A 46-year-old female with a history of rheumatoid arthritis presents with dry eyes and dry mouth. Physical examination reveals enlarged parotid glands. Based on the patient's presentation, history, and physical examination, which of the following is the most likely diagnosis?

(A) Scleroderma
(B) Sjogren's syndrome
(C) Fibromyalgia
(D) Polyarteritis nodosa
(E) Systemic lupus erythematosus

101. Which of the following vaccines contains antigens against 23 common strains of Pneumococcus?

(A) Polyvalent pneumococcal vaccine
(B) Pneumococcal conjugate vaccine
(C) Pneumococcal polysaccharide vaccine
(D) Bacille Calmette-Guerin vaccine
(E) Hib vaccine

102. A 48-year-old female health-care worker presents with a six-day history of cough, sweats, fever, chest pain, and chills. Physical examination reveals altered breath sounds, crackles, and bronchial breath sounds. Culture of respiratory secretions was positive for *Eschericia coli* bacteria. Based on the patient's presentation, physical examination, and test results, which of the following is the most appropriate diagnosis?

(A) Nosocomial pneumonia
(B) Pneumocystis pneumonia

(C) Cryptogenic organizing pneumonitis
(D) Tuberculosis
(E) Eosinophilic pneumonia

103. A 12-year-old girl presents with complaints of pain in the left eye, along with excessive tearing and light sensitivity of that eye. Physical examination reveals no foreign body within the eye. Which of the following is the proper diagnosis based on this information?
(A) Corneal abrasion
(B) Retinal detachment
(C) Central retinal vein occlusion
(D) Central retinal artery occlusion
(E) Blepharitis

104. Which of the following describes the clinical condition of severe cardiovascular failure caused by poor blood flow, inadequate distribution of blood flow, and inadequate oxygen delivery to the tissues?
(A) Cardiac arrest
(B) Hypovolemia
(C) Shock
(D) Congestive heart failure
(E) Cardiac ischemia

105. A 59-year-old female presents with persistent nausea and an excessively full feeling after meals. The patient was prescribed prokinetic medications, which partially relieved her symptoms. Based on the patient's presentation and response to medication, which of the following is the most appropriate diagnosis?
(A) Gastroesophageal reflux disease
(B) Gastritis
(C) Delayed gastric emptying
(D) Peptic ulcer disease
(E) Duodenal ulcer

106. A 69-year-old male with a history of diabetes and hypertension presents for a routine annual physical exam. As part of a thorough physical exam, which lab test would you order to evaluate for kidney damage secondary to diabetes and hypertension?
(A) Blood urea nitrogen
(B) Glomerular filtration rate
(C) Urinalysis for hematuria
(D) Urinalysis for pyuria
(E) Urinalysis for proteinuria

107. Which of the following types of anemia is classically diagnosed by an elevated reticulocyte count occurring simultaneously with a falling hematocrit level?
(A) Iron-deficiency anemia
(B) Pernicious anemia
(C) Hemolytic anemia
(D) Idiopathic ablastic anemia
(E) Sickle cell anemia

108. A 44-year-old nurse presents with an eight-day history of cough, sweats, fever, chest pain, and chills. Physical examination reveals altered breath sounds, crackles, and bronchial breath sounds. Culture of respiratory secretions was positive for *Pseudomonas aeruginosa* bacteria. You diagnose this patient with hospital-acquired pneumonia. Which of the following treatment options would you suggest?
(A) Bronchodilators
(B) Corticosteroids
(C) Broad-spectrum antibiotics
(D) Anti-inflammatories
(E) NSAIDs

109. For patients who have suffered a subarachnoid hemorrhage, which of the following describes the appearance of cerebrospinal fluid?
(A) Clear
(B) Yellowish
(C) Cloudy
(D) Bloody
(E) Viscous

110. Which of the following vaccines should be administered to a tuberculin-negative person at risk for intense, long-term exposure to tuberculosis?
(A) Polyvalent pneumococcal vaccine
(B) Pneumococcal conjugate vaccine
(C) Pneumococcal polysaccharide vaccine
(D) Bacille Calmette-Guerin vaccine
(E) Hib vaccine

111. A 20-year-old female presents with swelling in the left eye. The patient denies any pain associated with the swelling or disturbance with vision. Examination of the left eye reveals a yellowish, fleshy conjunctival mass on the sclera Which of the following is the proper diagnosis based on this information?
(A) Pterygium
(B) Pinguecula
(C) Blepharitis
(D) Viral conjunctivitis
(E) Bacterial conjunctivitis

112. A 58-year-old female presents with exertional dyspnea, non-productive cough, and fatigue. Auscultation of the chest reveals basilar rales and gallops. Chest X-ray reveals cardiomegaly, bilateral pleural effusions, and perivascular edema. Based on the patient's presentation, physical exam, and test results, which of the following is the most likely diagnosis?
(A) Primary pneumothorax
(B) Tension pneumothorax
(C) Cystic fibrosis
(D) Congestive heart failure
(E) Pulmonary embolism

113. Which of the following refers to the gastrointestinal disorder that is characterized by increased volume and frequency of stool?
(A) Malabsorption
(B) Diarrhea
(C) Volvulus
(D) Constipation
(E) Delayed gastric emptying

114. A 75-year-old male with a history of chronic prostatitis with prostatic calculi presents with increased frequency and urgency of urination. His prostatitis has shown no response to antibiotics. Which of the following treatment options is indicated for chronic, resistant prostatitis?
(A) Chemotherapy
(B) Hormone therapy
(C) Prostatectomy
(D) Radiation therapy
(E) Transurethral resection of the prostate

115. A 26-year-old female presents to the Intensive Care Unit after developing hemorrhaging during childbirth. Bloodwork reveals an extremely elevated d-dimer level and prolonged PT. You diagnose this patient with disseminated intravascular coagulopathy. Which of the following substances is most important for treatment of this disorder?
(A) Cryoprecipitate
(B) Prednisone
(C) Ferrous sulfate
(D) Fresh frozen plasma
(E) Prothrombin complex concentrate

116. Which of the following medications is used as treatment for generalized nonconvulsive, or absence, seizures?
(A) Clonazepam
(B) Felbamate
(C) Gabapentin
(D) Phenytoin
(E) Valproic Acid

117. Which of the following diagnostic techniques is successfully used to confirm the presence of fungus and confirm a diagnosis of dermatophytosis?
(A) Diascopy
(B) Scraping of the affected area
(C) Potassium hydroxide preparation
(D) Wood's light examination
(E) Culturing the suspected fungus

118. A 36-year-old pregnant female was diagnosed with severe preeclampsia. Her bloodwork reveals hemolysis, elevated liver enzymes, and low platelet count. Based on the patient's history and lab results, which of the following is the most appropriate diagnosis?
(A) Chronic hypertension
(B) Eclampsia
(C) HELLP syndrome
(D) Preterm labor
(E) Gestational diabetes

119. A 50-year-old female presents with dull pain, swelling, redness, and tenderness of the left leg. Bloodwork reveals a d-dimer level of 750 ng/dL. Based on the patient's presentation, which of the following diagnostic exams would you perform next?
(A) Lung ventilation-perfusion scan to rule out pulmonary embolism
(B) Intravenous venography to rule out deep venous thrombosis

(C) None; d-dimer level rules out thromboembolism

(D) Spiral CT scan of the chest to rule out pulmonary embolism

(E) Venous Doppler of the lower extremity to rule out deep venous thrombosis

120. A 38-year-old female presents with pain in the anatomical snuffbox after a fall on the ice. Physical examination reveals swelling and ecchymosis over the affected region. The X-ray of the patient's hand reveals a fracture in the area of pain. Based on the findings, which of the following is the most appropriate diagnosis?
(A) Carpal tunnel syndrome
(B) Colles's fracture
(C) De Quervain's disease
(D) Rheumatoid arthritis
(E) Scaphoid fracture

121. An 18-month-old infant presents with runny nose, sneezing, wheezing, and low-grade fever. Physical examination reveals nasal flaring, tachypnea, and retractions indicating respiratory distress. CBC was normal and chest X-ray was normal. Nasal washing was positive for respiratory syncytial virus. You diagnose this child with bronchiolitis. Which medication would you prescribe to treat this condition?
(A) Bactrim
(B) Erythromycin
(C) Ribavirin
(D) Cyclosporine
(E) Augmentin

122. A 62-year-old obese female presents with lower leg erythema, swelling, and tenderness. She also complains of shortness of breath occurring within the past 24 hours. Bloodwork reveals a d-dimer level of 300 ng/dL. Based on the patient's presentation, which of the following diagnostic exams would you perform next?
(A) Lung ventilation-perfusion scan to rule out pulmonary embolism
(B) Spiral CT scan of the chest to rule out pulmonary embolism
(C) Venous Doppler of the lower extremity to rule out deep venous thrombosis
(D) Intravenous venography to rule out deep venous thrombosis
(E) None; d-dimer level rules out thromboembolism

123. A newborn infant presents with excessive saliva and choking with attempts to feed. Attempt to drop a nasogastric tube for feedings was unsuccessful. Based on the patient's presentation, which of the following is the appropriate diagnosis?
(A) Esophageal atresia
(B) Pyloric stenosis
(C) Diaphragmatic hernia
(D) Hirschsprung's disease
(E) Nectrotizing enterocolitis

124. A 24-year-old athletic male presents with dull, aching discomfort in the hemiscrotum. Physical exam reveals a markedly swollen, very tender scrotal mass. The patient was recently diagnosed with the sexually transmitted disease gonorrhea. Ultrasound exam confirms a diagnosis of epididymitis. Which of the following medications would you prescribe to treat this condition?
(A) ACE inhibitors
(B) Ceftriaxone
(C) Tolterodine
(D) Ciprofloxacin
(E) Amoxicillin

125. Which of the following anti-diabetic medications decreases blood glucose by slowing gastric emptying?
(A) Metformin
(B) Glyburide
(C) Miglitol
(D) Exenatide
(E) Rosilitazone

126. A 42-year-old male presents with abnormal bleeding in the nasal sinus and GI mucous membranes. Bloodwork reveals normal PT and PTT. The bloodwork also reveals a reduced level of factor VIII antigen, which is characteristic of von Willebrand disease. Which of the following medications would you prescribe for treatment of this disorder?
(A) Bisphosphonates
(B) Ergocalciferol
(C) Desmopressin acetate
(D) Pegvisomant
(E) Prednisone

127. An otherwise healthy, 27-year-old male presents with non-productive cough, low-grade fever, fatigue, and muscle aches. Sputum culture was positive for Mycoplasma pneumonia. Based on the patient's presentation and sputum culture, which of the following is the most appropriate diagnosis?
(A) Community acquired-pneumonia
(B) Atypical community-acquired pneumonia
(C) Nosocomial pneumonia
(D) Pneumocystis pneumonia
(E) Tuberculosis

128. A 54-year-old male presents with memory loss, social withdrawal, and lack of interest in personal hygiene. Physical exam reveals increased rigidity in the muscles and loss of coordination. MRI reveals atrophy in the anterior temporal lobe. Based on the patient's presentation, physical examination, and test results, which of the following is the most likely diagnosis?
(A) Alzheimer's disease
(B) Vascular dementia
(C) Frontotemporal dementia
(D) Pseudodementia
(E) Psychosis

129. A 58-year-old obese male with a history of deep venous thrombosis presents with edema in the lower extremities and an ulcer on right ankle. The skin in the lower extremities appears shiny, thin, and discolored. The patient complains of lower leg itching and pain upon standing. Based on the patient's presentation and physical examination, which of the following is the most appropriate diagnosis?
(A) Peripheral arterial disease
(B) Varicose veins
(C) Deep venous thrombosis
(D) Chronic venous insufficiency
(E) Atherosclerosis

130. A 22-year-old female presents as underweight and emaciated. Physical examination reveals orthostatic hypotension, salivary gland hypertrophy, and dental erosion. The patient states she has a normal appetite but doesn't eat much because she is afraid of becoming overweight. Lab work reveals hypokalemia, hypochloremia, and elevated blood urea nitrogen. Based on the patient's history, physical examination, and test results, which of the following is the most appropriate diagnosis?

(A) Binge-eating disorder
(B) Anorexia nervosa
(C) Bulimia nervosa
(D) Narcissistic personality disorder
(E) Diabetes mellitus

131. A 55-year-old female presents with morning joint stiffness and swelling in the hands, wrists, and ankles that has persisted for approximately 8 weeks. Bloodwork reveals elevated erythrocyte sedimentation rate and C-reactive protein level. Bloodwork was also positive for anti-cyclic citrullinated peptide antibodies. Based on the patient's presentation and lab results, which of the following is the most appropriate diagnosis?
(A) Septic arthritis
(B) Rheumatoid arthritis
(C) Psoriatic arthritis
(D) Reactive arthritis
(E) Gout

132. Which of the following medications is indicated for maintenance therapy of chronic obstructive pulmonary disease?
(A) Antibiotics
(B) Anticholinergics
(C) Inhaled corticosteroids
(D) Beta-adrenergic agonists
(E) Theophylline

133. The most common injury of the wrist is a fracture that results from a fall onto a dorsiflexed hand. The X-ray of this fracture is characterized by a "silver fork deformity." Which of the following types of fracture is illustrated in this X-ray?
(A) Buckle (torus) fracture
(B) Greenstick fracture
(C) Colles's fracture
(D) Open fracture
(E) Smith's fracture

134. A 28-year-old female presents with a dark brown lesion on her neck. The lesion has an irregular border that has changed in size since her last visit. Based on the patient's presentation alone, which of the following is the most likely diagnosis?
(A) Pyogenic granuloma
(B) Malignant melanoma
(C) Basal cell carcinoma
(D) Squamous cell carcinoma
(E) Merkel cell carcinoma

135. A 24-year-old female presents with dysuria, increased urinary frequency and urgency, and a purulent urethral discharge. Physical exam reveals vaginitis and cervicitis. Gram stain of urethral discharge reveals Gram-negative intracellular diplococci. Based on the patient's presentation, physical examination, and test results, which of the following is the most appropriate diagnosis?
    (A) Syphilis
    (B) Gonorrhea
    (C) Chlamydia
    (D) HIV
    (E) Bacterial vaginosis

136. Which of the following diagnostic tests should be performed initially when evaluating the cause of infertility?
    (A) Ovulation prediction test
    (B) Semen analysis
    (C) Progesterone level analysis
    (D) Hysterosalpingogram
    (E) Serum FSH analysis

137. A 26-year-old female presents with a high degree of attention-seeking behavior. Her personality is described as excessively emotional, dramatic, and seductive. She is unable to maintain a long-term relationship and becomes angry if she is not the center of attention. Based on the patient's behavior and personality, which of the following is the most likely diagnosis?
    (A) Histrionic personality disorder
    (B) Narcissistic personality disorder
    (C) Dependent personality disorder
    (D) Schizotypal personality disorder
    (E) Borderline personality disorder

138. A 44-year-old male presents with pain, swelling, and redness in the joints of the lower extremities. Joint fluid analysis reveals rod-shaped, negatively birefringent urate crystals. Bloodwork reveals a uric acid level of 8.9 mg/dL. Based on the patient's presentation and test results, which of the following is the most appropriate diagnosis?
    (A) Septic arthritis
    (B) Reactive arthritis
    (C) Calcium pyrophosphate dehydrate disease
    (D) Rheumatoid arthritis
    (E) Gout

139. A 36-year-old male presents with non-productive cough, shortness of breath, fever, and substernal discomfort. Auscultation of the chest reveals expiratory rhonchi. Chest X-ray is normal. Based on the patient's presentation, physical examination, and test results, which of the following is the most appropriate diagnosis?
    (A) Pneumonia
    (B) Bronchitis
    (C) Tuberculosis
    (D) Bronchiolitis
    (E) Pulmonary hypertension

140. A 40-year-old male presents with lower leg pain and erectile dysfunction. Auscultation of the legs reveals an absent femoral and distal pulse and an iliac bruit. Doppler study reveals an ankle-brachial index of 0.7. Based on the patient's presentation, physical examination, and test results, which of the following is the most appropriate diagnosis?
    (A) Peripheral arterial disease
    (B) Varicose veins
    (C) Deep venous thrombosis
    (D) Chronic venous insufficiency
    (E) Atherosclerosis

141. Which of the following diagnostic studies is used to monitor bodily functions when a patient is asleep?
    (A) Electromyogram
    (B) Electroencephalogram
    (C) Electrocardiogram
    (D) Polysomnogram
    (E) Echocardiogram

142. A 24-year-old female presents with itchy, bleeding, non-healing lesions on the face and neck. Biopsy of affected areas reveals the presence of basal cell carcinoma. Which of the following courses of treatment would you prescribe for this disorder?
    (A) Liquid nitrogen therapy
    (B) Chemotherapy
    (C) Debridement of the lesions
    (D) Complete eradication of the lesions
    (E) Topical corticosteroids

143. Which of the following medications, used to stop preterm uterine contractions, stimulates beta-adrenergic receptors to relax smooth muscle, thereby decreasing uterine contractions?
(A) Calcium channel blockers
(B) Calcium gluconate
(C) Magnesium sulfate
(D) Methotrexate
(E) Ritodrine

144. During the diagnostic process, which of the following medical conditions must be ruled out before confirming a diagnosis of polymyalgia rheumatica?
(A) Systemic lupus erythematosus
(B) Giant cell arteritis
(C) Fibromyalgia
(D) Scleroderma
(E) Myasthenia gravis

145. A 40-year-old female is diagnosed with labyrinthitis. Which of the following medications would you prescribe for treatment of this disorder?
(A) Scopolamine
(B) Meclizine
(C) Otic antibacterial drops
(D) Diazepam
(E) Droperidol

146. A 62-year-old female who is being treated for gastroesophageal reflux disease (GERD) presents with progressively worsening symptoms of heartburn and regurgitation. The patient is currently being treated with histamine blockers, with no relief of symptoms. Endoscopy reveals severe disease with evidence of erosive gastritis. Which of the following medications would you prescribe to effectively manage this patient's gastroesophageal reflux disease?
(A) Antacids
(B) Proton pump inhibitors
(C) Nitrates
(D) Calcium channel blockers
(E) Corticosteroids

147. A 68-year-old male presents with dull, aching discomfort in the hemiscrotum. Physical exam reveals a markedly swollen, very tender scrotal mass. Ultrasound exam confirms a diagnosis of epididymitis. Which of the following medications would you prescribe to treat this condition?
(A) ACE inhibitors
(B) Ceftriaxone

(C) Tolterodine
(D) Ciprofloxacin
(E) Amoxicillin

148. A 60-year-old male presents with severely impaired bowel and bladder function along with leg pain and numbness. MRI reveals large midline disk herniation at L4-L5 that is compressing several nerve roots. You diagnose this patient with cauda equina syndrome. Which of the following treatment options would you suggest to treat this disorder?
(A) Epidural injection
(B) High-dose corticosteroids
(C) Biopsy
(D) Immediate surgery
(E) Physical therapy

149. Which of the following medications is indicated for maintenance therapy of chronic asthma?
(A) Antibiotics
(B) Anticholinergics
(C) Inhaled corticosteroids
(D) Beta-adrenergic agonists
(E) Theophylline

150. Which of the following medications are used to decrease the frequency of relapses of moderate or severe attacks stemming from multiple sclerosis?
(A) Corticosteroids
(B) Interferon-β
(C) Cyclophosphamide
(D) Amantadine
(E) Mitoxantrone

151. Which of the following classes of medication are indicated for maintenance therapy of rheumatoid arthritis?
(A) NSAIDs
(B) SSRIs
(C) MAOIs
(D) DMARDs
(E) Corticosteroids

152. Which of the following medications can be administered in order to reverse the effects of an overdose of opiates?
(A) Diazepam
(B) Antabuse
(C) Naloxone
(D) Bupropion
(E) Oxycodone

153. Which of the following vaccines is given as a series of four doses and is recommended for children aged 6 weeks to 15 months?
    (A) Polyvalent pneumococcal vaccine
    (B) Pneumococcal conjugate vaccine
    (C) Pneumococcal polysaccharide vaccine
    (D) Bacille Calmette-Guerin vaccine
    (E) Hib vaccine

154. A 60-year-old woman presents with sudden, abrupt, right-side facial muscle weakness, along with one-sided facial paralysis in which she cannot close her right eye or raise her right brow. Based on the patient's presentation, which of the following is the most likely diagnosis?
    (A) Bell's palsy
    (B) Diabetic peripheral neuropathy
    (C) Guillain-Barré syndrome
    (D) Myasthenia gravis
    (E) Fibromyalgia

155. A 10-year-old boy presents with poor appetite, abdominal pain, nausea, and vomiting. Physical exam reveals hypertension and a palpable abdominal mass. Bloodwork reveals an elevated renin level. Ultrasound of the kidneys reveals a mass in the left kidney. Based on the patient's presentation, physical exam, and test results, which of the following is the proper diagnosis?
    (A) Interstitial nephritis
    (B) Nephrolithiasis
    (C) Polycystic kidney disease
    (D) Renal cell carcinoma
    (E) Wilm's tumor

156. The leading cause of blindness in adults is retinopathy. Which of the following lifestyle habits is most critical in preventing progression of retinopathy?
    (A) Low-fat diet
    (B) Controlled blood glucose
    (C) Cessation of tobacco use
    (D) Avoidance of caffeine
    (E) Avoidance of sunlight

157. A 70-year-old female with a history of portal hypertension from chronic viral hepatitis presents with hematamesis. Endoscopy reveals dilatation of the veins of the esophagus. Based on the patient's presentation and test results, which of the following is the most appropriate diagnosis?
    (A) Mallory-Weiss tear
    (B) Esophageal varices
    (C) Budd-Chiari syndrome
    (D) Esophageal neoplasm
    (E) Boerhaave's syndrome

158. A 40-year-old female presents with muscle weakness in the pelvic girdle and generalized bone pain. She has a history of several fractures stemming from minor traumas. X-rays reveal generalized decrease in bone density with Looser zones. Bloodwork reveals vitamin D deficiency. Based on the patient's presentation, history, and test results, the likeliest diagnosis is:
    (A) Osteomalacia
    (B) Rickets
    (C) Paget's disease
    (D) Osteoporosis
    (E) Fibrous dysplasia

159. Which of the following medications is indicated to reduce systemic arterial pressure for patients who have been diagnosed with pulmonary hypertension?
    (A) Beta blockers
    (B) Bronchodilators
    (C) Calcium channel blockers
    (D) Corticosteroids
    (E) Diuretics

160. A 48-year-old male presents with progressive loss of vision. Physical examination reveals bilateral thickening of the bulbar conjunctiva and vascular, triangular masses encroaching on the corneas. You diagnose this patient with bilateral pterygium. Which of the following treatment options would you prescribe for treatment of this condition?
    (A) Application of ophthalmic antibiotics
    (B) Application of ophthalmic steroids
    (C) Administration of ophthalmic antibiotic
    (D) IV administration of antibiotics
    (E) Surgical excision of the masses

161. A 24-year-old female presents with a seven-day history of cough, purulent sputum, shortness of breath, chest pain, fever, and sweats. Auscultation of the chest reveals altered breath sounds with crackles, dullness to percussion, and bronchial breath sounds over an area of consolidation. Chest X-ray was performed, which reveals bilateral pleural consolidations. Based on patient symptoms and physical examination, which of the following is the proper diagnosis?
    (A) Acute bronchitis
    (B) Acute epiglottitis
    (C) Tuberculosis
    (D) Pneumonia
    (E) Pulmonary edema due to contusion

162. Which of the following is the Gram-negative, spiral-shaped bacillus that is responsible for most gastric ulcers and chronic gastritis?
    (A) *Lactobacillus rhamnosus*
    (B) *Lactobacillus acidophilus*
    (C) *Helicobacter pylori*
    (D) *Streptococcus agalactiae*
    (E) *Escherichia coli*

163. Which of the following pneumonia vaccines is indicated for children between 2 to 5 years of age who have not previously been immunized?
    (A) Polyvalent pneumococcal vaccine
    (B) Pneumococcal conjugate vaccine
    (C) Pneumococcal polysaccharide vaccine
    (D) Bacille Calmette-Guerin vaccine
    (E) Hib vaccine

164. Which of the following medications is commonly used in order to hasten the maximum recovery from acute exacerbations of multiple sclerosis?
    (A) Corticosteroids
    (B) Interferon-β
    (C) Cyclophosphamide
    (D) Amantadine
    (E) Mitoxantrone

165. A 36-year-old female presents with muscle weakness, bone pain, and history of several fractures. Bloodwork reveals a vitamin D deficiency. X-rays reveal generalized decrease in bone density and Looser lines, characteristic of pseudofractures. You diagnose this patient with osteomalacia. Which of the following medications would you prescribe to treat this disorder?

    (A) Bisphosphonates
    (B) Desmopressin acetate
    (C) Ergocalciferol
    (D) Ketoconazole
    (E) Pegvisomant

166. Which of the following preventative treatments are indicated for individuals who have tested negative for tuberculosis in the past, but have recently tested positive with known or unknown exposure?
    (A) Isoniazid
    (B) Rifampin
    (C) Pyrazinamide
    (D) Ethambutol
    (E) Streptomycin

167. A 22-year-old female presents with a throbbing, pulsating headache on the left side of her head. The patient also complains of nausea, vomiting, light sensitivity, and inability to eat while the headaches are in progress. Based on the patient's presentation, which of the following is the most appropriate diagnosis?
    (A) Tension headache
    (B) Migraine headache
    (C) Cluster headache
    (D) Subarachnoid hemorrhage
    (E) Sinus headache

168. A 14-year-old boy presents with blow-out fractures to the orbital floor after being hit with a baseball. Which of the following are critical to prevent further damage from this injury?
    (A) Ophthalmic antibiotics
    (B) IV antibiotics
    (C) Nasal decongestants
    (D) Ophthalmic steroids
    (E) IV steroids

169. Which of the following describes the type of shock that is the result of hemorrhage, loss of plasma, or loss of fluids and electrolytes?
    (A) Distributive shock
    (B) Cardiogenic shock
    (C) Compensated shock
    (D) Hypovolemic shock
    (E) Obstructive shock

170. A 44-year-old female hospital worker presents with a productive, bloody cough that has persisted for several weeks. She also complains of fever, night sweats, anorexia, and weight loss. Auscultation of the chest reveals post-tussive rales. Based on the patient's presentation and physical examination, the most appropriate diagnosis is:
(A) Nosocomial pneumonia
(B) Pneumocystis pneumonia
(C) Cryptogenic organizing pneumonitis
(D) Tuberculosis
(E) Eosinophilic pneumonia

171. Which of the following courses of treatment would you prescribe for treatment of a buckle fracture of the distal radius?
(A) Closed reduction
(B) Open-reduction internal fixation
(C) Pinning in situ
(D) Immobilization in a cast
(E) Osteotomy

172. A 46-year-old obese male presents in the emergency room with acute myocardial infarction. The patient's initial blood pressure is 140/70 mmHg. Shortly after presentation, the patient's blood pressure drops to 80/40 mmHg, heart rate is 130 beats per minute, and he becomes agitated and confused. Based on the presentation and patient's condition, which of the following is the best diagnosis?
(A) Congestive heart failure
(B) Orthostatic hypotension
(C) Cardiogenic shock
(D) Cardiac arrest
(E) Pulmonary embolism

173. Which advice would you give to a patient if he or she is concerned about developing cataracts?
(A) Stop tobacco use.
(B) Control blood glucose.
(C) Follow a low fat diet.
(D) Avoid sunlight.
(E) Take vitamin E supplements.

174. A 6-year-old female presents with pain in the distal radius after falling on her outstretched hand. Her X-ray depicts a buckle or bulge on one side of the distal radius, about 3 cm from the end. Based on the type of injury and the radiographic evidence, which

of the following types of fractures is illustrated on this girl's X-ray?
(A) Greenstick fracture
(B) Colles's fracture
(C) Open fracture
(D) Smith's fracture
(E) Torus fracture

175. A 48-year-old female presents to the emergency room with a tension pnuemothorax. Initial blood pressure is 140/90 mmHg. Prior to decompression with a large bore needle, the patient's blood pressure falls to 70/40 mmHg, heart rate rises to 140 beats per minutes, and mental status becomes altered. Based on the presentation and patient's condition, which of the following is the most likely diagnosis?
(A) Distributive shock
(B) Cardiogenic shock
(C) Compensated shock
(D) Hypovolemic shock
(E) Obstructive shock

176. A 26-year-old female is diagnosed with tinea versicolor. Which of the following treatments is required to prevent recurrence of yeast growth on the skin?
(A) Head-to-waist application of selenium sulfide shampoo
(B) Head-to-waist application of topical insecticides
(C) Head-to-waist application of topical corticosteroids
(D) Head-to-waist application of 1% lindane lotion
(E) Head-to-waist application of isopropyl alcohol

177. An 80-year-old female presents with unexplained neck pain, scalp tenderness, headache, and vision difficulties. Her bloodwork reveals marked elevations in erythrocyte sedimentation rate and C-reactive protein. You suspect this patient is suffering from giant cell arteritis. Which of the following exams would you perform to confirm your diagnosis?
(A) Carotid vascular ultrasound
(B) Carotid angiogram
(C) Echocardiogram
(D) Electrocardiogram
(E) Temporal artery biopsy

178. A 46-year-old African-American female presents with a persistent non-specific headache. Physical examination reveals her blood pressure to be 230/130 mmHg. Which of the following refers to the disorder that is characterized by blood pressure readings of this range?
(A) Primary hypertension
(B) Malignant hypertension
(C) Hypertensive urgency
(D) Hypertensive emergency
(E) Accelerated hypertension

179. A 44-year-old male with a history of alcoholism presents with forceful vomiting and hematemesis. Endoscopy reveals an esophageal tear at the gastroesophageal junction. Based on the patient's presentation and test results, which of the following is the most appropriate diagnosis?
(A) Mallory-Weiss tear
(B) Esophageal varices
(C) Budd-Chiari syndrome
(D) Esophageal neoplasm
(E) Boerhaave's syndrome

180. A 23-year-old male presents with fever, headache, and a stiff neck. Physical examination reveals a petechial rash. You suspect meningitis. Which of the following clinical interventions must be performed to confirm the diagnosis?
(A) Insert pledgets into nose to evaluate CSF
(B) Lumbar puncture to evaluate CSF
(C) Angiogram to confirm meningeal inflammation
(D) CT scan with contrast to confirm meningeal inflammation
(E) Blood titer to confirm meningitis infection

181. A 55-year-old male presents to the emergency room in hypovolemic shock. Which of the following laboratory tests will assist in revealing the cause of shock?
(A) CBC, d-dimer, troponin, urinalysis
(B) CBC, blood type and cross match, and coagulation parameters
(C) CBC, lipid panel, and troponin
(D) D-dimer, troponin, cpk, and mb
(E) Electrolytes, glucose, urinalysis, and serum creatinine

182. A 48-year-old man presents with a series of severe, unilateral, periorbital headaches lasting from 30 to 90 minutes, several times a day over the past month. Physical exam reveals myosis and ptosis. Patient states his headaches are not relieved by rest. Based on the patient's presentation and physical examination, which of the following is the most appropriate diagnosis?
(A) Cluster headache
(B) Migraine headache
(C) Subarachnoid hemorrhage
(D) Sinus headache
(E) Tension headache

183. A 29-year-old female presents with hearing loss, tinnitus, vertigo, nausea, and vomiting. Examination of the ears reveal distention of the endolymphatic compartment of the inner ear, but no inflammation. Based on the symptoms and examination, which of the following is the proper diagnosis?
(A) Acoustic neuroma
(B) Labyrinthitis
(C) Meniere's disease
(D) Otitis externa
(E) Otitis media

184. Which of the following is the clinical term for a deep-seated infection of a single hair follicle, commonly known as a boil?
(A) Abscess
(B) Carbuncle
(C) Cyst
(D) Foruncle
(E) Pimple

185. A 49-year-old patient presents with abdominal pain, distention, fever, and tachycardia. Physical exam reveals abdominal tympany. Abdominal X-ray reveals colonic distention, confirming a diagnosis of volvulus. Which of the following clinical procedures would you use to treat this disorder?
(A) Abdominal angiogram
(B) Colon cleansing
(C) Dietary restriction
(D) Endoscopic decompression
(E) Surgical correction

186. A 60-year-old male presents with shortness of breath, retrosternal chest pain, weakness, fatigue, cyanosis, and syncope. Auscultation of the chest reveals a systolic ejection click. Chest X-ray reveals enlarged pulmonary arteries. Based on the patient's

presentation, history, and test results, which of the following is the most accurate diagnosis?
(A) Bronchiectasis
(B) Cystic fibrosis
(C) Pulmonary edema
(D) Pulmonary embolism
(E) Pulmonary hypertension

187. A 52-year-old female presents with proximal muscle weakness, difficulty swallowing, skin rash, multiple joint pain, and muscle atrophy. Lab work reveals elevated levels of creatine phosphokinase and aldolase. Based on the patient's presentation and lab results, which of the following is the most appropriate diagnosis?
(A) Polyarteritis nodosa
(B) Polymyalgia rheumatica
(C) Polymyositis
(D) Systemic sclerosis
(E) Systemic lupus erythematosus

188. You diagnose a 40-year-old female patient with seasonal affective disorder. Which of the following treatment options would you suggest for treatment of this disorder?
(A) Electroconvulsive therapy
(B) Light therapy
(C) Monoamine oxidase inhibitors
(D) Psychotherapy
(E) Tricyclic antidepressants

189. A 72-year-old female presents with fatigue, nausea, weakness, muscle cramps, and weight loss. Physical exam reveals elevated blood pressure. You suspect chronic kidney disease. Which of the following laboratory tests is the gold standard for diagnosing chronic kidney disease?
(A) Blood urea nitrogen
(B) Glomerular filtration rate
(C) Hemoglobin and hematocrit
(D) Serum creatinine
(E) Urinalysis for proteinuria

190. Which of the following medical interventions is commonly used for emergency post-coital contraception?
(A) Ethynodiol diacetate
(B) Ethinyl estradiol
(C) Clomiphene citrate
(D) Progestin
(E) Topical 5-flurouracil

191. A 38-year-old male presents with lightheadedness when transferring from a sitting position to a standing position. Blood pressure reading in the sitting position is 130/80 mmHg. Blood pressure reading in the standing position is 100/60 mmHg. Based on the patient's presentation and blood pressure readings, which of the following is the most accurate diagnosis?
(A) Hypertension
(B) Hypoglycemia
(C) Malignant hypotension
(D) Postural hypotension
(E) Primary hypotension

192. A 32-year-old male presents, in the summer time, with a spotted tan on the face, chest, and arms. Potassium hydroxide preparation confirms the presence of hyphae and spores on the non-tanning areas of skin. Based on the patient's presentation and test results, which of the following is the most appropriate diagnosis?
(A) Dermatophytosis
(B) Melasma
(C) Scabies
(D) Tinea versicolor
(E) Vitiligo

193. A 28-year-old obese male presents with muscle weakness, headache, backache, acne, and erectile dysfunction. Laboratory results reveal free cortisol in the urine measuring 142 mg/dL and plasma cortisol of 13 mg/dL. CT scan of the abdomen reveals the presence of an adrenocortical tumor. Based on the patient's presentation, lab results, and diagnostic studies, which of the following is the most accurate diagnosis?
(A) Acromegaly
(B) Addison's disease
(C) Cushing's disease
(D) Diabetes insipidus
(E) Diabetes mellitus

194. Which of the following medical interventions is indicated to provide pain relief from spinal stenosis?
(A) Intrathecal steroid injection
(B) Lumbar epidural injection
(C) Physical therapy
(D) Surgical decompression
(E) Surgical fusion

195. A 27-year-old pregnant female presents with dizziness, one-sided uterine pain, and amenorrhea. Physical pelvic examination reveals a mass. Serial human chorionic gonadotropin values are less than expected. A transvaginal ultrasound reveals no uterine pregnancy. Based on the patient's presentation, physical examination, and test results, which of the following is the most accurate diagnosis?
(A) Ectopic pregnancy
(B) Gestational trophoblastic disease
(C) Ovarian cyst
(D) Spontaneous abortion
(E) Uterine cancer

196. Which of the following treatment options is indicated for a patient who was diagnosed with squamous cell carcinoma?
(A) Chemotherapy
(B) Hormonal therapy
(C) Immunotherapy
(D) Radiation therapy
(E) Surgery

197. A 17-year-old boy who was recently diagnosed with mumps presents with fever, tachycardia, and testicular swelling and tenderness. You diagnose him with orchitis secondary to the mumps virus. Which of the following is recommended for treatment of this disorder?
(A) Anti-inflammatories
(B) Ceftriaxone
(C) Doxycycline
(D) Ciprofloxacin
(E) Ice packs and analgesics

198. A 45-year-old male presents with chronic peritonsillar cellulitis. His symptoms include severe sore throat pain and an airway obstruction that has precipitated sleep apnea. Physical examination reveals persistent, marked asymmetry of the tonsils. What would be the most appropriate course of treatment for this patient?
(A) Aspiration of the tonsils followed by antibiotics
(B) Surgical incision and drainage of the tonsils followed by a course of antibiotics
(C) Tonsillectomy
(D) Tracheotomy
(E) Treat medically with penicillin or erythromycin

199. Which of the following anti-diabetic medications is contraindicated in patients with gastropareisis?
(A) Exenatide
(B) Glyburide
(C) Metformin
(D) Miglitol
(E) Rosilitazone

200. A 49-year-old female presents with personality traits of being haughty and arrogant, lacking empathy, having a sense of entitlement, and considering herself as being special. She is having a difficult time with the physical changes associated with the aging process. Based on this patient's behavior and personality, which of the following is the most likely diagnosis?
(A) Borderline personality disorder
(B) Dependent personality disorder
(C) Histrionic personality disorder
(D) Narcissistic personality disorder
(E) Schizotypal personality disorder

201. A 44-year-old female presents with dizziness and syncopal episodes when transferring from a sitting to a standing position. Blood pressure in the sitting position is 130/80 mmHg. Blood pressure in the standing position is noted to be 90/50 mmHg. It is noticed that her pulse rate in the sitting position is 80 beats per minute, while it is 105 beats per minute when standing. Based on this information, which of the following is the cause of the patient's postural hypotension?
(A) Central nervous system disease
(B) Depleted blood volume
(C) Hypoglycemia
(D) Peripheral neuropathy
(E) Medication

202. A 44-year-old obese female presents with fever, chills, and a swollen, hot and tender rash on the left lower extremity. Based on the patient's presentation, which of the following is the most likely diagnosis?
(A) Abscess
(B) Cellulitis
(C) Erythema multiforme
(D) Osteomyelitis
(E) Systemic lupus erythematosus

203. A 26-year-old female with history of diarrhea, steatorrhea, weight loss, and weakness has a positive

small bowel biopsy for celiac disease. Which of the following treatments must this patient adhere to in order to avoid flare-ups from this disorder?
(A) Casien-free diet
(B) Fat-free diet
(C) Gluten-free diet
(D) Lactose-free diet
(E) Low-glycemic diet

204. Which of the following medications is prescribed for maintenance therapy for panic attacks and panic disorder?
(A) Benzodiazepines
(B) Beta blockers
(C) Monoamine oxidase inhibitors
(D) Selective serotonin reuptake inhibitors
(E) Tricyclic antidepressants

205. Within what time period after unprotected sexual intercourse is emergency contraception most effective?
(A) 12 hours
(B) 24 hours
(C) 36 hours
(D) 48 hours
(E) 72 hours

206. A 24-year-old Caucasian male presents for a routine physical exam. His blood pressure has been routinely elevated with little or no reduction in response to dietary adjustments or diuretic therapy. Which of the following is the class of medication you would prescribe to control blood pressure?
(A) ACE inhibitors
(B) Alpha-adrenergic antagonists
(C) Beta-adrenergic antagonists
(D) Calcium channel blockers
(E) Diuretics

207. Which of the following diagnostic techniques would be most effective in confirming the diagnosis of melasma?
(A) Cell culture
(B) Diascopy
(C) Potassium hydroxide preparation
(D) Scraping of the affected area
(E) Wood's light examination

208. A 17-year-old male presents with fever, hearing loss, and pain in the right ear. Examination reveals an immobile eardrum that is erythematous and bulging. Based on the findings of the examination and the patient's symptoms, which of the following is the proper diagnosis?
(A) Acoustic neuroma
(B) Labyrinthitis
(C) Meniere's disease
(D) Otitis externa
(E) Otitis media

209. Which of the following gastrointestinal disorders is characterized by the twisting of any part of the bowel on itself, and normally involves the sigmoid or cecal area of the bowel?
(A) Bowel obstruction
(B) Celiac disease
(C) Crohn's disease
(D) Irritable bowel syndrome
(E) Volvulus

210. A 22-year-old female presents with fatigue, weakness, muscle aches, and weight loss. Physical exam reveals hypotension at 100/60 mm/Hg, hyperpigmentation, and delayed deep tendon reflexes. Bloodwork reveals hyperkalemia, low blood urea nitrogen, low plasma cortisol at 2 μg/dL, and serum DHEA of 875 ng/mL. Based on the patient's presentation, physical examination, and test results, which of the following is the most likely diagnosis?
(A) Acromegaly
(B) Addison's disease
(C) Cushing's disease
(D) Diabetes insipidus
(E) Diabetes mellitus

211. Which of the following gastrointestinal disorders involves the invagination of a proximal segment of the bowel into the portion just distal to it?
(A) Abdominal adhesion
(B) Bowel obstruction
(C) Intussusception
(D) Ulcerative colitis
(E) Volvulus

212. A 38-year-old obese white female presents with feeling of vaginal fullness, lower abdominal aching, lower back pain, and a sensation of "sitting on a ball". Physical examination reveals mild dropping of the uterus. Based on the patient's presentation and physical examination, which of the following is the most appropriate diagnosis?
(A) Adenomyosis
(B) Endometrial polyps
(C) Endometriosis
(D) Leiomyomata
(E) Uterine prolapse

213. A 40-year-old white male with a history of diabetes presents for his annual physical examination. His blood pressure is moderately elevated at 150/90 mmHg. Diuretic therapy has proven to be ineffective in controlling the patient's blood pressure. Which of the following is the class of medication you would prescribe to this patient to control his blood pressure?
(A) ACE inhibitors
(B) Alpha-adrenergic antagonists
(C) Beta-adrenergic antagonists
(D) Calcium channel blockers
(E) Diuretics

214. A 58-year-old female with a known history of sinusitis presents with severe congestion and pain without significant discharge. History obtained from the patient reveals she is a prior cocaine abuser who has been continuously using the nasal sprays prescribed to treat her sinusitis. Physical examination did not reveal opacification of the sinuses with transillumination. Based on the symptoms, history, and examination, which of the following is the appropriate diagnosis?
(A) Allergic rhinitis
(B) Chronic atrophic rhinitis
(C) Rhinitis medicamentosa
(D) Sinusitis
(E) Vasomotor rhinitis

215. A 29-year-old male presents with abdominal pain, diarrhea, low-grade fever, and fatigue. Colonoscopy and biopsy confirm the diagnosis of Crohn's disease. Which of the following medications are indicated for maintenance of Crohn's disease?
(A) Aminosalicylates
(B) Antacids

(C) Immunodilators
(D) Mesalamine
(E) Proton channel blockers

216. A 68-year-old male presents with abdominal pain, bloating, belching, weight loss, and intermittent gastrointestinal bleeding. Bloodwork reveals iron-deficiency anemia and elevated liver enzymes. Endoscopy reveals a neoplasm near the pylorus. Based on the patient's presentation and test results, which of the following is the most appropriate diagnosis?
(A) Barrett's esophagus
(B) Carcinoid stomach tumor
(C) Gastric adenocarcinoma
(D) Gastric lymphoma
(E) Zollinger-Ellison syndrome

217. A 48-year-old male presents with cough, hemoptysis, focal wheezing, and recurrent pneumonia. Bronchoscopy reveals a pink/purple, well-vascularized central lesion. Based on the patient's presentation and test results, which of the following is the most appropriate diagnosis?
(A) Carcinoid tumor
(B) Non-small cell lung carcinoma
(C) Sarcoma
(D) Small cell lung carcinoma
(E) Solitary pulmonary nodule

218. Which of the following treatment options is recommended for treatment of carcinoid tumor?
(A) Chemotherapy
(B) Hormonal therapy
(C) Immunotherapy
(D) Radiation therapy
(E) Surgical excision

219. A 26-year-old female presents with diarrhea, weight loss, weakness, and abdominal distention. You suspect Celiac disease. Which of the following clinical procedures would you perform to confirm the diagnosis?
(A) Barium enema
(B) Colonoscopy
(C) CT scan of the abdomen
(D) Gastrointestinal bleeding study
(E) Small bowel biopsy

220. A 24-year-old female with a history of thrombocytopenia presents with petechiae on the skin and mucous membranes. She also complains of

abnormal bleeding in the gums. Bloodwork reveals a decreased platelet count of 40,000 platelets/mcL. This patient has been prescribed a steroid regimen to treat her thrombocytopenia, which has failed. Which of the following options would offer a definitive treatment for her disorder?
(A) Bone marrow transplant
(B) Continued higher-dose prednisone treatment
(C) Immunosuppressive therapy
(D) Splenectomy
(E) Stem cell transplantation

221. A 70-year-old male presents with erectile dysfunction. Which class of medications is useful in treating this disorder?
(A) 5-alpha-reductase inhibitors
(B) Alpha-adrenergic agonists
(C) Beta-adrenergic agonists
(D) Phosphodiesterase-5 inhibitors
(E) Fluoroquinolones

222. A 44-year-old male presents with headache, purulent drainage, fever, malaise, and pain in the face when bending over. Physical examination reveals tenderness to palpation of the sinuses and opacification of the sinuses with transillumination. Based on the patient's presentation and physical examination, which of the following is the most appropriate diagnosis?
(A) Allergic rhinitis
(B) Chronic atrophic rhinitis
(C) Rhinitis medicamentosa
(D) Sinusitis
(E) Vasomotor rhinitis

223. A 29-year-old female presents with excessive hair growth, truncal obesity, acne, and irregular menstruation. Physical examination reveals skin discoloration. Ultrasound examination reveals a "string of pearls" appearance within the ovaries. Based on the patient's presentation, physical examination, and test results, which of the following is the most appropriate diagnosis?
(A) Endometrial cancer
(B) Endometrial polyps
(C) Polycystic ovary syndrome
(D) Ovarian cancer
(E) Ovarian cysts

224. Which of the following areas of an electrocardiogram represent the posterior wall of the heart muscle?

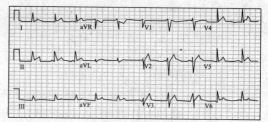

(A) Leads II, III, and aVF
(B) Leads V1 and V2
(C) Leads V1, V2, and V3
(D) Leads V1, V2, and VF
(E) Leads V4, V5, and V6

225. A 28-year-old intravenous drug user presents with jaw, neck, and back stiffness, difficulty swallowing, and irritability. Physical exam reveals hyperreflexia and muscle spasms to the face and jaw. Based on the patient's presentation and physical examination, which of the following is the most appropriate diagnosis?
(A) Botulism
(B) Diptheria
(C) Rabies
(D) Shigellosis
(E) Tetanus

226. Which of the following medications is the most appropriate treatment for gonorrhea for men and women?
(A) Acyclovir
(B) Ceftriaxone
(C) Chloroquine
(D) Mebendazole
(E) Penicillin

227. Which of the following treatment options would you suggest to treat a patient who has been diagnosed with pulmonary embolism?
(A) Anticoagulation
(B) Hyperbaric treatment
(C) Surgical clot removal
(D) Thrombolysis
(E) Vena cava interruption

228. Which of the following medications is the only drug that is FDA-approved specifically for the treatment of fibromyalgia?
(A) Leflunomide
(B) Methotrexate
(C) Naloxene
(D) Prednisone
(E) Pregabalin

229. A 9-year-old boy presents with sudden onset of severe testicular pain on the right side. Physical exam reveals a swollen scrotum. You suspect testicular torsion. Which of the following is the best diagnostic procedure in order to confirm this diagnosis?
(A) CT angiogram of the testicles
(B) MRI angiogram of the testicles
(C) Nuclear medicine testicular scan
(D) Testicular ultrasound
(E) X-ray of the testicles

230. A 15-year-old male presents with pain in the left ear for 3 days. Physical examination reveals pain when the tragus or auricle is manipulated. The exam also reveals an ear canal that is obscured and edematous, with purulent debris. Based on the symptoms and physical examination, which of the following is the most appropriate diagnosis?
(A) Acoustic neuroma
(B) Labyrinthitis
(C) Meniere's disease
(D) Otitis externa
(E) Otitis media

231. A 40-year-old male presents with recurrent, abrupt attacks of pain and swelling in the wrists and knees. Joint aspiration reveals rhomboid-shaped crystals that are negatively birefringent. Radiographs performed on the affected areas reveal chondro-calcinosis. Based on the patient's presentation and test results, which of the following is the most appropriate diagnosis?
(A) Calcium pyrophosphate dehydrate disease
(B) Gout
(C) Reactive arthritis
(D) Rheumatoid arthritis
(E) Septic arthritis

232. A 44-year-old diabetic female presents with pain in the wrist and base of the thumb, with radiation into the forearm. Physical examination reveals swelling and thickening of the tendon sheath. The examination also reveals a positive Finkelstein's test. Based on the patient's presentation and physical examination, which of the following is the most appropriate diagnosis?
(A) Carpal tunnel syndrome
(B) Colles's fracture
(C) De Quervain's disease
(D) Rheumatoid arthritis
(E) Scaphoid fracture

233. Which of the following classes of medications has been proven successful for the treatment of fibromyalgia?
(A) Corticosteroids
(B) DMARDs
(C) MAOIs
(D) NSAIDs
(E) SSRIs

234. Which of the following forms of childhood-onset idiopathic arthritis is characterized by spiking fevers of 102.2-104 °F with an associated salmon-pink maculopapular rash?
(A) Juvenile rheumatoid arthitis
(B) Osteoarthritis
(C) Pauciarticular arthritis
(D) Polyarticular arthritis
(E) Septic arthritis

235. A 55-year-old male presents with a sudden high fever, difficulty swallowing, sore throat, and drooling. You performed a lateral soft tissue c-spine X-ray, which reveals the classic thumb sign indicating epiglottitis. Which of the following is the proper course of treatment?
(A) Controlled intubation followed by IV fluids and antibiotics
(B) Tracheotomy to assist breathing
(C) Treatment with oral anti-inflammatories and antibiotics
(D) Treatment with epinephrine to assist with opening the airways
(E) Treatment with oral steroids and antibiotics

236. A 39-year-old male presents with fever, chills, vomiting, muscle pains, insomnia, and irritability. Physical examination reveals flushing of the face and faint maculopapules on the wrists, ankles, trunk, and extremities. Laboratory results reveals leukocytosis, thrombocytopenia, hyponatremia,

and proteinuria. CSF reveals pleocytosis and hypo-glycorrhachia. Based on the patient's presentation, physical examination, and test results, which of the following is the most appropriate diagnosis?
(A) Lyme disease
(B) Malaria
(C) Meningitis
(D) Rocky mountain spotted fever
(E) Syphilis

237. Which of the following radiologic modalities is most effective in visualizing white matter lesions in the central nervous system associated with multiple sclerosis?
(A) Angiography
(B) CT scanning
(C) Nuclear medicine
(D) MRI
(E) Ultrasound

238. A 53-year-old male is diagnosed with aseptic necrosis of the hip. Which of the following medications would you prescribe for maintenance therapy to avoid collapse of the femoral head?
(A) Alendronate
(B) High-dose corticosteroids
(C) Human growth hormone
(D) Methotrexate
(E) NSAIDs

239. A 26-year-old female presents with episodes of unexplained muscle weakness and muscle fatigue that fluctuate throughout the day and are resolved with rest. She also complains of double vision and difficulty chewing. Lab work reveals elevated levels of circulating acetylcholine receptor anti-bodies. Physical examination reveals ptosis, normal sensation in the limbs, and no reflex changes. Based on the patient's presentation and physical examination, which of the following is the most appropriate diagnosis?
(A) Bell's palsy
(B) Diabetic peripheral neuropathy
(C) Fibromyalgia
(D) Guillain-Barré syndrome
(E) Myasthenia gravis

240. Which of the following radiologic imaging modalities are useful to differentiate frontotemporal dementia from Alzheimer's disease?
(A) Angiography
(B) CT scan

(C) PET scan
(D) MRI
(E) Ultrasound

241. Which of the following anti-diabetic medications are contraindicated in patients with elevated serum creatinine?
(A) Exenatide
(B) Glyburide
(C) Metformin
(D) Miglitol
(E) Rosilitazone

242. A 55-year-old African-American male presents with recurrent back pain, flank pain, and head-aches. He also complains of blood in his urine and weight loss. Physical exam reveals hypertension and palpable, tender, nodular kidneys. You suspect polycystic kidney disease. Which of the following diagnostic exams would you perform in order to confirm your diagnosis?
(A) Biopsy of the kidney
(B) CT scan of the abdomen
(C) Renal angiography
(D) Ultrasound of the kidneys
(E) X-ray of the abdomen

243. A 60-year-old female who is being treated for pneumonia and a history of diabetes presents with a sudden high fever, difficulty swallowing, sore throat, and drooling. You need to rule out epiglottitis, which is a potentially life-threatening infection. Which of the following diagnostic pro-cedures would you do immediately?
(A) Bacterial culture
(B) CT scan of the neck
(C) MRI of the neck
(D) Ultrasound of the neck
(E) X-ray of the neck

244. A 40-year-old HIV-positive male is diagnosed with pneumocystis pneumonia. Which of the following medications is appropriate for treatment of this disorder?
(A) Bactrim
(B) Cefadroxil
(C) Clarithromycin
(D) Doxycycline
(E) Erythromycin

245. Which of the following radiographic procedures will allow you to differentiate croup from epiglottitis?
(A) CT scan of the neck
(B) Lateral neck radiograph
(C) MRI of the neck
(D) Posteroanterior neck radiograph
(E) Water's view radiograph

246. A 50-year-old obese white male presents with chest pain, shortness of breath, and non-specific headache. Physical examination reveals his blood pressure to be 240/140 mmHg. Which of the following refers to the disorder that is characterized by blood pressure readings of this range?
(A) Essential hypertension
(B) Hypertensive emergency
(C) Hypertensive urgency
(D) Malignant hypertension
(E) Primary hypertension

247. A 42-year-old male presents for routine examination. His blood pressure was mildly elevated at his last examination and he was advised to adjust his diet to reduce sodium. Although he was very compliant with his dietary adjustments, his blood pressure is still elevated. Which of the following is the class of medication you would initially prescribe to control blood pressure?
(A) ACE inhibitors
(B) Alpha-adrenergic antagonists
(C) Beta-adrenergic antagonists
(D) Calcium channel blockers
(E) Diuretics

248. An 80-year-old male presents post right-hip arthroplasty with pleuritic chest pain, dyspnea, and hemoptysis. Electrocardiogram reveals tachycardia and non-specific ST-T wave changes. Chest X-ray reveals basilar atelectasis. Auscultation of the chest reveals crackles and accentuation of the pulmonary component of the second heart sound. Based on the patient's presentation, history, and test results, which of the following is the most accurate diagnosis?
(A) Bronchiectasis
(B) Cystic fibrosis
(C) Pulmonary edema
(D) Pulmonary embolism
(E) Pulmonary hypertension

249. A 28-year-old female presents with abdominal pain and delayed menstruation. You suspect ovarian cysts. Which of the following diagnostic procedures would you use to confirm this diagnosis?
(A) CT scan of the abdomen
(B) CT scan of the pelvis
(C) Gynecological exam
(D) MRI of the abdomen
(E) Ultrasound of the pelvis

250. Which of the following diagnostic exams is frequently used to monitor seizure activity?
(A) Electrocardiogram
(B) Electromyogram
(C) Electroencephalogram
(D) Blood prolactin test
(E) Signal average electrocardiogram

251. A 65-year-old female presents with intermittent heart palpitations, fatigue, and dizziness. Auscultation of the chest reveals an irregular heart rhythm. Electrocardiogram confirmed the presence of an irregular heart rhythm.

Which cardiac arrhythmia is denoted on the patient's electrocardiogram?
(A) Atrial fibrillation
(B) Atrial flutter
(C) Atrial tachycardia
(D) Normal sinus rhythm with occasional premature atrial contractions
(E) Sinus tachycardia

252. A 15-year-old boy is diagnosed with slipped capital femoral epiphysis. Which of the following treatments would you suggest for treatment of this disorder?
(A) IV high-dose corticosteroids
(B) IV high-dose antibiotics
(C) Physical therapy
(D) Pinning of the hip in situ
(E) Total hip arthroplasty

253. A 22-year-old male presents with left lower-quadrant pain, weight loss, fever, and pus-filled diarrhea. Abdominal X-ray reveals colonic dilatation. Colonoscopy confirms the diagnosis of ulcerative colitis. Which of the following medications are indicated for the maintenance of ulcerative colitis?
    (A) Aminosalicylates
    (B) Antacids
    (C) Immunodilators
    (D) Mesalamine
    (E) Proton channel blockers

254. Which of the following laboratory tests can be used to confirm the diagnosis of diabetes insipidus?
    (A) Glucose tolerance test
    (B) Red cell mass test
    (C) Schilling's test
    (D) Urinalysis
    (E) Vasopressin challenge test

255. A 44-year-old female presents with abdominal pain that gets worse after eating, nausea, and weight loss. The patient also complains of black tarry stools. Endoscopy reveals the presence of small ulcers. Based on the patient's presentation and test results, which of the following is the most appropriate diagnosis?
    (A) Chronic gastritis
    (B) Duodenal ulcer
    (C) Esophageal achalasia
    (D) Gastric ulcer
    (E) Mallory-Weiss tear

256. A 29-year-old female presents with ectopic pregnancy. Her serum HCG is 4625 mU, the ectopic mass measures 2.8 cm on ultrasound, and she is hemodynamically stable and compliant with physician advice. Which of the following treatments is most appropriate for resolution of her ectopic pregnancy?
    (A) Laparoscopy
    (B) Laparotomy
    (C) Magnesium sulfate
    (D) Methotrexate
    (E) Oophrectomy

257. Which diagnostic imaging modality can be useful in the diagnosis of schizophrenia?
    (A) CT scan
    (B) Electoencephalogram
    (C) MRI
    (D) PET scan
    (E) SPECT scan

258. A newborn male infant presents with extreme cyanosis, hyperpnea, and agitation. Physical examination reveals clubbing of the fingers. Auscultation of the chest reveals increased right ventricle impulse at lower left sternal border and a loud S2. Based on the presentation and physical examination, which of the following is the proper diagnosis?
    (A) Hypoplastic left heart syndrome
    (B) Pulmonary atresia
    (C) Tetralogy of Fallot
    (D) Transposition of the great vessels
    (E) Ventricular outflow tract obstruction

259. Which of the following medications is contraindicated for treatment of anorexia nervosa?
    (A) Amitryptyline
    (B) Bupropion
    (C) Fluoxetine
    (D) Mirtazapine
    (E) Paroxetine

260. A 41-year-old pregnant woman presents at 32 weeks' gestation with painful vaginal bleeding, abdominal pain, and back pain. She has had six previous childbirths and a history of diabetes and hypertension. Based on the patient's history and presentation, which of the following is the most likely diagnosis?
    (A) Abruptio placentae
    (B) Ectopic pregnancy
    (C) Miscarriage
    (D) Placenta previa
    (E) Preeclampsia

261. A 27-year-old female presents with periodic episodes of moody, erratic, impulsive, and violent behavior. The patients states these episodes have been occurring for the past several years with associated symptom-free periods that last greater than two months. Based on the patient's history, which of the following is the most appropriate diagnosis?
    (A) Adjustment disorder
    (B) Alexithymia
    (C) Cyclothymic disorder
    (D) Bipolar disorder
    (E) Dysthymia

262. A 35-year-old male presents with early, recent onset of male pattern baldness. His area of hair loss is relatively small. Which of the following medications is the safest, most effective treatment to slow the progression of this patient's male pattern baldness?
(A) Aromatase inhibitor
(B) Finasteride
(C) Minoxidil
(D) Topical steroid creams
(E) Vitamin A

263. A newborn male infant presents with cyanosis, shock, heart failure, and respiratory distress. Auscultation of the chest reveals a single S2 sound. Based on the presentation and physical examination, which of the following is the proper diagnosis?
(A) Hypoplastic left heart syndrome
(B) Pulmonary atresia
(C) Tetralogy of Fallot
(D) Transposition of the great vessels
(E) Ventricular outflow tract obstruction

264. A chronically ill, 85-year-old female presents to the emergency room unresponsive and without a pulse. The patient's electrocardiogram is shown below. Based on the EKG findings, which is the most appropriate course of treatment?

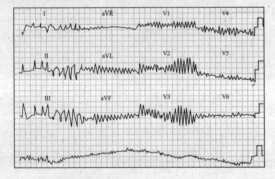

(A) Cardiac ablation
(B) Cardioversion
(C) Electrical defibrillation
(D) IV lidocaine
(E) IV adenosine

265. A 6-week-old infant presents with projectile vomiting, weight loss, and dehydration. Physical examination reveals an olive-shaped mass to the right of the umbilicus. You suspect pyloric stenosis.

Which of the following diagnostic exams would you order to confirm the diagnosis?
(A) Abdominal X-ray
(B) Biopsy of the mass
(C) CT scan of the abdomen
(D) MRI of the abdomen
(E) Ultrasound of the abdomen

266. Diseases involving defective bone mineralization, such as osteomalacia and rickets, are most often caused by a deficiency of which of the following vitamins?
(A) Vitamin B5
(B) Vitamin B6
(C) Vitamin B12
(D) Vitamin C
(E) Vitamin D

267. A 64-year-old female presents with generalized bone and muscle pain. Blood values reveal markedly elevated serum calcium levels. Nuclear medicine parathyroid exam reveals the presence of a parathyroid adenoma. Which of the following courses of treatment would you prescribe for this disorder?
(A) Calcium channel blockers
(B) Chemotherapy
(C) Hormonal therapy
(D) Radiation therapy
(E) Surgical removal

268. A 45-year-old businessman who spends a significant amount of time in airplanes complains of recurrent pain in the inner ear during flights. Which of the following disorders is likely the cause of his discomfort?
(A) Barotrauma
(B) Benign paroxysmal positional vertigo
(C) Central vertigo
(D) Labyrinthitis
(E) Tympanic membrane rupture

269. A 75-year-old female with a history of chronic renal disease presents with nausea, vomiting, and difficulty breathing. History obtained from the patient reveals she had been using milk of magnesia for the past few days for an intestinal disorder. Physical exam reveals reduced deep tendon reflexes and low blood pressure. Bloodwork reveals a plasma magnesium level of 3.1 mEq/L, confirming the diagnosis of hypermagnesemia. Which of the

following medications would you administer to this patient to treat her condition?

(A) IV 5% dextrose solution
(B) IV calcium gluconate
(C) IV potassium chloride
(D) IV sodium chloride
(E) Lactated Ringer's solution

270. A 72-year-old African-American male with a history of alcoholism presents with progressive shortness of breath. Auscultation of the chest reveals S1 gallop, rales, and increased jugular venous pressure. Chest X-ray reveals cardiomegaly with vascular congestion. Echocardiogram reveals dilated left ventricle, low cardiac output, and high diastolic pressure. Based on the patient's presentation, physical examination, and test results, which of the following is the most appropriate diagnosis?

(A) Congestive heart failure
(B) Dilated cardiomyopathy
(C) Hypertrophic cardiomyopathy
(D) Pulmonary hypertension
(E) Restrictive cardiomyopathy

271. A 19-year-old athletic female presents for annual physical exam. Blood pressure is normal at 120/80 mmHg. Auscultation of the chest is unremarkable. Electrocardiogram reveals the following rhythm. Which cardiac rhythm is denoted on the electrocardiogram?

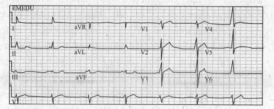

(A) Junctional rhythm
(B) Normal sinus rhythm with first-degree AV block
(C) Normal sinus rhythm
(D) Sinus bradycardia
(E) Ventricular escape rhythm

272. A normally healthy 45-year-old male presents with shortness of breath that is getting progressively worse. Chest X-ray reveals bilateral pleural effusions. Without knowing the underlying cause of the pleural effusions, which of the following is the proper course of treatment?

(A) Insertion of chest tube
(B) Treatment with antibiotics
(C) Treatment with diuretics
(D) Tracheotomy
(E) Thoracentesis

273. A 26-year-old female presents with excessive thirst and a craving for ice water, although she drinks in excess of 10 liters per day. Bloodwork reveals hyponatremia and dehydration. Urinalysis reveals a low specific gravity of 1.003. The patient had a positive vasopressin challenge test. Based on the patient's presentation and lab results, the correct diagnosis is:

(A) Acromegaly
(B) Addison's disease
(C) Cushing's disease
(D) Diabetes insipidus
(E) Diabetes mellitus

274. An 8-month-old child presents with severe colicky pain and mucous-filled, bloody stools. Physical examination reveals a sausage-like mass in the abdomen. Barium enema was positive for intussusception. Which of the following clinical procedures would you perform in order to correct this disorder?

(A) Abdominal angiogram
(B) Barium or air enema
(C) Colostomy
(D) Endoscopic decompression
(E) Surgical correction

275. A 70-year-old female presents to the emergency room with disorientation and convulsions. Physical exam reveals tachycardia, hypotension, fever, and dry mucous membranes. Lab work reveals a plasma sodium level of 226 mEq/L. With a plasma sodium elevation of this nature, what course of treatment would you prescribe to regulate this condition?

(A) Dialysis
(B) Increase intake of water
(C) IV 5% dextrose solution
(D) IV saline solution
(E) Oral rehydration therapy

276. A 72-year-old African-American male with a history of alcoholism presents with progressive shortness of breath. Auscultation of the chest reveals S1 gallop, rales, and increased jugular venous pressure. Chest X-ray reveals cardiomegaly with vascular congestion. Echocardiogram reveals dilated left ventricle, low cardiac output, and high diastolic pressure. Based on the patient's presentation, physical examination, and test results, which of the following is the most appropriate diagnosis?
(A) Congestive heart failure
(B) Dilated cardiomyopathy
(C) Hypertrophic cardiomyopathy
(D) Pulmonary hypertension
(E) Restrictive cardiomyopathy

277. Which of the following medications is administered to enhance fetal lung maturity in premature infants?
(A) 17a-hydroxyprogesterone caproate
(B) Beta-mimetic adrenergic agents
(C) Betamethisone
(D) Calcium gluconate
(E) Magnesium sulfate

278. A 36-year-old female presents with progressive hearing loss, tinnitus, and dizziness. You diagnose this patient with Meniere's disease. Which of the following treatment options would you prescribe for treatment of this disorder?
(A) Diuretics and salt restriction
(B) Intravenous antibiotics
(C) Oral antibiotics
(D) Otic antibacterial drops
(E) Vasopressin analog

279. Which of the following types of medication is commonly used for treatment of binge eating and obesity?
(A) Benzodiazepines
(B) Monoamine oxidase inhibitors
(C) Selective serotonin reuptake inhibitors
(D) Sympathomimetics
(E) Tricyclic antidepressants

280. A 40-year-old male sustains a scaphoid fracture with displacement greater than 1 mm. Which of the following treatment options would you suggest for treatment of this patient?
(A) Closed reduction
(B) Long-arm thumb spica cast

(C) Open-reduction internal fixation
(D) Osteotomy of the scaphoïd bone
(E) Short-arm thumb spica cast

281. A 22-year-old female presents with lower abdominal pain, fever, painful urination, and a foul-smelling vaginal discharge. Physical examination reveals cervicitis and salpingitis. Based on the patient's presentation and physical examination, which of the following is the most likely diagnosis?
(A) Bacterial vaginosis
(B) Chlamydia
(C) Gonorrhea
(D) HIV
(E) Syphilis

282. A 74-year-old male presents with shortness of breath, persistent non-productive cough, orthopnea, and exercise intolerance. Auscultation of the chest reveals basilar rales and gallops. Chest X-ray reveals bilateral pleural effusions, venous dilatation, and alveolar fluid. Based on the patient's presentation, physical exam, and test results, which of the following is the most accurate diagnosis?
(A) Cystic fibrosis
(B) Left-sided congestive heart failure
(C) Primary pneumothorax
(D) Right-sided congestive heart failure
(E) Tension pneumothorax

283. A 16-year-old Asian male presents with chest pain and shortness of breath. Auscultation of the chest reveals loud S4 gallop, variable systolic murmur, and jugular venous pulsations with a prominent "a" wave. Chest X-ray is essentially normal. Echocardiogram reveals left ventricular hypertrophy, asymmetric septal hypertrophy, and a small left ventricle. Based on the patient's presentation, physical examination, and test results, which of the following is the most appropriate diagnosis?
(A) Congestive heart failure
(B) Dilated cardiomyopathy
(C) Hypertrophic cardiomyopathy
(D) Pulmonary hypertension
(E) Restrictive cardiomyopathy

284. An 18-year-old male who was a victim of a motor vehicle accident presents to the emergency room with chest pain and shortness of breath. Chest X-ray reveals the accumulation of air in the pleural space with mediastinal shift to the left. Physical

exam reveals impaired ventilation. Which of the following is the proper diagnosis?
(A) Acute myocardial infarction
(B) Primary pneumothorax
(C) Pulmonary edema
(D) Pulmonary embolism
(E) Tension pneumothorax

285. A 44-year-old male presents with altered, bloody bowel movements, left lower quadrant pain, nausea, and vomiting. Physical exam reveals abdominal tenderness. CT scan confirms a diagnosis of diverticulitis. Which of the following treatments is recommended in order to avoid complications from diverticulitis?.
(A) Fat-free diet
(B) Gluten-free diet
(C) High-fiber diet
(D) Lactose-free diet
(E) Low-fiber diet

286. A 14-year-old male presents with tenderness, redness, and purulent drainage of the penis. Patient also complains of obstructed urinary stream and inability to retract the foreskin over the glans penis. Your diagnosis is phimosis. Which of the following is the most definitive treatment for symptomatic phimosis?
(A) Application of steroidal creams
(B) Circumcision
(C) No treatment required, will resolve when patient gets older
(D) Oral antibiotics
(E) Topical antibiotics

287. Which of the following medications is used to induce labor when the cervix is dilated more than one centimeter and some effacement has occurred?
(A) 17a-hydroxyprogesterone caproate
(B) Calcium gluconate
(C) Magnesium sulfate
(D) Oxytocin
(E) Progestin

288. A 70-year-old female, currently being treated for congestive heart failure, presents with nausea and leg swelling. Physical examination reveals distended neck veins, tender hepatomegaly, and pitting edema. Chest X-ray reveals cardiomegaly with bilateral pleural effusions. Based on the patient's presentation, physical exam, and test results, which of the following is the most accurate diagnosis?
(A) Cystic fibrosis
(B) Left-sided congestive heart failure
(C) Primary pneumothorax
(D) Right-sided congestive heart failure
(E) Tension pneumothorax

289. A patient currently taking an antidepressant complains of diminished sex drive and expresses an interest in switching or adding an antidepressant that will not cause this side effect. Which of the following types of antidepressant is least likely to cause diminished sexual function?
(A) Monoamine-oxidase inhibitor
(B) Norepinephrine-dopamine reuptake inhibitor
(C) Selective serotonin reuptake inhibitor
(D) Serotonin-norepinephrin reuptake inhibitor
(E) Tri-cyclic antidepressant

290. A 55-year-old male presents with progressive dyspnea. The patient's history reveals he worked in a coal mine for several years. Physical examination reveals inspiratory crackles. Chest X-ray reveals small opacities in the upper lung fields. Based on the patient's presentation, history, and test results, which of the following is the most accurate diagnosis?
(A) Coalworker's pneumoconiosis
(B) Cystic fibrosis
(C) Sarcoidosis
(D) Silicosis
(E) Tuberculosis

291. A 6-year-old female presents with excessive thirst and craving for ice water. Urinalysis reveals a low specific gravity of 1.004. Further testing confirmed a diagnosis of diabetes insipidus. Which of the following medications would you prescribe for treatment of this disorder?
(A) Desmopressin acetate
(B) Ergocalciferol
(C) Ketoconazole
(D) Parenteral octreotide
(E) Pegvisomant

292. Which of the following refers to the gastrointestinal condition that is characterized by a painful, fluctuant area at the sacrococcygeal cleft?
(A) Anal fissure
(B) Anorectal abscess
(C) Hemorrhoid
(D) Keratosis pilaris
(E) Pilonidal cyst

293. Which of the following types of tumors of the genitourinary system is resistant to radiation therapy?
(A) Nonseminomatous testicular tumor
(B) Prostate adenocarcinoma
(C) Renal cell carcinoma
(D) Seminomatous testicular tumor
(E) Wilms's tumor

294. A 48-year-old female presents with acute episodes of vertigo. Which of the following treatment options would you suggest for treatment of this disorder?
(A) Diazepam
(B) Dimenhydrinate
(C) Droperidol
(D) Meclizine
(E) Scopolamine

295. A 50-year-old female is diagnosed with Sjogren's syndrome. Which of the following medications is indicated to treat symptoms of this disorder by increasing salivary flow?
(A) Ketoconazole
(B) Leflunomide
(C) Methotrexate
(D) Pilocarpine
(E) Pregabalin

296. A 35-year-old female presents with ectopic pregnancy. Her serum HCG is 3870 mU, the ectopic mass is 3.7 cm as measured by ultrasound, several abdominal adhesions are documented, and she is hemodynamically unstable. Which of the following treatments is most appropriate for resolution of her ectopic pregnancy?
(A) Laparoscopy
(B) Laparotomy
(C) Methotrexate
(D) Magnesium Sulfate
(E) Oophrectomy

297. A newborn female infant presents with severe cyanosis and tachypnea at birth. Auscultation of the chest reveals a hyperdynamic apical impulse and a single S1 and S2 sound. Based on the presentation and physical examination, which of the following is the proper diagnosis?
(A) Hypoplastic left heart syndrome
(B) Pulmonary atresia
(C) Tetralogy of Fallot
(D) Transposition of the great vessels
(E) Ventricular outflow tract obstruction

298. A 55-year-old active white female presents with lower leg pain with exercise. Pain is relieved with rest. Auscultation of the legs reveal a weak femoral and distal pulse and a femoral bruit. Doppler study reveals an ankle-brachial index of 0.8. Based on the patient's presentation, physical examination, and test results, which of the following is the most appropriate diagnosis?
(A) Atherosclerosis
(B) Chronic venous insufficiency
(C) Deep venous thrombosis
(D) Peripheral arterial disease
(E) Varicose veins

299. A 60-year-old male presents with progressive shortness of breath. Physical examination reveals inspiratory crackles, clubbing, and cyanosis. Chest X-ray reveals small opacities throughout the lung fields with calcified hilar lymph nodes. The patient's history reveals he worked in a stone quarry for 35 years. Based on the patient's presentation, history, and test results, which of the following is the most accurate diagnosis?
(A) Coalworker's pneumoconiosis
(B) Cystic fibrosis
(C) Sarcoidosis
(D) Silicosis
(E) Tuberculosis

300. Diseases involving defective bone mineralization, such as osteomalacia and rickets, are most often caused by a deficiency of which of the following vitamins?
(A) Vitamin B5
(B) Vitamin B6
(C) Vitamin B12
(D) Vitamin C
(E) Vitamin D

301. Which of the following medical signs is an indication of acute appendicitis in which the patient is supine and attempts to raise the leg against resistance?
(A) Levine's sign
(B) McBurney's sign
(C) Obturator sign
(D) Psoas sign
(E) Rovsing's sign

302. A 63-year-old male presents with gross hematuria and flank pain. Physical examination reveals a palpable mass. Laboratory test results and diagnostic studies lead to a diagnosis of localized renal cell carcinoma without metastases. Which of the following treatments is required to adequately treat this disorder?
(A) Chemotherapy
(B) Hormonal therapy
(C) Immunotherapy
(D) Radical nephrectomy
(E) Radiation therapy

303. A 34-year-old male presents with difficulty focusing, hearing loss in the left ear, dizziness, and vertigo. Physical examination reveals inflammation of the inner ear and involuntary eye movements. Based on the patient's presentation and physical examination, which of the following is the most appropriate diagnosis?
(A) Barotrauma
(B) Benign paroxysmal positional vertigo
(C) Central vertigo
(D) Labyrinthitis
(E) Tympanic membrane rupture

304. Which of the following muscles is affected in "tennis elbow"?
(A) Extensor carpi radialis brevis
(B) Extensor carpi radialis longus
(C) Flexor digitorum
(D) Palmarus longus
(E) Pronator teres

305. Which of the following medications, used to stop pre-term uterine contractions, inhibits myometrial contractility mediated by calcium?
(A) Calcium channel blockers
(B) Calcium gluconate
(C) Magnesium sulfate
(D) Methotrexate
(E) Ritodrine

306. A 35-year-old male patient complains of intrusive thoughts of a graphic and disturbing nature. He is bothered by these thoughts, but cannot seem to eliminate them. He complains that the thoughts and images occur repeatedly and often distract him from accomplishing daily tasks. The thoughts are not memories of an event or scene, and were not triggered by a precipitating event. The most likely diagnosis for this patient is
(A) Major depressive disorder
(B) Obsessive-compulsive disorder
(C) Obsessive-compulsive personality disorder
(D) Post-traumatic stress disorder
(E) Schizophrenia

307. A 75-year-old man presents with shortness of breath that is becoming progressively worse. The man's history, exam, and test results lead to a diagnosis of silicosis. In addition to oxygen therapy, which of the following is the proper course of treatment for this disorder?
(A) Treat with anti-immunoglobulin
(B) Treat with antibiotics
(C) Treat with corticosteroids
(D) Treat with bronchodilators
(E) Treat with diuretics

308. A 46-year-old male with a history of Crohn's disease presents with severe abdominal cramping, fever, and abdominal distention. Physical examination reveals rigid abdomen and rebound abdominal tenderness. Abdominal X-ray reveals colonic dilation confirming the diagnosis of toxic megacolon. Which of the following clinical procedures is indicated for treatment of this disorder?
(A) Abdominal angiogram
(B) Colon cleansing
(C) Colonic decompression
(D) Colostomy
(E) Surgical correction

309. A 38-year-old male presents with pain in the pelvis, femurs, and tibias. Bloodwork reveals normal calcium, normal phosphates, and an elevated alkaline phosphatase. Nuclear medicine bone scan reveals increased radiotracer uptake in the pelvis and lower extremities confirming the diagnosis of Paget's disease. Which of the following medications would you prescribe to treat this disorder?
(A) Bisphosphonates
(B) Desmopressin acetate
(C) Ergocalciferol
(D) Parenteral octreotide
(E) Pegvisomant

310. A 36-year-old male presents with uncharacteristic heaviness in the right testicle. Ultrasound examination reveals an intratesticular echogenic focus. Laboratory results reveal normal levels of a-fetoprotein and a-human chorionic gonadotropin, confirming the diagnosis of a stage I seminomatous testicular tumor. Which of the following is the appropriate course of treatment for a stage I seminomatous testicular tumor?
(A) Chemotherapy
(B) Corticosteroids
(C) Hormone therapy
(D) Orchiectomy
(E) Radiation therapy

311. Which of the following medications, used to stop preterm uterine contractions, relax the uterine muscles by decreasing the intracellular concentration of calcium ions?
(A) Calcium channel blockers
(B) Calcium gluconate
(C) Magnesium sulfate
(D) Methotrexate
(E) Ritodrine

312. A 66-year-old male, currently being treated with diuretics for congestive heart failure, presents for a follow-up visit and complains of intermittent chest pain. Physical exam reveals a new onset of hypertension. Which of the following medications would you prescribe in addition to diuretics to treat his associated symptoms?
(A) ACE inhibitors
(B) Alpha-adrenergic antagonists
(C) Beta-adrenergic antagonists
(D) Calcium channel blockers
(E) Corticosteroids

313. A 59-year-old African-American female presents with chest discomfort, cough, and shortness of breath. In addition, the patient states she has an unusual lack of energy. Lab work reveals leukopenia, elevated erythrocyte sedimentation rate, and hypercalcemia. Chest X-ray reveals symmetrical bilateral hilar adenopathy. Based on the patient's presentation, history, and test results, which of the following is the most accurate diagnosis?
(A) Coalworker's pneumoconiosis
(B) Cystic fibrosis
(C) Sarcoidosis
(D) Silicosis
(E) Tuberculosis

314. Which of the following medical signs is an indication of acute appendicitis detectable by having the patient lie supine with the right knee bent at a right angle, holding the right ankle, and attempting to rotate the right hip internally by moving the knee inward?
(A) Levine's sign
(B) McBurney's sign
(C) Obturator sign
(D) Psoas sign
(E) Rovsing's sign

315. Which of the following laboratory tests is a classic diagnostic indicator of hyperparathyroidism?
(A) Decreased parathyroid hormone
(B) Decreased thyroid stimulating hormone
(C) Elevated serum calcium
(D) Elevated T4
(E) Elevated TSH

316. A middle-aged man states that he feels as if he has something stuck in his throat. His voice sounds muffled, and others have commented that he sounds different than usual. The patient is a non-smoker and does not have difficulty breathing. Examination of the throat reveals a pale, swollen, and translucent uvula, but no peritonsillar involvement. Rapid strep screen is negative. When asked, the patient revealed that he had recently ingested a fruit salad that may have contained apricots, which have in the past precipitated mild allergic reactions. Based on the patient's presentation and physical examination, the patient most likely has:
(A) GERD
(B) Glossitis

(C) Uvulitis

(D) Uvular hydrops

(E) Viral sore throat

317. Which of the following medications is used to counteract the effects of an overdose of magnesium sulfate (MgSO4)?

(A) Calcium channel blockers

(B) Calcium gluconate

(C) Neloxone

(D) Methotrexate

(E) Ritodrine

318. A 59-year-old female presents with progressive shortness of breath and non-productive cough. Chest X-ray reveals cardiomegaly and right-sided pleural effusions. Auscultation of the lungs reveals right-sided rales. You diagnose this patient with congestive heart failure. Which of the following is the proper initial course of treatment for this disorder?

(A) ACE inhibitors

(B) Alpha-adrenergic antagonists

(C) Beta-adrenergic antagonists

(D) Calcium channel blockers

(E) Diuretics

319. A 62-year-old male who sustained multiple traumas as the result of a motor vehicle accident develops sudden, profound shortness of breath. The physical examination and radiographic findings lead to a diagnosis of adult respiratory distress syndrome. Which of the following is the proper course of treatment?

(A) Insert chest tube.

(B) Insert large bore needle in the chest

(C) Intubate the patient.

(D) Perform a tracheotomy.

(E) Perform thoracentesis.

320. Which of the following treatments is effective in resolving chronic pancreatitis?

(A) Cessation of smoking

(B) Decrease alcohol consumption

(C) Low-fat/high-fiber diet

(D) Oral anti-inflammatories

(E) Reduction of stomach acid

321. A 64-year-old female presents with generalized bone and muscle pain. Blood values reveal markedly elevated serum calcium levels. Nuclear medicine parathyroid exam reveals the presence of a parathyroid adenoma. Which of the following courses of treatment would you prescribe for this disorder?

(A) Chemotherapy

(B) Hormonal therapy

(C) Immunotherapy

(D) Radiation therapy

(E) Surgical removal

322. Which of the following medications can reduce the risk of recurrent preterm birth in women with a history of preterm delivery?

(A) 17a-hydroxyprogesterone caproate

(B) Beta-mimetic adrenergic agents

(C) Betamethisone

(D) Calcium gluconate

(E) Magnesium sulfate

323. Which of the following radiological procedures is the most definitive for diagnosing coronary artery disease?

(A) Cardiac stress testing

(B) Coronary angiography

(C) Echocardiogram

(D) Myocardial perfusion SPECT imaging

(E) Myocardial perfusion PET imaging

324. A prematurely born infant begins to exhibit typical signs of respiratory distress. Chest X-ray reveals air bronchograms, bilateral atelectasis that gives a "ground glass" appearance, and a domed diaphragm. Based on the patient's presentation and test results, which of the following is the most accurate diagnosis?

(A) Acute asphyxia

(B) Acute respiratory failure

(C) Cystic fibrosis

(D) Hyaline membrane disease

(E) Transient tachypnea

325. Which of the following refers to the gastrointestinal disorder characterized by extreme dilation and immobility of the colon? This disorder is a true emergency.

(A) Acute mesenteric ischemia

(B) Appendicitis

(C) Intussesception

(D) Toxic megacolon

(E) Ulcerative colitis

326. A 92-year-old female with a history of diabetes presents to the Intensive Care Unit following total hip arthroplasty. Vital signs are normal with a blood pressure of 120/80 mmHg and a heart rate of 78. The day following the procedure, the patient's blood pressure drops to 80/50 mmHg, heart rate increases to 115 beats per minute, and she is unresponsive.

Based on the presentation and patient's condition, which of the following is the accurate diagnosis?
(A) Cardiogenic shock
(B) Compensated shock
(C) Hypovolemic shock
(D) Obstructive shock
(E) Septic shock

327. Which of the following interventions is used to prevent premature labor and delivery in women who have a history of preterm birth or with confirmed diagnosis of cervical incompetence?
(A) Bed rest
(B) Cervical cerclage
(C) Cervical laparoscopy
(D) Cervical laparotomy
(E) Hysterectomy

328. A 16-year-old male presents with maladaptive behavioral and emotional problems that have occurred since his parents divorced two months previously. Based on this history, which of the following is the most appropriate diagnosis?
(A) Adjustment disorder
(B) Alexithymia
(C) Bipolar disorder
(D) Cyclothymic disorder
(E) Dysthymia

329. A 45-year-old female presents with pain in the right wrist. She states the pain occurs even through the night. She also complains of loss of coordination and loss of strength in her right hand. Physical examination reveals a positive Tinel's sign and positive Phalen's test. Based on the patient's presentation and physical examination, which of the following is the most appropriate diagnosis?
(A) Carpal tunnel syndrome
(B) Colles's fracture
(C) De Quervain's disease
(D) Rheumatoid arthritis
(E) Scaphoid fracture

330. A 25-year-old male presents with a history of several manic episodes alternating with several depressive episodes. You diagnose this patient with bipolar disorder. Which of the following medications would you prescribe for treatment of this disorder?
(A) Amitryiptyline
(B) Bupropion
(C) Fluoxetine
(D) Lithium
(E) Paroxetine

331. Which of the following types of anemia is clinically diagnosed by the presence of hemoglobin S in red blood cells?
(A) Hemolytic anemia
(B) Idiopathic ablastic anemia
(C) Iron-deficiency anemia
(D) Pernicious anemia
(E) Sickle cell anemia

332. A 12-year-old girl presents with eye symptoms. You diagnose this patient with orbial cellulitis. Which of the following treatment options is indicated for this disorder?
(A) Application of ophthalmic antibiotics
(B) Application of ophthalmic steroids
(C) Administration of ophthalmic antibiotic
(D) Hospitalization and IV antibiotics
(E) Surgical intervention

333. A 52-year-old female presents with fatigue and occasional heart palpitations. Auscultation of the chest reveals mid-diastolic murmur, accentuated S1, and an opening snap following S2 without radiation. Chest X-ray reveals atrial enlargement. Based on the presentation and physical examination, which of the following is the proper diagnosis?
(A) Aortic stenosis
(B) Aortic regurgitation
(C) Mitral stenosis
(D) Mitral regurgitation
(E) Tricuspid regurgitation

334. Which of the following laboratory values is clinically diagnostic for the onset of menopause?
(A) Estradiol level above 75 pg/mL
(B) FSH level greater than 30 mIU/mL
(C) FSH level less than 30 mIU/mL
(D) HCG level greater than 1500 mU/mL
(E) HCG level less than 1500 mU/mL

335. A 67-year-old female with a family history of pancreatic cancer presents with abdominal pain, jaundice, and a palpable gallbladder. Which of the following diagnostic studies would you perform to rule out or confirm the presence of pancreatic cancer?
(A) Abdominal angiography
(B) Abdominal chest X-ray
(C) Biopsy of the pancreas
(D) CT scan of the abdomen
(E) Endoscopic retrograde cholangiopancreatogram

336. A 66-year-old gentleman presents with complaints of memory problems. He appears to be upset or distressed. Examination reveals attention span and concentration to be intact. Based on patient's presentation and examination, which of the following is the most likely diagnosis?
(A) Alzheimer's disease
(B) Frontotemporal dementia
(C) Pseudodementia
(D) Psychosis
(E) Vascular dementia

337. A 45-year-old obese sedentary female presents with tired, aching legs. Physical exam reveals superficial dilated, tortuous veins in the distribution of the long saphenous vein. Based on the patient's presentation and physical examination, which of the following is the most appropriate diagnosis?
(A) Atherosclerosis
(B) Chronic venous insufficiency
(C) Deep venous thrombosis
(D) Peripheral arterial disease
(E) Varicose veins

338. A 48-year-old female presents with pain in the throat area radiating to the ears with difficulty eating. Physical exam reveals an enlarged thyroid gland, low-grade fever, and fatigue. Bloodwork and radiologic exam lead to a diagnosis of subacute thyroiditis. Which of the following medications would you prescribe to treat this disorder?
(A) Thyroid hormones
(B) Aspirin
(C) Propanolol
(D) Antibiotics
(E) Prednisone

339. A 70-year-old female presents with headache, scalp tenderness, jaw pain, throat pain, and visual disturbances. Bloodwork reveals a markedly elevated erythrocyte sedimentation rate and C-reactive protein level. Based on the patient's presentation and lab results, which of the following is the most appropriate diagnosis?
(A) Abdominal aortic aneurysm
(B) Chronic venous insufficiency
(C) Giant cell arteritis
(D) Peripheral arterial disease
(E) Varicose veins

340. A 50-year-old obese diabetic male presents with a deep lesion in the area of the lateral malleolus of the right ankle. Physical examination of the lesion reveals localized necrotic tissue. Which of the following treatment options would you initially perform to give this lesion the best chance of healing?
(A) Debridement
(B) Topical antibiotics
(C) Topical steroids
(D) Vasodilator medication
(E) Whirlpool treatment

341. A 38-year-old women experiencing her first pregnancy presents in her 25th week of gestation with swelling of the face and hands, sudden weight gain, headache, visual disturbances, nausea, and decreased urine output. Physical examination reveals high blood pressure, proteinuria, and hyperreflexia. Based on the patient's presentation and physical examination, which of the following is the most appropriate diagnosis?
(A) Chronic hypertension
(B) Eclampsia
(C) Preeclampsia
(D) Gestational diabetes
(E) Premature labor

342. A 31-year-old female presents with persistent mild depression with symptoms including loss of interest, social withdrawal, overeating, over-sleeping, and lack of self-esteem for over 2 years. The patient denies any psychotic, manic, or hypo-manic episodes. Based on the patient's history, which of the following is the most appropriate diagnosis?
(A) Adjustment disorder
(B) Alexithymia
(C) Bipolar disorder
(D) Cyclothymic disorder
(E) Dysthymia

343. A 55-year-old diabetic male with history of shoulder injuries presents with pain in the left shoulder. Physical examination reveals restricted glenohumeral movement. Arthrography reveals decreased volume of the joint capsule and capsular contraction. Based on the patient's presentation, which of the following is the most appropriate diagnosis?
(A) Adhesive capsulitis
(B) Bankart's lesion
(C) Hills-Sachs lesion
(D) Impingement syndrome
(E) Rotator cuff syndrome

344. A 44-year-old man presents with shortness of breath on exertion and occasional heart palpitations. Auscultation of the chest reveals a soft systolic and diastolic decrescendo murmur with radiation to the right sternal border and arterial pulses that are large and bounding. Chest X-ray reveals left-sided atrial enlargement with ventricular hypertrophy. Based on the presentation and physical examination, which of the following is the proper diagnosis?
(A) Aortic stenosis
(B) Aortic regurgitation
(C) Mitral stenosis
(D) Mitral regurgitation
(E) Tricuspid regurgitation

345. An 18-year-old female presents with right upper quadrant pain that primarily occurs after she eats a fatty meal. An ultrasound exam of the abdomen was positive for multiple gallstones. The patient does not want to have surgery to remove the gallbladder. Which of the following would be the most appropriate medication to treat the presence of gallstones?

(A) Dilaudid
(B) Morphine
(C) Toradol
(D) Ox bile extract
(E) Ursadiol

346. Which of the following types of thyroiditis is caused by a bacterial, fungal, or parasitic agent?
(A) De Quervain's thyroiditis
(B) Hashimoto's thyroiditis
(C) Postpartum thyroiditis
(D) Suppurative thyroiditis
(E) Subacute lymphocytic thyroiditis

347. Which of the following is the common name for frontotemporal lobe dementia?
(A) Alzheimer's disease
(B) Huntington's disease
(C) Parkinson's disease
(D) Pick's disease
(E) Wilson's disease

348. Which of the following diagnostic techniques incorporates acetic acid in order to facilitate the examination of warts?
(A) Acetowhitening
(B) Biopsy
(C) Diascopy
(D) Potassium hydroxide preparation
(E) Wood's light examination

349. Which of the following medications is the appro-priate treatment for a three-year-old male who has been diagnosed with hookworms?
(A) Albendazole
(B) Ceftriaxone
(C) Penicillin
(D) Pyrantel
(E) Mebendazole

350. Which of the following characteristics distinguishes eclampsia from preeclampsia?
(A) Elevated liver enzymes
(B) Hemolysis
(C) Low platelet count
(D) Proteinuria
(E) Seizures

351. A 45-year-old female with a history of rheumatic fever presents with the complaint of exercise intol-erance. Physical examination reveals jugular venous distention, peripheral edema, and hepatomegaly.

Auscultation of the chest reveals a pancystolic murmur along the left lower sternal border with radiation to the right sternum, and xiphoid and increased jugular venous pressures. Chest X-ray reveals prominent right heart border and dilatation of the superior vena cava. Electrocardiogram reveals right axis deviation. Based on the presentation and physical examination, which of the following is the proper diagnosis?

(A) Aortic regurgitation
(B) Mitral regurgitation
(C) Mitral valve prolapse
(D) Pulmonic stenosis
(E) Tricuspid regurgitation

352. Which of the following medications is an alcohol deterrent medication that causes nausea when alcohol is consumed?

(A) Antabuse
(B) Bupropion
(C) Diazepam
(D) Fluoxetene
(E) Naloxone

353. A newborn baby presents with immediate respiratory distress. Auscultation of the chest reveals bowel sounds in the chest. Chest X-ray reveals loops of bowel in the hemithorax with displacement of the heart. Based on the patient's presentation, physical examination, and test results, which of the following is the most accurate diagnosis?

(A) Esophageal atresia
(B) Diaphragmatic hernia
(C) Hirschsprung's disease
(D) Nectrotizing enterocolitis
(E) Pyloric stenosis

354. A 31-year-old female presents with ectopic pregnancy. Her serum HCG is 5190mU, the ectopic mass is 4.2 cm on ultrasound, and she is hemodynamically stable and compliant with physican advice. Which of the following treatments is most appropriate for resolution of her ectopic pregnancy?

(A) Laparoscopy
(B) Laparotomy
(C) Methotrexate
(D) Magnesium sulfate
(E) Oophrectomy

355. A 50-year-old male presents with occasional chest pain, fatigue, and intermittent dizzy spells. Auscultation of the chest reveals a murmur in the left intercostal space between the second and third ribs, with a midsystolic crescendo-decrescendo radiating to the left shoulder and neck. An early pulmonic ejection sound is also appreciated during chest auscultation. Based on the presentation and physical examination, which of the following is the proper diagnosis?

(A) Aortic regurgitation
(B) Mitral regurgitation
(C) Mitral valve prolapse
(D) Pulmonic stenosis
(E) Tricuspid regurgitation

356. Which of the following medical treatments is appropriate for maintenance therapy of pernicious anemia?

(A) Erythropoeitin
(B) Ferrous sulfate
(C) Folic acid
(D) Vitamin B12
(E) Vitamin D

357. A 24-year-old male presents with heart palpitations, dizziness, and shortness of breath. The patient's electrocardiogram is illustrated below. Which of the following is the proper treatment for the abnormal rhythm shown on the electrocardiogram?

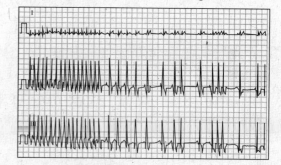

(A) Cardiac ablation
(B) Cardioversion
(C) Electrical defibrillation
(D) Intravenous adenosine
(E) Intravenous lidocaine

358. A 38-year-old male presents with upset stomach, indigestion, and abdominal pain. You suspect gastritis due to the presence of *Helicobacter pylori* bacteria. Which of the following diagnostic exams would you perform to confirm the presence of *H. pylori*?

(A) Barium swallow
(B) Endoscopy
(C) Gastric emptying study
(D) Urea breath test
(E) Stomach acid pH test

359. Which of the following laboratory values are indicative of a nonseminomatous germ cell testicular tumor?

(A) Elevated a-fetoprotein and a-human chorionic gonadotropin
(B) Elevated a-fetoprotein and decreased a-human chorionic gonadotropin
(C) Elevated carcinoembryonic antigen
(D) Normal levels of a-fetoprotein and a-human chorionic gonadotropin
(E) Normal levels of carcinoembryonic antigen

360. A 52-year-old female presents with pain in the throat area radiating to the ears and difficulty eating. Physical exam reveals an enlarged thyroid gland, low-grade fever, and fatigue. Bloodwork reveals elevated thyroid stimulating hormone levels. Radioactive iodine thyroid uptake was normal. Based on the patient's presentation, physical examination, and test results, which of the following is the most likely diagnosis?

(A) De Quervain's thyroiditis
(B) Hashimoto's thyroiditis
(C) Postpartum thyroiditis
(D) Suppurative thyroiditis
(E) Subacute lymphocytic thyroiditis

ANSWER KEY AND EXPLANATIONS

1. D	37. A	73. B	109. D	145. B
2. C	38. B	74. A	110. D	146. B
3. D	39. D	75. D	111. B	147. D
4. A	40. A	76. D	112. D	148. D
5. B	41. B	77. D	113. B	149. C
6. A	42. D	78. D	114. E	150. B
7. C	43. D	79. B	115. A	151. D
8. C	44. A	80. D	116. E	152. C
9. B	45. D	81. B	117. C	153. B
10. C	46. D	82. A	118. C	154. A
11. C	47. E	83. A	119. E	155. E
12. C	48. B	84. B	120. E	156. B
13. D	49. B	85. C	121. C	157. B
14. D	50. C	86. C	122. E	158. A
15. C	51. B	87. E	123. A	159. C
16. B	52. C	88. A	124. B	160. E
17. E	53. C	89. B	125. D	161. D
18. A	54. B	90. D	126. C	162. C
19. C	55. A	91. A	127. B	163. C
20. A	56. D	92. A	128. C	164. A
21. C	57. D	93. C	129. D	165. C
22. C	58. E	94. A	130. B	166. A
23. A	59. B	95. A	131. B	167. B
24. D	60. A	96. B	132. B	168. C
25. C	61. D	97. D	133. C	169. D
26. C	62. D	98. C	134. B	170. D
27. C	63. B	99. C	135. B	171. D
28. B	64. C	100. D	136. D	172. C
29. B	65. B	101. A	137. A	173. D
30. D	66. B	102. A	138. D	174. A
31. B	67. C	103. A	139. B	175. E
32. C	68. C	104. C	140. A	176. A
33. B	69. B	105. C	141. D	177. E
34. B	70. A	106. E	142. D	178. C
35. A	71. B	107. C	143. E	179. A
36. B	72. D	108. C	144. B	180. B

181. E	217. A	253. A	289. B	325. D
182. A	218. E	254. E	290. A	326. E
183. C	219. E	255. D	291. A	327. B
184. D	220. D	256. D	292. E	328. A
185. D	221. A	257. A	293. A	329. A
186. E	222. D	258. C	294. A	330. D
187. C	223. C	259. B	295. D	331. E
188. B	224. B	260. A	296. B	332. D
189. B	225. E	261. C	297. B	333. C
190. D	226. B	262. C	298. D	334. B
191. D	227. A	263. A	299. D	335. A
192. D	228. E	264. C	300. E	336. C
193. C	229. D	265. E	301. D	337. B
194. B	230. D	266. E	302. D	338. B
195. A	231. A	267. E	303. D	339. B
196. E	232. C	268. C	304. A	340. A
197. E	233. E	269. B	305. C	341. C
198. C	234. A	270. B	306. B	342. B
199. A	235. A	271. D	307. C	343. A
200. D	236. D	272. E	308. C	344. B
201. B	237. D	273. D	309. A	345. E
202. B	238. A	274. E	310. E	346. D
203. C	239. A	275. A	311. C	347. D
204. D	240. C	276. B	312. D	348. A
205. D	241. C	277. C	313. C	349. E
206. C	242. D	278. A	314. D	350. D
207. E	243. E	279. D	315. C	351. E
208. E	244. A	280. C	316. D	352. A
209. E	245. B	281. B	317. B	353. B
210. B	246. B	282. B	318. A	354. A
211. C	247. E	283. C	319. A	355. D
212. E	248. D	284. E	320. B	356. D
213. A	249. E	285. C	321. E	357. D
214. C	250. C	286. B	322. A	358. D
215. D	251. A	287. D	323. A	359. A
216. B	252. D	288. D	324. D	360. E

1. **The correct answer is (D).** Pulmonary embolism is the primary concern in this situation due to the elevated d-dimer, low pulse oximetry reading, and relatively normal electrocardiogram. A lung ventilation and perfusion study is the appropriate choice to rule out pulmonary embolism because it involves no contrast to be administered to the patient. The normal troponin level and relatively normal electrocardiogram should rule out a cardiac emergency. The elevated BUN and creatinine levels, along with depressed GFR, contraindicate the use of contrast because it may cause kidney failure.

2. **The correct answer is (C).** The physical act of yawning or swallowing can auto-inflate the auditory tube and equalize pressure in response to rapid changes in altitude. Equalizing pressure in the inner ear is critical because increased pressure can lead to rupture of the tympanic membrane.

3. **The correct answer is (D).** The patient's abnormal electrocardiogram with ST segment elevation indicates the patient is experiencing an acute myocardial infarction. Coronary angiography is the appropriate choice because the performing cardiologist can place a stent during the procedure to prevent permanent coronary damage. Coronary angiography is the best choice because it is the quickest, most effective way to diagnose and treat the patient.

4. **The correct answer is (A).** Addison's disease is a disorder characterized by weight loss, muscle weakness, fatigue, and darkening of the skin, and can also cause low blood pressure. The disorder is caused by the inability of adrenal glands to produce sufficient amounts of cortical hormones.

5. **The correct answer is (B).** A Water's view X-ray is routinely ordered for the diagnosis of sinusitis. Positive X-rays for this disorder will reveal opacities in the sinus area. A CT scan may also be required for further evaluation of this disorder.

6. **The correct answer is (A).** Multiple myeloma is a malignancy of plasma cells, possibly caused by exposure to the herpes virus. This disorder primarily occurs in individuals around 65 years of age. Patients with multiple myeloma can present with anemia, pain in the back or ribs, and recurrent infections.

7. **The correct answer is (C).** When a patient presents with chemical burns to the eyes, either acid or alkali, the eyes should immediately be irrigated with water or saline solution for a period of 30 minutes.

8. **The correct answer is (C).** Brugada syndrome is a genetic disorder most common among men of Asian descent. The rhythm on the patient's electrocardiogram is ventricular tachycardia.

9. **The correct answer is (B).** Due to the emergent nature of a tension pneumothorax, if this is confirmed or even suspected, a large bore needle should be inserted directly into the chest in order to release the accumulation of air in the pleural space. After this has been performed, a chest tube should then be inserted.

10. **The correct answer is (C).** Stasis dermatitis is a skin irritation of the lower legs caused by circulatory problems and congestion of leg veins. This condition is characterized by light brown or purplish-red discoloration of the lower legs due to back up of blood in the lower extremities. Individuals with varicose veins are particularly susceptible to this disorder.

11. **The correct answer is (C).** Fluoroquinolone medications, such as norfloxacin, are antibiotic medications commonly used as a first line of defense against infections of the urinary tract and prostate.

12. **The correct answer is (C).** Serotonin is a neurotransmitter that regulates mood, sleep and appetite. Serotonin modulating medications, such as fluoxetine and clomipramine, have been proven effective for the majority of patients who suffer from body morphic disorder.

13. **The correct answer is (D).** Alpha-glucosidase inhibitors, such as acarbose and miglitol, delay absorption of carbohydrates from the intestine, thus lowering blood glucose levels. GI symptoms are often side effects of these medications.

14. **The correct answer is (D).** While patients are hospitalized after a cardiogenic transient ischemic attack, anticoagulation is required with intravenous heparin. A long-term, maintenance regimen is obtained through the use of warfarin.

15. **The correct answer is (C).** A form of orthostatic hypertension occurs in young people when they are active or standing for long periods of time. The body responds with a drop in heart rate and blood pressure causing dizziness, nausea, and sometimes fainting.

16. **The correct answer is (B).** Acute respiratory syndrome is most likely caused by sepsis, multiple trauma, or aspiration of stomach contents. This disorder is characterized by rapid onset of profound dyspnea, tachypnea, frothy pink or red sputum, and diffuse crackles. Many patients with this disorder also present with cyanosis. A chest X-ray may initially be normal; however, most patients develop peripheral infiltrates with air bronchograms.

17. **The correct answer is (E).** Surgical revascularization is the only treatment option for chronic mesenteric ischemia and acute mesenteric ischemia. For both of these disorders, patients will generally be over the age of 50 and have other signs of cardiovascular or collagen vascular disease.

18. **The correct answer is (A).** Dyshidrotic eczema is characterized by severe itching on the palms of the hands and sometimes the soles of the feet. This disorder is also characterized by clear, deep blisters that itch and burn, and is sometimes referred to as a tapioca-like rash.

19. **The correct answer is (C).** The object should not be removed from the eye. Arrange for the patient to be transported to the nearest emergency room for a consult with an opthalmologist, who can arrange for removal with minimal lasting damage to the eye. Choices A, D, and E are incorrect because removing the object has the potential to cause further damage to the eye and risks vision loss. Choice B is incorrect because a penetrating trauma to the eye is considered emergent and should be treated immediately in an emergency room by a qualified opthalmologist.

20. **The correct answer is (A).** Individuals with Wolff-Parkinson-White syndrome are born with an extra connection in the heart called an accessory pathway, which allows electrical signals of the heart to bypass the AV node and move from the atria to the ventricles much more rapidly. Wolff-Parkinson-White syndrome is detectable on an electrocardiogram by the presence of a delta wave in the QRS complex.

21. **The correct answer is (C).** Restrictive cardiomyopathy results from fibrosis of the ventricular wall most commonly due to amyloidosis, radiation, and diabetes. Patients usually present with reduced exercise capacity and possibly right-sided congestive heart failure. Chest X-ray shows mildly enlarged cardiac silhouette. Echocardiogram reveals mildly reduced left ventricular function.

22. **The correct answer is (C).** Felbamate, marketed under the name Felbatol, is an anti-convulsant used in children and adults with epilepsy whose seizures have not improved with other treatments. This medication has serious side effects, such as aplastic anemia and hepatic failure.

23. **The correct answer is (A).** ACE inhibitors are the proper medical treatment for chronic kidney disease. These medications offer protection for the kidneys and are effective at slowing the progression of chronic kidney disease.

24. **The correct answer is (D).** A boxer's fracture is a fracture of the metacarpal neck of the fourth or fifth finger. Examination reveals loss of prominence of the knuckle with tenderness and pain. Puncture wounds may be evident if the fist came into contact with another person's mouth.

25. **The correct answer is (C).** Polycythemia vera is classically diagnosed with splenomegaly, normal arterial oxygen saturation, and elevated red cell mass. Patients with this disorder may present with headache, dizziness, weakness, fatigue, tinnitus, and blurred vision. Physical examination will reveal plethora, systolic hypertension, engorged retinal veins, and splenomegaly.

26. **The correct answer is (C).** If puncture wounds are present as a result of a patient's fist coming into contact with another person's mouth, antibiotics should be prescribed to avoid infection in the puncture wounds. *Eikenella carrodens* is an organism specific to the human mouth that can promote infection if it comes into contact with an open wound.

27. **The correct answer is (C).** Conversion disorder is defined as a complaint of one or more neurologic symptoms that cannot be explained clinically.

The most common symptoms of this disorder is blindness, paralysis, inability to speak, and tingling in the extremities. Patients with this disorder may display indifference and lack of concern for their symptoms.

28. **The correct answer is (B).** Micturition syncope is a temporary drop in blood pressure that occurs during urination. This condition usually occurs in elderly people. Orthostatic hypertension would occur following urination when going from sitting to standing position. Septicemia would be a consideration if the patient had an elevated white blood cell count. A vasovagal reaction is associated with fear, anxiety, or digestive tract stress.

29. **The correct answer is (B).** Fever of greater than 100.4°F, tender anterior cervical adenopathy, lack of cough, and pharyngotonsillar exudates are the critera for diagnosis of streptococcal pharyngitis. Presence of 3 of the 4 criteria is highly suggestive of streptococcal pharyngitis. Presence of 2 of the 4 criteria indicates a need for a culture. Presence of 1 of the 4 criteria makes streptococcal pharyngitis highly unlikely.

30. **The correct answer is (D).** The only curative treatment for a pilonidal cyst is surgical drainage. The surgical drainage may be supplemented with antibiotics to ensure complete, uncomplicated resolution of the disorder.

31. **The correct answer is (B)**. Rovsing's sign is a medical sign that indicates acute appendicitis. It occurs when pressure on the left lower quadrant of the abdomen causes pain in the right lower quadrant of the abdomen.

32. **The correct answer is (C).** Prinzmetal's angina is defined as angina, or chest pain, that occurs only at rest. This disorder is caused by vasospasm of the coronary arteries, leading to significant constriction of the vessels and causing chest discomfort. Once the spasm ceases, the arteries return to normal and the chest pain subsides. The patient's exercise capacity will remain intact and cardiac stress testing will be normal.

33. **The correct answer is (B).** Individuals with seasonal affective disorder usually experience lethargy, depression, and loss of interest, with onset of symptoms primarily occurring in the fall and winter months. This disorder is caused by the lessening of daylight hours and usually goes into remission in the spring.

34. **The correct answer is (B).** Slipped capital femoral epiphysis, or SCFE, is a weakening of the epiphyseal plate of the femur, resulting in displacement of the femoral head. This disorder occurs primarily in boys ages 10-16. Patients will present with pain in the hip, thigh, or knee associated with a painful limp. X-rays will reveal posterior and medial displacement of the epiphysis.

35. **The correct answer is (A).** Scopolamine is the required medication for treatment of severe vertigo or severe motion sickness. Scopolamine is most often administered via transdermal patch, which releases a dose of 330 micrograms per day.

36. **The correct answer is (B).** Hyperkalemia refers to an elevated level of potassium in the blood. Blood potassium levels greater than 6 mEq/L can cause changes in the electrocardiogram. An electrocardiogram in patients with hyperkalemia can reveal peaking T-waves, flattened P-waves, prolonged PR interval, and widening of the QRS complexes.

37. **The correct answer is (A).** Acute bronchitis presents with cough (with or without sputum), shortness of breath, fever, sore throat, headache, and body aches. Acute epiglottitis may be eliminated from consideration by the lack of characteristic sudden fever, sore throat, and muffled voice. Tuberculosis may be ruled out by the absence of anorexia, weight loss, and hemoptysis. Pulmonary edema due to contusion may be ruled out based on lack of trauma in medical history. Pneumonia and pulmonary edema should be ruled out due to the negative chest X-ray.

38. **The correct answer is (B).** Bronchiectasis is characterized by chronic purulent sputum that is often foul-smelling, hemoptysis, chronic cough, and recurrent pneumonia. Asthma and COPD may be ruled out by the presence of foul-smelling sputum and hemoptysis. The age of the patient rules out cystic fibrosis, which is diagnosed in childhood or adolescence. Tuberculosis may be ruled out by the absence of anorexia and weight loss.

39. **The correct answer is (D).** MRI of the hips is the study of choice for early detection of aseptic necrosis. X-ray results may appear normal early in the disease. A nuclear medicine bone scan may be of some use; however, MRI is much more sensitive for this disorder.

40. **The correct answer is (A).** Computerized tomography, commonly known as CT scanning, is the recommended imaging modality to use during the acute phase in order to differentiate between ischemic and hemorrhagic strokes.

41. **The correct answer is (B).** Aortic stenosis is characterized by chest pain, shortness of breath, and even sudden death. Fluid in the lungs may accompany aortic stenosis if the condition is severe enough to cause heart failure. Classic echocardiogram of aortic stenosis reveals a calcified, poorly functioning aortic valve.

42. **The correct answer is (D).** A pneumothorax is characterized by acute onset of chest pain and shortness of breath. Physical exam can show one-sided chest expansion, hyperresonance, and decreased breath sounds. This differs from a tension pneumothorax, which is characterized by a mediastinal shift to the opposite side.

43. **The correct answer is (D).** Hyperparathyroidism is characterized by generalized weakness, body aches, nausea, loss of appetite, and increased thirst along with an elevated serum calcium level. The parathyroid glands produce parathyroid hormone (PTH), which regulate calcium levels in the body. Overfunctioning parathyroid glands lead to elevated serum calcium levels.

44. **The correct answer is (A).** Water, caffeine, and salt will all cause blood pressure to elevate and reduce the effects of orthostatic hypotension. Beta blockers are effective in treating hypertension and can cause already low blood pressure to become dangerously low. ACE inhibitors are also effective in treating hypertension and can also cause an already decreased blood pressure to become dangerously low. Exercise is not an effective treatment for orthostatic hypotension. The proper treatment for this condition is to increase fluids, caffeine, and salts.

45. **The correct answer is (D).** For individuals with pyogenic granulomas, excision is the only successful course of treatment. Cryosurgery and cauterization have not been proven effective for this disorder.

46. **The correct answer is (D).** Mastoiditis can result from an inner ear infection (otitis media) that is inadequately treated or unresponsive to treatment. Mastoiditis is an infection of the mastoid bone of the skull and can cause drainage from the ear, spiking temperatures, ear pain, redness behind the ear, and swelling around the ear.

47. **The correct answer is (E).** Acute myocardial infarction is classically diagnosed with S-T segment elevation recorded on an electrocardiogram. Emergency treatment must be initiated when S-T elevation is discovered, as irreversible cardiac damage may occur if this condition is not resolved immediately.

48. **The correct answer is (B).** Glyburide, as well as glipizide and glimepiride, belong to a class of medications called sulfonylureas. Sulfonylureas stimulate insulin secretion, and are among the most commonly used anti-diabetic medications. This class of medications has very few drug interactions. Side effects are weight gain and increased risk of hypoglycemia.

49. **The correct answer is (B).** Gastroesophageal reflux disease, otherwise referred to as GERD, is characterized by heartburn, regurgitation, and dysphagia. Other symptoms could include hoarseness, halitosis, cough, hiccups, and chest pain. Classic diagnosis of GERD is made if symptoms are relieved with antacids. If patient presents with chest pain, an electrocardiogram is warranted to rule out any potential cardiac abnormality.

50. **The correct answer is (C).** COPD is characterized by progressive shortness of breath and excessive cough with sputum production. Auscultation of the chest should reveal decreased breath sounds, early inspiratory crackles, and prolonged expiration. Chest X-ray should reveal hyperinflation and flat diaphragm.

51. **The correct answer is (B).** Tolterodine is a member of a class of medications called antimuscarinics. Tolterodine is effective in preventing unwanted

bladder contractions and alleviating urinary difficulties such as frequency of urination and inability to control urine.

52. **The correct answer is (C).** Chronic thrombocytopenia will rarely resolve spontaneously like the acute version of thrombocytopenia. It is classically treated with high doses of prednisone.

53. **The correct answer is (C).** An enchondroma of the proximal phalanx is a cartilaginous tumor and the most common primary benign bone neoplasm of the hand. Enchondroma is often asymptomatic unless complicated by a pathologic fracture.

54. **The correct answer is (B).** Pneumocystis pneumonia is the most common infection occurring in HIV-positive patients. CD4 counts less than 200 cells/mL are typical with this disorder. Patients may present with fever, tachypnea, dyspnea, and a non-productive cough. Chest X-ray will typically show diffuse or perihilar infiltrates, but no pleural effusions. Bloodwork will show lymphopenia and low CD4 count.

55. **The correct answer is (A).** A total hysterectomy combined with bilateral salpingo-oopherectomy is the indicated treatment for endometrial cancer. Recurrence of endometrial cancer may be treated with high-dose progestins or anti-estrogens.

56. **The correct answer is (D).** Disease of the heart valves can cause all of the symptoms the patient is exhibiting: chest pressure, dizziness, shortness of breath, and heart palpitations. CT scan to rule out pulmonary embolism is unnecessary because the normal d-dimer level makes pulmonary embolism unlikely. Myocardial perfusion imaging is also not optimal because a normal EKG in the presence of symptoms makes cardiac ischemia unlikely. Cardiac catheterization is an invasive procedure that is not required in this patient because of a normal EKG. A stress test is not indicated, as it could aggravate symptoms.

57. **The correct answer is (D).** To avoid transmission of pediculosis, or lice, one must avoid sharing contact items such as hats, hairbrushes, and combs. If transmission is suspected, all shared items should be examined for infestation.

58. **The correct answer is (E).** When the condition of mastoiditis is unresponsive to treatment with antibiotics, mastoidectomy is the indicated course of treatment. Mastoidectomy is defined as surgical removal of all or part of the mastoid bone. This procedure will allow for proper drainage of the affected area and resolution of symptoms.

59. **The correct answer is (B).** Atrial flutter is characterized by a normal, regular ventricular response. The atrium will contract at regular intervals also, but much more rapidly than the ventricles. The ratio of atrial contractions to ventricular contractions can be 2:1, 3:1, or greater. Atrial flutter is easily recognized due to the classic "sawtooth" appearance of the atrial activity.

60. **The correct answer is (A).** Metformin is effective because it reduces hepatic glucose production. It effectively lowers blood glucose levels without risk of hypoglycemia. This medication is also effective in promoting weight loss and lowering triglycerides.

61. **The correct answer is (D).** A right-heart cardiac catheterization is the diagnostic study that is most useful and offers the most precise hemodynamic monitoring for evaluation of pulmonary arterial pressures. Echocardiography can also be useful in order to estimate pulmonary arterial pressures.

62. **The correct answer is (D).** Cystic fibrosis is characterized by cough, excess sputum, sinus pain, nasal discharge, diarrhea, and abdominal pain. Steatorrhea and decreased exercise tolerance may also be presented. Physical exam can reveal clubbing, apical crackles, and increased anteroposterior chest diameter. CT scan can reveal bronchiectasis. Chest X-ray can reveal hyperinflation, mucous plugging, peribronchial cuffing, focal atelectasis, or pneumothorax.

63. **The correct answer is (B).** Shigellosis, more commonly known as dysentery, is a food-borne illness caused by the infection of bacteria from the genus Shigella. Patients may present with diarrhea, abdominal cramps, tenesmus, fever, chills, headache, anorexia, and malaise. Stools will be loose and mixed with blood and mucous. Stool samples will be positive for leukocytes and erythrocytes. Sigmoidoscopy will reveal inflamed engorged mucosa, punctate, lesions, or ulcers.

64. **The correct answer is (C).** Psoriatic arthritis is an inflammatory arthritis with skin involvement. This disorder resembles rheumatoid arthritis;

however, rheumatoid factor will be normal. The pencil-in-cup deformity on X-ray is characteristic of psoriatic arthritis.

65. **The correct answer is (B).** *Klebsiella pneumoniae* is a Gram-negative, non-motile, rod-shaped bacterium that is an uncommon cause of pneumonia. However, prolonged abuse of alcohol will suppress the immune system and allow *K. pneumoniae* to colonize and cause pneumonia.

66. **The correct answer is (B).** Adenomyosis is the extension of the endometrial glands into the uterine musculature. This disorder has not been proven to be related to endometriosis. Adenomyosis is asymptomatic in many patients. Patients with this disorder may experience severe secondary dysmenorrhea.

67. **The correct answer is (C).** A "swishing" sound upon auscultation of the heart is a classic signal of mitral valve prolapse. An echocardiogram is the easiest, non-invasive method to evaluate the function of the heart valves.

68. **The correct answer is (C).** The most effective method to avoid the occurrence of decubitus ulcers in nursing home patients is to reposition, or turn, the patients periodically throughout the day. This method will eliminate prolonged pressure and friction on the same areas of the body, which will inhibit the formation of decubitus ulcers. Meticulous hygiene and proper nutrition can also help.

69. **The correct answer is (B).** Orbital cellulitis is more common in children than in adults, with a median age between 7 and 12 years. Patients with this disorder may present with ptosis, eyelid edema, exopthalmos, purulent discharge, and conjunctivitis. Physical examination will reveal fever, decreased range of motion of the eye muscles, and sluggish pupillary response. CT scan will reveal broad infiltration of the orbital soft tissue.

70. **The correct answer is (A).** Croup is classically diagnosed by the presence of the steeple sign on a posteroanterior neck radiograph. The steeple sign is due to subglottic narrowing associated with croup.

71. **The correct answer is (B).** The basilar and vertebral arteries are responsible for perfusion of the posterior aspect of the brain. These arteries supply the brain stem, cerebellum, thalamus, and portions of the occipital and temporal lobes. Strokes occurring in these vessels are commonly associated with evidence of brain stem dysfunction such as coma, drop attacks, vertigo, nausea, vomiting, and ataxia.

72. **The correct answer is (D).** Placenta previa is a condition in which the placenta partially or completely covers the cervical os. Patients normally present with painless vaginal bleeding and diagnosis is usually made within the first 20 weeks of gestation through a routine ultrasound examination.

73. **The correct answer is (B).** Individuals who are prescribed monoamine oxidase inhibitors are required to adopt a tyramine-free diet to avoid major side effects, such as a hypertensive crisis. Some common foods that contain tyamine include wine, beer, nearly all cheeses, aged foods, and smoked meats.

74. **The correct answer is (A).** Nitrates are a common initial treatment for chest pain. Nitrates can be administered in a variety of methods including patches, sprays, and tablets. This type of medication acts to relax the coronary arteries and alleviate chest pain.

75. **The correct answer is (D).** Perintonsillar cellulitis is characterized by severe sore throat, pain when swallowing and opening mouth widely, and muffled voice. Physical examination should reveal deviation of the soft palate and uvula.

76. **The correct answer is (D).** Acute myologenous leukemia is the primary form of acute leukemia found in adults. This disorder is classically diagnosed with bloodwork revealing decreased white cells, decreased red cells, and 22% blasts. Urinalysis reveals hyperuricemia. Patients with this disorder can present with bleeding from the gums, epistaxis, menorrhagia, lethargy, and shortness of breath.

77. **The correct answer is (D).** Precordial catch syndrome (PCS), or Texidor's twinge, is one of the most common causes of chest pain in adolescents. PCS manifests as a sudden, sharp pain localized to the left, anterior chest, typically near the lower ribs. The pain usually resolves completely in under a minute, or in a few minutes, although in rare cases

it may last up to 30 minutes. In some patients, the pain is resolved by a physical action, such as a sharp inhalation or exhalation, which is accompanied by a popping or cracking sensation in the chest. PCS can persist into young adulthood. The exact cause of PCS is unknown, but patients should be reassured that there is no cardiac involvement.

78. **The correct answer is (D).** Rabies is caused by transmission of the rhabdovirus from infected saliva via an animal bite or an open wound. An animal bite may or may not be present. Most common animals that transmit rabies are dogs, bats, skunks, foxes, raccoons, and coyotes. If an animal bite is present, patients may experience pain and paresthesia at the site and the skin may be sensitive to changes in temperature. Hydrophobia associated with painful spasms while drinking water may also be presented.

79. **The correct answer is (B).** Pulmonary hypertension occurs when pulmonary arterial pressure is too high for the cardiac output. Patients with this disorder will experience dyspnea, retrosternal chest pain similar to angina, weakness, fatigue, edema, ascites, cyanosis, and syncope. Auscultation of the chest will reveal narrow splitting and accentuation of the second heart sound and a systolic ejection click. A chest X-ray can reveal enlarged pulmonary arteries.

80. **The correct answer is (D).** Supraventricular tachycardia appears as rapid sinus rhythm without the presence of p-waves. Supraventricular tachycardia can cause symptoms such as shortness of breath, dizziness, and chest pressure.

81. **The correct answer is (B).** Hordeolum, commonly known as a sty, is characterized by acute onset of pain and swelling in the affected eye. In addition, there is a palpable, indurate area with a central area of purulence and surrounding redness.

82. **The correct answer is (A).** Although many patients with sarcoidosis require no treatment at all, the gold standard for treatment of sarcoidoisis symptoms is corticosteroids. Corticosteroids are effective at controlling inflammation associated with sarcoidosis as well as controlling granuloma formation, which may also occur with this disorder.

83. **The correct answer is (A).** Zollinger-Ellison syndrome is characterized by a gastrin-secreting tumor called a gastrinoma, and causes hypergastrinemia which results in a resistant form of peptic ulcer disease. A patient may present with the same symptoms as peptic ulcer disease, including abdominal pain that feels like a burning or gnawing, belching, bloating, heartburn, nausea, and black tarry stools. A fasting gastrin level greater than 150 pg/mL indicates hypergastrinemia. Endoscopy is useful in localizing the tumor.

84. **The correct answer is (B).** Rickets is a disease of defective bone mineralization that occurs in children. Children can present with skull deformity and rib-breastbone joint enlargement and may have developmental issues such as delays in sitting, walking, and crawling. Bloodwork will reveal decreased calcium and vitamin D. X-rays can reveal flattened skull, bowing of long bones, and dorsal kyphosis.

85. **The correct answer is (C).** Patients with community acquired pneumonia will present with a one- to ten-day history of cough, purulent sputum, dyspnea, chest pain, fever, chills, and sweats. Auscultation of the chest will reveal altered breath sounds or crackles, dullness to percussion if there is an effusion, or bronchial breath sounds over an area of consolidation. Specific causative organisms can be derived by conventional stain or sputum culture. Chest X-ray will reveal lobar or segmental infiltrates, air bronchograms, and pleural effusions.

86. **The correct answer is (C).** Alteplase is a form of thrombolytic therapy known as recombinant tissue plasminogen activator. Recombinant tissue plasminogen activator is a protein involved in the breakdown of blood clots. Types of recombinant tissue plasminogen activators include alteplase, reteplase, and tenecteplase. Alteplase is the indicated treatment of acute ischemic strokes, whereas reteplase is indicated for acute myocardial infarction.

87. **The correct answer is (E).** Koebner's phenomenon is associated with the skin disorder of psoriasis. Also referred to as isomorphic response, it is seen as the induction of new skin lesions following local trauma or injury to the skin.

88. The correct answer is (A). Short-term pharmacotherapy is indicated for treatment of adjustment disorder when this condition is associated with insomnia, anxiety, and depression. Adjustment disorders without these particular symptoms are treated with supportive psychotherapy or group therapy.

89. The correct answer is (B). Patients with ankylosing spondylitis are commonly under the age of 40 and present with back pain that is worse in the morning and resolves with exercise. Periods of inactivity will make pain worse. Classic radiographic sign of ankylosing spondylitis is a "bamboo" appearance of the vertebral spine and sacroiliac region.

90. The correct answer is (D). Ischemic heart disease is classically diagnosed with associated S-T segment depression. During cardiac stress testing, S-T depression of greater than 1mm is often a sign of ischemic heart disease.

91. The correct answer is (A). Blepharitis is characterized by itchy eyelids, burning eyes, and light sensitivity. It is also characterized by red eyelid margins, swollen eyelids, frothy tears, and crusting of the eyelashes. Cataracts is incorrect because this disorder is a clouding of the lens of the eye and vision is adversely affected. Glaucoma is incorrect because this disorder involves a disease of the optic nerve that negatively affects vision. Chalazion and hordeola are incorrect because they are characterized by a lump on the eyelid, not itching and redness. Blepharitis is the most accurate diagnosis in this instance.

92. The correct answer is (A). For pregnant women who develop severe preeclampsia or eclampsia, prompt, emergency delivery of the baby is indicated regardless of gestational age.

93. The correct answer is (C). Mitral regurgitation is the most common valvular abnormality, characterized by abnormal leaking of blood from the left ventricle, through the mitral valve, and into the left atrium. Auscultation of the chest will reveal a pancystolic murmur, decreased S2 sound, prolonged apical impulse with radiation to the left axilla. Chest X-ray reveals atrial enlargement.

94. The correct answer is (A). On a standard electrocardiogram, leads II, III, and aVF represent the inferior wall of the heart muscle. Any electrocardiographic abnormalities seen in these leads correspond to the area of the heart that is affected. For example, S-T elevation in lead III indicates a myocardial infarction currently occurring in the inferior wall of the heart.

95. The correct answer is (A). Stroke therapy with recombinant tissue plasminogen activator is most effective when administered within 3 hours after the initial onset of symptoms. Complications associated with this type of medication include an increased risk of bleeding. This type of medication is contraindicated in patients with suspicion of intracranial bleeding, recent intracranial surgery, serious head trauma, or previous stroke.

96. The correct answer is (B). Daily use of sunscreens is indicated for treatment of skin that has lost pigmentation due to vitiligo. Depigmented skin is more susceptible to damage from the sun than skin with normal pigmentation. In addition, sun darkening of normal skin around areas of depigmented skin makes the appearance of vitiligo more pronounced.

97. The correct answer is (D). Reye's syndrome is defined as a fatty liver with encephalopathy. This disorder usually manifests 2-3 weeks after onset of influenza or varicella infection. Most common age of onset is between 5-14 years. Patients will present with vomiting, lethargy, jaundice, seizures, and altered mental status. Laboratory results will reveal increased liver enzymes, elevated ammonia levels, hypoglycemia, and prolonged prothrombin time.

98. The correct answer is (C). The indicated infertility intervention for anovulatory women to promote ovulation is the administration of 50 to 100 mg of clomiphene citrate for 5 days beginning on day 3, 4, or 5 of the menstrual cycle.

99. The correct answer is (C). For individuals who are diagnosed with conversion disorder, psychotherapy such as insight-oriented or behavioral therapy is the indicated first-line treatment. Other forms of treatment for this disorder would include hypnosis, anxiolytics, and relaxation therapy.

100. **The correct answer is (B).** Sjogren's syndrome is an autoimmune disorder that destroys the salivary and lacrimal glands. This disorder is often a complication from rheumatoid arthritis, polymyositis, or scleroderma. Dry mouth, dry eyes, and enlarged parotid glands are characteristic of this disorder.

101. **The correct answer is (A).** The polyvalent pneumococcal vaccine, commonly referred to as Pneumovax, contains antigens against 23 common strains of the pneumococcus. Studies have shown this vaccine to be 51% to 86% effective in reducing serious pneumococcal disease.

102. **The correct answer is (A).** Nosocomial pneumonia, otherwise known as hospital-acquired pneumonia, is caused by organisms that colonize ill patients, staff, and equipment. Signs and symptoms are similar to community acquired pneumonia, such as cough, sweats, fever, chest pain, and chills. Physical examination will reveal altered breath sounds, crackles, and bronchial breath sounds over an area of consolidation. Pneumonias caused by *Pseudomonas aeruginosa, Eschericia coli,* and *Enterobacter sp.* are seen only in hospital-acquired, nosocomial forms of pneumonia.

103. **The correct answer is (A).** A corneal abrasion can cause pain, sensations of a foreign body, tearing, photophobia, and blepharospasm. Corneal abrasion is normally caused by minor trauma from a fingernail, contact lens, eyelash, or other small foreign body.

104. **The correct answer is (C).** Shock is defined as severe cardiovascular failure caused by poor blood flow, inadequate distribution of blood flow, and inadequate oxygen delivery to the tissues. Shock can lead to multi-system organ failure or even death.

105. **The correct answer is (C).** Delayed gastric emptying is defined as alteration in gastric motility due to myopathic diseases of the smooth muscles or neurologic dysfunction. Patients will present with nausea and excessive fullness after meals. Adminstration of prokinetic medications can allow food to move through the stomach more rapidly. A nuclear medicine gastric emptying study can be used to confirm diagnosis.

106. **The correct answer is (E).** Urinalysis for proteinuria is the proper lab test when evaluating for kidney damage. Normal, healthy kidneys filter out proteins because they are usually too large to pass into the urine. If kidneys are damaged, the filters or glomeruli allow proteins to leak out of the blood and into the urine.

107. **The correct answer is (C).** Hemolyic anemia is classified by episodic or continuous red blood cell destruction. A classic sign of hemolytic anemia is the presence of an elevated reticulocyte count in the presence of a falling hematocrit level. A peripheral smear can show immature red cells, nucleated red cells, or morphologic changes of red cells.

108. **The correct answer is (C).** For treatment of hospital-acquired, or nosocomial, pneumonia, broad spectrum antibiotics such as cefipime, peperacillin, or meropenem are indicated until the causing organism is identified. Once the causative organism is identified, appropriate therapy based on the culture results can be initiated.

109. **The correct answer is (D).** Bloody cerebrospinal fluid is often observed in patients who have suffered a subarachnoid hemorrhage. Cerebrospinal fluid evaluation will reveal markedly elevated opening pressures and grossly bloody fluid.

110. **The correct answer is (D).** The Bacille Calmette-Guerin vaccine (BCG) can and should be administered to a tuberculin-negative person who is at a high risk for intense, prolonged exposure to untreated or improperly treated cases of tuberculosis.

111. **The correct answer is (B).** Pinguecula is characterized by a yellowish, fleshy mass on the conjunctiva adjacent to the cornea and can lead to painless inflammation. Pterygium is a vascular, triangular shaped mass that can interfere with vision, not a yellowish fleshy mass. Viral conjunctivitis can be ruled out due to the fact that this disorder is characterized by redness of the conjunctiva and watery discharge. Blepharitis can be ruled out based on lack of pain and redness. Bacterial conjunctivitis can be ruled out because it affects both eyes.

112. **The correct answer is (D).** Congestive heart failure is characterized by dyspnea and the abnormal retention of water and sodium. Patients may

experience exertional dyspnea, non-productive cough, and fatigue. Patients may also experience orthopnea, paroxysmal nocturnal dyspnea, and exercise intolerance. Chest X-ray should reveal cardiomegaly, bilateral pleural effusions, and perivascular or interstitial edema. Auscultation of the chest should reveal basilar rales and gallops. Symptoms and patient presentation may vary according to the side of the heart that is failing.

113. **The correct answer is (B).** Diarrhea is the gastro-intestinal disorder that is characterized by increased volume and frequency of stools. Diarrhea may be caused by infectious, toxic, or dietary agents. Typically, diarrhea is diagnosed after a period of 2-3 days of 3 or more liquid or semisolid stools per day.

114. **The correct answer is (E).** A surgical intervention called transurethral resection of the prostate is required for ultimate resolution of chronic, recurrent, and resistant prostatitis. Radiation therapy and hormone therapy have not been proven effective in reducing symptoms associated with this disorder.

115. **The correct answer is (A).** Cryoprecipitate is a frozen blood product that is prepared from plasma. Each unit of cryoprecipitate contains 250 mg of fibrinogen, which is essential for treatment of disseminated intravascular coagulopathy.

116. **The correct answer is (E).** Valproic acid is a common treatment for epilepsy and is the indicated drug of choice for generalized nonconvulsive seizures. This medication also serves as a mood stabilizer in disorders such as bipolar disorder and depression.

117. **The correct answer is (C).** A potassium hydroxide preparation, or KOH prep, is a microscopic examination of scrapings that are mounted on microscope slides containing potassium hydroxide and gently heated. Potassium hydroxide will dissolve keratin and cellular material, but will leave fungi intact.

118. **The correct answer is (C).** HELLP syndrome is defined as severe preeclampsia with the addition of hemolysis, elevated liver enzymes, and low platelets. HELLP syndrome is a life-threatening complication associated with pregnancy and it can even occur after childbirth. Patients may

present with headache, nausea, vomiting, band-like pressure around the abdomen, blurred vision, and tingling in the extremities.

119. **The correct answer is (E).** The patient's presentation of dull pain, swelling, redness, and tenderness of the left leg along with an elevated d-dimer level is classically suspicious for deep venous thrombosis. Ultrasonic venous Doppler study of the lower extremities is the logical diagnostic exam to perform.

120. **The correct answer is (E).** A scaphoid fracture presents with pain in the anatomic snuffbox associated with swelling and ecchymosis over the affected area. This fracture is commonly misdiagnosed as a sprain because X-rays may initially be negative.

121. **The correct answer is (C).** Bronchiolitis with the presence of respiratory syncytial virus (RSV) is an indication for treatment with ribavirin. A 3- to 7-day regimen of ribavirin has been proven to reduce mortality, length of hospitalization, and duration of mechanical ventilation for patients with RSV-induced bronchiolitis.

122. **The correct answer is (E).** Although the patient presents with lower leg erythema, swelling, tenderness, and shortness of breath, all of which are classic signs for deep venous thrombosis and pulmonary embolism, no further diagnostic studies are required because a d-dimer less than 500 ng/dL is sufficient to rule out thromboembolism.

123. **The correct answer is (A).** Esophageal atresia is commonly associated with tracheoesophageal fistulae. Infants with this disorder present with excessive saliva, choking, or coughing when attempts are made to feed. Failed attempts to insert a nasogastric tube for feedings will actually confirm the diagnosis of esophageal atresia.

124. **The correct answer is (B).** Ceftriaxone is recommended for gonorrhea and Chlamydia. The Centers for Disease Control and Prevention states that ceftriaxone administered in conjunction with doxycycline twice a day for 10 days is an effective regimen for epididymitis that occurs as a result of sexually transmitted diseases.

125. **The correct answer is (D).** Exenatide is effective in lowering blood glucose levels due to the fact

that it decreases gastric emptying, stimulating pancreatic insulin response to glucose and preventing glucagon release after meals. This medication must be injected.

126. **The correct answer is (C).** Desmopressin acetate is the most effective medication in the treatment Von Willebrand disease. This medication is usually used in conjunction with factor VIII concentrates for maximum benefit.

127. **The correct answer is (B).** Atypical community-acquired pneumonia typically presents with a low-grade fever and mild pulmonary symptoms occurring in young, otherwise healthy adults. Other common symptoms include non-productive cough, myalgia, and fatigue.

128. **The correct answer is (C).** Frontotemporal dementia presents similarly to Alzheimer's dementia except this disorder is characterized by degeneration of the frontal lobe of the brain, and may include the temporal lobe. Patients with this disorder may present with memory loss, abrupt mood swings, inability to function in social situations, lack of personal hygiene, and obsessive/compulsive behavior. Physical examination will reveal increased rigidity in the muscles and loss of coordination. MRI will reveal atrophy in the frontal lobe and/or anterior temporal lobe.

129. **The correct answer is (D).** Chronic venous insufficiency is characterized by loss of venous wall tension, which results in stasis of venous blood. This disorder is common in individuals with a history of deep venous thrombosis or varicose veins. Patients may present clinically with edema in the lower extremities, ulcers just above the ankle, itching and dull leg pain when standing, and shiny, thin, discolored skin on the lower extremities.

130. **The correct answer is (B).** Individuals suffering from anorexia nervosa have a distorted body image and an intense fear of becoming overweight, even though they may be underweight. Physical signs of this disorder include emaciation, orthostatic hypotension, bradycardia, hypothermia, and dry skin. Lab work can reveal leukopenia, hypochloremia, hypokalemia, elevated blood urea nitrogen, and metabolic acidosis.

131. **The correct answer is (B).** Rheumatoid arthritis

is commonly characterized by morning stiffness lasting for over an hour, arthritis and soft tissue swelling in 3 or more joints, and arthritis in the joints of the hand, all lasting for greater than 6 weeks. Bloodwork will reveal an elevated erythrocyte sedimentation rate and C-reactive protein level. In addition, bloodwork will be positive for rheumatoid factor and anti-CCP antibodies.

132. **The correct answer is (B).** For patients with chronic obstructive pulmonary disease (COPD), such as emphysema or chronic bronchitis, anticholinergic medications (such as ipratropium or tiotropium) are superior to beta-adrenergic agonists in achieving bronchodilation. Short-acting bronchodilators should be on hand to treat acute exacerbations of dyspnea.

133. **The correct answer is (C).** A Colles's fracture is a distal radius fracture with dorsal angulation. This type of fracture is the most common injury of the wrist, and results from a fall onto the dorsiflexed hand. Silver fork deformity on X-ray is characteristic of this type of fracture.

134. **The correct answer is (B).** Malignant melanoma usually presents as black or dark brown lesions, but can be flesh-colored with blue, pink, or red components. The lesions associated with malignant melanoma have an irregular border with outward spreading pigment. These lesions also change in size over a relatively short period of time.

135. **The correct answer is (B).** Gonorrhea is caused by *Neisseria gonorrheae*, which is a Gram-negative diplococcus bacterium transmitted during sexual activity. This disease manifests in men as painful urination and a serous or milky discharge that becomes yellow and tinged with blood over time. In females, gonorrhea presents with dysuria, increased urinary frequency and urgency, and a purulent urethral discharge. Physical exam reveals vaginitis and cervicitis.

136. **The correct answer is (B).** When evaluating causes of infertility among couples, a male semen analysis should precede all other testing. Normal results from a semen analysis can effectively eliminate most of the male factors associated with infertility.

137. **The correct answer is (A).** Individuals diagnosed with histrionic personality disorder exude a high

degree of attention-seeking behavior. They tend to be overly dramatic, emotional, seductive, and excitable. They become angry if they are not the center of attention, and they are unable to maintain long-term relationships. They also tend to be flamboyant and extroverted.

138. **The correct answer is (D).** Gout is a systemic disease of altered purine metabolism, resulting in sodium urate crystal precipitation into the synovial fluid. It most commonly presents as pain, swelling, redness, and tenderness in the great toe. However, other joints of the lower extremities can be affected. Joint fluid analysis will reveal rod-shaped, negatively birefringent urate crystals. Serum uric acid levels will be greater than 8 mg/dL.

139. **The correct answer is (B).** Bronchitis presents very similarly to pneumonia, as the patients will experience cough, shortness of breath, fever, and substernal discomfort. Auscultation of the chest will reveal expiratory rhonchi or wheezes. The chest X-ray will be normal for acute bronchitis.

140. **The correct answer is (A).** Peripheral arterial disease usually presents initially with intermittent claudication, or lower leg pain that is relieved by rest. As disease progresses, discomfort will occur at rest also. Auscultation of the legs will reveal weak or absent distal and femoral pulses. An aortic, iliac, or femoral bruit may also be noted. An ankle-brachial reflex of 0.9 or lower is an indication of significant peripheral artery disease. When erectile dysfunction occurs in individuals with disease of the iliac artery, this disorder is known as Leriche's syndrome.

141. **The correct answer is (D).** A polysomnogram, also known as a sleep study, is often used to monitor bodily functions during sleep. A polysomnogram assesses EEG activity, heart rate, respiratory movement, and oxygen saturation.

142. **The correct answer is (D).** Basal cell carcinoma is a slow growing form of skin cancer. Lesions predominantly appear on exposed areas of the face, head, and neck. Complete eradication of the lesions is the only course of treatment. Eradication can be achieved by excision with clear margins, electrodissection with curettage, cryosurgery, and radiation therapy.

143. **The correct answer is (E).** Ritodrine is a member of a class of medications called beta-2 adrenergic receptor agonists. Beta-mimetic adrenergic agents stimulate beta-adrenergic receptors to relax smooth muscle and decrease uterine contractions. Side effects of these medications include maternal and fetal tachycardia, emesis, headaches, and pulmonary edema.

144. **The correct answer is (B).** Giant cell arteritis must be ruled out. Polymyalgia rheumatica will often present with pain and stiffness in the neck, shoulder, and pelvis, along with fever, fatigue, and weight loss. Giant cell arteritis presents with similar symptoms and must be ruled out before confirming diagnosis of polymyalgia rheumatic. Normal lab values of C-reactive protein and liver enzymes should rule out giant cell arteritis.

145. **The correct answer is (B).** Labyrinthitis is commonly treated with meclizine. Promethazine or dimenhydrate may also be used. The underlying cause of labyrinthitis is unknown but it is believed to be caused by an otitis or viremia.

146. **The correct answer is (B).** Proton pump inhibitors are very effective and offer long-lasting reduction of gastric acid production. This group of medications is the most powerful treatment of gastroesophageal reflux disease. Proton pump inhibitors are used in treatment of moderate to severe disease, patients who are unresponsive to histamine blockers, and patients with evidence of erosive gastritis.

147. **The correct answer is (D).** Ciprofloxacin is a powerful antibiotic that is a member of the fluoroquinolone family of medications. For older men, epididymitis is generally caused by a bacterial infection rather than a sexually transmitted disease. Ciprofloxacin will effectively eliminate the bacteria causing the epididymitis.

148. **The correct answer is (D).** Individuals who are diagnosed with cauda equina syndrome should have immediate, emergent surgery to correct this condition. Cauda equina is considered a medical emergency because, if left untreated, permanent dysfunction of the bowels and bladder and paralysis of the lower extremities can result.

149. **The correct answer is (C).** For everyday maintenance therapy for chronic asthma, inhaled

corticosteroids provide the greatest anti-inflammatory result and allow for best management of this disorder. Beta-adrenergic agonists should be available as rescue medication as they provide greatest degree of bronchodilation during acute asthma attacks.

150. **The correct answer is (B).** Interferon-b is the medication primarily used to prevent relapses of moderate or severe attacks stemming from multiple sclerosis. Mild attacks are generally treated with daily subcutaneous injections of glatiramer acetate.

151. **The correct answer is (D).** DMARDs, short for disease-modifying anti-rheumatic drugs, are indicated immediately following the diagnosis of rheumatoid arthritis. These medications will slow the progression of rheumatoid arthritis, unlike NSAIDs, which treat inflammation but not the underlying disease. Methotrexate, Ciclosporin, Rituximab, and Sulfasalazine are all examples of disease-modifying anti-rheumatic drugs.

152. **The correct answer is (C).** Naloxone is the medication that is used to counteract the effects of an overdose of opiates, such as heroin or morphine. This medication is specifically used to counteract the life-threatening depression of the central nervous and respiratory systems associated with overdose of opiates.

153. **The correct answer is (B).** The pneumococcal conjugate vaccine, or PCV, is administered in a series of four doses and is recommended for children aged 6 weeks to 15 months. This vaccine is intended to protect infants and young children from disease caused by Streptococcus pneumonia.

154. **The correct answer is (A).** Bell's palsy is characterized by unilateral facial weakness without evidence of other neurological disorders. This disorder occurs on the right side 60% of the time. Paralysis can occur in the forehead and lower facial area, leaving the patient unable to close the eye, raise the brow, or smile on the affected side.

155. **The correct answer is (E).** Wilm's tumor, or nephroblastoma, is a renal cancer that typically occurs in children. Patients may present with anorexia, nausea, vomiting, fever, abdominal pain, or hematuria. Physical exam will reveal a palpable abdominal mass. Hypertension will also be evident due to elevated renin levels.

156. **The correct answer is (B).** The main cause of retinopathy among adults in the United States is diabetes. Controlling blood glucose levels is critical in preventing retinopathy from progressing. Patients with this disorder should have yearly dilated opthalmoscopic examinations.

157. **The correct answer is (B).** Esophageal varices are dilatations of the veins of the esophagus. Varices normally occur at the distal end of the esophagus and are caused by portal hypertension due to cirrhosis from alcoholism or chronic viral hepatitis. Diagnosis is made with the presence of hematamesis. Endoscopy can confirm presence of esophageal varices.

158. **The correct answer is (A).** Osteomalacia is a disease of defective bone mineralization similar to rickets that occurs in adults. Patients may present with muscle weakness in the pelvic girdle, generalized bone pain, and a history of several fractures. X-rays will reveal generalized decrease in bone density and Looser lines, which are characteristic of pseudofractures. Bloodwork will reveal vitamin D deficiency.

159. **The correct answer is (C).** Treatment with calcium channel blockers is indicated for patients diagnosed with primary pulmonary hypertension. Calcium channel blockers act to reduce the systemic arterial pressure. Other medical treatments may include chronic oral anticoagulant and a potent pulmonary vasodilator called prostacyclin.

160. **The correct answer is (E).** If masses associated with pterygium have progressed to the point that they are encroaching on the corneas and impeding vision, excision of the masses is the indicated course of treatment.

161. **The correct answer is (D).** Pneumonia classically presents with a 1- to 10-day history of cough, purulent sputum, tachycardia, shortness of breath, chest pain, fever, and sweats. Auscultation of the chest reveals altered breath sounds with crackles, dullness to percussion, and bronchial breath sounds over an area of consolidation.

162. **The correct answer is (C).** *Helicobacter pylori* is the Gram-negative, spiral-shaped bacillus that is responsible for most gastric ulcers and chronic gastritis. This type of bacteria can inhabit many

areas of the stomach, but is primarily found in the antrum.

163. **The correct answer is (C).** The pneumococcal polysaccharide vaccine is indicated for children 2-5 years of age who have not previously been immunized. This vaccine is also indicated for individuals over the age of 65 who have a chronic illness that increases the risk of community-acquired pneumonia.

164. **The correct answer is (A).** The intravenous administration of corticosteroids is indicated for patients to achieve maximum recovery from acute exacerbations of multiple sclerosis. High-dose intravenous corticosteroids are indicated if optic neuritis is associated with the exacerbation.

165. **The correct answer is (C).** Ergocalciferol is required at a dose of 50,000 units orally twice a week for 6-12 months, followed by 1,000 to 2,000 units daily, to treat the vitamin D deficiency that causes osteomalacia.

166. **The correct answer is (A).** Isoniazid, commonly referred to as INH, should be administered for a period of 6-12 months for prophylaxis in patients who have tested negative in the past, but have recently tested positive with known or unknown exposure to tuberculosis.

167. **The correct answer is (B).** Migraine headaches often present unilaterally with throbbing or pulsing discomfort. Migraine headaches occur more often in women than in men and often follow the menstrual cycle pattern. Patients who suffer from migraines can present with aura (visual changes), nausea, vomiting, photophobia, phonophobia, and anorexia.

168. **The correct answer is (C).** Nasal decongestants are critical to patients with blow-out fractures of the orbital floor. Decreasing nasal congestion decreases pressure in the nasal and sinus cavities, which will decrease pain associated with this injury. In addition, these medications will decrease the need for the patient to blow his/her nose, which can cause further damage from the injury.

169. **The correct answer is (D).** Hypovolemic shock is the result of conditions that result in a life-threatening loss of blood volume. This type of shock is commonly caused by hemorrhage, loss

of plasma, or loss of fluids and electrolytes. This type of shock can also be the result of "third space" sequestration.

170. **The correct answer is (D).** Tuberculosis classically presents as a cough that begins dry that progresses to productive, with or without hemoptysis. Other classic symptoms of tuberculosis include fever, night sweats, anorexia, weight loss, chest pain, and shortness of breath. Auscultation of the chest will reveal post-tussive rales.

171. **The correct answer is (D).** For incomplete fractures such as buckle fractures and greenstick fractures, surgical intervention is seldom required for proper healing of the injury. Immobilization of the affected area in a cast for a period of time of four to six weeks should be sufficient for proper healing of the injury.

172. **The correct answer is (C).** Cardiogenic shock is a type of shock that can arise from myocardial infarctions, arrythmias, heart failure, valvular abnormalities, myocarditis, cardiac contusions, and myocardiopathies. Shock can cause low blood pressure, tachycardia, orthostatic changes, and altered mental status.

173. **The correct answer is (D).** Excessive exposure to sunlight can predispose to cataract development and enhance progression of cataracts. Individuals who are concerned with cataract development should decrease their exposure to sunlight.

174. **The correct answer is (A).** A torus, or buckle, fracture occurs when one side of the cortex buckles as a result of a compression injury, like falling on an outstretched hand. This injury differs from a greenstick fracture by the mechanism of the injury and the fact that a buckle fracture can sometimes buckle on both sides of the bone.

175. **The correct answer is (E).** Obstructive shock is a type of shock that can arise from tension pnuemothorax, pericardial tamponade, and massive pulmonary embolism. Shock can cause low blood pressure, tachycardia, orthostatic changes, and altered mental status.

176. **The correct answer is (A).** For patients diagnosed with tinea versacolor, a monthly head-to-waist application of selenium sulfide shampoo is indicated to prevent re-growth of yeast on the skin. For

initial treatment of tinea versacolor, daily head-to-waist application of selenium sulfide shampoo is indicated for 7 consecutive days to eliminate the present yeast growth.

177. **The correct answer is (E).** Giant cell arteritis is a systemic, inflammatory condition of the medium and large vessels. A temporal artery biopsy is required to positively confirm a diagnosis of giant cell arteritis. This procedure involves the surgical removal of a tissue sample from the wall of the temporal artery. The sample is then examined under a microscope to evaluate for signs of inflammation and damage.

178. **The correct answer is (C).** Hypertensive urgency refers to a situation in which the systolic blood pressure is greater than 220 mmHg and diastolic blood pressure is greater than 125 mmHg. Hypertensive urgency must be treated within hours to avoid further health consequences.

179. **The correct answer is (A).** A Mallory-Weiss tear is a linear mucosal tear in the esophagus, generally at the gastroesophageal junction. Patient presents with forceful vomiting and hematemesis. A Mallory-Weiss tear is most often associated with alcoholism; however, it should be considered in all cases of upper gastrointestinal bleeding. Endoscopy is the only method to accurately confirm diagnosis of Mallory-Weiss tear.

180. **The correct answer is (B).** When meningitis is suspected, a prompt lumbar puncture must be performed to evaluate the cerebrospinal fluid. CSF may appear cloudy to purulent, CSF pressure will be elevated, white blood cells will be increased, protein concentrations will be increased, and glucose levels will be decreased. Gram stain and culture is diagnostic in 80% of the cases.

181. **The correct answer is (E).** Electrolytes, glucose, urinalysis, and serum creatinine are required to reveal hypovolemic shock. All patients in shock will require a CBC, blood type and cross match, and coagulation parameters to ensure proper treatment and status of the patient. In addition, all patients should require pulse oximetry or arterial blood gases to monitor the patient's oxygenation. Electrolytes, glucose, urinalysis, and serum creatinine are required to determine the nature and cause of the shock.

182. **The correct answer is (A).** Cluster headaches are severe, unilateral, periorbital headaches that last for 30 to 90 minutes and occur several times a day over a period of weeks to months. These headaches are often accompanied by ipsilateral lacrimation, conjunctival injection, nasal congestion, myosis, and ptosis.

183. **The correct answer is (C).** Meniere's disease can cause hearing loss, tinnitus, vertigo, nausea, and vomiting. Episodes of nausea and vomiting, as well as the other symptoms, can last from minutes to hours. Meniere's disease is also characterized by distention of the endolymphatic compartment of the inner ear.

184. **The correct answer is (D).** A foruncle is defined as an infection of a single hair follicle, commonly referred to as a boil. The lesions commonly present as red, hard, tender lesions in the hair-bearing regions of the head, neck, and body. A carbuncle is an infection of more than one hair follicle as a conglomerate mass.

185. **The correct answer is (D).** A high percentage of volvulus cases can be resolved with endoscopic decompression; therefore, this procedure should be attempted initially. Surgical correction of the volvulus is indicated only after failure of endoscopic decompression.

186. **The correct answer is (E).** Pulmonary hypertension presents clinically with shortness of breath, retrosternal chest pain, weakness, fatigue, cyanosis, and syncope. Edema and ascites may also be present. Auscultation of the chest can reveal narrow splitting and accentuation of the second heart sound and a systolic ejection click. Chest X-ray will reveal enlarged pulmonary arteries.

187. **The correct answer is (C).** Polymyositis is an inflammatory disease affecting the proximal limbs, neck, and pharynx. This disorder may also be associated with a skin rash. Patients may present with proximal muscle weakness, dysphagia, skin rash, polyarthralgia, and muscle atrophy. Bloodwork should reveal elevated muscle enzymes of creatinine phosphokinase and aldolase.

188. **The correct answer is (B).** Light therapy, otherwise known as phototherapy or heliotherapy,

has proven successful for patients who suffer from seasonal affective disorder. Light therapy consists of exposure to daylight or to specific wavelengths of light using lasers, light-emitting diodes, or fluorescent lamps. Light therapy treatments are administered for a prescribed amount of time and/or during a certain time of day.

189. **The correct answer is (B).** The glomerular filtration rate, or GFR, is the laboratory test that is the gold standard for diagnosis of chronic kidney disease. Normal GFR value is 90 mL per minute per 1.73 m^2 of body surface area. GFR values below this value indicate loss of renal function.

190. **The correct answer is (D).** Under the circumstances in which emergency contraception is indicated, the medical intervention of choice is high dose progestin. High dose progestin-estrogen has also been proven effective for emergency contraception.

191. **The correct answer is (D).** Postural hypotension, otherwise known as orthostatic hypotension, is characterized by a drop in blood pressure greater than 20 mmHg when transferring from a supine to a sitting position or from a sitting to standing position. Postural hypotension is a major cause of syncope and a leading cause of falls among the elderly.

192. **The correct answer is (D).** Tinea versicolor is caused by a type of yeast found on the skin of humans that manifests itself in the spore and hyphal form. Most patients are asymptomatic and only recognize the disorder in the summer time, when areas of the skin will not tan due to overgrowth of yeast on the skin.

193. **The correct answer is (C).** Patients with Cushing's disease may present with obesity, hypertension, excessive thirst, headache, backache, and muscle weakness. Fat deposition may cause a characteristic buffalo hump. Dysmenorrhea may occur in females and erectile dysfunction may occur in males. MRI can reveal a pituitary tumor. CT scan may reveal an adrenocortical tumor. Urinalysis will reveal free cortisol in excess of 125 mg/dL. Bloodwork will reveal plasma cortisol in excess of 10 mg/dL.

194. **The correct answer is (B).** Individuals who experience pain associated with spinal stenosis can obtain relief following a lumbar epidural injection of corticosteroids. Approximately 25% of patients with spinal stenosis who undergo lumbar epidural corticosteroid injections experience sustained relief of symptoms.

195. **The correct answer is (A).** Ectopic pregnancy is the implantation of an embryo anywhere but the endometrium, and 95% of ectopic pregnancies occur in the fallopian tubes. Women may present with dizziness, syncope, unilateral adnexal pain, amenorrhea or spotting, and tenderness or mass detectable on physical pelvic examination. Serial HCG levels are lower than expected and transvaginal ultrasound will not reveal pregnancy.

196. **The correct answer is (E).** For individuals diagnosed with squamous cell carcinoma, surgery is a viable treatment option. Non-small cell lung carcinomas such as squamous cell carcinoma, adenocarcinoma, and large cell carcinoma grow slowly and have a greater chance of treatment via surgery than small cell carcinoma. The 5-year survival rate after resection is 35%-40%.

197. **The correct answer is (E).** Ice packs and analgesics are the appropriate treatment measures for orchitis that occurs secondary to the mumps virus. Antibiotics are only indicated if orchitis is caused by bacteria.

198. **The correct answer is (C).** Tonsillectomy is indicated in cases of peritonsillar cellulitis in the event that symptoms have progressed to include airway obstruction causing sleep apnea and persistent marked asymmetry of the tonsils. Treatment with penicillin or erythromycin is not sufficient when peritonsillar cellulitis has progressed to the extent as described above. Tracheotomy is recommended if the infection has spread into the neck, which is not the case here.

199. **The correct answer is (A).** Exenatide is effective in reducing blood glucose levels by stimulating pancreatic insulin response to glucose and preventing glucagon release after meals. However, this medication also slows gastric emptying, so it is contraindicated for patients with a history of gastroparesis.

200. **The correct answer is (D).** Individuals diagnosed with narcissistic personality disorder normally

exude an inflated self image, have a need for admiration, and lack empathy toward others. They consider themselves special and expect to be treated as such. They tend to be haughty and arrogant. The aging process is difficult for these individuals and makes them prone to midlife crises.

201. **The correct answer is (B).** If a patient diagnosed with postural hypotension experiences a pulse rate increase over 15 beats per minute from sitting to standing, depleted blood volume is the likely cause of the postural hypotension. If the patient experiences no change in pulse rate, the cause of postural hypotension may include medications, central nervous system disease, or peripheral neuropathy.

202. **The correct answer is (B).** Cellulitis is an acute, spreading inflammation of the dermis and subcutaneous tissue. The area of inflammation may appear to be swollen, red, hot, and tender. An individual with cellulitis may also exhibit lymphadenopathy, fever, chills, and malaise.

203. **The correct answer is (C).** A gluten-free diet is imperative for individuals diagnosed with celiac disease. Celiac disease is characterized by small bowel inflammation due to the digestion of gluten-containing products such as wheat, rye, and barley. A gluten-free diet will allow individuals diagnosed with celiac disease to avoid flare-ups.

204. **The correct answer is (D).** Selective serotonin reuptake inhibitors (SSRIs) are a class of compounds regularly prescribed for depression, anxiety, and personality disorders. They act by increasing levels of extracellular serotonin by preventing reuptake of serotonin into the presynaptic cell.

205. **The correct answer is (D).** In order to achieve maximum effectiveness from emergency contraception, the intervention must occur within 72 hours of unprotected intercourse. However, emergency contraception may be effective up to 5 days after unprotected intercourse.

206. **The correct answer is (C).** Beta-adrenergic antagonists, or beta blockers, have been proven effective in decreasing heart rate and cardiac output. This class of medication has proven most effective in younger white males.

207. **The correct answer is (E).** The Wood's light examination is used to assess changes in pigment or to fluoresce infectious lesions. This diagnostic technique is most useful in confirming the diagnosis of melasma because this exam will accentuate the hyperpigmented macules associated with this disorder.

208. **The correct answer is (E).** Otitis media is characterized by fever, pressure, pain, and hearing loss in the affected ear. The examination will reveal an immobile eardrum that is erythematous and bulging.

209. **The correct answer is (E).** A volvulus is a twisting of any part of the bowel on itself. This disorder usually involves the sigmoid or cecal areas of the bowel. Patients with volvulus may present with abdominal pain, distention, nausea, vomiting, fever, or tachycardia.

210. **The correct answer is (B).** Patients with Addison's disease usually present with fatigue, weakness, muscle aches, and weight loss. Physical exam will reveal hyperpigmentation, orthostatic hypotension, and delayed deep tendon reflexes. Bloodwork can reveal hyperkalemia, hyponatremia, hypoglycemia, hypercalcemia, and low BUN. Low plamsa cortisol (< 3 μg/dL) and serum dehydroepiandrosterone (DHEA) below 1000 ng/ml are associated with Addison's disease. DHEA levels above 1000 ng/ml will exclude a diagnosis of Addison's disease.

211. **The correct answer is (C).** Intussusception is the gastrointestinal disorder characterized by the invagination of a proximal segment of the bowel into the portion just distal to it, like pieces of a telescope. This disorder can cause inflammation, bowel obstruction, and decreased blood flow to the affected part of the colon.

212. **The correct answer is (E).** Uterine prolapse is more common among Caucasian women than those of African-American or Asian descent. Conditions that increase intra-abdominal pressure, such as obesity and chronic cough, may facilitate prolapse. Symptoms associated with prolapse are vaginal fullness, lower abdominal aching, low back pain, and the sensation of sitting on a ball.

213. **The correct answer is (A).** ACE inhibitors exhibit bradykinin degradation and stimulate vasodilating

prostaglandins. This class of medications is the initial medication of choice for hypertensive individuals with diabetes, younger white males, and patients for whom diuretics are insufficient therapy.

214. **The correct answer is (C).** Rhinitis medicamentosa is characterized by severe congestion and pain without significant discharge. This disorder is caused by overzealous use of prescribed drops and sprays, which in turn causes rebound congestion.

215. **The correct answer is (D).** Mesalamine is an anti-inflammatory agent, which inhibits the body from producing substances that cause pain or inflammation. Mesalamine is effective for the treatment of Crohn's disease because it inhibits inflammation in the entire colon. Prednisone is only indicated with acute attacks of Crohn's disease.

216. **The correct answer is (B).** Gastric adenocarcinoma is among the most common cancers, occurs in males twice as often as in women, and almost never occurs in people under the age of 40. Patients can present with abdominal pain, bloating, belching, weight loss, and intermittent gastrointestinal bleeding. Bloodwork will reveal iron-deficiency anemia. Liver enzymes may be elevated if metastases are present. Endoscopy will confirm the presence of the neoplasm.

217. **The correct answer is (A).** Carcinoid tumors, also known as bronchial gland tumors, are well differentiated neuroendocrine tumors that usually occur in patients under 60. These tumors are low-grade malignant neoplasms that grow slowly and rarely metastasize. Patients may present with hemolysis, cough, focal wheezing, and recurrent pneumonia. Bleeding and airway obstruction may also occur. Bronchoscopy will reveal a pink or purple, centrally located, well-vascularized lesion.

218. **The correct answer is (E).** For patients diagnosed with a carcinoid tumor, surgical excision of the tumor is the indicated course of treatment. The slow-growing and rarely-metastasizing characteristics of this tumor make surgery a viable option. Carcinoid tumors are resistant to radiation therapy and chemotherapy.

219. **The correct answer is (E).** Celiac disease is characterized by inflammation of the small bowel. A small bowel biopsy is needed in order to confirm the diagnosis of celiac disease.

220. **The correct answer is (D).** For individuals who have been diagnosed with thrombocytopenia and have undergone a prednisone therapy regimen that has failed, splenectomy is the indicated treatment. Splenectomy offers a definitive resolution for this disorder.

221. **The correct answer is (A).** Phosphodiesterase-5 inhibitors are recognized as the drug of choice for treatment of erectile dysfunction. Sildenafil, vardenafil, and tadalafil are drugs in the phosphodiesterase-5 inhibitor family most commonly prescribed for treatment of erectile dysfunction.

222. **The correct answer is (D).** Sinusitis is characterized by headache, purulent drainage, fever, malaise, and pain in the face when bending over. Physical exam should reveal tenderness to palpation of the sinuses and opacification of the sinuses with transillumination.

223. **The correct answer is (C).** Polycystic ovary syndrome is the most common cause of androgen excess and hirsutism. Patients may present with hirsutism, infertility, truncal obesity, irregular menstruation, and skin discoloration.

224. **The correct answer is (B).** On a standard electrocardiogram, leads V1 and V2 represent the posterior wall of the heart muscle. Any electrocardiographic abnormalities seen in these leads correspond to the area of the heart that is affected. For example, S-T depression in lead V1 indicates the presence of myocardial ischemia in the posterior wall of the heart.

225. **The correct answer is (E).** Tetanus is infection of the nervous system by the bacteria *Clostridium tetani*, which is found in soils around the world. Patients who contract tetanus often present with stiffness in the jaw, neck and back, difficulty swallowing, and irritability. Examination will reveal hyperreflexia and muscle spasms of the jaw and face. Patients may also experience drooling, fever, excessive sweating, and uncontrolled urination and defecation.

226. **The correct answer is (B).** Ceftriaxone is the treatment of choice for men and women infected with gonorrhea. There is much evolved resistance to

other medications such as penicillin, tetracyclines, and fluoroquinolones, making ceftriaxone the drug of choice.

227. **The correct answer is (A).** For individuals diagnosed with pulmonary embolism, anticoagulation therapy, preferably with heparin, should be initiated immediately. For individuals at risk of recurrence of pulmonary embolism or intolerant of anticoagulants, vena cava filter is the indicated intervention.

228. **The correct answer is (E).** Pregabalin, sold under the brand name Lyrica, is the only FDA-approved drug for the treatment of fibromyalgia pain. Fibromyalgia symptoms can include pain, muscle stiffness, muscle tenderness, fatigue, difficulty falling asleep, and difficulty staying asleep.

229. **The correct answer is (D).** Testicular ultrasound is now the gold standard in evaluation of testicular torsion. A nuclear medicine testicular scan would be an alternative to a testicular ultrasound if ultrasound is unavailable; however, testicular ultrasound is the study of choice for this disorder.

230. **The correct answer is (D).** Otitis externa is characterized by pain in the affected ear as well as pain when the tragus or auricle is manipulated. Physical exam should reveal an ear canal that is obscured and edematous, with purulent debris.

231. **The correct answer is (A).** Calcium pyrophosphate dehydrate disease (CPPD or pseudogout) is a result of deposition of calcium pyrophosphate. This disorder is characterized as recurrent, abrupt attacks of pain that mimic gout. CPPD most commonly affects the wrists, knees, and elbows. Joint aspiration will reveal rhomboid-shaped crystals that are negatively birefringent. Radiographs will reveal fine, linear calcifications of the cartilage, known as chondrocalcinosis.

232. **The correct answer is (C).** De Quervain's disease is a stenosing tenosynovitis involving the abductor pollicis and extensor pollicis brevis. This disorder is more common in women and diabetics. Patient will present clinically with pain in the wrist and base of the thumb with radiation into the forearm. Physical examination reveals swelling and thickening of the tendon sheath. The examination also reveals a positive Finkelstein's test.

233. **The correct answer is (E).** Selective serotonin reuptake inhibitors (SSRIs) have been proven effective in lessening the effects associated with fibromyalgia. Studies have shown that patients with fibromyalgia have low levels of serotonin and disturbed sleep patterns that lead to fatigue and increased pain. SSRIs function to regulate serotonin levels and regulate sleep patterns, thus alleviating symptoms.

234. **The correct answer is (A).** Juvenile rheumatoid arthritis, also referred to as Still's disease or systemic childhood-onset idiopathic arthritis, is characterized by spiking fevers, myalgias, polyarthralgias, and a typical salmon-pink maculopapular rash associated with fever.

235. **The correct answer is (A).** The proper course of treatment for this disorder is controlled intubation followed by IV fluids and antibiotics. This is imperative with epiglottitis because this disorder can cause a spontaneous closing off of the airways. An airway must immediately be established and medications must be administered to rid the body of the infection and reduce the inflammation of the epiglottis.

236. **The correct answer is (D).** Rocky Mountain spotted fever is an infectious disease that occurs primarily in the western United States that is transmitted by the wood tick. Patients will present with fever, chills, headache, nausea, vomiting, myalgias, restlessness, insomnia, and irritability. Physical exam will reveal flushing of the face, injected conjunctiva, and faint macules to maculopapules to petechiae on the wrists, ankles, trunk and extremities.

237. **The correct answer is (D).** Magnetic resonance imaging, or MRI, with gadolinium enhancement is the most effective diagnostic tool for the visualization of white matter lesions in the central nervous system associated with multiple sclerosis.

238. **The correct answer is (A).** Alendronate, more commonly known as Fosamax, is commonly prescribed for treatment and prevention of osteoporosis. This medication is also indicated for prevention of early collapse of the femoral head from aseptic necrosis.

239. The correct answer is (A). Myasthenia gravis is characterized by muscle weakness and fatigability that improves with rest. Patients may present with ptosis, diplopia, difficulty in chewing or swallowing, respiratory difficulties, and limb weakness. Physical examination will reveal normal sensation and reflexes. This disorder can occur at any age, but is more common in young women and older men.

240. The correct answer is (C). Positron Emission Tomography, or PET scan, will routinely reveal hypometabolism in the frontal and/or anterior temporal region of the brain, whereas Alzheimer's disease is indicated by biparietal hypometabolism.

241. The correct answer is (C). Metformin is a very effective first-line medication for diabetes. This medication will lower blood glucose levels without risk of hypoglycemia. However, metformin is contraindicated in patients with elevated serum creatine and for patients with lactic acidosis. Gastrointestinal side effects are also common while taking metformin.

242. The correct answer is (D). An ultrasound of the kidneys is the diagnostic method of choice for evaluation of polycystic kidney disease. A positive ultrasound for polycystic kidney disease will reveal several fluid-filled cysts bilaterally.

243. The correct answer is (E). A lateral soft tissue X-ray of the neck shows a classic thumb sign if epiglottitis is present. A simple lateral soft tissue X-ray of the neck is the most appropriate diagnostic study to order to rule out epiglottitis.

244. The correct answer is (A). Bactrim is the treatment of choice for pneumocystitis pneumonia. Bactrim is a combination of sulfamethoxazole and trimethoprim. It is commonly prescribed for treatment of confirmed pneumocystis pneumonia and for prevention against its occurrence in immunosuppressed patients.

245. The correct answer is (B). A lateral neck radiograph will differentiate between a diagnosis of the croup and epiglottitis. Epiglottitis is characterized by the thumb sign, indicating inflammation of the epiglottis. Croup will be visualized as subglottic haziness and narrowing with distention of the hypopharynx.

246. The correct answer is (B). A hypertensive emergency refers to a situation in which the diastolic pressure is in excess of 130 mmHg. A hypertensive emergency must be treated within one hour to avoid further health consequences.

247. The correct answer is (E). Diuretics initially reduce plasma volume and chronically reduce peripheral resistance. Diuretics are the recommended initial therapy for hypertension.

248. The correct answer is (D). Pulmonary embolism presents clinically with pleuritic chest pain, dyspnea, and hemoptysis. Cough and diaphoresis may also be present. Physical examination reveals tachycardia, tachypnea, low-grade fever, crackles, and accentuation of the pulmonary component of the second heart sound.

249. The correct answer is (E). Ovarian cysts are diagnostically confirmed with the use of a pelvic ultrasound. Ultrasound is also useful in differentiating between cancerous and non-cancerous lesions.

250. The correct answer is (C). An electroencephalogram, or EEG, is the most definitive exam for monitoring seizure activity. In generalized absence seizures, EEG will show generalized spikes and associated slow waves. In partial seizures, EEG will show focal rhythmic discharge at the onset of the seizure. In complex partial seizures, EEG shows interictal spikes or spikes associated with slow waves in the temporal or frontotemporal areas.

251. The correct answer is (A). Atrial fibrillation is the most common chronic arrhythmia. It can be noticed on an electrocardiogram because QRS complexes do not occur in a regular rhythm; the P-waves are absent on an electrocardiogram tracing of atrial fibrillation.

252. The correct answer is (D). Surgical pinning of the hip in situ is the only definitive treatment for slipped capital femoral epiphysis. This procedure will prevent further slipping of the femoral epiphysis and reduce the risk of avascular necrosis to the affected area.

253. The correct answer is (A). Topical or oral aminosalicylates used in conjunction with corticosteroids are the proper medical treatment for the maintenance of ulcerative colitis. Immunodilators are only indicated if the disease does not respond to topical or oral aminosalicylates.

254. The correct answer is (E). Diabetes insipidus is an uncommon disorder caused by a deficiency of or resistance to vasopressin, an antidiuretic hormone. The only way to confirm a diagnois of diabetes insipidus is by obtaining a vasopressin challenge test.

255. The correct answer is (D). The classic characteristic of a gastric ulcer, as opposed to a duodenal ulcer, is that the abdominal discomfort intensifies after eating. For this reason, gastric ulcers can lead to anorexia and weight loss. Patients can present with symptoms such as abdominal pain that feels like a burning or gnawing, belching, bloating, heartburn, nausea, and black tarry stools. Endoscopy can confirm diagnosis.

256. The correct answer is (D). Methotrexate can be used to treat up to 80% of ectopic pregnancies. Criteria for methotrexate treatment is a serum HCG under 5000 mU, ectopic mass less than 3.5 cm as measured by ultrasound, hemodynamically stable patient, and a patient who is compliant for follow-up treatments.

257. The correct answer is (A). If you suspect a patient is suffering from schizophrenia, a CT scan of the brain should be obtained in order to confirm the diagnosis. Individuals who suffer from schizophrenia will show enlarged ventricles and cortical atrophy on a CT scan, which are indicative of chronic schizophrenic disease.

258. The correct answer is (C). Tetralogy of Fallot is a congenital heart defect that is an emergency medical condition. This condition is characterized by extreme cyanosis, hyperpnea, and agitation. Physical examination will reveal clubbing of the extremities. Auscultation of the chest will reveal increased right ventricle impulse at the lower left sternal border and a loud S2 sound.

259. The correct answer is (B). Bupropion, commonly marketed as Wellbutrin, is an antidepressive medication most commonly used as a smoking cessation aid, as well as in treatment of other psychological disorders. This medication is contraindicated for treatment of anorexia nervosa because it may exacerbate the anorexic condition and lower the seizure threshold for patients with anorexia.

260. The correct answer is (A). Abruptio placentae is defined as the premature separation of a normally implanted placenta after the 20th week of gestation, but before childbirth. Risk factors for this disorder include trauma, smoking, hypertension, decreased folic acid, high parity, cocaine abuse, and alcohol abuse. Patients usually experience painful vaginal bleeding, uterine pain, abdominal pain, and back pain.

261. The correct answer is (C). Patients with cyclothymic disorder can best be described as moody, erratic, impulsive and somewhat violent. This disorder is characterized by recurring symptoms over a 2-year period with symptom-free periods lasting for greater than 2 months at any one time.

262. The correct answer is (C). Minoxidil is an antihypertensive, vasodilator medication that is known for its ability to slow or stop hair loss and promote regrowth. This medication is the safest, most effective treatment for male pattern baldness. Finasteride may also be effective to treat male pattern baldness; however, loss of libido and erectile dysfunction may occur with use of this drug.

263. The correct answer is (A). Hypoplastic left heart syndrome is a congenital heart defect in which the left side of the heart including the aorta, aortic valve, left ventricle, and mitral valve fail to develop properly. The patient will present with cyanosis, shock, heart failure, and respiratory distress. Auscultation of the chest reveals a single S2 sound.

264. The correct answer is (C). The rhythm shown on this patient's electrocardiogram is ventricular fibrillation. Ventricular fibrillation is an extreme medical emergency and electrical defibrillation must be attempted as soon as the defibrillator is available.

265. The correct answer is (E). When an olive-shaped mass suggestive for pyloric stenosis is detected on a physical examination, the appropriate diagnostic study is an ultrasound of the abdomen. An ultrasound will be extremely effective at locating the lesion and will not expose the infant to radiation.

266. **The correct answer is (E).** Diseases of defective bone mineralization, such as osteomalacia and rickets, are most commonly caused by a vitamin D deficiency. Other causes may include deficiencies of calcium or phosphate and aluminum toxicity. Vitamin D regulates calcium and phosphate serum levels, and also plays a role in immune function.

267. **The correct answer is (E).** For patients who are symptomatic and have a confirmed diagnosis of parathyroid adenoma, surgical removal of the affected parathyroid gland is the recommended treatment. Radiation therapy and chemotherapy have not been proven effective for treatment of this disorder.

268. **The correct answer is (C).** Barotrauma is defined as the inability to equalize barometric stress on the inner ear, resulting in pain. This disorder is caused by an auditory tube dysfunction as a result of congenital narrowing or acquired mucosal edema.

269. **The correct answer is (B).** Intravenous administration of 10-20 mL of 10% calcium gluconate over 10 minutes should remedy this situation. Calcium directly antagonizes neuromuscular and cardiovascular effects of magnesium. This treatment is used for patients with symptomatic hypermagnesemia that is causing cardiac effects or respiratory distress.

270. **The correct answer is (B).** Dilated cardiomyopathy comprises approximately 95% of all cardiomyopathies and is associated with reduced strength of ventricular contractions, resulting in dilatation of the left ventricle. Chest auscultation can reveal S1 gallop, rales, and increased jugular venous pressure. Chest X-ray reveals cardiomegaly with vascular congestion. Echocardiogram reveals dilated left ventricle, low cardiac output, and high diastolic pressures.

271. **The correct answer is (D).** Sinus bradycardia is simply a normal sinus rhythm with a heart rate below 60 beats per minute. This rhythm is common among young, athletic individuals or other individuals with well-conditioned hearts. This rhythm is also common for patients who are being administered medications to reduce heart rate.

272. **The correct answer is (E).** Unless the cause of the effusions has been discovered, the presence of fluid in the lungs is an indication for thoracentesis. Performing a thoracentesis allows for the fluid to be examined, symptoms to be relieved and an adequate imaging procedure of the lungs to be performed.

273. **The correct answer is (D).** Diabetes insipidus is an uncommon disorder caused by a deficiency of or resistance to vasopressin, an antidiuretic hormone. The only way to confirm a diagnois of diabetes insipidus is by obtaining a vasopressin challenge test. Patients may present with excessive thirst and a craving for ice water, consume 2 to 20 liters of water per day, and have high volume urination. Bloodwork can show hyponatremia and dehydration. Urinalysis will show a decreased specific gravity, <1.006.

274. **The correct answer is (E).** In children, a barium or air enema can be both diagnostic and curative for the disorder of intussusception. Surgical correction of intussusception is only indicated if the air or barium enema fails to cure the disorder.

275. **The correct answer is (A).** Dialysis is the proper course of treatment when the plasma sodium level is in excess of 200 mEq/L. Rapid correction of this disorder via dialysis is required in order to avoid complications that may arise due to excessively high plasma sodium.

276. **The correct answer is (B).** Dilated cardiomyopathy comprises approximately 95% of all cardiomyopathies and is associated with reduced strength of ventricular contractions, resulting in dilatation of the left ventricle. Chest auscultation can reveal S1 gallop, rales, and increased jugular venous pressure. Chest X-ray reveals cardiomegaly with vascular congestion. Echocardiogram reveals dilated left ventricle, low cardiac output, and high diastolic pressures.

277. **The correct answer is (C).** Betamethisone is administered to women who are further than 24 weeks and less than 34 weeks into gestation and whose births are going to occur within 7 days. Betamethisone is adminstered via two injections, 24 hours apart. Betamethisone will cause the lungs of a premature infant to produce surfactant, which enhances the infant's ability to breathe independently and reduces the need for respiratory treatment.

278. **The correct answer is (A).** Most individuals who are diagnosed with Meniere's disease can easily manage this disorder by restricting their salt consumption and taking diuretic medication. If this treatment option is unsuccessful, surgical intervention is required.

279. **The correct answer is (D).** Sympathomimetic drugs are substances that mimic the effects of the sympathetic nervous system. These types of medications are commonly used to treat cardiac arrest and low blood pressure, and delay preterm labor. Sympathomimetic drugs have an anorexic effect in humans, which makes them a preferred treatment for obesity. Medications included in this class of drugs are amphetamine, dextroamphetamine, phentermine, phendimetrazine, and bezphetamine.

280. **The correct answer is (C).** For displaced fractures of the scaphoid, the proper course of treatment is a surgical open reduction with internal fixation. Nondisplaced scaphoid fractures are treated with a short-arm thumb spica cast and referral to an orthopaedic surgeon.

281. **The correct answer is (B).** Chlamydia is the leading cause of infertility in females and may be totally asymptomatic. Symptomatic chlamydia may present with symptoms associated with pelvic inflammatory disease, such as painful urination, fever, lower abdominal pain, and a foul-smelling vaginal discharge. Physical examination will reveal cervicitis and salpingitis.

282. **The correct answer is (B).** Left-sided congestive heart failure occurs when the left side of the heart begins to fail and fluid begins to accumulate in the lungs. Left-sided congestive heart failure can lead to symptoms such as exertional dyspnea, non-productive cough, orthopnea, and exercise intolerance. Auscultation of the chest should reveal bilateral rales and gallops. Chest X-ray should reveal cardiomegaly, bilateral pleural effusions, and perivascular or interstitial edema.

283. **The correct answer is (C).** Hypertrophic cardiomyopathy is characterized by hypertrophy of the septum and small left ventricle. This disorder is primarily transmitted genetically and is much more common in individuals of Asian descent. Individuals with this disorder can experience sudden death under the age of 30. Auscultation of the chest reveals S4 gallop, variable systolic murmur, and jugular venous pulsations with a prominent "a" wave. Chest X-ray will be essentially normal. Echocardiogram will reveal left ventricular hypertrophy, asymmetric septal hypertrophy, diastolic dysfunction, and a small left ventricle.

284. **The correct answer is (E).** A tension pneumothorax is secondary to a chest wound or pulmonary laceration. It is characterized by chest pain and shortness of breath. Chest X-ray will reveal an accumulation of air in the pleural space with mediastinal shift to the opposite side. Physical exam will reveal impaired ventilation leading to compromised cardiac function.

285. **The correct answer is (C).** For patients diagnosed with diverticulitis, a high fiber diet and avoidance of obstructing or constipating foods, such as nuts, is indicated to avoid complications from diverticulitis. Failure to adhere to a high fiber diet may irritate the disorder, and surgical intervention may then be required to treat diverticulitis.

286. **The correct answer is (B).** Circumcision is the most definitive for symptomatic phimosis. If phimosis is asymptomatic, it can be left alone and should resolve as patient gets older. Antibiotics and steroid creams may be useful to relieve symptoms, but the only true way to remedy a symptomatic phimosis is through circumcision.

287. **The correct answer is (D).** Oxytocin, sold under the brand name Pitocin, is administered intravenously to induce labor when the cervix is dilated more than one centimeter and some effacement has occurred. Dosages of oxytocin are increased periodically until strong contractions are occurring approximately every 3 minutes.

288. **The correct answer is (D).** Right-sided congestive heart failure is often caused by left-sided congestive heart failure. Symptoms may include distended neck veins, tender or non-tender hepatic congestion, hepatomegaly, and pitting edema.

289. **The correct answer is (B).** Norepinephrine-dopamine reuptake inhibitors, such as buproprion (Wellbutrin), do not cause sexual dysfunction commonly experienced with typical atidepressents, such as SSRIs, MAOIs, and tri-cyclics.

290. The correct answer is (A). Coalworker's pneumoconiosis, or black lung disease, is an occupational and restrictive lung disease caused by the inhalation of dust, which is very common among coal miners. This disorder is characterized by progressive shortness of breath with inspiratory crackles. A chest X-ray will reveal small opacities in the upper lung fields.

291. The correct answer is (A). Desmopressin acetate is the treatment of choice for all forms of diabetes insipidus, including central diabetes insipidus and diabetes insipidus associated with pregnancy and the puerperium. It is a vasopressin analog and therefore compensates for diminished vasopressin production.

292. The correct answer is (E). A pilonidal cyst is an abscess on the sacrococcygeal cleft associated with subsequent sinus tract development. Pilonidal cysts are most likely in obese, hairy males under the age of 40.

293. The correct answer is (A). Nonseminomatous testicular tumors are radioresistant, which means they will not respond to radiation therapy. Treatment for this type of tumor, depending on the stage of the disease, includes retroperitoneal lymph node dissection, chemotherapy, and surgery.

294. The correct answer is (A). For individuals who suffer from acute episodes of vertigo, intravenous or rectal administration of diazepam is the preferred treatment. Bed rest may also be required with acute episodes of vertigo.

295. The correct answer is (D). Pilocarpine is used to increase salivary flow for patients who experience dry mouth as a result of Sjogren's syndrome. This medication is used when other therapies such as artificial tears, artificial saliva, and increasing oral fluid intake fail to provide adequate treatment.

296. The correct answer is (B). Laparotomy is a form of surgical removal of the ectopic gestation. Laparotomy is only indicated for patients with significant abdominal adhesions and those who are hemodynamically unstable.

297. The correct answer is (B). Pulmonary atresia is a congenital heart defect in which the pulmonary valve fails to develop properly, preventing blood flow from the right ventricle to the pulmonary artery. Patients are born with severe cyanosis and tachypnea without dyspnea. Auscultation of the chest should reveal a hyperdynamic apical impulse and a single S1 and S2 sound.

298. The correct answer is (D). Peripheral arterial disease usually presents initially with intermittent claudication, or lower leg pain that is relieved by rest. As disease progresses, discomfort will occur at rest also. Auscultation of the legs will reveal weak or absent distal and femoral pulses. An aortic, iliac, or femoral bruit may also be noticed. An ankle-brachial reflex of 0.9 or lower is indicative of significant peripheral artery disease.

299. The correct answer is (D). Silicosis is a form of a pneumoconiosis that is common among stone workers or quarry workers. It is characterized by shortness of breath, inspiratory crackles, clubbing, and cyanosis. Chest X-ray for this disorder is characterized by small opacities throughout the lung fields and calcified hilar lymph nodes.

300. The correct answer is (E). Diseases of defective bone mineralization, such as osteomalacia and rickets, are most commonly caused by a vitamin D deficiency. Other causes may include deficiencies of calcium or phosphate and aluminum toxicity. Vitamin D regulates calcium and phosphate serum levels, and also plays a role in immune function.

301. The correct answer is (D). The psoas sign is determined by having the patient lie in a supine position and attempt to raise the leg against resistance. The right ileopsoas muscle lies under the appendix when the patient is supine. Therefore, inability to raise the right leg is indicative of appendicitis.

302. The correct answer is (D). The most effective treatment option for a localized renal cell carcinoma is a radical nephrectomy. Radiation therapy has not been proven effective to prolong survival in early stage, localized renal cell carcinoma.

303. The correct answer is (D). Labyrinthitis is a disorder that involves irritation and inflammation of the inner ear. Patients may present with difficulty focusing due to involuntary eye movements, dizziness, vertigo, one-sided hearing loss, nausea, and vomiting.

304. The correct answer is (A). Tennis elbow, scientifically known as lateral epicondylitis, is a disorder that involves the tendinous insertion of the extensor carpi radialis brevis muscle. This disorder is the most common overuse injury associated with the elbow. Patients with tennis elbow experience pain when lifting objects or when the arm is pronated.

305. The correct answer is (C). Magnesium sulfate, MgSO4, inhibits myometrial contractility mediated by calcium. Side effects include nausea, fatigue, and muscle weakness. Toxicity from magnesium sulfate can lead to decreased reflexes, respiratory depression, and cardiac collapse.

306. The correct answer is (B). Obsessive-compulsive disorder is characterized by recurring thoughts that provoke anxiety (obsessions), although it may also consist of repeated actions aimed at reducing anxiety (compulsions) or a combination of the two. It is not to be confused with obsessive-compulsive personality disorder, which is characterized by rigid adherence to order and routine.

307. The correct answer is (C). Supportive cortico-steroid treatment is really the only option when treating pneumoconioses such as silicosis. Oxygen therapy is indicated as a supportive treatment for silicosis. In addition, treatment with corticosteroids can relieve the chronic alveolitis that is associated with silicosis.

308. The correct answer is (C). Emergency colonic decompression is required in order to treat the disorder of toxic megacolon. In the case that colonic decompression fails to cure toxic mega-colon, a colostomy or complete colonic resection is required.

309. The correct answer is (A). Bisphosphonates are the treatment of choice for Paget's disease. Bisphosphonates include alendronate, tiludronate, risedronate, zoledronic acid, and pamidronate.

310. The correct answer is (E). Seminomatous testicular tumors are radiosensitive which means they will respond to radiation therapy. Radiation therapy is the indicated treatment for stage I and stage II seminomatous testicular tumors. Chemotherapy is not indicated unless the disease progresses to stage III.

311. The correct answer is (C). Calcium channel blockers inhibit smooth muscle contractility and relax the uterine muscles by decreasing intracellular calcium ions. Side effects associated with calcium channel blockers include hypotension and tachycardia.

312. The correct answer is (D). Calcium channel blockers are commonly prescribed to lessen the load on the heart, thus alleviating symptoms such as chest pain and hypertension. This is no different when treating congestive heart failure. Diuretics are the appropriate initial treatment; however, calcium channel blockers may also be necessary if chest pain and hypertension are associated with congestive heart failure.

313. The correct answer is (C). Sarcoidosis is a disorder characterized by inflammation of diverse organs and tissues such as lymph nodes, lungs, liver, eyes, and skin. It commonly includes respiratory symptoms such as cough, shortness of breath, and chest pain. Some patients may experience excessive fatigue and a persistent low-grade fever. Lab tests can reveal leukopenia, eosino-philia, elevated erythrocyte sedimentation rate, hypercalcemia, and hypercalciuria. Chest X-ray can reveal symmetric bilateral hilar adenopathy, right paratracheal adenopathy, and bilateral diffuse reticular infiltrates.

314. The correct answer is (D). The obturator sign is determined with the patient in the supine position and an attempt is made to flex and internally rotate the right hip with the knee bent. If an inflamed appendix comes into contact with the obturator internus muscle, the obturator sign will cause spasm of the obturator internus muscle, causing pain in the hypogastrium.

315. The correct answer is (C). Elevated serum calcium, or hypercalcemia, is a classic diagnostic indicator of hyperparathyroidism. Hyperthyroidism is primarily caused by a parathyroid adenoma, a malignant tumor of the parathyroid gland.

316. The correct answer is (D). Uvular hydrops, or uvular edema, is a non-inflammatory swelling of the uvular that may cause a feeling of enlargement or of a foreign body in the throat, change in voice quality (muffled voice), gagging, and in severe cases, difficulty breathing. Uvular hydrops is usually caused by an allergic reaction, and may present with hypopharyngular edema.

317. The correct answer is (B). Calcium gluconate is the medication used to counteract the effects of an overdose of magnesium sulfate. Magnesium sulfate is also administered to pregnant women who are experiencing premature labor in order to slow down or stop uterine contractions. Signs of magnesium sulfate overdose, or toxicity, include respiratory depression and loss of deep tendon reflexes.

318. The correct answer is (A). The most appropriate initial treatment for congestive heart failure is treatment with diuretics. Diuretics are effective in reducing the fluid volume in the lungs, which will relieve the symptoms associated with congestive heart failure.

319. The correct answer is (A). Due to the extreme respiratory dysfunction patients experience with adult respiratory distress syndrome, oxygen must be delivered via endotracheal intubation with positive pressure ventilation and low levels of positive end-expiratory pressure. In addition to intubation, the underlying cause of adult respiratory distress syndrome must also be treated.

320. The correct answer is (B). Approximately 90% of cases of chronic pancreatitis in the United States are caused by alcohol abuse. Because alcohol abuse is the principal cause of this disorder, a high percentage of chronic pancreatitis cases can be resolved by decreasing alcohol consumption.

321. The correct answer is (E). For patients who are symptomatic and have a confirmed diagnosis of parathyroid adenoma, surgical removal of the affected parathyroid gland is the recommended treatment. Radiation therapy and chemotherapy have not been proven effective for treatment of this disorder.

322. The correct answer is (A). Weekly injections of 17a-hydroxyprogesterone caproate from 16 to 36 weeks' gestation can substantially reduce the rate of recurrent preterm births in women with a history of preterm delivery.

323. The correct answer is (A). Coronary angiography is unequivocally the most definitive diagnostic procedure for the diagnosis of coronary artery disease. Coronary angiography, however, is not the most cost effective or least invasive method to diagnose coronary artery disease. It is normally used only after myocardial perfusion imaging indicates an obstruction of coronary vessels.

324. The correct answer is (D). Hyaline membrane disease is the most common cause of respiratory disease in the newborn infant. It is characterized by typical signs of respiratory distress. Chest X-rays for this disorder will typically show air broncho-grams, bilateral atelectasis that gives a "ground glass" appearance, and a domed diaphragm.

325. The correct answer is (D). Toxic megacolon is a life-threatening, emergent condition characterized by extreme dilation and immobility of the colon. This disorder is usually a complication from other bowel diseases such as ulcerative colitis or Crohn's disease. If left untreated, perforation of the colon may occur.

326. The correct answer is (E). Septic shock is a type of distributive shock and is caused by poorly regulated blood volume. Septic shock is most associated with Gram-negative sepsis in patients of advanced age, diabetics, immunosuppressed patients, and patients who have recently undergone an invasive procedure. Shock can cause low blood pressure, tachycardia, orthostatic changes, and altered mental status.

327. The correct answer is (B). Cervical cerclage is defined as closure of the cervix by mechanical means. This technique involves placing a strong suture into and around the cervix and is normally performed during weeks 12 to 14 of pregnancy. The suture is removed later in the pregnancy when the risk of miscarriage has passed and the fetus is full term.

328. The correct answer is (A). Adjustment disorder is characterized by maladaptive behavioral or emotional symptoms that develop within three months after a stressful life event. It normally ends within 6 months of the event. Among adolescent children, these stressors can include parental rejection, divorce, problems at school, or leaving home.

329. The correct answer is (A). Carpal tunnel syndrome is a mononeuropathy that involves compression of the median nerve under the transverse carpal ligament. Patients may experience night pain, numbness, paresthesia, loss of coordination, and loss of strength in the affected wrist and hand. Tinel's sign and Phalen's test may be positive. Electromyography may assist with confirming the diagnosis.

330. **The correct answer is (D).** Lithium is a member of the class of medications known as anti-manic agents. This class of medications is used to decrease abnormal activity in the brain. Lithium is commonly used in the treatment and prevention of manic episodes in those individuals diagnosed with bipolar disorder.

331. **The correct answer is (E).** Sickle cell anemia is an autosomal hemolytic anemia. Diagnosis is made via electrophoresis, which demonstrates hemoglobin S in red blood cells.

332. **The correct answer is (D).** Orbital cellulitis is considered a medical emergency. Patients diagnosed with orbital cellulitis should be hospitalized and IV antibiotics should be initiated immediately. Antibiotics should be of the broad-spectrum variety until the underlying cause of the condition is identified.

333. **The correct answer is (C).** Mitral stenosis is a valvular disorder that impedes the flow of blood from the left ventricle to the left atrium. Symptoms can include fatigue, shortness of breath, and heart palpitations. Auscultation of the chest will reveal mid-diastolic murmur, accentuated S1, and an opening snap following S2 without radiation. Chest X-ray reveals atrial enlargement

334. **The correct answer is (B).** Menopause is clinically confirmed when the level of follicle stimulating hormone exceeds 30 mIU/mL. The rise in follicular stimulating hormone level is a consequence of the ovaries slowing down the production of estrogen.

335. **The correct answer is (A).** An abdominal angiogram is the only diagnostic exam proven to accurately depict vascular invasion of the pancreas and thereby confirm a diagnosis of pancreatic cancer. Studies are now being performed with newer modalities, such as CT angiogram, but evidence thus far is inconclusive.

336. **The correct answer is (C).** Pseudodementia is defined as a psychiatric illness in which the patient appears to have dementia. It is often due to a pre-existing psychiatric condition. Patients will present with the appearance of being distressed or upset and will complain of memory problems, but examination will reveal concentration and attention span to be intact.

337. **The correct answer is (B).** Varicose veins classically present with superficial dilated, tortuous veins in the distribution of the long saphenous vein. This venous abnormality can be asymptomatic or may occur with fatigue and aching in the legs.

338. **The correct answer is (B).** The recommended treatment for subacute thyroiditis is simply aspirin. Aspirin will act as an anti-inflammatory to reduce the swelling of the thyroid gland and will also work as an analgesic to lessen the pain associated with this disorder.

339. **The correct answer is (B).** Giant cell arteritis primarily occurs in individuals over the age of 50. Classic symptoms of this disorder are headache, scalp tenderness, jaw pain, throat pain, and visual disturbances. Pain and stiffness in the shoulder and pelvis can occur in approximately 50 percent of patients. Bloodwork will reveal marked elevations in erythrocyte sedimentation rate and C-reactive protein.

340. **The correct answer is (A).** Debridement is defined as the medical removal of dead, damaged, or infected tissue in order to improve the healing process of the remaining living, healthy tissue. Debridement may occur surgically, mechanically, or chemically.

341. **The correct answer is (C).** Preeclampsia is diagnosed with the classic triad of hypertension, edema, and proteinuria. Patients may present with edema in the face and hands, sudden weight gain, headache, visual disturbances, nausea, vomiting, right upper quadrant pain, and decreased urine output.

342. **The correct answer is (B).** Dysthymia is characterized by a patient being in a depressed mood for most of the day, more days than not, for a period exceeding over 2 years. Symptoms may include poor concentration, indecisiveness, hopelessness,

poor appetite, overeating, insomnia, hypersomnia, low energy, fatigue, and lack of self-esteem.

343. The correct answer is (A). Adhesive capsulitis, commonly referred to as a frozen shoulder, is an inflammatory process that can occur after a shoulder injury, or may occur spontaneously in diabetic patients. Patients usually present with pain and restricted glenohumeral movement. Arthrography may reveal decreased volume of the joint capsule and capsular contraction.

344. The correct answer is (B). Aortic regurgitation, also referred to as aortic insufficiency, is a disorder of the aortic valve that causes blood to flow in the reverse direction during ventricular diastole, from the aorta into the left ventricle. Symptoms can include shortness of breath on exertion and occasional heart palpitations. Auscultation of the chest should reveal soft systolic and diastolic decrescendo murmur with radiation to the right sternal border and arterial pulses that are large and bounding. Chest X-ray reveals left-sided atrial enlargement with ventricular hypertrophy.

345. The correct answer is (E). Ursadiol is a bile acid. It acts to decrease the production of cholesterol and dissolve the cholesterol already present in the bile so that it cannot form gallstones. Ursadiol is prescribed for patients who do not want surgery or cannot have surgery to remove gallstones.

346. The correct answer is (D). Patients with suppurative thyroiditis present with fever, pain, redness, and a fluctuant neck mass. Suppurative thyroiditis is caused either by a bacterial, fungal, or parasitic agent.

347. The correct answer is (D). Pick's disease is a rare, but permanent, form of dementia that is similar to Alzheimer's disease except it only affects the frontal and temporal lobes of the brain. Individuals with this disorder have abnormal substances called Pick cells or Pick bodies inside the affected nerve cells.

348. The correct answer is (A). Acetowhitening is the process of blanching the skin with 3% to 5% acetic acid solution. This diagnostic technique is used primarily on genital skin, including the uterine cervix and mucous membrane, in order to identify areas of squamous cell change for biopsy.

349. The correct answer is (E). For individuals diagnosed with hookworms, mebendazole administered twice a day for three days is the appropriate treatment. Pyrantel, which is also effective for hookworms, cannot be administered to children less than five years of age.

350. The correct answer is (D). Eclampsia is defined as severe preeclampsia with the presence of seizures. Eclampsia is an acute, life-threatening pregnancy-associated disorder. Although seizures and even coma can occur with eclampsia, this disorder is not associated with any pre-existing or organic brain disorder.

351. The correct answer is (E). Tricuspid regurgitation is a disorder in which the tricuspid valve does not close properly, causing an abnormal backflow of blood into the right atrium when the right ventricle contracts. Physical examination could reveal jugular venous distention, peripheral edema and hepatomegaly. Auscultation of the chest reveals a pancystolic murmur along the left lower sternal border with radiation to the right sternum and xiphoid and increased jugular venous pressures. Chest X-ray reveals prominent right heart border and dilatation of the superior vena cava. Electrocardiogram reveals right axis deviation.

352. The correct answer is (A). Disulfiram, most commonly referred to as Antabuse, is commonly prescribed for treatment of chronic alcoholism. Antabuse will cause unpleasant reactions when even small amounts of alcohol are consumed. The unpleasant symptoms may include flushing of the face, headache, nausea, vomiting, chest pain, blurred vision, sweating, shortness of breath, and anxiety.

353. The correct answer is (B). A diaphragmatic hernia causes immediate respiratory distress because the affected lung is compressed by pressure of the abdominal contents. Auscultation of the chest will reveal bowel sounds in the chest. Chest X-ray will reveal loops of bowel in the hemithorax with displacement of the heart and mediastinal structures.

354. The correct answer is (A). Laparoscopy is a form of surgical removal of the ectopic gestation. Laparoscopy is indicated when the serum HCG is over 5000 mu, the ectopic mass is over 3.5 cm on ultrasound, and the patient is compliant and hemodyamically stable.

355. The correct answer is (D). Pulmonic stenosis is a disorder that disrupts the flow of blood from the heart to the lungs due to improper function of the pulmonic valve. Patients with pulmonic stenosis may exhibit symptoms of chest discomfort, fatigue, dizzy spells, and fainting.

356. The correct answer is (D). Pernicious anemia is defined as a decrease in red blood cells that occurs when the body is unable to properly absorb vitamin B12 from the gastrointestinal tract. This disorder requires lifelong, daily intramuscular injection of vitamin B12 for maintenance.

357. The correct answer is (D). The rhythm noted on the patient's electrocardiogram is supraventricular tachycardia. The proper treatment for supraventricular tachycardia is intravenous administration of 6 mg adenosine. Adenosine is effective in slowing conduction time through the AV node.

358. The correct answer is (D). A urea breath test is useful for indicating the presence of *H. pylori* in the stomach due to the fact that urea is the by-product of *H. pylori* metabolism. The presence of urea in the breath test confirms the presence of this bacterium in the stomach.

359. The correct answer is (A). Elevated a-fetoprotein and a-human chorionic gonadotropin levels are diagnostic for a nonseminomatous germ cell testicular tumor. Normal levels of a-fetoprotein and a-human chorionic gonadotropin, along with positive ultrasound, is diagnostic for a seminomatous testicular tumor.

360. The correct answer is (E). Subacute lymphocytic thyroiditis is characterized by acute, painful thyroid enlargement with radiation of pain to the ears, dyphagia, low-grade fever, fatigue, and malaise. This disorder is common among young and middle-aged females. Elevated blood levels of thyroid hormone and normal radioactive iodine uptake are also indicative of this disorder.

ANSWER SHEET PRACTICE TEST 3

1. Ⓐ Ⓑ Ⓒ Ⓓ Ⓔ	37. Ⓐ Ⓑ Ⓒ Ⓓ Ⓔ	73. Ⓐ Ⓑ Ⓒ Ⓓ Ⓔ	109. Ⓐ Ⓑ Ⓒ Ⓓ Ⓔ	145. Ⓐ Ⓑ Ⓒ Ⓓ Ⓔ
2. Ⓐ Ⓑ Ⓒ Ⓓ Ⓔ	38. Ⓐ Ⓑ Ⓒ Ⓓ Ⓔ	74. Ⓐ Ⓑ Ⓒ Ⓓ Ⓔ	110. Ⓐ Ⓑ Ⓒ Ⓓ Ⓔ	146. Ⓐ Ⓑ Ⓒ Ⓓ Ⓔ
3. Ⓐ Ⓑ Ⓒ Ⓓ Ⓔ	39. Ⓐ Ⓑ Ⓒ Ⓓ Ⓔ	75. Ⓐ Ⓑ Ⓒ Ⓓ Ⓔ	111. Ⓐ Ⓑ Ⓒ Ⓓ Ⓔ	147. Ⓐ Ⓑ Ⓒ Ⓓ Ⓔ
4. Ⓐ Ⓑ Ⓒ Ⓓ Ⓔ	40. Ⓐ Ⓑ Ⓒ Ⓓ Ⓔ	76. Ⓐ Ⓑ Ⓒ Ⓓ Ⓔ	112. Ⓐ Ⓑ Ⓒ Ⓓ Ⓔ	148. Ⓐ Ⓑ Ⓒ Ⓓ Ⓔ
5. Ⓐ Ⓑ Ⓒ Ⓓ Ⓔ	41. Ⓐ Ⓑ Ⓒ Ⓓ Ⓔ	77. Ⓐ Ⓑ Ⓒ Ⓓ Ⓔ	113. Ⓐ Ⓑ Ⓒ Ⓓ Ⓔ	149. Ⓐ Ⓑ Ⓒ Ⓓ Ⓔ
6. Ⓐ Ⓑ Ⓒ Ⓓ Ⓔ	42. Ⓐ Ⓑ Ⓒ Ⓓ Ⓔ	78. Ⓐ Ⓑ Ⓒ Ⓓ Ⓔ	114. Ⓐ Ⓑ Ⓒ Ⓓ Ⓔ	150. Ⓐ Ⓑ Ⓒ Ⓓ Ⓔ
7. Ⓐ Ⓑ Ⓒ Ⓓ Ⓔ	43. Ⓐ Ⓑ Ⓒ Ⓓ Ⓔ	79. Ⓐ Ⓑ Ⓒ Ⓓ Ⓔ	115. Ⓐ Ⓑ Ⓒ Ⓓ Ⓔ	151. Ⓐ Ⓑ Ⓒ Ⓓ Ⓔ
8. Ⓐ Ⓑ Ⓒ Ⓓ Ⓔ	44. Ⓐ Ⓑ Ⓒ Ⓓ Ⓔ	80. Ⓐ Ⓑ Ⓒ Ⓓ Ⓔ	116. Ⓐ Ⓑ Ⓒ Ⓓ Ⓔ	152. Ⓐ Ⓑ Ⓒ Ⓓ Ⓔ
9. Ⓐ Ⓑ Ⓒ Ⓓ Ⓔ	45. Ⓐ Ⓑ Ⓒ Ⓓ Ⓔ	81. Ⓐ Ⓑ Ⓒ Ⓓ Ⓔ	117. Ⓐ Ⓑ Ⓒ Ⓓ Ⓔ	153. Ⓐ Ⓑ Ⓒ Ⓓ Ⓔ
10. Ⓐ Ⓑ Ⓒ Ⓓ Ⓔ	46. Ⓐ Ⓑ Ⓒ Ⓓ Ⓔ	82. Ⓐ Ⓑ Ⓒ Ⓓ Ⓔ	118. Ⓐ Ⓑ Ⓒ Ⓓ Ⓔ	154. Ⓐ Ⓑ Ⓒ Ⓓ Ⓔ
11. Ⓐ Ⓑ Ⓒ Ⓓ Ⓔ	47. Ⓐ Ⓑ Ⓒ Ⓓ Ⓔ	83. Ⓐ Ⓑ Ⓒ Ⓓ Ⓔ	119. Ⓐ Ⓑ Ⓒ Ⓓ Ⓔ	155. Ⓐ Ⓑ Ⓒ Ⓓ Ⓔ
12. Ⓐ Ⓑ Ⓒ Ⓓ Ⓔ	48. Ⓐ Ⓑ Ⓒ Ⓓ Ⓔ	84. Ⓐ Ⓑ Ⓒ Ⓓ Ⓔ	120. Ⓐ Ⓑ Ⓒ Ⓓ Ⓔ	156. Ⓐ Ⓑ Ⓒ Ⓓ Ⓔ
13. Ⓐ Ⓑ Ⓒ Ⓓ Ⓔ	49. Ⓐ Ⓑ Ⓒ Ⓓ Ⓔ	85. Ⓐ Ⓑ Ⓒ Ⓓ Ⓔ	121. Ⓐ Ⓑ Ⓒ Ⓓ Ⓔ	157. Ⓐ Ⓑ Ⓒ Ⓓ Ⓔ
14. Ⓐ Ⓑ Ⓒ Ⓓ Ⓔ	50. Ⓐ Ⓑ Ⓒ Ⓓ Ⓔ	86. Ⓐ Ⓑ Ⓒ Ⓓ Ⓔ	122. Ⓐ Ⓑ Ⓒ Ⓓ Ⓔ	158. Ⓐ Ⓑ Ⓒ Ⓓ Ⓔ
15. Ⓐ Ⓑ Ⓒ Ⓓ Ⓔ	51. Ⓐ Ⓑ Ⓒ Ⓓ Ⓔ	87. Ⓐ Ⓑ Ⓒ Ⓓ Ⓔ	123. Ⓐ Ⓑ Ⓒ Ⓓ Ⓔ	159. Ⓐ Ⓑ Ⓒ Ⓓ Ⓔ
16. Ⓐ Ⓑ Ⓒ Ⓓ Ⓔ	52. Ⓐ Ⓑ Ⓒ Ⓓ Ⓔ	88. Ⓐ Ⓑ Ⓒ Ⓓ Ⓔ	124. Ⓐ Ⓑ Ⓒ Ⓓ Ⓔ	160. Ⓐ Ⓑ Ⓒ Ⓓ Ⓔ
17. Ⓐ Ⓑ Ⓒ Ⓓ Ⓔ	53. Ⓐ Ⓑ Ⓒ Ⓓ Ⓔ	89. Ⓐ Ⓑ Ⓒ Ⓓ Ⓔ	125. Ⓐ Ⓑ Ⓒ Ⓓ Ⓔ	161. Ⓐ Ⓑ Ⓒ Ⓓ Ⓔ
18. Ⓐ Ⓑ Ⓒ Ⓓ Ⓔ	54. Ⓐ Ⓑ Ⓒ Ⓓ Ⓔ	90. Ⓐ Ⓑ Ⓒ Ⓓ Ⓔ	126. Ⓐ Ⓑ Ⓒ Ⓓ Ⓔ	162. Ⓐ Ⓑ Ⓒ Ⓓ Ⓔ
19. Ⓐ Ⓑ Ⓒ Ⓓ Ⓔ	55. Ⓐ Ⓑ Ⓒ Ⓓ Ⓔ	91. Ⓐ Ⓑ Ⓒ Ⓓ Ⓔ	127. Ⓐ Ⓑ Ⓒ Ⓓ Ⓕ	163. Ⓐ Ⓑ Ⓒ Ⓓ Ⓔ
20. Ⓐ Ⓑ Ⓒ Ⓓ Ⓔ	56. Ⓐ Ⓑ Ⓒ Ⓓ Ⓔ	92. Ⓐ Ⓑ Ⓒ Ⓓ Ⓔ	128. Ⓐ Ⓑ Ⓒ Ⓓ Ⓔ	164. Ⓐ Ⓑ Ⓒ Ⓓ Ⓔ
21. Ⓐ Ⓑ Ⓒ Ⓓ Ⓔ	57. Ⓐ Ⓑ Ⓒ Ⓓ Ⓔ	93. Ⓐ Ⓑ Ⓒ Ⓓ Ⓔ	129. Ⓐ Ⓑ Ⓒ Ⓓ Ⓔ	165. Ⓐ Ⓑ Ⓒ Ⓓ Ⓔ
22. Ⓐ Ⓑ Ⓒ Ⓓ Ⓔ	58. Ⓐ Ⓑ Ⓒ Ⓓ Ⓔ	94. Ⓐ Ⓑ Ⓒ Ⓓ Ⓔ	130. Ⓐ Ⓑ Ⓒ Ⓓ Ⓔ	166. Ⓐ Ⓑ Ⓒ Ⓓ Ⓔ
23. Ⓐ Ⓑ Ⓒ Ⓓ Ⓔ	59. Ⓐ Ⓑ Ⓒ Ⓓ Ⓔ	95. Ⓐ Ⓑ Ⓒ Ⓓ Ⓔ	131. Ⓐ Ⓑ Ⓒ Ⓓ Ⓔ	167. Ⓐ Ⓑ Ⓒ Ⓓ Ⓔ
24. Ⓐ Ⓑ Ⓒ Ⓓ Ⓔ	60. Ⓐ Ⓑ Ⓒ Ⓓ Ⓔ	96. Ⓐ Ⓑ Ⓒ Ⓓ Ⓔ	132. Ⓐ Ⓑ Ⓒ Ⓓ Ⓔ	168. Ⓐ Ⓑ Ⓒ Ⓓ Ⓔ
25. Ⓐ Ⓑ Ⓒ Ⓓ Ⓔ	61. Ⓐ Ⓑ Ⓒ Ⓓ Ⓔ	97. Ⓐ Ⓑ Ⓒ Ⓓ Ⓔ	133. Ⓐ Ⓑ Ⓒ Ⓓ Ⓔ	169. Ⓐ Ⓑ Ⓒ Ⓓ Ⓔ
26. Ⓐ Ⓑ Ⓒ Ⓓ Ⓔ	62. Ⓐ Ⓑ Ⓒ Ⓓ Ⓔ	98. Ⓐ Ⓑ Ⓒ Ⓓ Ⓔ	134. Ⓐ Ⓑ Ⓒ Ⓓ Ⓔ	170. Ⓐ Ⓑ Ⓒ Ⓓ Ⓔ
27. Ⓐ Ⓑ Ⓒ Ⓓ Ⓔ	63. Ⓐ Ⓑ Ⓒ Ⓓ Ⓔ	99. Ⓐ Ⓑ Ⓒ Ⓓ Ⓔ	135. Ⓐ Ⓑ Ⓒ Ⓓ Ⓔ	171. Ⓐ Ⓑ Ⓒ Ⓓ Ⓔ
28. Ⓐ Ⓑ Ⓒ Ⓓ Ⓔ	64. Ⓐ Ⓑ Ⓒ Ⓓ Ⓕ	100. Ⓐ Ⓑ Ⓒ Ⓓ Ⓔ	136. Ⓐ Ⓑ Ⓒ Ⓓ Ⓕ	172. Ⓐ Ⓑ Ⓒ Ⓓ Ⓔ
29. Ⓐ Ⓑ Ⓒ Ⓓ Ⓔ	65. Ⓐ Ⓑ Ⓒ Ⓓ Ⓔ	101. Ⓐ Ⓑ Ⓒ Ⓓ Ⓔ	137. Ⓐ Ⓑ Ⓒ Ⓓ Ⓔ	173. Ⓐ Ⓑ Ⓒ Ⓓ Ⓔ
30. Ⓐ Ⓑ Ⓒ Ⓓ Ⓔ	66. Ⓐ Ⓑ Ⓒ Ⓓ Ⓔ	102. Ⓐ Ⓑ Ⓒ Ⓓ Ⓔ	138. Ⓐ Ⓑ Ⓒ Ⓓ Ⓔ	174. Ⓐ Ⓑ Ⓒ Ⓓ Ⓔ
31. Ⓐ Ⓑ Ⓒ Ⓓ Ⓔ	67. Ⓐ Ⓑ Ⓒ Ⓓ Ⓔ	103. Ⓐ Ⓑ Ⓒ Ⓓ Ⓔ	139. Ⓐ Ⓑ Ⓒ Ⓓ Ⓔ	175. Ⓐ Ⓑ Ⓒ Ⓓ Ⓔ
32. Ⓐ Ⓑ Ⓒ Ⓓ Ⓔ	68. Ⓐ Ⓑ Ⓒ Ⓓ Ⓔ	104. Ⓐ Ⓑ Ⓒ Ⓓ Ⓔ	140. Ⓐ Ⓑ Ⓒ Ⓓ Ⓔ	176. Ⓐ Ⓑ Ⓒ Ⓓ Ⓔ
33. Ⓐ Ⓑ Ⓒ Ⓓ Ⓔ	69. Ⓐ Ⓑ Ⓒ Ⓓ Ⓔ	105. Ⓐ Ⓑ Ⓒ Ⓓ Ⓔ	141. Ⓐ Ⓑ Ⓒ Ⓓ Ⓔ	177. Ⓐ Ⓑ Ⓒ Ⓓ Ⓔ
34. Ⓐ Ⓑ Ⓒ Ⓓ Ⓔ	70. Ⓐ Ⓑ Ⓒ Ⓓ Ⓔ	106. Ⓐ Ⓑ Ⓒ Ⓓ Ⓔ	142. Ⓐ Ⓑ Ⓒ Ⓓ Ⓔ	178. Ⓐ Ⓑ Ⓒ Ⓓ Ⓔ
35. Ⓐ Ⓑ Ⓒ Ⓓ Ⓔ	71. Ⓐ Ⓑ Ⓒ Ⓓ Ⓔ	107. Ⓐ Ⓑ Ⓒ Ⓓ Ⓔ	143. Ⓐ Ⓑ Ⓒ Ⓓ Ⓔ	179. Ⓐ Ⓑ Ⓒ Ⓓ Ⓔ
36. Ⓐ Ⓑ Ⓒ Ⓓ Ⓔ	72. Ⓐ Ⓑ Ⓒ Ⓓ Ⓔ	108. Ⓐ Ⓑ Ⓒ Ⓓ Ⓔ	144. Ⓐ Ⓑ Ⓒ Ⓓ Ⓔ	180. Ⓐ Ⓑ Ⓒ Ⓓ Ⓔ

181. (A)(B)(C)(D)(E)   217. (A)(B)(C)(D)(E)   253. (A)(B)(C)(D)(E)   289. (A)(B)(C)(D)(E)   325. (A)(B)(C)(D)(E)
182. (A)(B)(C)(D)(E)   218. (A)(B)(C)(D)(E)   254. (A)(B)(C)(D)(E)   290. (A)(B)(C)(D)(E)   326. (A)(B)(C)(D)(E)
183. (A)(B)(C)(D)(E)   219. (A)(B)(C)(D)(E)   255. (A)(B)(C)(D)(E)   291. (A)(B)(C)(D)(E)   327. (A)(B)(C)(D)(E)
184. (A)(B)(C)(D)(E)   220. (A)(B)(C)(D)(E)   256. (A)(B)(C)(D)(E)   292. (A)(B)(C)(D)(E)   328. (A)(B)(C)(D)(E)
185. (A)(B)(C)(D)(E)   221. (A)(B)(C)(D)(E)   257. (A)(B)(C)(D)(E)   293. (A)(B)(C)(D)(E)   329. (A)(B)(C)(D)(E)
186. (A)(B)(C)(D)(E)   222. (A)(B)(C)(D)(E)   258. (A)(B)(C)(D)(E)   294. (A)(B)(C)(D)(E)   330. (A)(B)(C)(D)(E)
187. (A)(B)(C)(D)(E)   223. (A)(B)(C)(D)(E)   259. (A)(B)(C)(D)(E)   295. (A)(B)(C)(D)(E)   331. (A)(B)(C)(D)(E)
188. (A)(B)(C)(D)(E)   224. (A)(B)(C)(D)(E)   260. (A)(B)(C)(D)(E)   296. (A)(B)(C)(D)(E)   332. (A)(B)(C)(D)(E)
189. (A)(B)(C)(D)(E)   225. (A)(B)(C)(D)(E)   261. (A)(B)(C)(D)(E)   297. (A)(B)(C)(D)(E)   333. (A)(B)(C)(D)(E)
190. (A)(B)(C)(D)(E)   226. (A)(B)(C)(D)(E)   262. (A)(B)(C)(D)(E)   298. (A)(B)(C)(D)(E)   334. (A)(B)(C)(D)(E)
191. (A)(B)(C)(D)(E)   227. (A)(B)(C)(D)(E)   263. (A)(B)(C)(D)(E)   299. (A)(B)(C)(D)(E)   335. (A)(B)(C)(D)(E)
192. (A)(B)(C)(D)(E)   228. (A)(B)(C)(D)(E)   264. (A)(B)(C)(D)(E)   300. (A)(B)(C)(D)(E)   336. (A)(B)(C)(D)(E)
193. (A)(B)(C)(D)(E)   229. (A)(B)(C)(D)(E)   265. (A)(B)(C)(D)(E)   301. (A)(B)(C)(D)(E)   337. (A)(B)(C)(D)(E)
194. (A)(B)(C)(D)(E)   230. (A)(B)(C)(D)(E)   266. (A)(B)(C)(D)(E)   302. (A)(B)(C)(D)(E)   338. (A)(B)(C)(D)(E)
195. (A)(B)(C)(D)(E)   231. (A)(B)(C)(D)(E)   267. (A)(B)(C)(D)(E)   303. (A)(B)(C)(D)(E)   339. (A)(B)(C)(D)(E)
196. (A)(B)(C)(D)(E)   232. (A)(B)(C)(D)(E)   268. (A)(B)(C)(D)(E)   304. (A)(B)(C)(D)(E)   340. (A)(B)(C)(D)(E)
197. (A)(B)(C)(D)(E)   233. (A)(B)(C)(D)(E)   269. (A)(B)(C)(D)(E)   305. (A)(B)(C)(D)(E)   341. (A)(B)(C)(D)(E)
198. (A)(B)(C)(D)(E)   234. (A)(B)(C)(D)(E)   270. (A)(B)(C)(D)(E)   306. (A)(B)(C)(D)(E)   342. (A)(B)(C)(D)(E)
199. (A)(B)(C)(D)(E)   235. (A)(B)(C)(D)(E)   271. (A)(B)(C)(D)(E)   307. (A)(B)(C)(D)(E)   343. (A)(B)(C)(D)(E)
200. (A)(B)(C)(D)(E)   236. (A)(B)(C)(D)(E)   272. (A)(B)(C)(D)(E)   308. (A)(B)(C)(D)(E)   344. (A)(B)(C)(D)(E)
201. (A)(B)(C)(D)(E)   237. (A)(B)(C)(D)(E)   273. (A)(B)(C)(D)(E)   309. (A)(B)(C)(D)(E)   345. (A)(B)(C)(D)(E)
202. (A)(B)(C)(D)(E)   238. (A)(B)(C)(D)(E)   274. (A)(B)(C)(D)(E)   310. (A)(B)(C)(D)(E)   346. (A)(B)(C)(D)(E)
203. (A)(B)(C)(D)(E)   239. (A)(B)(C)(D)(E)   275. (A)(B)(C)(D)(E)   311. (A)(B)(C)(D)(E)   347. (A)(B)(C)(D)(E)
204. (A)(B)(C)(D)(E)   240. (A)(B)(C)(D)(E)   276. (A)(B)(C)(D)(E)   312. (A)(B)(C)(D)(E)   348. (A)(B)(C)(D)(E)
205. (A)(B)(C)(D)(E)   241. (A)(B)(C)(D)(E)   277. (A)(B)(C)(D)(E)   313. (A)(B)(C)(D)(E)   349. (A)(B)(C)(D)(E)
206. (A)(B)(C)(D)(E)   242. (A)(B)(C)(D)(E)   278. (A)(B)(C)(D)(E)   314. (A)(B)(C)(D)(E)   350. (A)(B)(C)(D)(E)
207. (A)(B)(C)(D)(E)   243. (A)(B)(C)(D)(E)   279. (A)(B)(C)(D)(E)   315. (A)(B)(C)(D)(E)   351. (A)(B)(C)(D)(E)
208. (A)(B)(C)(D)(E)   244. (A)(B)(C)(D)(E)   280. (A)(B)(C)(D)(E)   316. (A)(B)(C)(D)(E)   352. (A)(B)(C)(D)(E)
209. (A)(B)(C)(D)(E)   245. (A)(B)(C)(D)(E)   281. (A)(B)(C)(D)(E)   317. (A)(B)(C)(D)(E)   353. (A)(B)(C)(D)(E)
210. (A)(B)(C)(D)(E)   246. (A)(B)(C)(D)(E)   282. (A)(B)(C)(D)(E)   318. (A)(B)(C)(D)(E)   354. (A)(B)(C)(D)(E)
211. (A)(B)(C)(D)(E)   247. (A)(B)(C)(D)(E)   283. (A)(B)(C)(D)(E)   319. (A)(B)(C)(D)(E)   355. (A)(B)(C)(D)(E)
212. (A)(B)(C)(D)(E)   248. (A)(B)(C)(D)(E)   284. (A)(B)(C)(D)(E)   320. (A)(B)(C)(D)(E)   356. (A)(B)(C)(D)(E)
213. (A)(B)(C)(D)(E)   249. (A)(B)(C)(D)(E)   285. (A)(B)(C)(D)(E)   321. (A)(B)(C)(D)(E)   357. (A)(B)(C)(D)(E)
214. (A)(B)(C)(D)(E)   250. (A)(B)(C)(D)(E)   286. (A)(B)(C)(D)(E)   322. (A)(B)(C)(D)(E)   358. (A)(B)(C)(D)(E)
215. (A)(B)(C)(D)(E)   251. (A)(B)(C)(D)(E)   287. (A)(B)(C)(D)(E)   323. (A)(B)(C)(D)(E)   359. (A)(B)(C)(D)(E)
216. (A)(B)(C)(D)(E)   252. (A)(B)(C)(D)(E)   288. (A)(B)(C)(D)(E)   324. (A)(B)(C)(D)(E)   360. (A)(B)(C)(D)(E)

Practice Test 3

1. A 37-year-old female presents with night pain, numbness, and loss of strength in the right wrist. Physical examination reveals a positive Tinel's sign and positive Phalen's test. Based on the patient's presentation and physical examination, which of the following is the most appropriate diagnosis?
   (A) Carpal tunnel syndrome
   (B) Colles's fracture
   (C) De Quervain's disease
   (D) Rheumatoid arthritis
   (E) Scaphoid fracture

2. A 22-year-old female presents with history of feigning signs and symptoms of several disease processes and attempting to gain hospital admission for these diseases by assuming several different names. Full work-up, including bloodwork and radiographic study, fail to find any clinical explanation for the symptoms she is feigning. Based on the patient's presentation and work-up, which of the following is the most appropriate diagnosis?
   (A) Body dysmorphic disorder
   (B) Conversion disorder
   (C) Factitious disorder
   (D) Hypochondriasis
   (E) Somatization disorder

3. The Bacille Calmette-Guerin vaccine is administered to prevent the occurrence of which of the following pulmonary disorders?
   (A) Bacterial pneumonia
   (B) Bronchitis
   (C) Emphysema
   (D) Tuberculosis
   (E) Viral pneumonia

4. Altering one's diet to include higher amounts of water, caffeine, and salt is the indicated treatment for which of the following disorders?
   (A) Diabetes insipidus
   (B) Essential hypertension
   (C) Orthostatic hypotension
   (D) Pulmonary hypertension
   (E) Vertigo

5. A 45-year-old white male presents with sudden onset of crushing sub-sternal chest pain and shortness of breath. Electrocardiogram reveals normal sinus rhythm at 78 beats per minute with no S-T segment abnormality. Pulse oximetry reveals a level of 89% on room air. Blood test results are as follows:

Troponin level	> 0.1
D-dimer level	0.59
Blood Urea Nitrogen	38
Serum Creatinine	2.2
GFR	52

Lung VQ scan showed normal ventilation and multiple perfusion defects. Based on the patient's presentation and test results, which of the following is the most appropriate diagnosis?
   (A) Bilateral pleural effusions
   (B) Lung cancer
   (C) Pneumonia
   (D) Pneumothorax
   (E) Pulmonary embolism

6. A 36-year-old male with a recent history of a severe laceration to the left calf presents with nausea, vomiting, and diarrhea. Examination of the left calf laceration reveals excessive pain in the area of injury. The skin around the injury has changed color and now appears violet. There are blisters on the surrounding skin and a clear yellow discharge issues from the wound. The pain and skin discoloration has spread both proximally and distally. Based on the patient's presentation and examination, which of the following is the most appropriate diagnosis?
   (A) Cellulitis
   (B) Osteomyelitis
   (C) Necrotizing fasciitis
   (D) Tetanus
   (E) Gangrene

7. A 14-year-old female presents with scattered yellow-to-gray colored macules and papules with a greasy appearance on the face and scalp. Examination of the scalp reveals the presence of dandruff. What is the appropriate diagnosis made from this examination?
   (A) Contact eczema
   (B) Discoid eczema
   (C) Neurodermatitis
   (D) Seborrheic eczema
   (E) Stasis dermatitis

8. A 50-year-old male presents with cough, purulent sputum, and rigors. The patient's sputum was noticed to be rust colored. Chest X-ray confirmed the diagnosis of pneumonia. Due to the presence of rust-colored sputum, which of the following pathogens is the most likely cause of this patient's pneumonia?
   (A) *Chlamydia pneumoniae*
   (B) *Klebsiella pneumoniae*
   (C) *Legionella pneumoniae*
   (D) *Mycoplasma pneumoniae*
   (E) *Streptococcus pneumoniae*

9. A 30-minute eye flush with water or normal saline is the proper clinical intervention for which of the following ocular disorders?
   (A) Blepharitis
   (B) Chemical burn
   (C) Corneal abrasion
   (D) Foreign object
   (E) Penetrating trauma

10. A 36-year-old male presents for routine examination. His blood pressure was noticed to be mildly elevated. He is very compliant with doctors' advice. Which of the following treatment options would you suggest to manage newly diagnosed, mild hypertension?
    (A) ACE inhibitors
    (B) Beta-adrenergic antagonists
    (C) Calcium channel blockers
    (D) Diuretics
    (E) Reduction of dietary sodium intake

11. In addition to oxygen therapy, chronic alveolitis associated with pneumoconioses, such as silicosis, is treated by which of the following medications?
    (A) Anti-inflammatories
    (B) Broad-spectrum antibiotics
    (C) Bronchodilators
    (D) Corticosteroids
    (E) NSAIDs

12. A 24-year-old male presents with pain in the left shoulder. Physical examination reveals a bump on the acromioclavicular joint. Based on the patient's presentation, which of the following is the most appropriate diagnosis?
    (A) Acromioclavicular separation
    (B) Adhesive capsulitis
    (C) Bankart's lesion
    (D) Hills-Sachs lesion
    (E) Rotator cuff syndrome

13. A 26-year-old female presents with anxiety, depression, and irrational fear of contracting a serious illness. She frequently misinterprets normal bodily sensations as manifestations of disease. Based on the patient's behavior and personality, which of the following is the most likely diagnosis?
    (A) Body dysmorphic disorder
    (B) Conversion disorder
    (C) Factitious disorder
    (D) Hypochondriasis
    (E) Somatization disorder

14. A 46-year-old obese African-American male presents with sudden onset of chest tightness radiating to his back and left arm, along with nausea. Chest X-ray was normal, and electrocardiogram is shown here. Troponin level was 0.4. D-dimer level was 0.42. Pulse oximetry was normal at 100% at room air. Blood pressure was 150/70. Patient

was administered nitroglycerin with no resolution of chest pain.

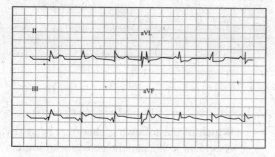

Based on the patient's electrocardiogram, which of the following diagnostic procedures would you perform?

(A) Coronary angiography to evaluate for myocardial infarction

(B) CT scan with contrast of the chest to rule out pulmonary embolism

(C) Echocardiogram to evaluate cardiac function

(D) Myocardial perfusion scan to evaluate for myocardial infarction

(E) Treadmill test to detect reduced blood supply to the heart

15. A healthy 28-year-old male presents with flesh-colored, waxy, dome-shaped, umbilicated lesions on the groin and lower abdomen. A white curd-like material can be expressed from under the depression of the lesions. What is the appropriate diagnosis made from this examination?

(A) Contact dermatitis

(B) Dyshidrotic eczema

(C) Molluscum contagiosum

(D) Neurodermatitis

(E) Seborrheic eczema

16. A 44-year-old female presents with weight loss, insomnia, exophthalmos, and a visible goiter. Chest X-ray is normal. CT scan and ultrasound exams of the abdomen both reveal abnormalities to the adrenal glands. Which is the appropriate diagnosis?

(A) Addison's disease

(B) Grave's disease

(C) Hashimoto's thyroiditis

(D) Pheochromocytoma

(E) Wilson's disease

17. A 45-year-old male presents with pterygium encroaching on the cornea and interfering with vision. What would be the most appropriate course of treatment for this patient?

(A) Excision

(B) Intravenous antibiotics

(C) Ophthalmic antibiotics

(D) Ophthalmic corticosteroids

(E) Warm compresses

18. Which of the following medications is the gold standard medicinal treatment for sarcoidosis?

(A) ACE inhibitors

(B) Alpha-adrenergic antagonists

(C) Beta-adrenergic antagonists

(D) Calcium channel blockers

(E) Corticosteroids

19. A 62-year-old chronically ill male with a history of alcohol abuse presents with cough, purulent sputum, and rigors. The patient's sputum is noted to be the color of currant jelly. Chest X-ray confirms the presence of pneumonia. Due to the presence of currant jelly–colored sputum, which of the following pathogens is the most likely cause of this patient's pneumonia?

(A) *Chlamydia pneumoniae*

(B) *Klebsiella pneumoniae*

(C) *Legionella pneumoniae*

(D) *Mycoplasma pneumoniae*

(E) *Streptococcus pneumoniae*

20. A 56-year-old Caucasian male presents for a routine physical exam. This gentleman complains of pain in his legs after walking a short distance, indicating claudication. Which of the following medications would you prescribe for maintenance therapy of this disorder?

(A) Cilostazol

(B) Diltiazem

(C) Felodipine

(D) Valsartan

(E) Verapamil

21. A 68-year-old male presents with cough, dyspnea, fever, chest discomfort, and sore throat. Auscultation of the chest reveals expiratory wheezes. Chest X-ray is normal. Based on the patient's presentation, physical examination, and test results, which of the following is the most appropriate diagnosis?
    (A) Bronchitis
    (B) Pulmonary hypertension
    (C) Pleural effusion
    (D) Pneumonia
    (E) Tuberculosis

22. A 29-year-old male with a history of chlamydial urethritis develops asymmetric arthritis. His physical examination reveals inflammation of the foreskin of the penis and conjunctivitis. Based on the patient's history and physical examination, which of the following is the most appropriate diagnosis?
    (A) Gout
    (B) Psoriatic arthritis
    (C) Reactive arthritis
    (D) Rheumatoid arthritis
    (E) Septic arthritis

23. Congestive heart failure is most effectively treated by which of the following medications?
    (A) ACE inhibitors
    (B) Alpha-adrenergic antagonists
    (C) Beta-adrenergic antagonists
    (D) Calcium channel blockers
    (E) Diuretics

24. Isoniazid, commonly referred to as INH, is a standard maintenance medication for treatment of tuberculosis. Which of the following vitamins should be administered concurrently with INH to reduce side effects associated with this therapy?
    (A) Vitamin A
    (B) Vitamin B6
    (C) Vitamin B12
    (D) Vitamin C
    (E) Vitamin D

25. A 66-year-old white male presents with dizziness, chest pressure, shortness of breath, and heart palpitations for several weeks. EKG is shown here. Cholesterol is borderline elevated at 210. Troponin levels are normal at 0.2 ng/mL. D-dimer level is normal at 0.37.

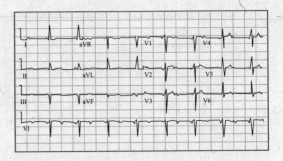

Which of the following abnormal heart rhythms is evident in the patient's electrocardiogram?
    (A) 2:1 AV block
    (B) Complete heart block
    (C) First-degree AV block
    (D) Normal sinus rhythm
    (E) Wenckebach

26. A 44-year-old female reports having had gradual decrease in vision, episodes of double vision, and reduced color perception. Examination reveals translucent, yellow discoloration of the lens. Based on the patient's presentation and examination, which of the following is the most appropriate diagnosis?
    (A) Blepharitis
    (B) Cataracts
    (C) Chalazion
    (D) Glaucoma
    (E) Hordeola

27. A 47-year-old male presents with chest pain on exertion that is relieved by rest. The patient describes his chest pain as chest pressure with the occasional "squeezing." No chest X-ray abnormalities, CT scan abnormalities, or bloodwork abnormalities are found. Which is the appropriate diagnosis?
    (A) Acute coronary syndrome
    (B) Prinzmetal's angina
    (C) Pulmonary hypertension
    (D) Stable angina
    (E) Unstable angina

28. Which of the following describes the type of shock that results from tension pneumothorax or pulmonary embolism?
    (A) Cardiogenic shock
    (B) Compensated shock
    (C) Distributive shock
    (D) Hypovolemic shock
    (E) Obstructive shock

29. A 27-year-old male presents with acute onset of copious, purulent discharge from both eyes. Gram stain showed presence of *Neisseria gonorrhoeae*. You diagnose this patient with bacterial conjunctivitis. Which of the following is the proper course of treatment?
   (A) Intravenous antibiotics
   (B) Ophthalmic antibiotics
   (C) Ophthalmic corticosteroids
   (D) Excision
   (E) Warm compresses

30. In addition to diuretics, which of the following medications would you add to a treatment regimen when congestive heart failure presents with additional symptoms of chest pain and hypertension?
   (A) ACE inhibitors
   (B) Alpha-adrenergic antagonists
   (C) Beta-adrenergic antagonists
   (D) Calcium channel blockers
   (E) Corticosteroids

31. Which of the following vaccines should be administered to all adults aged 19-64 who suffer from asthma?
   (A) Hib vaccine
   (B) Bacille Calmette-Guerin vaccine
   (C) Pneumococcal conjugate vaccine (PCV)
   (D) Pneumococcal polysaccharide vaccine (PPSV)
   (E) Polyvalent pneumococcal vaccine

32. A 26-year-old female presents with the behavior pattern of being dependent, clinging, and submissive. She has difficulty making her own decisions and will not disagree with anyone for fear of being disliked. Based on these characteristics, which of the following is the most appropriate diagnosis?
   (A) Adjustment disorder
   (B) Borderline personality disorder
   (C) Dependent personality disorder
   (D) Narcissistic personality disorder
   (E) Schizotypal personality disorder

33. A 36-year-old male presents with cough, fever, night sweats, anorexia, and weight loss. Chest X-ray reveals homogenous infiltrates, paratracheal lymph node enlargement, and cavitations. Based on the patient's presentation, physical examination, and test results, which of the following is the most appropriate diagnosis?
   (A) Bronchitis
   (B) Pleural effusion
   (C) Pneumonia
   (D) Pulmonary hypertension
   (E) Tuberculosis

34. Which of the following vaccines should be administered to high-risk children at least 2 years of age? These include children with heart problems, lung problems, sickle cell disease, and diabetes.
   (A) Hib vaccine
   (B) Bacille Calmette-Guerin vaccine
   (C) Pneumococcal conjugate vaccine
   (D) Pneumococcal polysaccharide vaccine
   (E) Polyvalent pneumococcal vaccine

35. A healthy 40-year-old male presents for routine, annual check-up. The patient does not complain of any symptoms. Electrocardiogram is normal. Blood pressure is normal. Auscultation of the heart reveals a "swishing" sound. You order an echocardiogram to evaluate the "swishing" sound. Which of the following abnormalities would you expect to find on the echocardiogram?
   (A) Cardiomyopathy
   (B) Carotid stenosis
   (C) Congestive heart failure
   (D) Mitral valve prolapse
   (E) Pericarditis

36. A 48-year-old male presents with thick, crusted, golden "honey" lesions on his skin. Based on patient symptoms and physical examination, which of the following is the proper diagnosis?
   (A) Cellulitis
   (B) Erysipelas
   (C) Impetigo
   (D) Scabies
   (E) Vitiligo

37. After a motor vehicle accident, a 58-year-old female presents with chest pain and shortness of breath. Her initial blood pressure is 140/90 mmHg. Suddenly, the patient's blood pressure falls to 70/40 mmHg, heart rate rises to 140 beats per minutes, and mental status becomes altered. The patient's chest X-ray reveals a left-side tension pneumo-thorax. The patient is most likely experiencing:
    (A) Cardiogenic shock
    (B) Distributive shock
    (C) Hypovolemic shock
    (D) Obstructive shock
    (E) Septic shock

38. *Helicobacter pylori* is the primary cause of which of the following disorders?
    (A) Celiac disease
    (B) Chronic gastritis
    (C) Crohn's disease
    (D) GERD
    (E) Diverticulitis

39. A normally healthy 42-year-old male presents with hemoptysis, cough, focal wheezing, and recurrent pneumonia. Bronchoscopy reveals a pink to purple well-vascularized central lesion. You diagnose this patient with a carcinoid tumor. Which of the following is the most appropriate treatment for this disorder?
    (A) Chemotherapy
    (B) Immunotherapy
    (C) Inhaled corticosteroids
    (D) Radiation therapy
    (E) Surgical excision

40. Quinidine and procainamide are maintenance medications for abnormal heart rhythms such as supraventricular tachycardia and symptomatic premature ventricular contractions. These medications belong to the class of drugs known as:
    (A) Angiotensin antagonists
    (B) Beta-adrenergic antagonists
    (C) Nitrates
    (D) Sodium channel blockers
    (E) Vasodilators

41. The condition of resting chest pain, also known as Prinzmetal's angina, is most effectively treated with which of the following medications?
    (A) Angiotensin antagonists
    (B) Beta-adrenergic antagonists

(C) Nitrates
(D) Sodium channel blockers
(E) Vasodilators

42. An ultrasound of the abdomen performed on a 3-year-old child reveals an olive-shaped mass to the right of the navel. Which of the following disorders does this mass indicate?
    (A) Bowel atresia
    (B) Diaphragmatic hernia
    (C) Esophageal etresia
    (D) Pyloric stenosis
    (E) Volvulus

43. A thin, 15-year-old male presents with acute chest pain, shortness of breath, and one-sided chest expansion. Auscultation of the chest reveals dimin-ished breath sounds on the right side. Chest X-ray reveals a visceral pleural line. Based on the patient's presentation, history, and test results, which of the following is the most accurate diagnosis?
    (A) Pleural effusion
    (B) Pneumothorax
    (C) Pulmonary edema
    (D) Pulmonary embolism
    (E) Pulmonary hypertension

44. A 58-year-old female presents with exertional dyspnea, non-productive cough, and fatigue. Auscultation of the chest reveals basilar rales and gallops. Patient's chest X-ray reveals cardiomegaly, bilateral pleural effusions, and perivascular edema. Based on the patient's presentation, physical exam, and test results, which of the following is the most accurate diagnosis?
    (A) Congestive heart failure
    (B) Cardiogenic shock
    (C) Cardiac arrest
    (D) Hypertensive emergency
    (E) Stroke

45. Large outpouchings of mucosa in the colon con-stitute the condition called:
    (A) Intussusception
    (B) Diverticulosis
    (C) Diverticulitis
    (D) Ulcerative colitis
    (E) Volvulus

46. A 22-year-old female presents to the emergency room with acute onset of ipsilateral chest pain and shortness of breath. The examination and chest X-ray reveal a large pneumothorax. Which of the following is the proper course of treatment?
(A) Insert chest tube.
(B) Insert large bore needle in the chest.
(C) Intubate the patient.
(D) Perform a tracheotomy.
(E) Perform thoracentesis.

47. Which of the following cardiac arrhythmias is most effectively treated with intravenous administration of a 6 mg dose of adenosine?
(A) Atrial fibrillation
(B) Atrial flutter
(C) Bradychardia
(D) Supraventricular tachycardia
(E) Ventricular tachycardia

48. Which of the following diagnostic procedures is the gold standard for diagnosing abnormalities of the testicles?
(A) CT angiogram of the testicles
(B) MRI angiogram of the testicles
(C) Nuclear medicine testicular scan
(D) Testicular ultrasound
(E) X-ray of the testicles

49. A 46-year-old patient experienced a myocardial infarction two weeks previously, and now presents with fever. Echocardiogram reveals pericarditis. Chest X-ray reveals pleural effusions. Based on the patient's presentation, physical exam, and test results, which of the following is the most accurate diagnosis?
(A) Cardiogenic shock
(B) Cardiac tamponade
(C) Congestive heart failure
(D) Dressler's syndrome
(E) Pneumothorax

50. A 66-year-old female with a history of congestive heart failure presents with nausea and leg swelling. Physical examination reveals distended neck veins, tender hepatomegaly, and pitting edema. Chest X-ray revealed cardiomegaly with bilateral pleural effusions. Based on the patient's presentation, physical exam, and test results, which of the following is the most accurate diagnosis?
(A) Cystic fibrosis
(B) Left-sided congestive heart failure

(C) Primary pneumothorax
(D) Right-sided congestive heart failure
(E) Tension pneumothorax

51. Which of the following conditions appears as a linear lesion on the posterior midline of the rectal wall?
(A) Anal fissure
(B) Anorectal abscess
(C) Hemorrhoid
(D) Pilonidal cyst
(E) Pruritis ani

52. A 62-year-old male presents with recurrent pulmonary embolism. His disorder has been resistant to anticoagulants. Due to this man's history and condition, which of the following treatment options would you suggest?
(A) Continue oral anticoagulants
(B) Intravenous anticoagulants
(C) Surgical clot removal
(D) Thrombolysis
(E) Vena cava filter

53. Which of the following types of medication is a first-line treatment for maintenance of mild gastro-esophageal reflux disease (GERD)?
(A) Antacids
(B) Calcium channel blockers
(C) Corticosteroids
(D) Histamine blockers
(E) Proton pump inhibitors

54. A 52-year-old female presents with fever, fatigue, weight loss, and bilateral morning stiffness in the neck, shoulders and pelvis. Lab work revealed a markedly erythrocyte sedimentation rate. Based on the patient's presentation and lab results, which of the following is the most appropriate diagnosis?
(A) Fibromyalgia
(B) Polyarteritis nodosa
(C) Polymyalgia rheumatica
(D) Polymyositis
(E) Systemic sclerosis

55. A 67-year-old male presents with dry cough, exertional dyspnea, fatigue, and malaise. Auscultation of the chest reveals inspiratory crackles. Chest X-ray reveals fibrosis that appears to have progressed in comparison to an X-ray taken several years previously. Based on the patient's presentation, physical examination, and test results, which of the following is the most appropriate diagnosis?
    (A) Community-acquired pneumonia
    (B) Idiopathic fibrosing interstitial pneumonia
    (C) Nosocomial pneumonia
    (D) Pneumocystis pneumonia
    (E) Tuberculosis

56. Which of the following medications is appropriate for treatment of the cardiac arrhythmia ventricular tachycardia?
    (A) ACE inhibitors
    (B) Adenosine
    (C) Beta-blockers
    (D) Calcium channel blockers
    (E) Lidocaine

57. Which of the following glomerular filtration rate values are indicative of impaired renal function?
    (A) 60 mL/1.73 m^2 of body surface area
    (B) 80 mL/min/1.73 m^2 of body surface area
    (C) 100 mL/min/1.73 m^2 of body surface area
    (D) 120 mL/min/1.73 m^2 of body surface area
    (E) 150 mL/min/1.73 m^2 of body surface area

58. A newborn male infant presents with extreme cyanosis and tachypnea without respiratory distress and poor feeding. Physical examination reveals absent lower extremity pulses. Auscultation of the chest reveals a single loud S2 and a systolic murmur. Based on the presentation and physical examination, which of the following is the proper diagnosis?
    (A) Hypoplastic left heart syndrome
    (B) Pulmonary atresia
    (C) Tetralogy of Fallot
    (D) Transposition of the great vessels
    (E) Ventricular outflow tract obstruction

59. A 47-year-old active white female reports that she has been experiencing lower leg pain with exercise. Pain is relieved with rest. Auscultation of the legs reveals a weak femoral pulse with an aortic bruit. Doppler study reveals an ankle-brachial index of 0.9. Based on the patient's presentation, physical

examination, and test results, which of the following is the most appropriate diagnosis?
    (A) Atherosclerosis
    (B) Chronic venous insufficiency
    (C) Deep venous thrombosis
    (D) Peripheral arterial disease
    (E) Varicose veins

60. The obturator or Cope sign is a classic medical sign for which of the following disorders?
    (A) Appendicitis
    (B) Cholecystitis
    (C) Gastritis
    (D) Hepatitis
    (E) Pancreatitis

61. A chronically ill 80-year-old emergency-room patient appears unresponsive. A pulse cannot be detected. The patient's electrocardiogram is illustrated below.

Based on the electrocardiographic findings, which is the most appropriate course of treatment?
    (A) Cardiac ablation
    (B) Cardioversion
    (C) Electrical defibrillation
    (D) IV lidocaine
    (E) IV adenosine

62. Decreasing alcohol consumption is the most effective treatment for which of the following gastrointestinal disorders?
    (A) Acute cholecystitis
    (B) Cirrhosis
    (C) Chronic pancreatitis
    (D) Duodenal ulcer
    (E) Gastric ulcer

63. An ultrasound examination revealing bilateral fluid-filled renal cysts is a classic diagnosis for which of the following disorders?
    (A) Interstitial nephritis
    (B) Nephrolithiasis

55. A 67-year-old male presents with dry cough, exertional dyspnea, fatigue, and malaise. Auscultation of the chest reveals inspiratory crackles. Chest X-ray reveals fibrosis that appears to have progressed in comparison to an X-ray taken several years previously. Based on the patient's presentation, physical examination, and test results, which of the following is the most appropriate diagnosis?
   (A) Community-acquired pneumonia
   (B) Idiopathic fibrosing interstitial pneumonia
   (C) Nosocomial pneumonia
   (D) Pneumocystis pneumonia
   (E) Tuberculosis

56. Which of the following medications is appropriate for treatment of the cardiac arrhythmia ventricular tachycardia?
   (A) ACE inhibitors
   (B) Adenosine
   (C) Beta-blockers
   (D) Calcium channel blockers
   (E) Lidocaine

57. Which of the following glomerular filtration rate values are indicative of impaired renal function?
   (A) 60 mL/1.73 m² of body surface area
   (B) 80 mL/min/1.73 m² of body surface area
   (C) 100 mL/min/1.73 m² of body surface area
   (D) 120 mL/min/1.73 m² of body surface area
   (E) 150 mL/min/1.73 m² of body surface area

58. A newborn male infant presents with extreme cyanosis and tachypnea without respiratory distress and poor feeding. Physical examination reveals absent lower extremity pulses. Auscultation of the chest reveals a single loud S2 and a systolic murmur. Based on the presentation and physical examination, which of the following is the proper diagnosis?
   (A) Hypoplastic left heart syndrome
   (B) Pulmonary atresia
   (C) Tetralogy of Fallot
   (D) Transposition of the great vessels
   (E) Ventricular outflow tract obstruction

59. A 47-year-old active white female reports that she has been experiencing lower leg pain with exercise. Pain is relieved with rest. Auscultation of the legs reveals a weak femoral pulse with an aortic bruit. Doppler study reveals an ankle-brachial index of 0.9. Based on the patient's presentation, physical examination, and test results, which of the following is the most appropriate diagnosis?
   (A) Atherosclerosis
   (B) Chronic venous insufficiency
   (C) Deep venous thrombosis
   (D) Peripheral arterial disease
   (E) Varicose veins

60. The obturator or Cope sign is a classic medical sign for which of the following disorders?
   (A) Appendicitis
   (B) Cholecystitis
   (C) Gastritis
   (D) Hepatitis
   (E) Pancreatitis

61. A chronically ill 80-year-old emergency-room patient appears unresponsive. A pulse cannot be detected. The patient's electrocardiogram is illustrated below.

   Based on the electrocardiographic findings, which is the most appropriate course of treatment?
   (A) Cardiac ablation
   (B) Cardioversion
   (C) Electrical defibrillation
   (D) IV lidocaine
   (E) IV adenosine

62. Decreasing alcohol consumption is the most effective treatment for which of the following gastrointestinal disorders?
   (A) Acute cholecystitis
   (B) Cirrhosis
   (C) Chronic pancreatitis
   (D) Duodenal ulcer
   (E) Gastric ulcer

63. An ultrasound examination revealing bilateral fluid-filled renal cysts is a classic diagnosis for which of the following disorders?
   (A) Interstitial nephritis
   (B) Nephrolithiasis

---

29. A 27-year-old male presents with acute onset of copious, purulent discharge from both eyes. Gram stain showed presence of *Neisseria gonorrhoeae*. You diagnose this patient with bacterial conjunctivitis. Which of the following is the proper course of treatment?
   (A) Intravenous antibiotics
   (B) Ophthalmic antibiotics
   (C) Ophthalmic corticosteroids
   (D) Excision
   (E) Warm compresses

30. In addition to diuretics, which of the following medications would you add to a treatment regimen when congestive heart failure presents with additional symptoms of chest pain and hypertension?
   (A) ACE inhibitors
   (B) Alpha-adrenergic antagonists
   (C) Beta-adrenergic antagonists
   (D) Calcium channel blockers
   (E) Corticosteroids

31. Which of the following vaccines should be administered to all adults aged 19-64 who suffer from asthma?
   (A) Hib vaccine
   (B) Bacille Calmette-Guerin vaccine
   (C) Pneumococcal conjugate vaccine (PCV)
   (D) Pneumococcal polysaccharide vaccine (PPSV)
   (E) Polyvalent pneumococcal vaccine

32. A 26-year-old female presents with the behavior pattern of being dependent, clinging, and submissive. She has difficulty making her own decisions and will not disagree with anyone for fear of being disliked. Based on these characteristics, which of the following is the most appropriate diagnosis?
   (A) Adjustment disorder
   (B) Borderline personality disorder
   (C) Dependent personality disorder
   (D) Narcissistic personality disorder
   (E) Schizotypal personality disorder

33. A 36-year-old male presents with cough, fever, night sweats, anorexia, and weight loss. Chest X-ray reveals homogenous infiltrates, paratracheal lymph node enlargement, and cavitations. Based on the patient's presentation, physical examination, and test results, which of the following is the most appropriate diagnosis?
   (A) Bronchitis
   (B) Pleural effusion
   (C) Pneumonia
   (D) Pulmonary hypertension
   (E) Tuberculosis

34. Which of the following vaccines should be administered to high-risk children at least 2 years of age? These include children with heart problems, lung problems, sickle cell disease, and diabetes.
   (A) Hib vaccine
   (B) Bacille Calmette-Guerin vaccine
   (C) Pneumococcal conjugate vaccine
   (D) Pneumococcal polysaccharide vaccine
   (E) Polyvalent pneumococcal vaccine

35. A healthy 40-year-old male presents for routine, annual check-up. The patient does not complain of any symptoms. Electrocardiogram is normal. Blood pressure is normal. Auscultation of the heart reveals a "swishing" sound. You order an echocardiogram to evaluate the "swishing" sound. Which of the following abnormalities would you expect to find on the echocardiogram?
   (A) Cardiomyopathy
   (B) Carotid stenosis
   (C) Congestive heart failure
   (D) Mitral valve prolapse
   (E) Pericarditis

36. A 48-year-old male presents with thick, crusted, golden "honey" lesions on his skin. Based on patient symptoms and physical examination, which of the following is the proper diagnosis?
   (A) Cellulitis
   (B) Erysipelas
   (C) Impetigo
   (D) Scabies
   (E) Vitiligo

37. After a motor vehicle accident, a 58-year-old female presents with chest pain and shortness of breath. Her initial blood pressure is 140/90 mmHg. Suddenly, the patient's blood pressure falls to 70/40 mmHg, heart rate rises to 140 beats per minutes, and mental status becomes altered. The patient's chest X-ray reveals a left-side tension pneumothorax. The patient is most likely experiencing:
(A) Cardiogenic shock
(B) Distributive shock
(C) Hypovolemic shock
(D) Obstructive shock
(E) Septic shock

38. *Helicobacter pylori* is the primary cause of which of the following disorders?
(A) Celiac disease
(B) Chronic gastritis
(C) Crohn's disease
(D) GERD
(E) Diverticulitis

39. A normally healthy 42-year-old male presents with hemoptysis, cough, focal wheezing, and recurrent pneumonia. Bronchoscopy reveals a pink to purple well-vascularized central lesion. You diagnose this patient with a carcinoid tumor. Which of the following is the most appropriate treatment for this disorder?
(A) Chemotherapy
(B) Immunotherapy
(C) Inhaled corticosteroids
(D) Radiation therapy
(E) Surgical excision

40. Quinidine and procainamide are maintenance medications for abnormal heart rhythms such as supraventricular tachycardia and symptomatic premature ventricular contractions. These medications belong to the class of drugs known as:
(A) Angiotensin antagonists
(B) Beta-adrenergic antagonists
(C) Nitrates
(D) Sodium channel blockers
(E) Vasodilators

41. The condition of resting chest pain, also known as Prinzmetal's angina, is most effectively treated with which of the following medications?
(A) Angiotensin antagonists
(B) Beta-adrenergic antagonists

(C) Nitrates
(D) Sodium channel blockers
(E) Vasodilators

42. An ultrasound of the abdomen performed on a 3-year-old child reveals an olive-shaped mass to the right of the navel. Which of the following disorders does this mass indicate?
(A) Bowel atresia
(B) Diaphragmatic hernia
(C) Esophageal etresia
(D) Pyloric stenosis
(E) Volvulus

43. A thin, 15-year-old male presents with acute chest pain, shortness of breath, and one-sided chest expansion. Auscultation of the chest reveals diminished breath sounds on the right side. Chest X-ray reveals a visceral pleural line. Based on the patient's presentation, history, and test results, which of the following is the most accurate diagnosis?
(A) Pleural effusion
(B) Pneumothorax
(C) Pulmonary edema
(D) Pulmonary embolism
(E) Pulmonary hypertension

44. A 58-year-old female presents with exertional dyspnea, non-productive cough, and fatigue. Auscultation of the chest reveals basilar rales and gallops. Patient's chest X-ray reveals cardiomegaly, bilateral pleural effusions, and perivascular edema. Based on the patient's presentation, physical exam, and test results, which of the following is the most accurate diagnosis?
(A) Congestive heart failure
(B) Cardiogenic shock
(C) Cardiac arrest
(D) Hypertensive emergency
(E) Stroke

45. Large outpouchings of mucosa in the colon constitute the condition called:
(A) Intussusception
(B) Diverticulosis
(C) Diverticulitis
(D) Ulcerative colitis
(E) Volvulus

46. A 22-year-old female presents to the emergency room with acute onset of ipsilateral chest pain and shortness of breath. The examination and chest X-ray reveal a large pneumothorax. Which of the following is the proper course of treatment?
(A) Insert chest tube.
(B) Insert large bore needle in the chest.
(C) Intubate the patient.
(D) Perform a tracheotomy.
(E) Perform thoracentesis.

47. Which of the following cardiac arrhythmias is most effectively treated with intravenous administration of a 6 mg dose of adenosine?
(A) Atrial fibrillation
(B) Atrial flutter
(C) Bradychardia
(D) Supraventricular tachycardia
(E) Ventricular tachycardia

48. Which of the following diagnostic procedures is the gold standard for diagnosing abnormalities of the testicles?
(A) CT angiogram of the testicles
(B) MRI angiogram of the testicles
(C) Nuclear medicine testicular scan
(D) Testicular ultrasound
(E) X-ray of the testicles

49. A 46-year-old patient experienced a myocardial infarction two weeks previously, and now presents with fever. Echocardiogram reveals pericarditis. Chest X-ray reveals pleural effusions. Based on the patient's presentation, physical exam, and test results, which of the following is the most accurate diagnosis?
(A) Cardiogenic shock
(B) Cardiac tamponade
(C) Congestive heart failure
(D) Dressler's syndrome
(E) Pneumothorax

50. A 66-year-old female with a history of congestive heart failure presents with nausea and leg swelling. Physical examination reveals distended neck veins, tender hepatomegaly, and pitting edema. Chest X-ray revealed cardiomegaly with bilateral pleural effusions. Based on the patient's presentation, physical exam, and test results, which of the following is the most accurate diagnosis?
(A) Cystic fibrosis
(B) Left-sided congestive heart failure

(C) Primary pneumothorax
(D) Right-sided congestive heart failure
(E) Tension pneumothorax

51. Which of the following conditions appears as a linear lesion on the posterior midline of the rectal wall?
(A) Anal fissure
(B) Anorectal abscess
(C) Hemorrhoid
(D) Pilonidal cyst
(E) Pruritis ani

52. A 62-year-old male presents with recurrent pulmonary embolism. His disorder has been resistant to anticoagulants. Due to this man's history and condition, which of the following treatment options would you suggest?
(A) Continue oral anticoagulants
(B) Intravenous anticoagulants
(C) Surgical clot removal
(D) Thrombolysis
(E) Vena cava filter

53. Which of the following types of medication is a first-line treatment for maintenance of mild gastroesophageal reflux disease (GERD)?
(A) Antacids
(B) Calcium channel blockers
(C) Corticosteroids
(D) Histamine blockers
(E) Proton pump inhibitors

54. A 52-year-old female presents with fever, fatigue, weight loss, and bilateral morning stiffness in the neck, shoulders and pelvis. Lab work revealed a markedly erythrocyte sedimentation rate. Based on the patient's presentation and lab results, which of the following is the most appropriate diagnosis?
(A) Fibromyalgia
(B) Polyarteritis nodosa
(C) Polymyalgia rheumatica
(D) Polymyositis
(E) Systemic sclerosis

(C) Nephrotic syndrome
(D) Polycystic kidney disease
(E) Renal cell carcinoma

64. A 56-year-old male presents with chest pain radiating down left arm and shortness of breath. Electrocardiogram is abnormal but inconclusive for myocardial infarction. Which of the following lab tests would you perform in order to confirm or rule out the diagnosis of myocardial infarction?
(A) Complete blood count
(B) D-dimer
(C) Erythrocyte sedimentation rate
(D) Hemoglobin/hematocrit
(E) Troponin

65. Which of the following is a component of a complete blood count (CBC)?
(A) C-reactive protein
(B) Hemoglobin
(C) LDL cholesterol
(D) Serum glucose
(E) Serum triglycerides

66. A 26-year-old female presents with abdominal cramps, diarrhea, low grade fever, muscle pain, and fatigue. You suspect Crohn's disease. Which of the following clinical procedures would you perform to confirm the diagnosis?
(A) Barium enema
(B) Colonoscopy
(C) CT scan of the abdomen
(D) Gastrointestinal bleeding study
(E) Small bowel biopsy

67. Which of the following disorders requires a gluten-free diet as maintenance therapy?
(A) Celiac disease
(B) Crohn's disease
(C) Diverticulitis
(D) Irritable bowel syndrome
(E) Ulcerative colitis

68. Which of the following gastrointestinal disorders can effectively be treated with Ursadiol?
(A) Diverticulitis
(B) Duodenal ulcer
(C) Gallstones
(D) Pancreatitis
(E) Ulcerative colitis

69. A 38-year-old female presents to the emergency room with shortness of breath and chest pain. The patient's electrocardiogram is shown below.

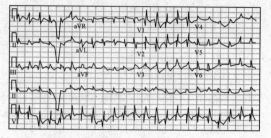

Which of the following disorders can be diagnosed from this electrocardiogram?
(A) Acute myocardial infarction
(B) Hypertensive emergency
(C) Hypertensive urgency
(D) Ischemic heart disease
(E) Pulmonary embolism

70. A 49-year-old patient presents with weight loss, malaise, fever, tenesmus, and pus-filled diarrhea. Sigmoidoscopy reveals colonic dilatation, confirming the diagnosis of ulcerative colitis. Which of the following interventions is most successful for treatment of ulcerative colitis?
(A) Aminosalicylates
(B) Colonic decompression
(C) Corticosteroids
(D) Segmental resection
(E) Total proctocolectomy

71. An 86-year-old female presents with a history of dizziness when going from a sitting to a standing position. Blood pressure in the sitting position is 140/90 mmHg. Blood pressure in the standing position is 110/70 mmHg. All lab values are within normal limits. Chest X-ray is normal and CT scans of chest, abdomen, and pelvis are all within normal limits. Which of the following is the best diagnosis?
(A) Labyrinthitis
(B) Micturition syncope
(C) Orthostatic hypotension
(D) Postural tachycardia syndrome
(E) Vasovagal reaction

72. Which of the following medications would you prescribe to effectively treat infections of the urinary tract or prostate?
    (A) ACE inhibitors
    (B) Ceftriaxone
    (C) Doxycycline
    (D) Fluoroquinolone
    (E) Methotrexate

73. Which of the following laboratory values are indicative of a seminomatous germ cell testicular tumor?
    (A) Elevated a-fetoprotein and a-human chorionic gonadotropin
    (B) Elevated a-fetoprotein and decreased a-human chorionic gonadotropin
    (C) Elevated carcinoembryonic antigen
    (D) Normal levels of a-fetoprotein and a-human chorionic gonadotropin
    (E) Normal levels of carcinoembryonic antigen

74. A 68-year-old male presents with abdominal pain occurring 10 to 30 minutes after eating. He reports that the pain is relieved by lying down. Colonoscopy confirms chronic mesenteric ischemia. Which of the following courses of treatment would you suggest for treatment of this disorder?
    (A) Oral anticoagulants
    (B) Intravenous anticoagulants
    (C) Intravenous hydration
    (D) Surgical resection
    (E) Surgical revascularization

75. Mesalamine is an anti-inflammatory agent that is also an effective maintenance therapy for which of the following gastrointestinal disorders?
    (A) Celiac disease
    (B) Crohn's disease
    (C) Diverticulitis
    (D) Irritable bowel syndrome
    (E) Ulcerative colitis

76. Which of the following medications is effective for the treatment of urinary incontinence?
    (A) ACE inhibitors
    (B) Desmopressin acetate
    (C) Doxycycline
    (D) Fluoroquinolone
    (E) Tolterodine

77. A vasopressin challenge test is used to confirm the diagnosis of which of the following disorders?
    (A) Diabetes insipidus
    (B) Gestational diabetes
    (C) Hypothyroidism
    (D) Type I diabetes
    (E) Type II diabetes

78. A 46-year-old male presents with fever, anorexia, weight loss, muscle aches, and peripheral neuropathy. Bloodwork reveals elevated C-reactive protein and erythrocyte sedimentation rate. Urinalysis reveals proteinuria. Based on the patient's presentation and test results, which of the following is the most appropriate diagnosis?
    (A) Fibromyalgia
    (B) Multiple sclerosis
    (C) Polyarteritis nodosa
    (D) Scleroderma
    (E) Sjogren's syndrome

79. A 28-year-old female with history of placenta previa presents three days post-caesarian section with a fever of 102.3°F and uterine tenderness. Physical exam reveals peritoneal irritation, ovarian tenderness, and decreased bowel sounds. White blood count is 24,000/mcL. Based on the patient's presentation and medical history, which of the following is the most appropriate diagnosis?
    (A) Adenomyosis
    (B) Endometrial polyps
    (C) Endometriosis
    (D) Endometritis
    (E) Leiomyomata

80. Which of the following clinical interventions is recommended for a kidney stone measuring less than 5 mm?
    (A) Elective lithotripsy
    (B) Elective ureteroscopy
    (C) Increased fluid intake
    (D) Percutaneous nephrostomy
    (E) Ureteral stent

81. Which of the following medications is used in combination with doxycycline to treat epididymitis that occurs as a result of a sexually transmitted disease such as gonorrhea and chlamydia?
    (A) Ceftriaxone
    (B) Ciproflaxin
    (C) Desmopressin acetate

(D) Fluoroquinolone

(E) Tolterodine

82. Hypercalcemia is a classic marker for which of the following endocrine disorders?
(A) Addison's disease
(B) Hyperparathyroidism
(C) Hyperthyroidism
(D) Hypoparathyroidism
(E) Hypothyroidism

83. Cigarette smoking may have protective effects against which of the following gastrointestinal disorders?
(A) Celiac disease
(B) Chronic gastritis
(C) Crohn's disease
(D) GERD
(E) Ulcerative colitis

84. Which of the following clinical interventions is required for a kidney stone measuring 5-10 mm?
(A) Elective lithotripsy
(B) Elective ureteroscopy
(C) Increased fluid intake
(D) Percutaneous nephrostomy
(E) Ureteral stent

85. A 26-year-old male who is an avid golfer presents with nagging, chronic pain in his right elbow. Physical examination revealed inflammation overlying the olecranon process. Based on the patient's presentation and physical examination, which of the following is the most appropriate diagnosis?
(A) Avascular necrosis
(B) Dislocation of the radial head
(C) Lateral epicondylitis
(D) Medial epicondylitis
(E) Olecranon bursitis

86. Which of the following types of medication is required for maintenance therapy for ulcerative colitis if the disease does not respond to aminosalicylates?
(A) Antacids
(B) Corticosteroids
(C) Immunodilators
(D) Mesalamine
(E) Vasodilators

87. Which of the following medications would you prescribe to treat epididymitis that occurs as a result of a bacterial infection?
(A) Ceftriaxone
(B) Ciproflaxin
(C) Doxycycline
(D) Fluoroquinolone
(E) Tolterodine

88. Macrocytic anemias are characterized by a mean corpuscular volume level of:
(A) <50 fL
(B) <80 fL
(C) 80-100 fL
(D) >100 fL
(E) >125 fL

89. A 44-year-old female presents with facial pain while eating. She also states she feels a click or pop in her jaw while she eats. Based on the patient's presentation, which of the following is the most appropriate diagnosis?
(A) Extension injury
(B) Mastoiditis
(C) Rheumatoid spondylitis
(D) Temperomandibular joint disorder
(E) Whiplash

90. A 41-year-old pregnant female, with 6 previous childbirths and a history of cigarette smoking, presents at 32 weeks with painless vaginal bleeding. Ultrasound reveals the placenta is covering the cervical os. Based on the patient's history, presentation, and test results, which of the following is the most likely diagnosis?
(A) Ectopic pregnancy
(B) Miscarriage
(C) Molar pregnancy
(D) Abruptio placentae
(E) Placenta previa

91. Which of the following clinical interventions is required for kidney stones measuring over 10 mm and in cases where kidney function is jeopardized?
(A) Elective lithotripsy
(B) Elective ureteroscopy
(C) Increased fluid intake
(D) Percutaneous nephrostomy
(E) Ureteral stent

92. Sildenafil, vardenafil, and tadalafil are members of which following families of medications for treatment of erectile dysfunction?
    (A) 5-alpha-reductase inhibitors
    (B) Alpha-adrenergic agonists
    (C) Beta-adrenergic agonists
    (D) Fluoroquinolones
    (E) Phosphodiesterase-5 inhibitors

93. Which of the following disorders of the ear can be diagnosed with either CT or MRI scanning?
    (A) Acoustic neuroma
    (B) Presbycusis
    (C) Mastoiditis
    (D) Meniere's disease
    (E) Tympanic membrane rupture

94. Which of the following clinical interventions is required for a patient with hypernatremia with a sodium level greater than 200 mEq/L?
    (A) Dialysis
    (B) Increase intake of water
    (C) Intravenous 5% dextrose solution
    (D) Intravenous saline solution
    (E) Oral rehydration therapy

95. Adopting a high-fiber diet is proper maintenance therapy for which of the following gastrointestinal disorders?
    (A) Celiac disease
    (B) Crohn's disease
    (C) Diverticulitis
    (D) Irritable bowel syndrome
    (E) Ulcerative colitis

96. The condition of hypermagnesemia is most effectively treated by intravenous administration of which of the following medications?
    (A) IV 5% dextrose solution
    (B) IV calcium gluconate
    (C) IV potassium chloride
    (D) IV sodium chloride
    (E) Lactated Ringer's solution

97. Which of the following diagnostic modalities is the most definitive for evaluating transient ischemic attacks?
    (A) Arteriogram
    (B) CT Scan
    (C) MRI
    (D) Nuclear medicine
    (E) Ultrasound

98. A 34-year-old female intravenous drug user presents with stiffness in the jaw and neck, difficulty eating, and irritability. Physical examination reveals muscle spasms of the jaw and face. Based on the patient's presentation, and physical examination, which of the following is the most appropriate diagnosis?
    (A) Anthrax
    (B) Bell's palsy
    (C) Botulism
    (D) Rhabdovirus
    (E) Tetanus

99. A 70-year-old female presents with hyperventilation, burning of the hands and feet, and light-headedness. Saliva reveals a body pH of 7.6, indicating respiratory alkalosis. Which of the following treatment options would you suggest for this patient?
    (A) Administration of CO_2 breathing mixtures
    (B) Administration of electrolytes
    (C) Breathing into a paper bag
    (D) Immediate oxygen therapy
    (E) Intubation

100. Body dysmorphic disorder is an example of a somatoform psychological disorder. Fluoxetine and clomipramine have been proven effective in the treatment of body dysmorphic disorder. Fluoxetine and clomipramine are what type of medications?
    (A) Antipsychotic medications
    (B) Monoamine oxidase inhibitor medications
    (C) Neuroleptic medications
    (D) Serotonin-modulating medications
    (E) Tricyclic antidepressant medications

101. Cerebrospinal fluid evaluations that reveal markedly opening pressures and grossly bloody fluid are a classic marker for which neurologic disorder?
    (A) Hydrocephalus
    (B) Meningitis
    (C) Subarachnoid hemorrhage
    (D) Stroke
    (E) Transient ischemic attack (TIA)

102. A 75-year-old female presents with dribbling after urination for a prolonged period of time. You diagnose this patient with overflow incontinence. Which of the following is the most appropriate course of treatment for this condition?

(A) Anticholinergic medications
(B) Catheterization
(C) Imipramine
(D) Surgical intervention
(E) Pelvic floor muscle training

103. A 26-year-old female presents with complaints of painful sexual intercourse, itching on the inner thighs, and a foul-smelling, frothy, yellow/green vaginal discharge. Physical examination reveals red macular lesions on the vagina and cervix. Based on the patient's presentation and physical examination, which of the following is the most appropriate diagnosis?
(A) Bacterial vaginosis
(B) Chlamydia
(C) Gonorrhea
(D) Syphilis
(E) Trichomoniasis

104. Which of the following medications is used for maintenance therapy for overactive bladder?
(A) Buproprion
(B) Ceftriaxone
(C) Ciproflaxin
(D) Doxycycline
(E) Oxybutynin

105. Glyburide is a medication that acts to increase insulin secretion. It has very few drug interactions and can cause weight gain. For which of the following disorders is glyburide the indicated treatment?
(A) Anorexia nervosa
(B) Bulimia nervosa
(C) Chronic pancreatitis
(D) Diabetes insipidus
(E) Diabetes mellitus

106. Electroencephalograms are commonly used to evaluate which of the following neurologic disorders?
(A) Hydrocephalus
(B) Migraine headaches
(C) Parkinson's disease
(D) Seizures
(E) Subarachnoid hemorrhage

107. A 50-year-old female presents with sudden, unilateral, painless loss of vision. Examination reveals an afferent pupillary defect and a "blood-and-thunder" retina. Which of the following is the proper diagnosis based on this information?
(A) Blepharitis
(B) Central retinal artery occlusion
(C) Central retinal vein occlusion
(D) Corneal abrasion
(E) Retinal detachment

108. A 70-year-old male presents with chest pain radiating to the neck and shoulder. The pain is relieved by sitting upright and leaning forward. Chest X-ray reveals pleural effusions. Echocardiogram reveals inflammation of the sac around the heart. Which of the following is the correct diagnosis?
(A) Aortic stenosis
(B) Carotid stenosis
(C) Mitral valve prolapse
(D) Pericarditis
(E) Pulmonary embolism

109. Which of the following classes of hypertensive medications is the best choice for peripheral vasodilatation and also most effective among the African-American and elderly populations?
(A) ACE inhibitors
(B) Alpha-adrenergic antagonists
(C) Beta-adrenergic antagonists
(D) Calcium channel blockers
(E) Diuretics

110. Which of the following is the proper course of treatment for individuals with recurrent bladder cancer?
(A) Chemotherapy
(B) Endoscopic resection
(C) Intravesical instillation of thiotepa
(D) Radiation therapy
(E) Radical cystectomy

111. Which of the following anti-diabetic medications is effective in lowering serum glucose and serum triglycerides, and promotes weight loss without risk of hypoglycemia?
(A) Glyburide
(B) Exenatide
(C) Metformin
(D) Miglitol
(E) Rosilitazone

112. Which of the following characteristics of multiple sclerosis can be visualized effectively with gadolinium-enhanced MRI scanning?
(A) Cerebral atrophy
(B) Gray matter lesions
(C) Hydrocephalus
(D) Subarachnoid hemorrhage
(E) White matter lesions

113. A 40-year-old man presents with a painless, indurated lesion deep from the palpebral margin. Which of the following is the proper diagnosis based on this information?
(A) Blepharitis
(B) Chalazion
(C) Dacrycystostenosis
(D) Glaucoma
(E) Hordeola

114. A 52-year-old female who has previously undergone thyroidectomy presents with irritability and distal extremity tingling. Physical examination reveals a positive Chvostek's sign and Trousseu's phenomenon. Bloodwork reveals decreased serum calcium and magnesium. Based on this information, what is the most appropriate initial diagnosis?
(A) Grave's disease
(B) Hyperparathyroidism
(C) Hyperthyroidism
(D) Hypoparathyroidism
(E) Hypothyroidism

115. Which of the following hypertensive medications, often used for initial therapy of essential hypertension, reduces plasma volume, and chronically reduces peripheral resistance?
(A) ACE inhibitors
(B) Alpha-adrenergic antagonists
(C) Beta-adrenergic antagonists
(D) Calcium channel blockers
(E) Diuretics

116. The administration of a combination of beta blockers, hydrocortisone, a thiourea drug, iodide, and symptom-specific medications constitutes the treatment for which of the following endocrine disorders?
(A) Hashimoto's thyroiditis
(B) Hyperthryoidism

(C) Myxedema
(D) Subacute thyroiditis
(E) Thyroid storm

117. Glomerulonephritis is a disorder in which the renal glomeruli are damaged due to deposition of inflammatory proteins in the glomerular membranes. Which of the following medications are used for maintenance therapy of this disorder?
(A) ACE inhibitors
(B) Desmopressin acetate
(C) Diuretics
(D) Sodium channel blockers
(E) Tolterodine

118. Miglitol is a member of the class of anti-diabetic medications called alpha-glucosidase inhibitors. This class of medications lowers blood glucose by which of the following mechanisms?
(A) Decreasing production of hepatic glucose
(B) Delaying absorption of carbohydrates from the intestine
(C) Delaying gastric emptying
(D) Promoting the breakdown of carbohydrates
(E) Stimulating insulin secretion

119. Positron emission tomography of the brain of patients with Alzheimer's disease will reveal hypometabolism in which area of the brain?
(A) Cerebellum
(B) Frontal lobe
(C) Occipital lobe
(D) Parietal lobe
(E) Temporal lobe

120. A 75-year-old female presents with her eyelids permanently turned outward. Which of the following is the proper diagnosis based on this information?
(A) Chalazion
(B) Ectropion
(C) Entropion
(D) Pinguecula
(E) Pterygium

121. A 58-year-old male with a history of cystic fibrosis presents with foul-smelling, purulent sputum, hemoptysis, and chronic cough. Auscultation of the chest reveals localized chest crackles and clubbing. High-resolution CT scan reveals dilated, tortuous airways. Chest X-ray reveals crowded bronchial markings and basal cystic spaces, tram-track lung markings, honeycombing, and atelectasis. Based

on the patient's presentation, history, and test results, which of the following is the most accurate diagnosis?
(A) Asthma
(B) Bronchiectasis
(C) COPD
(D) Cystic fibrosis
(E) Tuberculosis

122. A 58-year-old male presents with dyspnea, clubbing, and cyanosis. Auscultation of the chest reveals inspiratory crackles. Chest X-ray reveals interstitial fibrosis, thickened pleura, and calcified plaques on the diaphragm. Based on the patient's presentation, history, and test results, which of the following is the most accurate diagnosis?
(A) Asbestosis
(B) Coalworker's pneumoconiosis
(C) Sarcoidosis
(D) Silicosis
(E) Tuberculosis

123. Which of the following treatment options is the appropriate initial treatment for low-risk Hodgkin's lymphoma?
(A) Chemotherapy
(B) Cryotherapy
(C) Hormonal therapy
(D) Immunotherapy
(E) Radiation therapy

124. Exenatide is an example of an anti-diabetic medication. By which of the following mechanisms does exenatide function to decrease blood glucose?
(A) Decreasing production of hepatic glucose
(B) Delaying absorption of carbohydrates from the intestine
(C) Delaying gastric emptying
(D) Promoting the breakdown of carbohydrates
(E) Stimulating insulin secretion

125. A polysomnogram assesses bodily functions under which of the following conditions?
(A) Exertion
(B) Ingestion of food
(C) Rest
(D) Sleep
(E) Stress

126. Furosemide, commonly referred to as Lasix, is a member of which of the following classes of diuretic medications?
(A) Calcium-sparing diuretics
(B) Loop diuretics
(C) Osmotic diuretics
(D) Potassium-sparing diuretics
(E) Thyazides

127. A 29-year-old female presents with hearing loss, tinnitus, vertigo, and ataxia. MRI reveals a neoplasm in the ear. Based on the symptoms and examination, which of the following is the proper diagnosis?
(A) Acoustic neuroma
(B) Labyrinthitis
(C) Meniere's disease
(D) Otitis externa
(E) Otitis media

128. A 23-year-old female presents with cough, excess sputum, purulent nasal discharge, steatorrhea, and abdominal pain. This patient has a history of chronic lung disease, pancreatitis, and infertility. Physical examination reveals clubbing and apical crackles. Thin-section CT reveals bronchiectasis. Chest X-ray reveals hyperinflation and mucous plugging. Based on the patient's presentation, history, and test results, which of the following is the most accurate diagnosis?
(A) Chronic obstructive pulmonary disease
(B) Cystic fibrosis
(C) Pneumonia
(D) Sarcoidosis
(E) Tuberculosis

129. A 28-year-old male presents with pain in the left eye. Physical examination reveals a rust ring on the cornea, indicating the presence of a metallic foreign body. Which of the following course of treatment would you suggest for this condition?
(A) Application of ophthalmic antibiotics
(B) Application of ophthalmic steroids
(C) Removal with moistened cotton-tip swab
(D) Removal with rotating burr
(E) Flush with sterile saline

130. Administration of 325 mg of ferrous sulfate 3 times per day is appropriate maintenance therapy for which of the following forms of anemia?
(A) Folate-deficiency anemia
(B) Hemolytic anemia
(C) Hypochromic microcytic anemia
(D) Macrocytic anemia
(E) Normochromic normocytic anemia

131. Metformin, an anti-diabetic medication, is contraindicated for individuals with which of the following disorders?
(A) Elevated D-dimer
(B) Elevated LDL
(C) Elevated serum creatinine
(D) Elevated triglycerides
(E) Elevated troponin

132. A potassium hydroxide preparation is commonly used to rule out fungal infection during the diagnosis of which of the following skin conditions?
(A) Acne vulgaris
(B) Contact dermatitis
(C) Seborrheic dermatitis
(D) Lichen simplex chronicus
(E) Pityriasis rosea

133. A 12-year-old male presents with hearing loss and pain in the left ear. Examination reveals an immobile eardrum that is erythematous and bulging. Based on the findings of the examination and the patient's symptoms, which of the following is the correct diagnosis?
(A) Acoustic neuroma
(B) Labyrinthitis
(C) Meniere's disease
(D) Otitis externa
(E) Otitis media

134. A 62-year-old male presents with progressive dyspnea. The patient's history reveals he worked in a stone quarry for several years. Physical examination reveals inspiratory crackles. Chest X-ray reveals small rounded opacities throughout the lung and calcified hilar lymph nodes. Based on the patient's presentation, history, and test results, which of the following is the most accurate diagnosis?
(A) Asbestosis
(B) Coalworker's pneumoconiosis
(C) Sarcoidosis

(D) Silicosis
(E) Tuberculosis

135. A 54-year-old male presents with intermittent heart palpitations, fatigue, and dizziness. Electrocardiogram was performed and is illustrated below. Which cardiac arrhythmia is denoted on the patient's electrocardiogram?

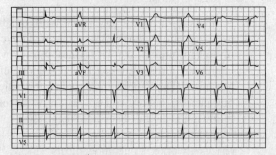

(A) Atrial fibrillation
(B) Junctional rhythm
(C) Normal sinus rhythm with first-degree AV block
(D) Sinus arrhythmia
(E) Sinus bradycardia

136. Which of the following is the proper initial treatment for the condition of strabismus?
(A) Application of ophthalmic antibiotics
(B) Application of ophthalmic steroids
(C) Corrective lenses
(D) Patch therapy
(E) Surgical correction

137. Exenatide, an anti-diabetic medication, is contraindicated in patients with which of the following disorders?
(A) Gastroparesis
(B) Hyperglycemia
(C) Hypertension
(D) Hypotension
(E) Lactic acidosis

138. A wood's light examination is commonly used to evaluate which of the following conditions?
(A) Extravasated blood
(B) Fungal presence
(C) Pigment changes
(D) Tinea versacolor
(E) Warts

139. Which of the following terms describes pre-cancerous whitish-gray, thick, hard, and slightly raised lesions on the tongue and inside of the cheeks?
    (A) Aphthous ulcers
    (B) Oral candidiasis
    (C) Oral leukoplakia
    (D) Oral herpes simplex
    (E) Peritonsillar abscess

140. A 71-year-old male presents with progressive shortness of breath. Physical examination reveals inspiratory crackles, clubbing, and cyanosis. Chest X-ray shows small opacities prominent in the upper lung fields. The patient's history reveals he worked in a coal mine for 35 years. Based on the patient's presentation, history, and test results, which of the following is the most accurate diagnosis?
    (A) Asbestosis
    (B) Coal worker's pneumoconiosis
    (C) Sarcoidosis
    (D) Silicosis
    (E) Tuberculosis

141. A 59-year-old man presents with intermittent dizzy spells. Electrocardiography was performed and the result is shown below.

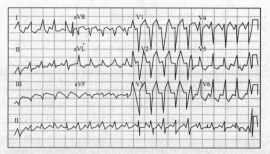

Which of the following abnormalities is perceived on this electrocardiogram?
    (A) Brugada syndrome
    (B) Left axis deviation
    (C) Left bundle branch block
    (D) Right bundle branch block
    (E) Sick sinus syndrome

142. Which of the following is the clinical intervention for presbycusis?
    (A) Diuretics
    (B) Hearing aid
    (C) Oral antibiotics
    (D) Oral anti-inflammatories
    (E) Surgical correction

143. Oral administration of 1 mg of folic acid per day is proper maintenance therapy for which of the following forms of anemia?
    (A) Folate-deficiency anemia
    (B) Hemolytic anemia
    (C) Hypochromic microcytic anemia
    (D) Macrocytic anemia
    (E) Normochromic normocytic anemia

144. A 40-year-old male presents with proximal muscle weakness, dysphagia, and malar skin rash. Bloodwork reveals elevated levels of creatinine phosphokinase and aldolase. Based on the patient's presentation and test results, which of the following is the most appropriate diagnosis?
    (A) Calcium pyrophosphate dehydrate disease
    (B) Gout
    (C) Myasthenia gravis
    (D) Polymyositis
    (E) Rheumatoid arthritis

145. A 27-year-old pregnant female presents with abnormal vaginal bleeding, uterine size greater than normal, nausea, vomiting, and hypertension. Bloodwork reveals a serum hCG level greater than 100,000 mU/mL. Ultrasound image has the appearance of grapelike vesicles. Based on the patient's presentation, physical examination, and test results, which of the following is the most accurate diagnosis?
    (A) Ectopic pregnancy
    (B) Gestational trophoblastic disease
    (C) Preeclampsia
    (D) Polycystic ovarian syndrome
    (E) Spontaneous abortion

146. Desmopressin acetate is the indicated medication for treatment of which of the following disorders?
    (A) Chronic obstructive pulmonary disease
    (B) Chronic pancreatitis
    (C) Diabetes insipidus
    (D) Diabetes mellitus
    (E) Hypertension

147. A 38-year-old female presents with sudden onset of shortness of breath and dizziness. An electrocardiogram is performed and is shown below.

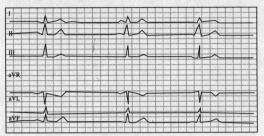

Which of the following describes this cardiac arrhythmia?
(A) Atrial fibrillation
(B) Normal sinus rhythm
(C) Normal sinus rhythm with first-degree AV block
(D) Junctional rhythm
(E) Sinus bradycardia

148. A 44-year-old male presents with bluish discoloration under the eyes, clear and watery nasal discharge, and itchy eyes. Patient states this occurs when he is exposed to pollen or mold. Based on the patient's presentation and physical examination, which of the following is the most appropriate diagnosis?
(A) Allergic rhinitis
(B) Chronic atrophic rhinitis
(C) Rhinitis medicamentosa
(D) Sinusitis
(E) Vasomotor rhinitis

149. A 50-year-old African-American woman presents with chest discomfort, cough, and shortness of breath. Lab work reveals eosinophilia, elevated erythrocyte sedimentation rate, and hypercalcemia. Physical examination reveals erythema nodosa on the shins and enlarged parotid glands. Chest X-ray shows symmetric bilateral hilar adenopathy. Based on the patient's presentation, history, and test results, which of the following is the most accurate diagnosis?
(A) Asbestosis
(B) Coalworker's pneumoconiosis
(C) Sarcoidosis
(D) Silicosis
(E) Tuberculosis

150. A 60-year-old male presents with episodes of fatigue, dizziness, and chest pain. Electrocardiogram was performed and is shown below.

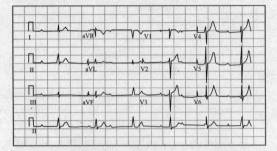

Which of the following abnormalities is perceived on this electrocardiogram?
(A) Complete heart block
(B) Second-degree AV block
(C) Sinus bradycardia
(D) Ventricular escape rhythm
(E) Wandering atrial pacemaker

151. Which of the following treatments for stroke victims is required if the internal or common carotid artery proves to have 70%-99% stenosis?
(A) Ablation
(B) Anticoagulant therapy
(C) Antiplatelet therapy
(D) Endarterectomy
(E) Thrombolytic therapy

152. A 44-year-old male presents with pain, swelling, and tenderness to palpation in the left ankle. The patient also has a fever. Synovial fluid exam was positive for the *Staphylococcus aureus* bacterium. Based on the patient's presentation and test results, which of the following is the most appropriate diagnosis?
(A) Calcium pyrophosphate dehydrate disease
(B) Psoriatic arthritis
(C) Reactive arthritis
(D) Rheumatoid arthritis
(E) Septic arthritis

153. A 24-year-old female in her 16th week of pregnancy presents with vaginal bleeding. Gynecological exam reveals an open cervix. Based on the patient's presentation and physical examination, which of the following is the most appropriate diagnosis?
(A) Ectopic pregnancy
(B) Gestational trophoblastic disease
(C) Preeclampsia

(D) Polycystic ovarian syndrome

(E) Spontaneous abortion

154. Ergocalciferol is the medication of choice for the treatment of osteomalacia. Osteomalacia is precipitated by a deficiency of which of the following vitamins?

(A) Vitamin A

(B) Vitamin B6

(C) Vitamin B12

(D) Vitamin C

(E) Vitamin D

155. A 6-year-old female presents with sudden high fever, difficulty swallowing, sore throat, and drooling. A lateral X-ray of the neck was obtained and a thumb sign was noted. The best diagnosis for this child is:

(A) Bronchiolitis

(B) Croup

(C) Epiglottitis

(D) Esophogeal obstruction

(E) Tracheal obstruction

156. A 58-year-old female presents with nasal stuffiness and rhinorrhea. She states this occurs when she is exposed to changes in temperature and humidity. Based on this patient's history, which of the following is the most appropriate diagnosis?

(A) Allergic rhinitis

(B) Chronic atrophic rhinitis

(C) Rhinitis medicamentosa

(D) Sinusitis

(E) Vasomotor rhinitis

157. An elderly, gravely ill 85-year-old male with a history of aspiration of stomach contents presents with rapid onset of profound dyspnea. Physical examination reveals tachypnea, frothy red sputum, diffuse crackles, and cyanosis. Based on the patient's presentation, history, and test results, which of the following is the most accurate diagnosis?

(A) Cystic fibrosis

(B) Adult respiratory distress syndrome

(C) Septic shock

(D) Acute respiratory failure

(E) Hypertensive emergency

158. A healthy 55-year-old male presents for his annual office visit. Electrocardiogram is performed and is shown here.

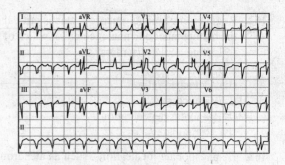

Which of the following abnormalities is shown on this electrocardiogram?

(A) Brugada syndrome

(B) Left axis deviation

(C) Left bundle branch block

(D) Right bundle branch block

(E) Sick sinus syndrome

159. Which of the following types of medications is used for treatment of tremors associated with Parkinson's disease?

(A) Anti-inflammatories

(B) Anticholinergics

(C) Beta-adrenergic antagonists

(D) Calcium channel blockers

(E) Lithium

160. A 27-year-old male presents with an abnormal suspicion and distrust of other people. The patient also tends to act hostile, angry, and blame problems on other people. Based on the patient's history, which of the following is the most appropriate diagnosis?

(A) Adjustment disorder

(B) Avoidant disorder

(C) Narcissistic personality disorder

(D) Obsessive compulsive disorder

(E) Paranoid disorder

161. A 22-year-old male presents with painful, burning urination associated with a profuse, creamy, bloody, yellow urethral discharge. Based on the patient's presentation, which of the following is the most likely diagnosis?

(A) Chlamydia

(B) Gonorrhea

(C) HIV

(D) Syphilis

(E) Trichomoniasis

162. Regulation of blood glucose levels is critical for the maintenance and management of which of the following ocular disorders?
    (A) Cataracts
    (B) Detached retina
    (C) Glaucoma
    (D) Macular degeneration
    (E) Retinopathy

163. Bisphosponate medications, such as alendronate and pamidronate, are the treatment of choice for which of the following disorders?
    (A) Fibrous dysplasia
    (B) Osteomalacia
    (C) Osteoporosis
    (D) Paget's disease
    (E) Rickets

164. When treating a patient who exhibits signs of shock, obtaining lab work including electrolytes, serum glucose, urinalysis, and serum creatinine will assist you in determining which of the following?
    (A) Cause of shock
    (B) Duration of shock
    (C) Proper treatment of shock
    (D) Severity of shock
    (E) Type of shock

165. A 32-year-old male presents with sore throat that is progressively worsening, low-grade fever, and symptoms of a head cold. Physical exam reveals cervical lymphadenopathy. Strep screen was negative. Based on the patient's symptoms and physical examination, which of the following is the most appropriate diagnosis?
    (A) Peritonsillar cellulitis
    (B) Sinusitis
    (C) Streptococcal pharyngitis
    (D) Tonsillitis
    (E) Viral pharyngitis

166. A prematurely-born infant begins to exhibit typical signs of respiratory distress. Chest X-ray shows air bronchograms, a "ground glass" appearance to the lungs, and a domed diaphragm. Based on the patient's presentation and test results, which of the following is the most accurate diagnosis?
    (A) Acute asphyxia
    (B) Acute respiratory failure
    (C) Hyaline membrane disease
    (D) Transient tachypnea
    (E) Respiratory distress syndrome

167. A 27-year-old female presents with palpitations. Electrocardiogram was performed and is shown below.

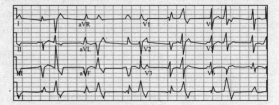

Which of the following abnormalities is perceived on this electrocardiogram?
    (A) Atrial bigeminy
    (B) Atrial fibrillation
    (C) Atrial flutter
    (D) Junctional rhythm
    (E) Ventricular bigeminy

168. Which of the following interventions is the most appropriate treatment for scabies?
    (A) Oral antibiotics
    (B) Hydrating agents
    (C) Topical antibiotics
    (D) Topical corticosteroids
    (E) Topical insecticides

169. Which of the following medications would you prescribe for the treatment of subacute thyroiditis?
    (A) Aspirin
    (B) Antibiotics
    (C) Corticosteroids
    (D) Propanolol
    (E) Thyroid hormone

170. The electrocardiogram shown below was obtained from a middle-aged patient admitted to the emergency room with chest pain.

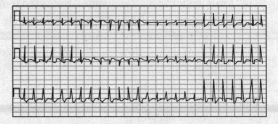

Based on the patient's symptoms and electrocardiographic findings, which of the following is the most accurate diagnosis?
    (A) Left-sided congestive heart failure
    (B) Right-sided congestive heart failure

(C) Cardiomyopathy
(D) Ischemic heart disease
(E) Acute myocardial infarction

171. A 31-year-old female presents with an excessive devotion to her job and excludes any leisure activities. She states she does not delegate any of her responsibilities because they will not be completed in the manner she desires. Based on the patient's history, which of the following is the most appropriate diagnosis?
(A) Adjustment disorder
(B) Avoidant disorder
(C) Narcissistic personality disorder
(D) Obsessive-compulsive disorder
(E) Paranoid disorder

172. A 14-year-old female presents with low-grade fever, malaise, headache, and muscle aches. Physical exam reveals erythematous macules that appear in crops. Based on the patient's presentation and physical examination, which of the following is the most likely diagnosis?
(A) Contact dermatitis
(B) Influenza
(C) Lyme disease
(D) Molluscum contagiosum
(E) Varicella zoster

173. A 37-year-old female presents with itchy, bleeding, non-healing lesions on the lips, mouth and tongue. Biopsy of affected areas reveals the presence of squamous cell carcinoma. Which of the following courses of treatment would you prescribe for this disorder?
(A) Chemotherapy
(B) Complete eradication of the lesions
(C) Debridement of the lesions
(D) Liquid nitrogen therapy
(E) Topical corticosteroids

174. Minimizing exposure to ultraviolet radiation is suggested to decrease the risk of developing which of the following ocular disorders?
(A) Cataracts
(B) Detached retina
(C) Glaucoma
(D) Macular degeneration
(E) Retinopathy

175. A 22-year-old female is underweight and emaciated. Physical examination reveals dental erosion, esophogitis, calluses on her knuckles, and atrophy of her salivary glands. Bloodwork reveals hypochloremia, hypokalemia, alkalosis, and hypomagnesemia. Based on the patient's history, physical examination, and test results, which of the following is the most appropriate diagnosis?
(A) Anorexia nervosa
(B) Atypical depression
(C) Binge eating disorder
(D) Bulimia nervosa
(E) Seasonal affective disorder

176. A 44-year-old female presents with a painful macular, fiery red rash with well-defined borders on her face. The rash has begun to spread to her extremities. Based on the patient's presentation, which of the following is the most appropriate diagnosis?
(A) Erysipelas
(B) Chlamydia
(C) Gonorrhea
(D) Shingles
(E) Systemic lupus erythematous

177. Which of the following medications is most effective for the treatment of chronic thrombocytopenia secondary to systemic lupus erythematosus?
(A) Erythropoietin
(B) Folic Acid
(C) Prednisone
(D) Vitamin B12
(E) Vitamin D

178. Which of the following pneumonia vaccines is indicated for individuals over the age of 65 who suffer from chronic illness and are at increased risk for community-acquired pneumonia?
(A) Hib vaccine
(B) Bacille Calmette-Guerin vaccine
(C) Pneumococcal conjugate vaccine
(D) Pneumococcal polysaccharide vaccine
(E) Polyvalent pneumococcal vaccine

179. Broad-spectrum antibiotics are the preferred treatment for which of the following conditions caused by the *Pseudomonas aeruginosa* bacterium?
(A) Community-acquired pneumonia
(B) Atypical community-acquired pneumonia
(C) Nosocomial pneumonia
(D) Pneumocystis pneumonia
(E) Tuberculosis

180. A 17-year-old male presents with chest pain and palpitations. Electrocardiogram performed in the emergency room is shown below.

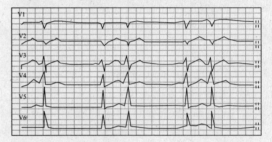

Based on the patient's symptoms and electrocardiographic findings, which of the following is the most accurate diagnosis?
(A) Acute myocardial infarction
(B) Brugada syndrome
(C) Left ventricular hypertrophy
(D) Pulmonary hypertension
(E) Wolff-Parkinson-White syndrome

181. A 24-year-old female presents with history of cough, purulent sputum, shortness of breath, and fever. Auscultation of the chest reveals expiratory rhonchi. Chest X-ray was performed and appeared normal. Based on patient symptoms and physical examination, which of the following is the proper diagnosis?
(A) Acute bronchitis
(B) Acute epiglottitis
(C) Croup
(D) Pneumonia
(E) Tuberculosis

182. A 72-year-old male presents to the emergency room with chest pain. The patient's initial blood pressure is 140/70 mmHg. Shortly after presentation, the patient's blood pressure drops to 80/40 mmHg and peripheral pulses are "thready." The patient's electrocardiogram is shown below.

Based on the presentation and patient's condition, which of the following is the accurate diagnosis?
(A) Congestive heart failure
(B) Cardiogenic shock
(C) Cardiac arrest
(D) Hypertensive emergency
(E) Stroke

183. An otherwise healthy 22-year-old male presents with episodes of heart palpitations. The patient's electrocardiogram is illustrated below.

Which of the following abnormalities is noted on this electrocadiogram?
(A) Atrial bigeminy
(B) Atrial fibrillation
(C) Atrial flutter
(D) Junctional rhythm
(E) Ventricular bigeminy

184. Which of the following is the most appropriate treatment for keratoderma?
(A) Topical steroids
(B) Fluconazole
(C) Lindane
(D) Liquid nitrogen
(E) Permethrin

185. Which of the following is used as an emergency treatment for the condition of disseminated intravascular coagulopathy?
(A) Cryoprecipitate
(B) Prednisone
(C) Ferrous sulfate
(D) Fresh frozen plasma
(E) Prothrombin complex concentrate

186. Which of the following radiological procedures is the most definitive for diagnosing viable myocardium after acute myocardial infarction?
(A) Cardiac stress testing
(B) Coronary angiography
(C) Echocardiogram

(D) Myocardial perfusion SPECT imaging

(E) Myocardial perfusion PET imaging

187. A 48-year-old male presents with cough, hemoptysis, chest pain, and weight loss. Chest X-ray reveals a centrally-located mass. Based on the patient's presentation and test results, which of the following is the most appropriate diagnosis?
(A) Carcinoid tumor
(B) Non-small cell lung carcinoma
(C) Sarcoma
(D) Small cell lung carcinoma
(E) Solitary pulmonary nodule

188. A 14-year-old female presents with a history of exaggerating illnesses to avoid going to school. Physical examination was completely normal; however, she insists she is ill. Based on this patient's behavior and personality, which of the following is the most likely diagnosis?
(A) Adjustment disorder
(B) Conversion disorder
(C) Factitious disorder
(D) Hypochondriasis
(E) Malingering

189. Which of the following medications is approved for treatment of gestational diabetes?
(A) Alpha-glucosidase inhibitors
(B) Glucophage
(C) Glyburide
(D) Insulin
(E) Metformin

190. Meniere's disease is characterized by distention of the endolymphatic compartment of the inner ear. Which of the following medications is used for maintenance therapy for Meniere's disease?
(A) Antibacterials
(B) Anti-inflammatories
(C) Antibiotics
(D) Corticosteroids
(E) Diuretics

191. A 42-year-old female presents by stating she finds no pleasure in anything in her life. Physically she is experiencing anorexia, weight loss, depression, and sleep disturbances. Based on the patient's history and presentation, which of the following is the most accurate diagnosis?
(A) Atypical depression
(B) Catatonic depression

(C) Dysthymia
(D) Melancholia
(E) Seasonal affective disorder

192. A 55-year-old man presents with a red, raspberry-like nodule that appeared on his neck. Based on the appearance of this lesion, which of the following is the most appropriate diagnosis?
(A) Cellulitis
(B) Erythema multiforme
(C) Pyogenic granuloma
(D) Malignant melanoma
(E) Squamous cell carcinoma

193. Von Willebrand disease is a disease of abnormal bleeding due to lack of factor VIII antigen. In addition to factor VIII, what medication would you prescribe for maximum resolution of this disorder?
(A) Bisphosphonates
(B) Ergocalciferol
(C) Desmopressin acetate
(D) Pegvisomant
(E) Prednisone

194. Which of the following medications is administered to a hypertensive pregnant female who must deliver her baby early, to ensure fetal lung maturity?
(A) Betamethisone
(B) Hydralazine
(C) Labetalol
(D) Magnesium sulfate
(E) Pitocin

195. Prolonged use of phenothiazine medications, such as compazine and thorazine, can cause which of the following eye disorders?
(A) Cataracts
(B) Glaucoma
(C) Macular degeneration
(D) Orbital cellulitis
(E) Retinopathy

196. A standard electrocardiogram is shown below.

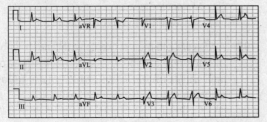

Which of the following areas of an electrocardiogram represents the lateral wall of the heart muscle?

(A) Leads I, aVL, V5, and V6
(B) Leads II, III, and aVF
(C) Leads V1 and V2
(D) Leads V1, V2, and V3
(E) Leads V4, V5, and V6

197. A 60-year-old male presents with progressively worsening shortness of breath, excessive cough, and sputum production. Physical examination reveals decreased breath sounds and early inspiratory crackles. Percussion yields increased resonance. Chest X-ray reveals hyperinflation of the lungs and a flat diaphragm. Based on the patient's presentation and test results, which of the following is the most appropriate diagnosis?

(A) Bronchiectasis
(B) Chronic obstructive pulmonary disease
(C) Emphysema
(D) Pulmonary hypertension
(E) Tuberculosis

198. A 65-year-old female who is undergoing chemotherapy and radiation therapy for lung cancer presents to the Intensive Care Unit. Vital signs are normal with a blood pressure of 130/70 mmHg and a heart rate of 64. The day following the procedure, the patient's blood pressure drops to 70/40 mmHg, heart rate increases to 130 beats per minute, and she is unresponsive. Blood culture is positive for Gram-negative bacteria. Based on the presentation and patient's condition, which of the following is the accurate diagnosis?

(A) Cardiogenic shock
(B) Compensated shock
(C) Hypovolemic shock
(D) Obstructive shock
(E) Septic shock

199. Which of the following forms of contraception can last up to ten years?

(A) Combined injectable contraceptive
(B) Copper-T IUD
(C) Hormone-impregnated vaginal ring
(D) Implanon system
(E) Mirena IUD

200. Which of the following medications is indicated for maintenance therapy for myasthenia gravis?

(A) ACE inhibitors
(B) Calcium channel blockers
(C) Cholinesterase inhibitors
(D) Proton pump inhibitors
(E) Selective serotonin reuptake inhibitors

201. A 60-year-old female presents with pain in the big toe and states she is unable to find shoes that fit her properly. The patient's X-ray reveals a deformity of the proximal phalanx at an angle of approximately 25 degrees. Based on the patient's presentation and X-ray, which of the following is the proper diagnosis?

(A) Arthritis
(B) Bunion
(C) Fracture
(D) Gout
(E) Sprain

202. Which of the following treatment options, along with antibiotics, would be indicated for a patient who presents with dacryocystitis?

(A) Anti-inflammatories
(B) Eyelid scrubs
(C) Nasal decongestants
(D) Ophthalmic steroids
(E) Warm compresses

203. A standard electrocardiogram is shown below.

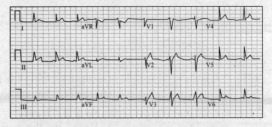

Which of the following areas of an electrocardiogram represent the anterior wall of the heart muscle?

(A) Leads II, III, and aVF
(B) Leads V1 and V2
(C) Leads V3 and V4
(D) Leads V2 and V4
(E) Leads V4, V5, and V6

204. A 46-year-old male with a history of atrial fibrillation presents with pleuritic chest pain, dyspnea, and hemoptysis. Electrocardiogram reveals tachycardia and non-specific ST-T wave changes. Chest X-ray reveals "Hampton's hump." Auscultation of the chest reveals accentuation of the pulmonary component of the second heart sound. Based on the patient's presentation, history, and test results, which of the following is the most accurate diagnosis?
(A) Bronchiectasis
(B) Cystic fibrosis
(C) Pulmonary hypertension
(D) Pulmonary embolism
(E) Tuberculosis

205. A 38-year-old male presents with intermittent headaches. His blood pressure reading is 150/94 mmHg. Similar readings were obtained on previous examinations. Based on the patient's presentation and blood pressure reading, which of the following is the most likely diagnosis?
(A) Hypertensive emergency
(B) Hypoglycemia
(C) Malignant hypertension
(D) Postural hypotension
(E) Primary hypertension

206. A 72-hour fecal fat test is commonly used to diagnose which of the following gastrointestinal disorders?
(A) Celiac disease
(B) Crohn's disease
(C) Diverticulitis
(D) Malabsorption
(E) Ulcerative colitis

207. Which of the following forms of contraception is characterized by the implantation of a single flexible rod, about the size of a matchstick, that releases about 40 mcg/day of etonorgestrel?
(A) Combined injectable contraceptive
(B) Copper-T IUD
(C) Hormone-impregnated vaginal ring
(D) Implanon system
(E) Mirena IUD

208. A 33-year-old male presents with redness of the eyelids associated with dandruff-like deposits and fibrous scales. You diagnose this patient with blepharitis. Which of the following treatment options would you prescribe?
(A) Anti-inflammatories
(B) Eyelid scrubs
(C) Nasal decongestants
(D) Ophthalmic steroids
(E) Warm compresses

209. A 50-year-old female presents with dull pain, swelling, redness, and tenderness of the left leg. Which of the following disorders can adequately be ruled out with an ultrasound examination?
(A) Contact dermatitis
(B) Cellulitus
(C) Deep venous thrombosis
(D) Osteomyelitis
(E) Phlebitis

210. A 24-year-old male was a victim of an occupational accident and presents in the emergency room with a sucking chest wound. Chest X-ray reveals the accumulation of air in the pleural space with mediastinal shift to the left. Physical exam reveals impaired ventilation. Which of the following is the proper diagnosis?
(A) Acute respitatory distress syndrome
(B) Congestive heart failure
(C) Primary pneumothorax
(D) Pulmonary embolism
(E) Tension pneumothorax

211. A 70-year-old female presents with shortness of breath, persistent non-productive cough, and nocturnal dyspnea. Auscultation of the chest reveals enlarged apical impulse, diminished first heart sound, an S3 gallop, and an S4 gallop. Chest X-ray reveals bilateral pleural effusions, venous dilatation, and alveolar fluid. Based on the patient's presentation, physical exam, and test results, which of the following is the most accurate diagnosis?
(A) Cystic fibrosis
(B) Left-sided congestive heart failure
(C) Primary pneumothorax
(D) Right-sided congestive heart failure
(E) Tension pneumothorax

212. Which of the following disorders is characterized by the appreciation of a sausage-like mass upon abdominal examination of a pediatric patient?
(A) Acute mesenteric ischemia
(B) Appendicitis
(C) Intussesception
(D) Toxic megacolon
(E) Ulcerative colitis

213. Methotrexate is the indicated form of treatment for ectopic pregnancy only if the hCG titer is less than:
(A) 4,500 mU
(B) 5,000 mU
(C) 5,500 mU
(D) 6,000 mU
(E) 6,500 mU

214. Which of the following vaccines can be administered to prevent the occurrence of genital warts?
(A) Cervarix
(B) Comvax
(C) Gardasil
(D) Mycobax
(E) Pentacel

215. Diazepam is the indicated medical treatment for which of the following disorders?
(A) Acute vertigo
(B) Labyrinthitis
(C) Motion sickness
(D) Otitis externa
(E) Presbycusis

216. Regardless of presentation and symptoms, which of the following is ruled out immediately with a negative d-dimer level?
(A) Blood clot
(B) Diabetes
(C) Acute myocardial infarction
(D) Aortic dissection
(E) Ischemia

217. Ranson's criteria is a commonly used formula to evaluate the prognosis for which of the following conditions?
(A) Appendicitis
(B) Cholecystitis
(C) Gastritis
(D) Hepatitis
(E) Pancreatitis

218. A 62-year-old female recently underwent coronary bypass graft surgery and now presents with sudden onset of chest pain with inspiration and shortness of breath. You suspect she has developed a pulmonary embolism. Which of the following lab tests would you perform in order to confirm the diagnosis of pulmonary embolism?
(A) Complete blood count
(B) D-dimer
(C) Erythrocyte sedimentation rate
(D) Hemoglobin/hematocrit
(E) Troponin

219. A 45-year-old obese sedentary female presents with dull pain in the right leg associated with swelling, redness, and tenderness. D-dimer level is elevated at 1,460 ng/dL. Based on the patient's presentation and physical examination, which of the following is the most appropriate diagnosis?
(A) Atherosclerosis
(B) Chronic venous insufficiency
(C) Deep venous thrombosis
(D) Peripheral arterial disease
(E) Varicose veins

220. Methotrexate is the indicated form of treatment for ectopic pregnancy only if the ectopic mass is less than:
(A) 3.5 cm
(B) 4.5 cm
(C) 5.5 cm
(D) 6.5 cm
(E) 7.5 cm

221. Scopolamine is the indicated medical treatment for which of the following disorders?
(A) Acute vertigo
(B) Labyrinthitis
(C) Motion sickness
(D) Otitis externa
(E) Presbycusis

222. A temporal artery biopsy is required to confirm the diagnosis of which of the following disorders?
(A) Abdominal aortic aneurysm
(B) Chronic venous insufficiency
(C) Giant cell arteritis
(D) Subarachnoid hemorrhage
(E) Transposition of the great vessels

223. A 33-year-old woman who has never been pregnant presents with dysmenorrhea, painful

sexual intercourse, painful bowel movements, and intermittent spotting. Based on the patient's presentation and physical examination, which of the following is the most appropriate diagnosis?
(A) Adenomyosis
(B) Endometriosis
(C) Endometrial polyps
(D) Leiomyomata
(E) Uterine prolapse

224. A 24-year-old female presents with redness, inflammation, burning, and small eruptions on her lower face, around the mouth. Based on the patient's presentation, which of the following is the most likely diagnosis?
(A) Cellulitis
(B) Erythema multiforme
(C) Perioral dermatitis
(D) Porphyria
(E) Seborrheic dermatitis

225. Laparotomy is indicated for treatment of ectopic pregnancy only in which of the following conditions?
(A) Abdominal adhesions
(B) Fetal mass greater than 2.5 cm
(C) Fetal mass less than 5.5 cm
(D) Serum hCG greater than 3,000 mU
(E) Serum hCG less than 5,000 mU

226. Which of the following preventative measures would you advise the staff of a nursing home to perform in order to avoid the occurrence of decubitus ulcers?
(A) Bathe the patients regularly.
(B) Change bed linens regularly.
(C) Check patients' blood glucose regularly.
(D) Massage the patients regularly.
(E) Reposition the patients regularly.

227. A 45-year-old female who has had 2 children presents with severe secondary dysmenorrhea and menorrhagia. Physical exam reveals a symmetrically enlarged uterus. Pregnancy test is negative. Based on the patient's history and physical examination, which of the following is the most appropriate diagnosis?
(A) Adenomyosis
(B) Endometrial polyps
(C) Endometriosis
(D) Endometritis
(E) Leiomyomata

228. A 32-year-old male with a respiratory tract infection presents with a "herald patch" on the abdomen with an associated rash. Based on the patient's presentation, which of the following is the most appropriate diagnosis?
(A) Dermatophytosis
(B) Pityriasis rosea
(C) Scabies
(D) Tinea versicolor
(E) Vitiligo

229. For which of the following disorders is Meclizine the most effective treatment?
(A) Acute vertigo
(B) Labyrinthitis
(C) Motion sickness
(D) Otitis externa
(E) Presbycusis

230. Which of the following diagnostic procedures is most effective to diagnose a hiatal hernia?
(A) Abdominal angiogram
(B) Barium swallow
(C) Chest X-ray
(D) CT scan of the chest
(E) Endoscopy

231. A patient presents with right upper quadrant pain. Which of the following symptoms would also have to be present to create Charcot's triad for cholangitis?
(A) Fever and swelling
(B) Jaundice and fever
(C) Jaundice and vomiting
(D) Nausea and fever
(E) Nausea and vomiting

232. Which of the following conditions would require you to obtain a creatinine phosphokinase lab test?
(A) Aortic dissection
(B) Myocardial infarction
(C) Pericardial effusion
(D) Pulmonary embolism
(E) Pulmonary hypertension

233. A 44-year-old male who had previously sustained a compound femur fracture presents with edema in the lower extremities and an ulcer on the right ankle. The skin in the lower extremities appears shiny, thin, and discolored. The patient complains of lower leg itching and pain when he stands. Based on the patient's presentation and physical examination, which of the following is the most appropriate diagnosis?
(A) Atherosclerosis
(B) Chronic venous insufficiency
(C) Deep venous thrombosis
(D) Peripheral arterial disease
(E) Varicose veins

234. Cervical cerclage is indicated to reduce the risk of miscarriage if the pregnant female has a history of which of the following disorders?
(A) Caesarian section
(B) Cervical incompetence
(C) Gestational diabetes
(D) Hypertension
(E) Preeclampsia

235. Recombinant tissue plasminogen activators, such as alteplase and reteplase, are commonly used to break down which of the following substances?
(A) Bile stones
(B) Blood clots
(C) Cholesterol
(D) Glucose
(E) Kidney stones

236. A Mallory-Weiss tear occurs most commonly secondary to which of the following disorders?
(A) Alcohol abuse
(B) Anorexia nervosa
(C) Binge eating disorder
(D) Bulimia nervosa
(E) Cocaine abuse

237. Nonseminomatous testicular tumors are resistant to which form of therapy?
(A) Chemotherapy
(B) Cryotherapy
(C) Hormonal therapy
(D) Immunotherapy
(E) Radiation therapy

238. A 52-year-old female arrives for yearly examination. Auscultation of the chest reveals a systolic murmur between the second and third left intercostal space, radiating to the left shoulder and neck. Auscultation also reveals an early pulmonic ejection sound. Based on presentation and physical examination, which of the following is the proper diagnosis?
(A) Aortic regurgitation
(B) Aortic stenosis
(C) Mitral stenosis
(D) Pulmonic stenosis
(E) Tricuspid regurgitation

239. A 70-year-old male presents with abdominal pain, back pain, and intermittent "pulses" in the center of the abdomen. Based on the patient's presentation, which of the following is the most appropriate diagnosis?
(A) Abdominal aortic aneurysm
(B) Aortic dissection
(C) Chronic venous insufficiency
(D) Giant cell arteritis
(E) Peripheral arterial disease

240. Which of the following clinical procedures can be performed to assess fetal lung maturity?
(A) Amniocentesis
(B) Chorionic villus sampling
(C) CT scan of the abdomen
(D) Fetal ultrasound
(E) X-Ray of the abdomen

241. Sunscreen is imperative to prevent against the progression of which of the following dermatologic disorders?
(A) Alopecia
(B) Acanthosis nigricans
(C) Impetigo
(D) Petechiae
(E) Vitiligo

242. Felbatol is commonly used as which type of medication?
(A) Anti-arrhythmic
(B) Anti-convulsant
(C) Anti-inflammatory
(D) Anti-psychotic
(E) Antibiotic

243. Esophageal varices are normally caused by which of the following disorders?
(A) Essential hypertension
(B) Orthostatic hypotension
(C) Portal hypertension

(D) Pulmonary hypertension

(E) Secondary hypertension

244. Deficiency of vitamin D is the cause of which of the following disorders?

(A) Osteoarthritis

(B) Osteogenesis imperfecta

(C) Osteomalacia

(D) Osteomyelitis

(E) Osteoporosis

245. A 44-year-old male presents with shortness of breath on exertion, fatigue, and sudden nocturnal dyspnea. Auscultation of the chest reveals a mid-diastolic murmur at the apex with little radiation. Auscultation also reveals S1 accentuated opening snap following S2. Based on the presentation and physical examination, which of the following is the proper diagnosis?

(A) Aortic regurgitation

(B) Aortic stenosis

(C) Mitral stenosis

(D) Pulmonic stenosis

(E) Tricuspid regurgitation

246. A 44-year-old male presents with difficult, painful swallowing. Endoscopy reveals multiple shallow ulcers. Culture was positive for herpes simplex virus. Based on the patient's presentation and test results, which of the following is the most appropriate diagnosis?

(A) Diffuse esophageal spasm

(B) Esophageal dysmotility

(C) Esophageal neoplasm

(D) Infectious esophagitis

(E) Reflux esophagitis

247. Antipsychotic drugs, such as haldol and seroquel, are commonly used to regulate which of the following psychological conditions?

(A) Anxiety

(B) Depression

(C) Hostility

(D) Mania

(E) Paranoia

248. Which of the following types of seizures are commonly treated with valproic acid?

(A) Absence seizures

(B) Simple partial seizures

(C) Complex partial seizures

(D) Generalized convulsive seizures

(E) Generalized nonconvulsive seizures

249. A urea breath test is commonly performed to confirm the presence of which of the following types of bacteria?

(A) *Helicobacter pylori*

(B) *Lactobacillus acidophilus*

(C) *Lactobacillus rhamnosus*

(D) *Pneumocystis joroveci*

(E) *Porphyromonas gingivalis*

250. Light therapy is indicated for treatment of which of the following psychological disorders?

(A) Atypical depression

(B) Catatonic depression

(C) Dysthymia

(D) Melancholia

(E) Seasonal affective disorder

251. Which of the following treatments are essential for protection of areas of hyperpigmented skin due to melasma?

(A) Hydrating agents

(B) Sunscreens

(C) Topical antibiotics

(D) Topical corticosteroids

(E) Topical insecticides

252. Interferon-b is commonly used to decrease the frequency of relapses of moderate or severe attacks associated with which of the following disorders?

(A) Fibromyalgia

(B) Muscular dystrophy

(C) Multiple sclerosis

(D) Scleroderma

(E) Systemic lupus erthythematosus

253. Zollinger-Ellison syndrome is characterized by a tumor that secretes which of the following digestive enzymes?

(A) Gastrin

(B) Hydrochloric acid

(C) Lipase

(D) Mucin

(E) Pepsinogen

254. Hypercalcemia is a classic marker for which of the following disorders?

(A) Addison's disease

(B) Hyperparathyroidism

(C) Hyperthyroidism

(D) Hypoparathyroidism

(E) Hypothyroidism

255. A 45-year-old female presents with decreased exercise tolerance, dyspnea, fatigue, and hoarseness. Auscultation of the chest reveals mid-systolic murmur at the second right intercostal space and radiating to the neck and left sternal border. Carotid pulse is "thready." Based on the presentation and physical examination, which of the following is the proper diagnosis?
   (A) Aortic regurgitation
   (B) Aortic stenosis
   (C) Mitral stenosis
   (D) Pulmonic stenosis
   (E) Tricuspid regurgitation

256. A 28-year-old male presents with difficulty swallowing. Barium swallow reveals a "parrot-beaked" esophageal appearance, which is a sign of achalasia. Based on the patient's presentation and test results, which of the following is the most appropriate diagnosis?
   (A) Diffuse esophageal spasm
   (B) Esophageal dysmotility
   (C) Esophageal neoplasm
   (D) Infectious esophagitis
   (E) Reflux esophagitis

257. Which of the following medications can be prescribed to halt nicotine cravings?
   (A) Disulfiram
   (B) Buproprion
   (C) Naloxone
   (D) Phenobarbital
   (E) Verenicline

258. Which symptom associated with multiple sclerosis is commonly treated with amantadine?
   (A) Balance problems
   (B) Fatigue
   (C) Muscle dystonia
   (D) Muscle spasticity
   (E) Urologic dysfunction

259. Which of the following medications is approved by the FDA for treatment and management of pregnancy-induced hypertension?
   (A) Aliskiren
   (B) Cozaar
   (C) Lopressor
   (D) Methyldopa
   (E) Pitocin

260. Which of the following types of bacteria is most likely to colonize and cause pneumonia as a result of exposure to contaminated water droplets from cooling and ventilation systems?
   (A) *Chlamydia pneumoniae*
   (B) *Klebsiella pneumoniae*
   (C) *Legionella pneumoniae*
   (D) *Mycoplasma pneumoniae*
   (E) *Streptococcus pneumoniae*

261. A 29-year-old female presents with abdominal pain associated with uterine hemorrhaging after a delay in menstrual cycle. Pregnancy test was negative. Based on the patient's presentation, which of the following is the most appropriate diagnosis?
   (A) Endometrial cancer
   (B) Endometrial polyps
   (C) Polycystic ovary syndrome
   (D) Ovarian cysts
   (E) Uterine fibroids

262. A 34-year-old male presents with involuntary, quick movements of the hands and feet, irritability, moodiness, and antisocial behavior. CT scan reveals cerebral atrophy as well as atrophy of the caudate nucleus. Based on the patient's presentation and test results, which of the following is the most appropriate diagnosis?
   (A) Alzheimer's disease
   (B) Huntington's disease
   (C) Parkinson's disease
   (D) Pseudodementia
   (E) Vascular dementia

263. Minoxidil is effective for promoting hair growth via which of the following mechanisms?
   (A) Transcription factor activation
   (B) Desquamation
   (C) Inhibiting bacterial growth
   (D) Vasoconstriction
   (E) Vasodilatation

264. An abdominal angiogram is the ONLY diagnostic procedure to accurately confirm the diagnosis of which of the following gastrointestinal disorders?
   (A) Hepatitis
   (B) Acute cholecystitis
   (C) Colorectal cancer
   (D) Pancreatic cancer
   (E) Volvulus

265. Ceftriaxone is the most effective treatment for both men and women afflicted with which of the following sexually transmitted diseases?
(A) Chlamydia
(B) Genital warts
(C) Gonorrhea
(D) Herpes
(E) Syphilis

266. A 24-year-old physically active female presents with abnormal pain in the posterior lower calf. X-ray of the lower extremity shows a soft tissue shadow and calcifications along the Achilles tendon and its insertions. Based on the patient's history and X-ray, which of the following is the most appropriate diagnosis?
(A) Achilles tendonitis
(B) Fibula stress fracture
(C) Medial tibial stress syndrome
(D) Plantar fasciitis
(E) Tibial stress fracture

267. Which of the following is the name of the sign that results in a facial muscle contraction after tapping a facial nerve, a common sign associated with hypoparathyroidism?
(A) Chvostek's sign
(B) Harrison's groove
(C) Dalrymple's sign
(D) Queen Anne's sign
(E) Trousseau's phenomenon

268. A 50-year-old male, with a history of rheumatic fever, complains of dyspnea, fatigue, and cough. Auscultation of the chest reveals rales in the lungs. Auscultation also reveals a soft systolic and diastolic decrescendo from the second to the fourth left intercostal space radiating to the apex and right sternal border. Based on the presentation and physical examination, which of the following is the proper diagnosis?
(A) Aortic regurgitation
(B) Aortic stenosis
(C) Mitral stenosis
(D) Pulmonic stenosis
(E) Tricuspid regurgitation

269. A 44-year-old female present with abdominal pain, distention, vomiting of partially digested food, and obstipation. Auscultation of the abdomen reveals high-pitched bowel sounds that come in rushes. Based on the patient's presentation and

examination, which of the following is the most appropriate diagnosis?
(A) Chronic gastritis
(B) Duodenal ulcer
(C) Gastric ulcer
(D) Pancreatitis
(E) Small bowel obstruction

270. Disulfiram is the clinical intervention to deter cravings to which of the following substances?
(A) Alcohol
(B) Caffeine
(C) Cocaine
(D) Opiates
(E) Tobacco

271. Xenical, a maintenance medication for the treatment of obesity, is an example of which of the following classes of medication?
(A) Alpha-glucosidase inhibitors
(B) Cholinesterase inhibitors
(C) Gastrin inhibitors
(D) Lipase inhibitors
(E) Proton pump inhibitors

272. Pyrantel is an effective treatment for hookworms affecting patients in which of the following age groups?
(A) 0-2 years
(B) 18 months to 3 years
(C) 3-5 years
(D) Over 5 years
(E) Over 12 years

273. The diagnostic technique of acetowhitening uses acetic acid to facilitate a thorough evaluation of which of the following skin disorders?
(A) Extravasated blood
(B) Fungal presence
(C) Hyperpigmented macules
(D) Vitiligo
(E) Warts

274. A 59-year-old male, with a history of diabetes, presents with numbness, burning sensations, and pain in the lower extremities. Based on the patient's history and presentation, which of the following is the most appropriate diagnosis?
(A) Bell's palsy
(B) Diabetic peripheral neuropathy
(C) Guillain-Barré syndrome
(D) Myasthenia gravis
(E) Fibromyalgia

275. A 2-year-old boy presents with sudden onset of fever, anorexia, listlessness, and bleeding gums. Physical exam reveals red, swollen mucosa and vesicles on the oral mucosa, tongue, and lips. Based on the patient's presentation and physical examination, which of the following is the most appropriate diagnosis?
   (A) Acute herpetic gingivostomatitis
   (B) Acute herpetic pharyngotonsillitis
   (C) Peritonsillar cellulitis
   (D) Streptococcal pharyngitis
   (E) Viral pharyngitis

276. A 42-year-old woman presents with tingling, creeping, and crawling sensations and subjective need to move her lower extremities. Based on the patient's presentation, which of the following is the most likely diagnosis?
   (A) Chronic venous insufficiency
   (B) Diabetic peripheral neuropathy
   (C) Myasthenia gravis
   (D) Peripheral arterial disease
   (E) Restless leg syndrome

277. Naloxone is commonly prescribed to counteract the effects from an overdose of which of the following substances?
   (A) Alcohol
   (B) Caffeine
   (C) Cocaine
   (D) Opiates
   (E) Tobacco

278. Clomiphene citrate is commonly prescribed for which reproductive purpose?
   (A) Emergency contraception
   (B) Oral contraception
   (C) Promotion of ovulation
   (D) Prevention of miscarriage
   (E) Transdermal contraception

279. A hysterosalpingography is a useful exam for the evaluation of infertility. Which of the following does this exam evaluate?
   (A) Cervical competency
   (B) Ovulation
   (C) Sperm survival
   (D) Sperm penetration
   (E) Tubal patency

280. Which of the following is the name of the clinical sign that results in a carpal spasm in response to inflation of a blood pressure cuff, a common sign associated with hypoparathyroidism?
   (A) Chvostek's sign
   (B) Harrison's groove
   (C) Dalrymple's sign
   (D) Queen Anne's sign
   (E) Trousseau's phenomenon

281. A 72-year-old Asian male presents with dyspnea and angina. Echocardiogram reveals left ventricular hypertrophy, asymmetric septal hypertrophy, small left ventricle, and diastolic dysfunction. Electrocardiogram reveals left ventricular hypertrophy and exaggerated septal Q-waves. Based on the patient's presentation, physical examination, and test results, which of the following is the most appropriate diagnosis?
   (A) Congestive heart failure
   (B) Dilated cardiomyopathy
   (C) Hypertrophic cardiomyopathy
   (D) Infective endocarditis
   (E) Restrictive cardiomyopathy

282. A 58-year-old male presents with abdominal pain, rectal discomfort, nausea, and vomiting. Physical examination revealed a palpable abdominal mass and rock hard stool in the rectal vault. Based on the patient's presentation and examination, which of the following is the most appropriate diagnosis?
   (A) Appendicitis
   (B) Colorectal polyps
   (C) Diverticulitis
   (D) Fecal impaction
   (E) Volvulus

283. A 60-year-old male presents painful kyphosis with a curve greater than 60 degrees. Which of the following treatments would you suggest for this patient?
   (A) Epidural corticosteroid injection
   (B) Exercises
   (C) Oral corticosteroids
   (D) Milwaukee brace
   (E) Surgical correction

284. Lithium, an anti-manic medication, is commonly used as a maintenance medication to prevent manic episodes for individuals with which of the following disorders?
   (A) Anxiety disorder
   (B) Bipolar disorder
   (C) Borderline personality disorder

(D) Major depressive disorder

(E) Schizophrenia

285. Magnesium sulfate effectively treats pre-term contractions through which of the following mechanisms?

(A) Decreasing intracellular calcium ions

(B) Decreasing estrogen levels

(C) Decreasing progestin levels

(D) Inhibiting myometrial contractility mediated by calcium

(E) Stimulating beta receptors to relax smooth muscle

286. A 28-year-old female has just returned from vacation in which she was scuba diving. She presents with severe pain in the inner ear. Based on the patient's history and presentation, which of the following is the most appropriate diagnosis?

(A) Barotrauma

(B) Benign paroxysmal positional vertigo

(C) Central vertigo

(D) Labyrinthitis

(E) Tympanic membrane rupture

287. Which of the following physical exams is useful in detecting a meniscal tear?

(A) Finkelstein's test

(B) Lachman's test

(C) McMurray's test

(C) Phalen's test

(E) Tinel's sign

288. A 40-year-old female presents with fever, malaise, headache, and sore throat. Physical examination reveals vesicles on the posterior pharynx and tonsils. In addition, a grayish exudate is appreciated over the posterior mucosa. Based on the patient's history, presentation, and physical examination, which of the following is the most appropriate diagnosis?

(A) Acute herpetic gingivostomatitis

(B) Acute herpetic pharyngotonsillitis

(C) Peritonsillar cellulitis

(D) Streptococcal pharyngitis

(E) Viral pharyngitis

289. A follicle stimulating hormone (FSH) level of 42 mIU/mL is classically indicative for which of the following conditions?

(A) Pregnancy

(B) Ectopic pregnancy

(C) Menopause

(D) Ovarian cancer

(E) Spontaneous abortion

290. Which of the following is a permanent side effect to surgical removal of Morton's neuroma?

(A) Discoloration of the toes

(B) Numbness of the foot

(C) Numbness of the third and fourth toes

(D) Pain between the third and fourth toes

(E) Parasthesia of the toes

291. The medication ritodrine stimulates which of the following mechanisms in order to stop pre-term uterine contractions?

(A) Decreasing intracellular calcium ions

(B) Decreasing estrogen levels

(C) Decreasing progestin levels

(D) Inhibiting myometrial contractility mediated by calcium

(E) Stimulating beta-receptors to relax smooth muscle

292. A CT scan of the brain can be a useful tool for the diagnosis of which of the following psychological disorders?

(A) Alzheimer's disease

(B) Bipolar disorder

(C) Dementia

(D) Obsessive-compulsive disorder

(E) Schizophrenia

293. Which of the following types of stroke is associated with hemispheric signs and symptoms such as aphasia, apraxia, hemipareisis, hemisensory losses, and visual field defects?

(A) Hemorrhagic strokes

(B) Silent strokes

(C) Strokes involving anterior circulation

(D) Strokes involving posterior circulation

(E) Transient ischemic attacks (TIAs)

294. A 66-year-old female with a history of diabetes and amyloidosis presents with shortness of breath, reduced exercise capacity, and right-sided congestive heart failure. Auscultation of the chest reveals right-side rales. Chest X-ray shows mildly enlarged cardiac silhouette. Echocardiogram reveals mildly reduced left ventricular function. Based on the patient's presentation, physical examination, and test results, which of the following is the most appropriate diagnosis?
(A) Congestive heart failure
(B) Dilated cardiomyopathy
(C) Hypertrophic cardiomyopathy
(D) Infective endocarditis
(E) Restrictive cardiomyopathy

295. A 59-year-old woman with a history of alcoholism presents with epigastric pain that radiates to the back. She states that the pain is relieved when she lies in the fetal position. Patient also presents with fat malabsorption and steatorrhea. Bloodwork reveals elevated lipase and amylase levels. Based on the patient's presentation and lab results, which of the following is the most appropriate diagnosis?
(A) Acute pancreatitis
(B) Chronic pancreatitis
(C) Mallory-Weiss tear
(D) Pancreatic neoplasm
(E) Cholelithiasis

296. Lumbar epidural injections are commonly used for pain relief caused by which of the following spinal disorders?
(A) Ankylosing spondylitis
(B) Kyphosis
(C) Lordosis
(D) Scoliosis
(E) Spinal stenosis

297. Methotrexate, Ciclosporin, Rituximab, and Sulfasalazine are all medications approved for maintenance therapy of which of the following disorders?
(A) Osteoarthritis
(B) Psoriatic arthritis
(C) Reactive arthritis
(D) Rheumatoid arthritis
(E) Septic arthritis

298. A 34-year-old male who was a victim of a motor vehicle accident presents with bright red blood coming from the nose. Bright red blood is also seen in the posterior pharynx. Based on the patient's presentation and physical examination, which of the following is the most likely source of the epistaxis?
(A) Epiglottitis
(B) Kiesselbach's plexus
(C) Maxillary sinus osteum
(D) Soft palate
(E) Woodruff's plexus

299. Which of the following ligaments is affected in the disorder called gamekeeper's thumb?
(A) Dorsal radiocarpal ligament
(B) Extensor retinaculum
(C) Palmar radiocarpal ligament
(D) Radial collateral ligament
(E) Ulnar collateral ligament

300. A 28-year-old male presents with double vision, drooping eyelids, impaired extraocular movements, and fixed, dilated pupils. Patient also complains of dry mouth, nausea, and vomiting. Based on the patient's presentation and physical examination, which of the following is the most appropriate diagnosis?
(A) Diptheria
(B) Botulism
(C) Shigellosis
(D) Tetanus
(E) Tetrodotoxin poisoning

301. Calcium channel blockers stimulate which of the following mechanisms in order to effectively stop premature uterine contractions?
(A) Decreasing estrogen levels
(B) Decreasing intracellular calcium ions
(C) Decreasing progestin levels
(D) Inhibiting myometrial contractility mediated by calcium
(E) Stimulating beta-receptors to relax smooth muscle

302. Which areas of the brain are affected in Pick's disease?
(A) Frontal and occipital lobes
(B) Frontal and parietal lobes
(C) Frontal and temporal lobes
(D) Occipital and temporal lobes
(E) Occipital and parietal lobes

303. An 80-year-old female presents with fever, cough, dyspnea, and back pain. Physical exam reveals painless red lesions on the palms and soles. In addition, exudative lesions are observed in the retina. Blood cultures are positive and a trans-esophageal echocardiogram reveals an oscillating intracardiac mass. Auscultation of the chest reveals a heart murmur that was not appreciated at her previous exam. Based on the patient's presentation, physical examination, and test results, which of the following is the most appropriate diagnosis?
(A) Congestive heart failure
(B) Dilated cardiomyopathy
(C) Hypertrophic cardiomyopathy
(D) Infective endocarditis
(E) Restrictive cardiomyopathy

304. A 56-year-old man with a history of Crohn's disease presents with jaundice, itching, fatigue, malaise, and weight loss. Physical examination reveals hepatomegaly and splenomegaly. Bloodwork reveals elevated liver enzymes. Based on the patient's presentation, physical examination, and test results, which of the following is the most appropriate diagnosis?
(A) Acute cholangitis
(B) Acute pancreatitis
(C) Choledocolithiasis
(D) Chronic pancreatitis
(E) Primary sclerosing cholangitis

305. A 15-year-old male presents with pain in the anatomical snuffbox after sustaining a fall. Physical examination reveals swelling and ecchymosis over the affected region. X-ray was negative for scaphoid fracture. Which of the following treatment options would you suggest for treatment of this patient?
(A) Closed reduction
(B) Long-arm thumb spica cast
(C) Open-reduction internal fixation
(D) Osteotomy of the scaphoid bone
(E) Short-arm thumb spica cast

306. Calcium gluconate is extremely effective for counteracting the effects from an overdose of which of the following medications?
(A) ACE inhibitors
(B) Calcium channel blockers
(C) Clomiphene citrate
(D) Magnesium sulfate
(E) Ritodrine

307. A pediatric patient's X-ray reveals a "rachitic rosary" abnormality on the chest. A rachitic rosary is a common finding with which of the following disorders?
(A) Cardiomyopathy
(B) Croup
(C) Hyaline membrane disease
(D) Pneumonia
(E) Rickets

308. Which of the following is the clinical term for a deep-seated infection of multiple hair follicles as a conglomerate mass?
(A) Abscess
(B) Carbuncle
(C) Cyst
(D) Foruncle
(E) Pimple

309. A 12-year-old boy presents with anterior knee pain with swelling over the tibial tubercle. Patient states that pain only occurs with exercise and is relieved by rest. Lateral X-ray of the knee shows fragmentation at the tibial tubercle. Based on the patient's history and test results, which of the following is the most appropriate diagnosis?
(A) Anterior cruciate ligament tear
(B) Medial collateral ligament tear
(C) Meniscal tear
(D) Osgood-Schlatter disease
(E) Patellar tendinitis

310. A newborn infant presents with projectile vomiting, dehydration, and weight loss. The child remains hungry and wants to be fed. Upper GI study reveals a "string sign." Based on the patient's presentation and test results, which of the following is the appropriate diagnosis?
(A) Bowel atresia
(B) Diaphragmatic hernia
(C) Esophogeal atresia
(D) Pyloric stenosis
(E) Volvulus

311. Which of the following orthopedic devices should be worn for management of golfer's elbow?
(A) Figure-eight sling
(B) Lateral counterforce brace
(C) Medial counterforce brace
(D) Milwaukee brace
(E) No orthopedic device should be worn.

312. Bisphosponate medications are currently approved for maintenance therapy of which of the following musculoskeletal disorders?
    (A) Osteoarthritis
    (B) Osteogenesis imperfecta
    (C) Osteomalacia
    (D) Osteomyelitis
    (E) Osteoporosis

313. The medication betamethisone will enable the lungs of a premature infant to produce which of the following substances?
    (A) Carbon dioxide
    (B) Growth factor
    (C) Mucous
    (D) Oxygen
    (E) Surfactant

314. A hip X-ray reveals a classic "crescent sign" along the acetabulofemoral joint. A crescent sign is a classic indication for which of the following disorders?
    (A) Acute hip dislocation
    (B) Avascular necrosis
    (C) Osgood-Schlatter disease
    (D) Septic arthritis
    (E) Slipped capital femoral epiphysis

315. Which of the following common skin lesions present as minute hemorrhagic spots that cannot be blanched by diascopy?
    (A) Bullae
    (B) Petechiae
    (C) Pustules
    (D) Vesicles
    (E) Wheals

316. A 40-year-old female presents with generalized bone and joint pain. Skeletal survey reveals kyphosis and bowed tibias. Blood reveals an abnormally high alkaline phosphatase level. Based on the patient's presentation, history, and test results, which of the following is the correct diagnosis?
    (A) Osteogenesis imperfecta
    (B) Osteomalacia
    (C) Osteoporosis
    (D) Paget's disease
    (E) Rickets

317. A 22-year-old male presents with a chronic, non-tender mass on the left side of the scrotum. Physical examination reveals the lesion has the consistency of a "bag of worms,'" increases in size with Valsalva maneuver, and decreases with elevation of the testicles. Based on the patient's presentation and physical exam, which of the following is the proper diagnosis?
    (A) Hydrocele
    (B) Orchiditis
    (C) Spermatocele
    (D) Testicular torsion
    (E) Varicocele

318. Which of the following treatment options is indicated for a patient who has been diagnosed with non-small cell carcinoma?
    (A) Chemotherapy
    (B) Hormonal therapy
    (C) Immunotherapy
    (D) Radiation therapy
    (E) Surgery

319. Oxytocin is commonly used for which of the following reproductive purposes?
    (A) Inducing labor
    (B) Inhibiting pre-term labor
    (C) Oral contraception
    (D) Promotion of ovulation
    (E) Transdermal contraception

320. A chest radiograph reveals a Hampton's hump sign. This sign indicates a diagnosis of which of the following disorders?
    (A) Croup
    (B) Lung cancer
    (C) Pulmonary embolism
    (D) Pneumonia
    (E) Tuberculosis

321. A 60-year-old female with a history of diabetes and hypertension presents with insidious, progressive loss of vision. Examination of the eye reveals venous dilatation and retinal edema. Based on the patient's presentation and physical examination, which of the following is the most likely diagnosis?
    (A) Dacryostenosis
    (B) Glaucoma
    (C) Retinopathy
    (D) Orbital cellulitis
    (E) Viral conjunctivits

322. The spinal abnormality characterized by increased convex curvature of the thoracic spine is known as:
    (A) Ankylosing spondylitis
    (B) Kyphosis
    (C) Lordosis
    (D) Scoliosis
    (E) Spinal stenosis

323. A 42-year-old male presents with fever, nausea, vomiting, abdominal cramps, and bloody diarrhea that has persisted for four days. Stool culture was positive for Salmonella. Based on the patient's presentation and test results, which of the following is the most appropriate diagnosis?
    (A) Dysentery
    (B) *E. coli* O157:H7 infection
    (C) Gastroenteritis
    (D) Pseudomembranous colitis
    (E) Ulcerative colitis

324. Selective estrogen receptor modulating medications, such as raloxifene and lasofoxifene, are somewhat effective for treatment of osteoporosis but increase risk of developing which of the following disorders?
    (A) Blood clots
    (B) Breast cancer
    (C) Cardiac arrhythmia
    (D) Diabetes
    (E) Hypertension

325. Foods that contain the amino acid tyramine are contraindicated with which of the following types of medications?
    (A) ACE inhibitors
    (B) DMARDs
    (C) MAOIs
    (D) NSAIDs
    (E) SSRIs

326. Which type of fracture is classically defined as a fracture in which one side of the bone is broken while the other side is bent?
    (A) Greenstick fracture
    (B) Colles's fracture
    (C) Open fracture
    (D) Smith's fracture
    (E) Torus fracture

327. Which of the following is the clinical term for the condition of uterine fibroids?
    (A) Adenomyosis
    (B) Endometrial hyperplasia
    (C) Endometriosis
    (D) Leiomyomata
    (E) Prolapse

328. A 23-year-old male presents with cervical lymph-adenopathy. The patient states that the relevant lymph nodes are painful after consumption of alcohol. Physical exam reveals an enlarged liver and spleen. Based on the patient's presentation, which of the following is the most appropriate diagnosis?
    (A) Acute myologenous leukemia
    (B) Hodgkin's lymphoma
    (C) Goiter
    (D) Non-Hodgkin's lymphoma
    (E) Parathyroid adenoma

329. A 39-year-old obese male presents with fatigue, itching, blurred vision, and poor wound healing. His fasting glucose level was measured at 141 mg/dL. Based on the patient's presentation and lab results, which of the following is the most accurate diagnosis?
    (A) Diabetes insipidus
    (B) Hypoglycemia
    (C) Hypothyroidism
    (D) Type I diabetes mellitus
    (E) Type II diabetes mellitus

330. The medication bupropion is contraindicated for treatment of which of the following conditions?
    (A) Anorexia nervosa
    (B) Binge eating disorder
    (C) Bulimia nervosa
    (D) Body dysmorphic disorder
    (E) Obesity

331. An ultrasound image of a 32-year-old woman's ovary denotes a characteristic "string of pearls" appearance. Which of the following disorders is characterized by this sign?
    (A) Endometriosis
    (B) Adenomyosis
    (C) Leiomyomata
    (D) Ovarian cancer
    (E) Polycystic ovary syndrome

332. Inhaled corticosteroids are the first-line choice for everyday, maintenance therapy for which of the following conditions?
    (A) Asthma
    (B) Bronchitis
    (C) Bronchiolitis
    (D) Emphysema
    (E) Pneumonia

333. Medications that mimic the effects of the sympathetic nervous system, called sympathomimetics, are commonly prescribed to treat which of the following conditions?
    (A) Anorexia nervosa
    (B) Binge eating disorder
    (C) Bulimia nervosa
    (D) Body dysmorphic disorder
    (E) Obesity

334. A pediatric chest X-ray reveals a boot-shaped heart. This appearance of the heart is a common finding for which of the following disorders?
    (A) Aortic stenosis
    (B) Atrial septal defect
    (C) Hypoplastic left heart syndrome
    (D) Tetralogy of Fallot
    (E) Transposition of the great vessels

335. Which of the following disorders is characterized by the presence of endometrial glands and stroma outside the endometrial cavity?
    (A) Adenomyosis
    (B) Endometrial hyperplasia
    (C) Endometriosis
    (D) Leiomyomata
    (E) Prolapse

336. A 22-year-old male with a history of chewing smokeless tobacco presents with painless white areas on the tongue and lower lip. Based on the patient's presentation, which of the following is the most appropriate diagnosis?
    (A) Candidiasis
    (B) Canker Sores
    (C) Leukoplakia
    (D) Oral herpetic lesions
    (E) Perioral dermatitis

337. A 12-year-old female presents with increased appetite with weight loss, blurred vision, and orthostatic hypotension. Bloodwork reveals a random blood glucose level of 248 mg/dL. Based on the patient's presentation and test results, which of the following is the most likely diagnosis?
    (A) Diabetes insipidus
    (B) Hypoglycemia
    (C) Hypothyroidism
    (D) Type I diabetes mellitus
    (E) Type II diabetes mellitus

338. Pregabalin is the only FDA-approved medication for the treatment of which of the following conditions?
    (A) Fibromyalgia
    (B) Muscular dystrophy
    (C) Multiple sclerosis
    (D) Scleroderma
    (E) Systemic lupus erthythematosus

339. You order a nuclear medicine scan of the testicles of a patient. The scan reveals a classic doughnut sign, which is indicative of which of the following disorders?
    (A) Epididymitis
    (B) Orchitis
    (C) Testicular atrophy
    (D) Testicular torsion
    (E) Testicular cancer

340. Anticholinergic medications, such as ipratropium or tiotropium, are indicated for everyday maintenance therapy for which of the following conditions?
    (A) Asthma
    (B) Bronchiectasis
    (C) COPD
    (D) Cystic fibrosis
    (E) Pulmonary edema

341. Selective serotonin reuptake inhibitors (SSRIs) are effective for reducing symptoms of fibromyalgia due to the fact they regulate which of the following?
    (A) Appetite
    (B) Bowel habits
    (C) Circadian rhythm
    (D) Mood
    (E) Sleep patterns

342. Which of the following lethal cardiac arrhythmias is noted on the electrocardiogram below?

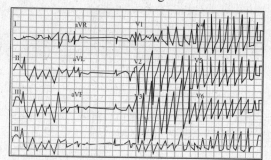

(A) Agonal rhythm
(B) Asystole
(C) Torsades de Pointes
(D) Ventricular escape rhythm
(E) Ventricular fibrillation

343. Which of the following personality disorders is characterized by an inferiority complex and extreme sensitivity to rejection?
(A) Antisocial personality disorder
(B) Avoidant personality disorder
(C) Depressive disorder
(D) Narcissistic personality disorder
(E) Schizotypal personality disorder

344. A 48-year-old man presents with unilateral, throbbing headaches, associated with nausea, vomiting, and visual aura. Based on the patient's presentation, which of the following is the most appropriate diagnosis?
(A) Cluster headache
(B) Migraine headache
(C) Sinus headache
(D) Subarachnoid hemorrhage
(E) Tension headache

345. A 26-year-old female with history of type I diabetes presents with rapid heartbeat, unexplained weight loss, and nervousness. The patient gave birth 3 months ago. Bloodwork reveals decreased thryoid-stimulating hormone (TSH) and increased T3 and T4 levels. Based on the patient's history and bloodwork, which of the following is the most appropriate diagnosis?
(A) Hashimoto's thyroiditis
(B) Hyperthyroidism
(C) Postpartum thyroiditis
(D) Subacute thyroiditis
(E) Suppurative thyroiditis

346. Salagen is prescribed to increase salivary flow for patients diagnosed with which of the following conditions?
(A) De Quervain's disease
(B) Hashimoto's disease
(C) Meniere's disease
(D) Sjogren's syndrome
(E) Wilson's disease

347. A urinalysis to evaluate for proteins in the urine would be obtained as an assessment for which of the following disorders?
(A) Diabetes insipudus
(B) Diabetes mellitus
(C) Hypertension
(D) Impaired renal function
(E) Kidney damage

348. Chemotherapy is the treatment of choice for which of the following types of lung neoplasms?
(A) Carcinoid tumor
(B) Non-small cell carcinoma
(C) Sarcoma
(D) Small cell carcinoma
(E) Solitary pulmonary nodule

349. Septic arthritis is characterized by yellow-to-green joint fluid and a white blood cell count that is:
(A) Between 200 and 300 /μl
(B) Between 500 and 2,000 /μl
(C) Between 2,000 and 3,000 /μl
(D) Between 3,000 and 50,000 /μl
(E) Greater than 50,000 /μl

350. A 26-year-old female presents with episodes of steady, aching, band-like pain around the head. Physical examination reveals tenderness of the posterior cervical and occipital muscles. Based on the patient's presentation and physical examination, which of the following is the most appropriate diagnosis?
(A) Cluster headache
(B) Migraine headache
(C) Sinus headache
(D) Subarachnoid hemorrhage
(E) Tension headache

351. A 52-year-old female presents with fatigue, depression, muscle stiffness, peripheral edema, weight gain, and thinning hair. Bloodwork revealed elevated thyroid stimulating hormone (TSH) and low T3 and T4 levels. Based on the patient's presentation, physical examination, and test results, which of the following is the most likely diagnosis?
   (A) Hyperparathyroidism
   (B) Hypoparathyroidsm
   (C) Hyperthyroidism
   (D) Hypothyroidism
   (E) Thyroid storm

352. Calcium channel blockers are indicated to reduce systemic arterial pressure for patients who have been diagnosed with which of the following disorders?
   (A) Essential hypertension
   (B) Orthostatic hypotension
   (C) Portal hypertension
   (D) Pulmonary hypertension
   (E) Secondary hypertension

353. Which of the following antibiotic medications is a combination of sulfamethoxazole and trimethoprim?
   (A) Amoxicillin
   (B) Bactrim
   (C) Ciprofloxin
   (D) Erythromycin
   (E) Doxycycline

354. A woman who is diagnosed with and treated for breast cancer is at increased risk of developing which of the following other form of cancer?
   (A) Cervical cancer
   (B) Bladder cancer
   (C) Endometrial cancer
   (D) Ovarian cancer
   (E) Uterine cancer

355. In addition to drainage, which of the following is required for proper treatment of malignant pleural effusions?
   (A) Insertion of large-bore needle
   (B) Intubation
   (C) Paracentesis
   (D) Pleurodesis
   (E) Thoracentesis

356. The medication ribavirin has been proven effective in reducing mortality in children who suffer from which of the following conditions?
   (A) Bronchiolitis
   (B) COPD
   (C) Epiglottitis
   (D) Respiratory distress syndrome
   (E) Hyaline membrane disease

357. Which of the following types of arthritis is characterized by yellow-to-opalescent joint color and a white blood count of 3,000-50,000/µl?
   (A) Osteoarthritis
   (B) Psoriatic arthritis
   (C) Reactive arthritis
   (D) Rheumatoid arthritis
   (E) Septic arthritis

358. A 74-year-old male with a history of chronic hypertension presents with forgetfulness and inattentiveness. The patient is not depressed and social graces are well maintained. Based on the patient's presentation, physical examination, and test results, which of the following is the most likely diagnosis?
   (A) Alzheimer's disease
   (B) Frontotemporal dementia
   (C) Pseudodementia
   (D) Psychosis
   (E) Vascular dementia

359. A 6-year-old girl presents with fever, headache, lethargy, and bone pain in the sternum, tibia, and femur. Bloodwork reveals pancytopenia with circulating blasts in which terminal deoxynucleotidyl transferase is detected. Based on the patient's presentation and lab results, which of the following is the most likely diagnosis?
   (A) Acute lymphocytic leukemia
   (B) Acute myelogenous leukemia
   (C) Polycythemia vera
   (D) Sickle cell disease
   (E) Thrombocytopenia

360. Immediate decompression with a large-bore needle is required for which of the following pulmonary conditions?
   (A) Hemopneumothorax
   (B) Primary pneumothorax
   (C) Pulmanary edema
   (D) Spontaneous pneumothorax
   (E) Tension pneumothorax

ANSWER KEY AND EXPLANATIONS

1. A	37. D	73. D	109. D	145. B
2. C	38. B	74. E	110. E	146. C
3. D	39. E	75. B	111. C	147. E
4. C	40. D	76. A	112. E	148. A
5. E	41. C	77. D	113. B	149. C
6. C	42. D	78. C	114. D	150. A
7. D	43. B	79. D	115. E	151. D
8. E	44. A	80. C	116. E	152. E
9. B	45. B	81. A	117. A	153. E
10. E	46. A	82. D	118. B	154. E
11. D	47. D	83. E	119. D	155. C
12. A	48. D	84. A	120. B	156. E
13. D	49. C	85. E	121. B	157. B
14. A	50. D	86. C	122. A	158. D
15. C	51. A	87. B	123. E	159. B
16. B	52. E	88. D	124. C	160. E
17. A	53. D	89. D	125. C	161. B
18. E	54. C	90. E	126. B	162. E
19. B	55. B	91. D	127. A	163. D
20. A	56. E	92. E	128. B	164. A
21. A	57. A	93. A	129. D	165. E
22. C	58. D	94. A	130. C	166. C
23. B	59. D	95. C	131. C	167. E
24. B	60. A	96. B	132. D	168. E
25. B	61. D	97. A	133. E	169. A
26. B	62. C	98. E	134. D	170. D
27. E	63. D	99. A	135. B	171. D
28. E	64. E	100. D	136. D	172. E
29. D	65. B	101. C	137. A	173. B
30. D	66. B	102. B	138. D	174. A
31. E	67. A	103. E	139. C	175. D
32. C	68. C	104. E	140. A	176. A
33. E	69. E	105. E	141. C	177. C
34. E	70. E	106. D	142. B	178. D
35. D	71. C	107. C	143. A	179. C
36. C	72. D	108. D	144. D	180. E

181. A	217. E	253. A	289. C	325. C
182. B	218. B	254. B	290. C	326. A
183. A	219. C	255. B	291. E	327. D
184. D	220. A	256. B	292. E	328. B
185. A	221. C	257. E	293. C	329. D
186. D	222. C	258. B	294. E	330. A
187. B	223. B	259. B	295. B	331. E
188. E	224. C	260. C	296. E	332. A
189. D	225. A	261. D	297. D	333. B
190. E	226. E	262. B	298. E	334. D
191. D	227. A	263. E	299. E	335. C
192. C	228. B	264. D	300. B	336. C
193. C	229. B	265. C	301. B	337. D
194. A	230. B	266. A	302. C	338. A
195. C	231. B	267. A	303. D	339. D
196. A	232. B	268. B	304. E	340. C
197. B	233. B	269. E	305. B	341. E
198. E	234. B	270. A	306. D	342. C
199. B	235. B	271. D	307. E	343. B
200. C	236. A	272. D	308. B	344. B
201. B	237. E	273. B	309. D	345. C
202. E	238. D	274. B	310. D	346. D
203. C	239. A	275. A	311. C	347. D
204. D	240. A	276. E	312. E	348. D
205. E	241. E	277. D	313. E	349. D
206. D	242. B	278. D	314. B	350. E
207. D	243. C	279. E	315. B	351. D
208. B	244. C	280. E	316. D	352. D
209. C	245. C	281. C	317. E	353. B
210. E	246. D	282. D	318. E	354. C
211. B	247. C	283. D	319. A	355. D
212. C	248. E	284. B	320. C	356. A
213. B	249. A	285. D	321. A	357. D
214. C	250. E	286. A	322. B	358. E
215. A	251. B	287. C	323. C	359. A
216. A	252. C	288. B	324. A	360. E

1. **The correct answer is (A).** Carpal tunnel syndrome is caused by compression of the median nerve under the transverse carpal ligament. Patients may experience night pain, numbness, paresthesias, loss of coordination, and loss of strength in the affected wrist and hand. Tinel's sign and Phalen's test may be positive.

2. **The correct answer is (C).** Individuals with factitious disorder intentionally fake signs and symptoms of medical or psychiatric disorders with the primary motivation of being taken care of and assuming the sick role. Patients will attempt to gain hospital admission under several different names with several different illnesses, and when confronted normally become angry and check themselves out. Patients are unable to provide reliable medical history. However, they are fairly knowledgeable about disease processes.

3. **The correct answer is (D).** The Bacille Calmette-Guerin vaccine is administered to prevent the spread of tuberculosis. The Bacille Calmette-Guerin vaccine (BCG) can and should be administered to a tuberculin negative person who is at a high risk for intense prolonged exposure to untreated or improperly treated cases of tuberculosis.

4. **The correct answer is (C).** Altering one's diet to include higher amount of water, caffeine, and salt is the indicated treatment for orthostatic hypotension. The reason for this is that water, caffeine, and salt all cause blood pressure to elevate and thereby reduce the effects of orthostatic hypotension.

5. **The correct answer is (E).** Pulmonary embolism is the correct diagnosis. The presence of normal ventilation and multiple perfusion defects on lung VQ scan is the classic indicator for pulmonary embolism.

6. **The correct answer is (C).** Necrotizing fasciitis is a deep, subcutaneous infection that results in destruction of fascia and fat. Presentation will include swelling, heat, erythema, and pain that spreads both distally and proximally. The skin around the wound will change color and will appear either red or violet. Blisters or bullae can form around the wound and a clear yellow fluid may emanate from the wound. This disorder will lead to gangrene and necrosis of the affected area. Patients may develop nausea, vomiting, and diarrhea in the early stages of this disorder.

7. **The correct answer is (D).** Seborrheic eczema is a skin disorder characterized by scattered yellowish or gray, scaly macules and papules with a greasy appearance. This disorder primarily occurs in where sebaceous glands are most active, such as skin folds, face, scalp, and genitalia. It can occur during infancy, puberty, and in young-to-middle-aged adults. This disorder manifests as dandruff in the adult population.

8. **The correct answer is (E).** The presence of rust-colored sputum and rigors are very typical manifestations that occur when the bacteria *Streptococcus pnuemoniae* is the causative agent for pneumonia.

9. **The correct answer is (B).** Chemical burns, either acid or alkali, of the eye should immediately be treated with a 30-minute flush of the eyes using either sterile water or saline solution. Chemical burns can continue to cause damage even after the flush has been performed.

10. **The correct answer is (E).** Non-pharmacologic therapies should be initiated for treatment of newly diagnosed hypertension. Reducing intake of sodium is one such non-pharmacologic method to initiate in an attempt to reduce hypertension. If diet changes are not effective, pharmacologic treatment should be initiated.

11. **The correct answer is (D).** Oxygen therapy is indicated as a supportive treatment for silicosis. In addition, treatment with corticosteroids can relieve the chronic alveolitis that is associated with silicosis. Supportive treatment is really the only option when treating pnuemoconioses such as silicosis.

12. **The correct answer is (A).** Acromioclavicular separation is commonly referred to as a separated shoulder. This injury involves a tearing of the acromioclavicular or coraclavicular ligaments and is normally caused by impact to the tip of the shoulder. A bump on the affected shoulder may appear during physical examination.

13. **The correct answer is (D).** Hypochondriasis is a disorder in which a patient has an irrational fear of contracting a serious illness. This disorder is commonly associated with anxiety and depression.

The patient continues to have fear of disease even though a physical examination reveals no cause.

14. **The correct answer is (A).** ST segment elevation as shown on the patient's electrocardiogram is the classic sign of acute myocardial infarction. Coronary angiography is the appropriate choice because the performing cardiologist can place a stent during the coronary angiography procedure to prevent permanent coronary damage.

15. **The correct answer is (C).** Molluscum contagiosum is a common viral disease of the skin and mucous membranes caused by a poxvirus. This disorder is common among children but can affect adults. The lesions associated with this disorder are discrete, flesh-colored, waxy, dome shaped, umbilicated papules on the face, trunk, and extremities. In adults, the lesions primarily occur in the groin area and the lower abdomen. A white curd-like material can be expressed from under the depression of the lesions.

16. **The correct answer is (B).** Grave's disease is an autoimmune disorder in which the thyroid is overactive and produces an excessive amount of thyroid hormones. Individuals with this disorder can present with weight loss, insomnia, exopthalmos, and a visible goiter.

17. **The correct answer is (A).** A pterygium is a highly vascular, triangular mass that grows from the nasal side of the eye toward the cornea. If the pterygium has progressed to the point where it interferes with vision, excision is the warranted course of treatment.

18. **The correct answer is (E).** The gold standard for treatment of symptomatic sarcoidosis is corticosteroids. Corticosteroids are effective at controlling inflammation associated with sarcoidosis as well as controlling granuloma formation that may also occur.

19. **The correct answer is (B).** *Klebsiella pneumoniae* is often the cause of pneumonia. Sputum the color of currant jelly is a classic manifestation of pneumonia caused by *K. pneumonia*.

20. **The correct answer is (A).** Cilostazol is used as first-line, maintenance medication for the reduction of symptoms associated with intermittent claudication. This medication will enable individuals to walk for a longer period of time prior to leg pain developing.

21. **The correct answer is (A).** Bronchitis is characterized by cough, dyspnea, fever, sore throat, headache, muscle aches, and chest pain. Auscultation of the chest will reveal expiratory rhonchi or wheezes. Patients with bronchitis will have a normal chest X-ray.

22. **The correct answer is (C).** Reactive arthritis presents with urethritis, conjunctivitis, oligoarthritis, and mucosal ulcers. This disorder is often the result of chlamydia infection or gastroenteritis. Patients may present with asymmetric arthritis in the large joints below the waist. Other common presentations are balanitis, stomatitis, urethritis, and conjunctivitis. This disorder affects males more than females.

23. **The correct answer is (B).** The most appropriate initial treatment for congestive heart failure is treatment with diuretics. Diuretics are effective in reducing the fluid volume in the lungs, which will relieve the symptoms associated with congestive heart failure.

24. **The correct answer is (B).** Isoniazid or INH is administered for treatment of tuberculosis. INH can cause side effects such as hepatitis and peripheral neuropathy. Administration of vitamin B6, known as pyroxidine, should be administered with INH to reduce the risk of these side effects.

25. **The correct answer is (B).** 2:1 AV Block, or second-degree AV block, is an abnormality of the conduction system of the heart. This means there is a conduction block between the atria and ventricle. 2:1 AV Block is demonstrated on an electrocardiogram by 2 P-waves to each QRS complex.

26. **The correct answer is (B).** A cataract is an opacity of the natural lens of the eye. Patients with cataracts may experience gradual loss of vision, episodes of double vision, fixed spots, and reduced color perception. Examination will reveal a yellow, translucent discoloration of the lens of the eye.

27. **The correct answer is (E).** Angina is characterized by sudden onset of chest pain that feels like pressure or "squeezing". Stable angina is classically diagnosed by chest pain brought on by physical activity and relieved spontaneously by rest.

28. **The correct answer is (E).** Obstructive shock is a form of shock that is associated with the physical obstruction of the great vessels or the heart itself. Some conditions that can potentially lead to obstructive shock are tension pneumothorax, pericardial tamponade, obstructive valvular disease, and massive pulmonary embolism.

29. **The correct answer is (D).** In the event the disorder of bacterial conjunctivitis is caused by a rare pathogen such as *Neisseria gonorrhoeae* or *Chlamydia trachomatis*, intravenous antibiotics are the proper course of treatment. If the disease is caused by common pathogens such as *Streptococcus pneumoniae*, topical antibiotics are sufficient to treat this disorder.

30. **The correct answer is (D).** Diuretics are the appropriate initial treatment; however, calcium channel blockers may also be necessary if chest pain and hypertension are associated with congestive heart failure. Calcium channel blockers are commonly prescribed to lessen the load on the heart, thus alleviating symptoms such as chest pain and hypertension. This is no different when treating congestive heart failure.

31. **The correct answer is (E).** The polyvalent pneumococcal vaccine, commonly referred to as Pneumovax, contains antigens of 23 common strains of the pneumococcus. All individuals who are aged 19–64 who suffer from asthma should receive a single dose of the pneumovax vaccine to prevent the occurrence of pneumonia.

32. **The correct answer is (C).** Dependent personality disorder is characterized by a behavior pattern of being dependent, clinging, and submissive. Patients have difficulty making their own decisions and avoid disagreements for fear of being disliked. Patients with this disorder often lack self-confidence and have difficulty being alone.

33. **The correct answer is (E).** Classic presentation for tuberculosis is dry cough progressing to productive cough, fever, night sweats, anorexia, and weight loss. Chest X-ray will reveal homogenous infiltrates, hilar or paratracheal lymph node enlargement, segmental atelectasis, or cavitations.

34. **The correct answer is (E).** The polyvalent pneumococcal vaccine, commonly referred to as Pneumovax, contains antigens of 23 common strains of the pneumococcus. This vaccine should be administered to prevent pneumonia in high-risk children, including those with heart problems, lung problems, sickle cell disease, and diabetes.

35. **The correct answer is (D).** A "swishing" sound upon auscultation of the heart is a classic signal of mitral valve prolapse. An echocardiogram is the easiest, least-invasive method to evaluate the function of the heart valves.

36. **The correct answer is (C).** Impetigo is characterized by thick, crusted, golden "honey" lesions. This disorder is more prevalent is individuals with poor hygiene or malnutrition. Impetigo is caused by *Streptococcus pyoderma* bacteria, which colonizes unbroken skin and enters the skin when an abrasion or insect bite is sustained.

37. **The correct answer is (D).** Obstructive shock is a type of shock that can arise from tension pnuemothorax, pericardial tamponade, or massive pulmonary embolism. Shock can cause low blood pressure, tachycardia, orthostatic changes, and altered mental status.

38. **The correct answer is (B).** *Helicobacter pylori* is the Gram-negative, spiral-shaped bacillus that is responsible for most cases of chronic gastritis. This type of bacteria can inhabit many areas of the stomach, but it is primarily found in the antrum.

39. **The correct answer is (E).** For carcinoid tumors, surgical excision is the only reasonable course of treatment. Surgical excision of carcinoid tumors carries a good prognosis and this form of tumor is resistant to chemotherapy and radiation therapy.

40. **The correct answer is (D).** Quinidine and procainamide are drugs known as sodium channel blockers. Sodium channel blockers depress phase zero depolarization, slow conduction, and prolong repolarization in an effort to prevent cardiac arrhythmias.

41. **The correct answer is (C).** Nitrates are a common initial treatment for chest pain. Nitrates can be administered in a variety of methods including patches, sprays, and tablets. This type of medication acts to relax the coronary arteries and alleviate chest pain.

42. **The correct answer is (D).** An olive-shaped mass appreciated on physical examination and confirmed with ultrasound is the classic diagnosis for pyloric stenosis.

43. **The correct answer is (B).** A pneumothorax is characterized by acute onset of chest pain and shortness of breath. Physical exam can show one-sided chest expansion, hyperresonance, and decreased breath sounds. Chest X-ray may show presence of pleural air, although a visceral pleural line is often the only radiographic evidence of a small pleural effusion.

44. **The correct answer is (A).** Congestive heart failure is characterized by dyspnea and the abnormal retention of water and sodium. Patients may experience exertional dyspnea, non-productive cough, and fatigue. Patients may also experience orthopnea, paroxysmal nocturnal dyspnea, and exercise intolerance. Chest X-ray should reveal cardiomegaly, bilateral pleural effusions, and perivascular or interstitial edema. Auscultation of the chest should reveal basilar rales and gallops. Symptoms and patient presentation may vary according to the side of the heart that is failing.

45. **The correct answer is (B).** Diverticulosis is the condition of having large outpouchings of the mucosa of the colon, called diverticula. Patients with this disorder may experience bloating, change in bowel habits, and pain in the left lower abdomen. Diverticulitis refers to an inflammation of the diverticula.

46. **The correct answer is (A).** For pnuemothoraces that are large and/or symptomatic, insertion of a chest tube is the proper course of treatment. Smaller pneumothoraces usually resolve spontaneously.

47. **The correct answer is (D).** The proper treatment for supraventricular tachycardia is intravenous administration of 6 mg adenosine. Adenosine is effective in slowing conduction time through the AV node.

48. **The correct answer is (D).** Ultrasound examinations are currently the gold standard for evaluating disorders pertaining to the testicles. Ultrasound exams are the most effective diagnostic procedures for diagnosis of testicular disorders such as torsion and epididymitis. A Nuclear Medicine testicular scan would be an alternative to a testicular ultrasound if ultrasound is unavailable.

49. **The correct answer is (C).** Dressler's syndrome, also referred to as post-MI syndrome, usually occurs one to two weeks after a myocardial infarction. Patients with Dressler's syndrome can experience pericarditis, fever, leukocytosis, pericardial effusions, and pleural effusions.

50. **The correct answer is (D).** Right-sided congestive heart failure is often caused by left-sided congestive heart failure. Symptoms may include distended neck veins, tender or non-tender hepatic congestion, hepatomegaly, and pitting edema.

51. **The correct answer is (A).** An anal fissure is defined as a linear lesion of the rectal wall that most commonly occurs on the posterior midline. Individuals with an anal fissure may experience a severe, tearing pain with defecation and bright red blood may be visible in the stool.

52. **The correct answer is (E).** For patients who are at risk for developing recurrent pulmonary embolism and are unable to tolerate or are resistant to anticoagulants, the insertion of a vena cava filter will prevent blood clots from progressing to the lungs.

53. **The correct answer is (D).** Histamine blockers are often used as first-line treatment for maintenance of mild gastro-esophageal reflux disease. These medications decrease the production of stomach acid by blocking the action of histamine on the parietal cells of the stomach. Cimetidine and zantac are examples of histamine blocker medications.

54. **The correct answer is (C).** Polymyalgia rheumatica is characterized by bilateral pain and stiffness in the neck, shoulder, and pelvic girdles. Patients with this disorder often experience fever, fatigue, weight loss, and depression. The pain and stiffness most often occurs, and is most severe, after rest and in the morning.

55. **The correct answer is (B).** Idiopathic fibrosing interstitial pneumonia is characterized by a dry cough, exertional dyspnea, fatigue, and malaise. Physical examination will reveal clubbing and inspiratory crackles. Chest X-rays will demonstrate progressive fibrosis over several years.

56. **The correct answer is (E).** Lidocaine, otherwise known as Xylocaine, is a commonly used anti-arrythmic medication as well as a local anesthetic. Lidocaine is indicated for the treatment of ventricular tachycardia.

57. **The correct answer is (A).** A glomerular filtration rate of 60 mL/1.73 m^2 of body surface area is indicative of impaired renal function. Normal GFR value is 90mL/min/1.73 m^2 of body surface area. GFR values below 90mL/min/1.73 m^2 of body surface area indicate some loss of renal function.

58. **The correct answer is (D).** Transportation of the great vessels is a congenital abnormality in which the aorta and the pulmonary artery are transposed, or switched. Patients with this condition present with blue skin, clubbing of fingers and toes, poor feeding, and shortness of breath. Auscultation of the chest will reveal a single loud S2 and a systolic murmur.

59. **The correct answer is (D).** Peripheral artery disease usually presents initially with intermittent claudication, or lower leg pain that is relieved by rest. As disease progresses, discomfort will occur at rest also. Auscultation of the legs will reveal weak or absent distal and femoral pulses. An aortic, iliac, or femoral bruit may also be appreciated. An ankle-brachial reflex of 0.9 or lower indicates significant peripheral artery disease.

60. **The correct answer is (A).** The obturator sign, or Cope sign, is a classic medical sign for the presence of acute appendicitis. The obturator sign is assessed when a patient is placed in the supine position and an attempt is made to flex and internally rotate the right hip with the knee bent. If pain is present, inflammation associated with appendicitis is confirmed.

61. **The correct answer is (D).** Lidocaine is the most important class 1B antiarrhythmic medication. Lidocaine is administered intravenously for treatment of ventricular arrhythmias such as the ventricular tachycardia shown in the electrocardiogram.

62. **The correct answer is (C).** Approximately 90% of cases of chronic pancreatitis in the United States are caused by alcohol abuse. Because alcohol abuse is the cause of this disorder, if alcohol consumption is decreased, a high percentage of chronic pancreatitis cases can be resolved.

63. **The correct answer is (D).** Several fluid-filled cysts appearing on an ultrasound examination is classic for the diagnosis of polycystic kidney disease. An ultrasound of the kidneys is the diagnostic method of choice for evaluation of polycystic kidney disease.

64. **The correct answer is (E).** Cardiac troponin levels are very sensitive and specific indicators of heart muscle damage stemming from a myocardial infarction. This laboratory test is often used to differentiate between diagnoses of unstable angina and myocardial infarction.

65. **The correct answer is (B).** Hemoglobin is a component of a complete blood count (CBC), along with total red cells, mean corpuscular volume, hematocrit, mean corpuscular hemoglobin, mean corpuscular hemoglobin concentration, red blood cell distribution width, total white blood cells with differential, platelets, and mean platelet volume.

66. **The correct answer is (B).** Colonoscopy is the most useful tool for confirming the diagnosis, determining the extent and severity, and guiding the treatment of Crohn's disease. Contrast studies and endoscopy procedures should be avoided because of the possibility of inducing toxic megacolon or perforation.

67. **The correct answer is (A).** A gluten-free diet is imperative for individuals diagnosed with celiac disease. Celiac disease is characterized by small bowel inflammation due to the digestion of gluten-containing products such as wheat, rye, and barley. A gluten-free diet will allow individuals diagnosed with celiac disease to avoid flare-ups.

68. **The correct answer is (C).** Ursadiol is a bile acid. It acts to decrease the production of cholesterol and dissolves the cholesterol already present in the bile so that it cannot form gallstones. Ursadiol is prescribed for patients who do not want surgery or cannot have surgery to remove gallstones.

69. **The correct answer is (E).** An electrocardiogram that shows an S wave in lead I, a Q wave in lead II, and an inverted-T wave in lead III is a classic electrocardiographic pattern for pulmonary embolism. This electrocardiogram is evident for

right ventricular overload, which is primarily caused by pulmonary embolism.

70. The correct answer is (E). For patients with ulcerative colitis, a total proctocolectomy is the most curative surgical cure. Segmental resection may be indicated for some cases.

71. The correct answer is (C). Orthostatic hypertension is characterized by a 20 mmHg change in blood pressure when transferring from a sitting to a standing position. This disorder is the most common cause of syncope and falls among the elderly.

72. The correct answer is (D). Fluoroquinolone medications, such as norflaxacin, are antibiotic medications commonly used for first-line of defense against infections of the urinary tract and prostate.

73. The correct answer is (D). Normal levels of a-fetoprotein and a-human chorionic gonadotropin, along with positive ultrasound, is diagnostic for a seminomatous testicular tumor. Elevated a-fetoprotein and a-human chorionic gonadotropin levels are diagnostic for a nonseminomatous germ cell testicular tumor.

74. The correct answer is (E). For cases of mesenteric ischemia, whether acute or chronic in nature, surgical revascularization is the only treatment option. Hydration is a critical factor for the management of this disease; however, surgical revascularization is the only chance for a cure.

75. The correct answer is (B). Mesalamine is an anti-inflammatory agent used primarily for maintenance therapy of Crohn's disease. Mesalamine inhibits inflammation in part of or the entire colon. Prednisone is only indicated with acute attacks of Crohn's disease.

76. The correct answer is (A). Tolterodine is a member of a class of medications called antimuscarinics. It is effective in preventing unwanted bladder contractions and alleviating urinary difficulties such as frequency of urination and inability to control urine.

77. The correct answer is (D). The only way to confirm a diagnosis of diabetes insipidus is by obtaining a vasopressin challenge test. Diabetes insipidus is an uncommon disorder caused by a deficiency

of or resistance to vasopressin, an anti-diuretic hormone.

78. The correct answer is (C). Polyarteritis nodosa is a disorder characterized by inflammation of the small-to-medium arteries involving the skin, kidney, peripheral nerves, and muscles. This disorder affects men to women by a 3:1 ratio. Patients may present with fever, anorexia, weight loss, muscle aches, and peripheral neuropathy. Bloodwork may reveal elevated C-reactive protein and erythrocyte sedimentation rate. Urinalysis will reveal proteinuria.

79. The correct answer is (D). Endometritis most commonly occurs two to three days after a caesarian section. Patients with this disorder present with fever greater than 101°F and uterine tenderness. Patients may also experience ovarian tenderness, peritoneal irritation, and decreased bowel sounds. White blood count is commonly greater than 20,000/mcL.

80. The correct answer is (C). Kidney stones measuring less than 5 mm will often pass spontaneously and can be managed on an outpatient basis. Increasing fluid intake should increase kidney function and urine output, which will allow the stone to pass more quickly and relieve associated symptoms more rapidly.

81. The correct answer is (A). Ceftriaxone is recommended for epididymitis that occurs as a result of sexually transmitted diseases such as gonorrhea and chlamydia. The Centers for Disease Control and Prevention states that ceftriaxone administered in conjunction with doxycycline twice a day for 10 days is an effective regimen for epididymitis that occurs as a result of sexually transmitted diseases.

82. The correct answer is (D). Hyperparathyroidism is classically diagnosed by elevated levels of serum calcium, or hypercalcemia. The parathyroid glands regulate blood calcium levels. Hyperthyroidism is primarily caused by a parathyroid adenoma, a malignant tumor of the parathyroid gland.

83. The correct answer is (E). Cigarette smoking may offer protection and relieve symptoms associated with ulcerative colitis. The causal bacterium for ulcerative colitis produces toxic hydrogen sulfide gas. Hydrogen cyanide obtained from cigarette smoking reacts with hydrogen sulfide to produce nontoxic isothiocyanate, thus reducing symptoms associated with ulcerative colitis.

84. **The correct answer is (A).** Elective lithotripsy is warranted for treatment of kidney stones that measure between 5-10 mm. Kidney stones of this size are less likely to pass spontaneously and should be directed for elective intervention if no contraindicating factors are present.

85. **The correct answer is (E).** Olecranon bursitis is caused by an acute injury or repetitive trauma to the olecranon bursa. The most common finding is inflammation overlying the olecranon bursa. There may or may not be pain associated with this condition.

86. **The correct answer is (C).** Immunodilators are indicated for maintenance therapy of ulcerative colitis if the disease does not respond to topical or oral aminosalicylates. Immunodilatory medications such as azathioprine and 6-mercaptopurine are used to maintain remission of ulcerative colitis without the harmful effects of long-term use of corticosteroids.

87. **The correct answer is (B).** Ciproflaxin is a powerful antibiotic and a member of the fluoroquinolone family of medications. For cases caused by bacteria rather than a sexually transmitted disease, Ciproflaxin will effectively eliminate the bacteria causing the epididymitis.

88. **The correct answer is (D).** Macrocytic anemias are characterized by mean corpuscular volumes greater than 100 fL. These forms of anemia are caused by acute hemorrhage and hemolysis. This form of anemia also includes deficiencies that ultimately lead to megaloblastic states.

89. **The correct answer is (D).** Temperomandibular joint disorder (TMJ) is the most common cause of facial pain. Facial pain is aggravated by movement of the jaw, such as when eating. In addition, a click or pop may be felt or heard while eating. The jaw may have limited range of motion.

90. **The correct answer is (E).** Placenta previa is a disorder of pregnancy in which the placenta partially or completely covers the cervical os. This disorder will prevent a natural childbirth and caesarian section is required for women with this condition. This disorder routinely occurs in women who have had several pregnancies, are of advanced age, and smoke cigarettes.

91. **The correct answer is (D).** For kidney stones measuring greater than 10 mm and when kidney function is jeopardized, percutaneous nephrostomy is the gold standard for treatment. A percutaneous nephrostomy consists of the renal pelvis being punctured and a nephrostomy tube inserted, and allows for drainage and release of the calcifications.

92. **The correct answer is (E).** Phosphodieterase-5 inhibitors are recognized as the drug of choice for treatment of erectile dysfunction. Sildenafil, vardenafil, and tadalafil are the most common drugs in the phosphodieterase-5 inhibitor family that are prescribed for treatment of erectile dysfunction.

93. **The correct answer is (A).** Acoustic neuroma, otherwise known as vestibular schwannoma, is a neoplastic cause of hearing loss. Acoustic neuroma can be diagnosed either by CT scanning or MRI imaging.

94. **The correct answer is (A).** Dialysis is the treatment of choice when a patient presents with sodium levels greater than 200 mEq/L. A high mortality rate is associated with sodium levels in this range, so rapid reduction of serum sodium is warranted. Extreme care should be taken when using rapid reduction techniques because the human body becomes accustomed to the higher sodium levels and rapid reduction may cause pulmonary or cerebral edema.

95. **The correct answer is (C).** A high-fiber diet and avoidance of obstructing or constipating foods, such as nuts, is indicated to avoid complications from diverticulitis. Surgical intervention may be required to treat this condition if a high-fiber diet is not adopted.

96. **The correct answer is (B).** Intravenous administration of 10-20 mL of 10% calcium gluconate over 10 minutes should remedy hypermagnesemia. Calcium directly antagonizes neuromuscular and cardiovascular effects of magnesium. Use for patients with symptomatic hypermagnesemia that is causing cardiac effects or respiratory distress.

97. **The correct answer is (A).** An arteriogram is the most definitive diagnostic study to evaluate for a transient ischemic attack. MRI can also be of use,

and is less invasive. However, arteriogram is the most definitive method.

98. **The correct answer is (E).** Tetanus is caused by a spore that germinates in wounds and produces a neurotoxin that causes uncontrolled spasms and exaggerated reflexes. Puncture wounds are most susceptible and intravenous drug users are at a high risk for tetanus. This disorder is characterized by jaw and neck stiffness, difficulty eating, and irritability. Pain and tingling at the site of the wound is common and is associated with spasticity of the nearby muscles. Physical exam will reveal hyperreflexia and muscle spasms of the jaw and face.

99. **The correct answer is (A).** For treatment of severe respiratory alkalosis with pH levels at 7.6 or greater, administration of CO_2 breathing mixtures is indicated for rapid reduction in body pH. If patient is unable to breathe on her own, mechanically-controlled ventilation of CO_2 breathing mixtures should be administered.

100. **The correct answer is (D).** Serotonin is a neurotransmitter that regulates mood, sleep, and appetite. Serotonin-modulating medications, such as fluoxetine and clomipramine, have proven effective for the majority of patients who suffer from body dysmorphic disorder.

101. **The correct answer is (C).** Cerebrospinal fluid is often examined in patients who have suffered a subarachnoid hemorrhage. Cerebrospinal fluid evaluation will reveal markedly elevated opening pressures and grossly bloody fluid.

102. **The correct answer is (B).** Overflow incontinence is characterized by an individual experiencing prolonged dribbling after urination. The patient's bladder is like a constantly overflowing pan. This condition is caused by loss of urinary muscle tone, past surgery, or spinal cord injuries. Catheterization is the best treatment option for this condition because the patient is unable to completely empty the bladder on his or her own.

103. **The correct answer is (E).** Trichomoniasis is a sexually transmitted disease caused by the parasite *Trichomonas vaginalis*. Women with this disorder complain of painful sexual intercourse, itching on the inner thighs, and a foul-smelling, frothy, yellow/green vaginal discharge. Physical examination will reveal red macular lesions on the vagina and cervix. Men with this disorder will complain of pain following urination or ejaculation, urethral itching, and minor urethral discharge.

104. **The correct answer is (E).** Oxybutynin is an anticholinergic medication. These medications are used as preventative and maintenance treatment of urinary incontinence and overactive bladder. Tolterodine is another medication of this class that can be used for this purpose.

105. **The correct answer is (E).** Glyburide, as well as glipizide and glimepiride, belong to a class of medications called sulfonylureas that are indicated for the treatment of diabetes mellitus. Sulfonylureas stimulate insulin secretion, and are among the most commonly used anti-diabetic medications. This class of medications has very few drug interactions. Side effects are weight gain and increased risk of hypoglycemia.

106. **The correct answer is (D).** An electroencephalogram, or EEG, is the most definitive exam for monitoring seizure activity. In generalized absence seizures, EEG will show generalized spikes and associated slow waves. In partial seizures, EEG will show focal rhythmic discharge at the onset of the seizure. In complex partial seizures, EEG shows interictal spikes or spikes associated with slow waves in the temporal or frontotemporal areas.

107. **The correct answer is (C).** Central retinal vein occlusion occurs secondary to a blood clot. Individuals who suffer from this disorder experience sudden, unilateral, painless blurred vision or complete vision loss. Examination will reveal an afferent pupillary defect and a "blood-and-thunder" retina, which consists of dilated veins, hemorrhages, edema, and exudates.

108. **The correct answer is (D).** Pericarditis is a condition in which the sac covering the heart becomes inflamed. This condition is characterized by chest pain that radiates to the neck, back, shoulder, or abdomen that is relieved by sitting up and leaning forward. Chest X-ray will reveal pleural effusions. Echocardiogram will confirm the inflammation of the pericardium.

109. **The correct answer is (D).** Calcium channel blocker medications such as Cardizem, Norvasc, and Procardia prevent calcium from entering cells of the heart and blood vessel walls. These medications relax and widen the blood vessels by affecting the muscle cells of arterial walls, and are the best choice for peripheral vasodilatation. Calcium channel blockers are also the best choice among the African-American and the elderly population.

110. **The correct answer is (E).** For patients who suffer from recurrent bladder cancer, a radical cystectomy is the only viable treatment option. Radical cystectomy is also indicated for individuals with transitional cell carcinoma in situ and for tumors that have invaded the surrounding muscles.

111. **The correct answer is (C).** Metformin is effective because it reduces hepatic glucose production. It effectively lowers blood glucose levels without risk of hypoglycemia. This medication is also effective in promoting weight loss and lowering triglycerides.

112. **The correct answer is (E).** White matter lesions of the central nervous system, which are characteristic of multiple sclerosis, can best be visualized with the performance of an MRI enhanced with gadolinium.

113. **The correct answer is (B).** A chalazion is characterized by a relatively painless, indurated lesion deep from the palpebral margin. This disorder has an insidious onset and minimal irritation. Chalazions may become pruritic and cause redness in the affected eyelid.

114. **The correct answer is (D).** Hypoparathryoidism is a condition that most commonly occurs after a patient undergoes a thyroidectomy. Hypoparathyroidism may present with irritability and distal extremity tingling. Facial muscle contraction after tapping a facial nerve, Chvostek's sign, may be evident. Physical examination may also reveal a carpal spasm in response to a blood pressure cuff being inflated, Trousseau's phenomenon.

115. **The correct answer is (E).** A diuretic medication is any medication that forces the release of excess fluids from the body by increasing the rate of urination. These medications reduce plasma volume and chronically reduce peripheral resistance. Diuretics are frequently the initial treatment for essential hypertension.

116. **The correct answer is (E).** Thyroid storm is a potentially life-threatening condition that may follow a stressful illness, thyroid surgery, or radioactive thyroid ablation. This disorder is characterized by high fever, tachycardia, vomiting, dehydration, confusion, and delirium. Treatment for thyroid storm requires prompt and specific treatment with beta blockers and hydrocortisone, a thiourea drug to control hyperthyroidism followed by iodide, plus medications to treat the other various symptoms associated with thyroid storm.

117. **The correct answer is (A).** ACE inhibitors are the proper medical treatment for glomerulonephritis. ACE inhibitors are extremely renoprotective and reduce the amount of urinary protein loss associated with chronic glomerulonephritis.

118. **The correct answer is (B).** Alpha-glucosidase inhibitors, such as acarbose and migilitol, delay absorption of carbohydrates from the intestine, thereby lowering blood glucose levels. GI symptoms are often side effects of these medications.

119. **The correct answer is (D).** Positron Emission Tomography, or PET scan, will routinely reveal biparietal hypometabolism in patients with Alzheimer's dementia. This differs from frontotemporal dementia, which will exhibit hypometabolism to the frontal or anterior temporal lobe.

120. **The correct answer is (B).** Ectropion is a condition characterized by the eyelids permanently turned outward, primarily the lower eyelid, so that the inner surface is exposed. This condition occurs secondary to advanced age, trauma, infection, or palsy of the facial nerve.

121. **The correct answer is (B).** Bronchiectasis is characterized by chronic purulent sputum which is often foul-smelling, hemoptysis, chronic cough, and recurrent pneumonia. Physical examination will reveal localized chest crackles and clubbing. High resolution CT scan will reveal dilated tortuous airways. Chest X-ray can reveal crowded bronchial markings and basal cystic spaces, tram-track lung markings, honeycombing and atelectasis.

122. The correct answer is (A). Individuals with asbestosis can present with dyspnea, clubbing, and cyanosis. Auscultation of the chest will reveal inspiratory crackles. Chest X-ray will reveal interstitial fibrosis, thickened pleura, and calcified plaques on the diaphragm or lateral chest wall.

123. The correct answer is (E). Radiation therapy is the appropriate initial treatment choice for individuals diagnosed with low-risk stage IA or IIA Hodgkin's lymphoma. The 10-year survival rate for this course of treatment exceeds 80%.

124. The correct answer is (C). Exenatide is effective in lowering blood glucose levels due to the fact that it decreases gastric emptying, stimulating pancreatic insulin response to glucose and preventing glucagon release after meals. This medication must be injected.

125. The correct answer is (C). A polysomnogram assesses EEG activity, heart rate, respiratory movement, and oxygen saturation while the patient is asleep. A polysomnogram is commonly referred to as a sleep study.

126. The correct answer is (B). Furosemide is a loop diuretic. Loop diuretics inhibit the reabsorption of sodium at the ascending loop of the nephron. These medications cause substantial diuresis, up to 20% of the entire filtered load of NaCl and water.

127. The correct answer is (A). Acoustic neuroma, otherwise known as vestibular schwannoma, is hearing loss due to a neoplasm in the ear. This disorder is most predominant in females. Individuals may present with hearing loss, tinnitus, vertigo, ataxia, and brain stem dysfunction. CT or MRI can confirm the diagnosis.

128. The correct answer is (B). Cystic fibrosis is characterized by cough, excess sputum, sinus pain, nasal discharge, diarrhea, and abdominal pain. Steatorrhea and decreased exercise tolerance may also be presented. Physical exam can reveal clubbing, apical crackles, and increased anteroposterior chest diameter. CT scan can reveal bronchiectasis. Chest X-ray can reveal hyperinflation, mucous plugging, peribronchial cuffing, focal atelectasis, or pneumothorax.

129. The correct answer is (D). The rust ring on the cornea is a classic indicator of the presence of a metallic foreign body. Metallic foreign bodies can be removed with a surgical device known as a rotating burr. If extraction with the rotating burr fails, a referral should be made to an ophthalmologist.

130. The correct answer is (C). Hypochromic mirocytic anemia, otherwise known as iron-deficiency anemia, can easily be treated and maintained by oral administration of ferrous sulfate. An oral dose of 325 mg of ferrous sulfate taken 3 times a day prior to meal times should be sufficient to maintain this disorder.

131. The correct answer is (C). Metformin is a very effective first-line medication for type II diabetes. This medication will lower blood glucose levels without risk of hypoglycemia. However, metformin is contraindicated in patients with elevated serum creatinine and for patients with lactic acidosis. Gastrointestinal side effects are also common while taking metformin.

132. The correct answer is (D). This diagnostic technique is an excellent way to confirm the presence of a fungus, such as with dermatophytosis. When diagnosing the disorder of lichen simplex chronicus, a potassium hydroxide preparation is commonly used to rule out fungal infection associated with this disorder.

133. The correct answer is (E). Otitis media is characterized by fever, pressure, pain, and hearing loss in the affected ear. The examination will reveal an immobile eardrum that is erythematous and bulging.

134. The correct answer is (D). Silicosis is an occupational disease common among coal miners, stone quarry workers, and construction workers. Patients with silicosis present with progressive dyspnea, cough, cyanosis, and clubbing. Auscultation of the chest will reveal inspiratory crackles. Chest X-ray will reveal small rounded opacities throughout the lung and calcified hilar lymph nodes.

135. The correct answer is (B). Junctional rhythm is caused by a profound sinus node dysfunction. No atrial activity is noted on the electrocardiogram and P-waves are absent. Individuals who have this rhythm abnormality can experience fatigue, shortness of breath, heart palpitations, and dizziness.

136. **The correct answer is (D).** Strabismus is a condition in which binocular fixation is not present. This condition is commonly referred to as lazy eye or cross-eye, depending on whether strabismus is inward or outward. Patch therapy (covering the unaffected eye) is the recommended treatment of this disorder, as this will force the affected eye muscles to focus properly.

137. **The correct answer is (A).** Exenatide is effective in reducing blood glucose levels by stimulating pancreatic insulin response to glucose and preventing glucagon release after meals. However, this medication also slows gastric emptying, so it is contraindicated for patients with a history of gastroparesis.

138. **The correct answer is (D).** The Wood's light examination is used to assess changes in pigment or to detect infectious lesions, which fluoresce under blacklight. A Wood's light examination is extremely useful for accentuating hyperpigmented macules that are associated with the disorder of melasma.

139. **The correct answer is (C).** Oral leukoplakia is a pre-cancerous condition that results from excessive irritation to the oral cavity. This condition is common among individuals who routinely use smokeless tobacco. Oral leukoplakia appears as whitish/gray, thick, hard and slightly raised lesions on the tongue and inside of the cheeks.

140. **The correct answer is (A).** Coal worker's pneumoconiosis is characterized by shortness of breath, inspiratory crackles, clubbing, and cyanosis. Chest X-rays for this disorder is characterized by small opacities prominent in the upper lung fields.

141. **The correct answer is (C).** The left bundle branch block is a conduction abnormality in which the left ventricle contracts before the right ventricle. Most patients with this abnormality are asymptomatic. However, dizziness can occur. This abnormality is characterized on an electrocardiogram by a wide QRS complex and the T-wave deflecting in the opposite direction as the QRS complex.

142. **The correct answer is (B).** Presbycusis is the most common form of sensorineural hearing loss. This condition involves higher frequencies and may be associated with tinnitus. Presbycusis is age related and occurs more in men than women. Hearing aids are used to remedy hearing loss for individuals with presbycusis; they may or may not be an effective treatment.

143. **The correct answer is (A).** Folate deficiency anemia is a form of macrocytic anemia caused by a deficiency of folic acid. Oral administration of 1 mg of folic acid per day is proper first-line maintenance therapy for treatment of this disorder.

144. **The correct answer is (D).** Polymyositis is an inflammatory disease of striated muscles affecting the proximal limbs, neck, and pharynx. Patients may present with proximal muscle weakness, dysphagia, malar or heliotrope skin rash, muscle aches, or muscle atrophy. Serum creatinine, phosphokinase, and aldolase will be elevated.

145. **The correct answer is (B).** Gestational trophoblastic disease is commonly referred to as a molar pregnancy. It is characterized by an abnormal growth in the uterus that forms at the beginning of pregnancy. A molar pregnancy is also associated with an empty egg and the appearance of grapelike vesicles on ultrasound. Females who experience a molar pregnancy may present with abnormal vaginal bleeding, increased uterine size, nausea, vomiting, and hypertension. Serum hCG levels are often greater than 100,000 mU/mL.

146. **The correct answer is (C).** Desmopressin acetate is the treatment of choice for all forms of diabetes insipidus, including central diabetes insipidus and diabetes insipidus associated with pregnancy and the puerperium.

147. **The correct answer is (E).** Sinus bradycardia is defined as a normal sinus heart rhythm with a rate less than 60 beats per minute. Patients usually do not become symptomatic until the heart rate drops below 50 beats per minute. Patients with sinus bradycardia may experience chest pain, shortness of breath, dizziness, lightheadedness, and syncope.

148. **The correct answer is (A).** Allergic rhinitis is a response to airborne antigens such as pollen, mold, dander, and dust. Individuals with allergic rhinitis will present with bluish discoloration under the eyes known as allergic shiners, rhinorrhea with a clear and watery discharge, itchy or watery eyes,

sneezing, and dry cough. Symptoms of this disorder can mimic those of the common cold.

149. **The correct answer is (C).** Sarcoidosis is a disorder characterized by inflammation of different organs such as lymph nodes, lungs, liver, eyes, skin, or other tissues. Common respiratory symptoms such as cough, shortness of breath, and chest pain also occur. Some patients may experience excessive fatigue and a persistent low-grade fever. Lab tests can reveal leukopenia, eosinophilia, elevated erythrocyte sedimentation rate, hypercalcemia, and hypercalciuria. Patients may also present with erythema nodosum or enlargement of the parotid glands, lymph nodes, liver, or spleen. Chest X-ray can reveal symmetric bilateral hilar adenopathy, right paratracheal adenopathy, and bilateral diffuse reticular infiltrates.

150. **The correct answer is (A).** Complete heart block is classically noted on an electrocardiogram by lack of association between the P-wave and the QRS complex. Notice the random pattern of contraction of both atria and ventricles. Patients in complete heart block often experience chest pain, palpitations, fatigue, and dizziness.

151. **The correct answer is (D).** For stroke victims whose internal carotid or common carotid artery has been proven to have 70%-99% stenosis, endarterectomy is the most appropriate treatment. An endarterectomy is a surgical procedure performed to remove plaque from the stenotic artery.

152. **The correct answer is (E).** Septic arthritis is caused by a systemic spread of bacteria. This disorder tends to affect a single joint such as hip, shoulder, ankle, or wrist. Patients usually present with swelling, fever, joint warmth, effusion, tenderness to palpation, and increased pain with minimal range of motion. Evaluation of the synovial fluid will be positive for bacteria.

153. **The correct answer is (E).** Spontaneous abortion is defined as the termination of pregnancy, by any means, before 20 weeks of gestation. Vaginal bleeding is a classic sign for spontaneous abortion. An open cervix does not permit the female to maintain the pregnancy, so termination of the pregnancy is inevitable.

154. **The correct answer is (E).** Ergocalciferol is required at a dose of 50,000 units orally twice a week for 6-12 months, followed by 1,000 to 2,000 units daily, to treat the vitamin D deficiency that causes osteomalacia.

155. **The correct answer is (C).** A lateral soft tissue X-ray of the neck shows a classic thumb sign if epiglottitis is present. CT scan of the neck, MRI of the neck, and ultrasound of the neck are all viable options in order to diagnose epiglottitis.

156. **The correct answer is (E).** Vasomotor rhinitis is rhinorrhea caused by increased secretion of mucous from the nasal mucosa. This condition is often caused by changes in temperature or humidity, odors, or alcohol. Patients with vasomotor rhinitis may present with bogginess of the nasal mucosa associated with stuffiness and rhinorrhea.

157. **The correct answer is (B).** Adult respiratory distress syndrome is most likely caused by sepsis, multiple trauma, or aspiration of stomach contents. This disorder is characterized by rapid onset of profound dyspnea, tachypnea, frothy pink or red sputum, and diffuse crackles. Many patients with this disorder also present with cyanosis. Chest X-ray may initially be normal; however, most patients develop peripheral infiltrates with air bronchograms.

158. **The correct answer is (D).** A right bundle branch block is most often asymptomatic. Bundle branch blocks are partial interruptions of electrical pathways inside the wall of the heart, between the ventricles. A right bundle branch block is classically noted on an electrocardiogram with a characteristic "bunny ear pattern" in the QRS complexes in V1 and V2.

159. **The correct answer is (B).** Anticholinergic medications such as benzatropine and trihexyphenidyl are particularly helpful in treating the tremor associated with Parkinson's disease. These medications, however, are less helpful for the bradykinesia associated with Parkinson's disease.

160. **The correct answer is (E).** Paranoid disorder is characterized by an abnormal suspicion and distrust of other people. Individuals with this disorder tend to be hostile and angry and blame their problems on others.

161. The correct answer is (B). Gonorrhea is a sexually transmitted disease that occurs in men and women primarily between the ages of 15 and 29. This disorder is caused by the *Neisseria gonorrhoeae* bacterium. Men afflicted with gonorrhea complain of painful, burning urination and a serous or milky-white discharge. One to three days after symptoms begin, the pain and burning becomes more pronounced and the discharge becomes yellow, creamy, profuse, and tinged with blood.

162. The correct answer is (E). Regulation of blood glucose levels is critical to prevent the progression of retinopathy. The main cause of retinopathy among adults in the United States is diabetes. Individuals with this disorder should have yearly dilated ophthalmoscopic examinations.

163. The correct answer is (D). The treatment of choice for Paget's disease is prompt administration of bisphosphonates such as alendronate, tiludronate, risedronate, zoledronic acid, or pamidronate.

164. The correct answer is (A). Electrolytes, glucose, urinalysis, and serum creatinine are required to determine the nature and cause of the shock. All patients in shock will require a CBC, blood type and cross match, and coagulation parameters to ensure proper treatment and status of the patient. In addition, all patients should require pulse oximety or arterial blood gases to monitor the patient's oxygenation.

165. The correct answer is (E). Viral pharyngitis is characterized by a sore throat that progressively worsens, low-grade fever, and symptoms of a head cold. Lymphadenopathy may or may not be present. Strep screen will be negative.

166. The correct answer is (C). Hyaline membrane disease is the most common cause of respiratory disease in the newborn infant. It is characterized by typical signs of respiratory distress. Chest X-rays for this disorder will typically show air bronchograms, bilateral atelectasis that gives a "ground glass" appearance, and a domed diaphragm.

167. The correct answer is (E). Ventricular bigeminy is the condition of the heart having a premature ventricular contraction, or skipped beat, after each normal heartbeat. Patients with this condition often experience heart palpitations.

168. The correct answer is (E). Scabies is a parasitic infection caused by Sarcoptes scabiei, an eight-legged mite that burrows into the skin to deposit its eggs. This condition is best treated with topical creams or lotions that contain insecticides such as lindane or permethrine. These creams should be applied from the chin to the feet, left on overnight and then washed off in the morning. This should be repeated for a period of seven days to ensure proper treatment of this condition.

169. The correct answer is (A). The recommended treatment for subacute thyroiditis is simply aspirin. Aspirin will act as an anti-inflammatory to reduce the swelling of the thyroid gland and will also work as an analgesic to lessen the pain associated with this disorder.

170. The correct answer is (D). Ischemic heart disease is classically diagnosed with associated S-T segment depression. S-T segment depression of greater than 1 mm is often a sign of ischemic heart disease.

171. The correct answer is (D). Obsessive-compulsive disorder, or OCD, can manifest itself in many different ways, from perfectionism to obsessive cleanliness to constant rechecking everyday tasks such as locking the door. An excessive devotion to one's profession combined with excluding any leisure activities and unwillingness to delegate is also a form of obsessive-compulsive disorder.

172. The correct answer is (E). Varicella zoster, commonly referred to as chickenpox, is a highly contagious condition that commonly occurs during childhood. Patients present with low-grade fever, malaise, muscle aches, and headache. Varicella zoster is characteristic for erythematous macules and papules that form superficial vesicles and later crust over.

173. The correct answer is (B). Squamous cell carcinoma is a slow-growing form of cancer. Lesions can appear on the skin, lips, mouth, esophagus, bladder, prostate, lungs, vagina, and cervix. Unlike basal cell carcinoma, squamous cell carcinoma does have the ability to metastasize. Complete eradication of the lesions is the only course of treatment. Eradication can be achieved by excision with clear margins, electrodissection with curettage, cryosurgery, and radiation therapy.

174. The correct answer is (A). Exposure to ultraviolet radiation, or sunlight, can drastically increase risk of developing cataracts. Excessive exposure to sunlight can predispose to cataract development and enhance progression of cataracts. Individuals who are concerned with cataract development should decrease their exposure to sunlight.

175. The correct answer is (D). Bulimia nervosa is binge eating followed by induced vomiting or otherwise purging by using laxatives and diuretics. Individuals with bulimia nervosa due to vomiting present with dental erosion, esophagitis, calluses on the knuckles, and atrophy of the salivary glands. Bloodwork reveals electrolyte deficiencies.

176. The correct answer is (A). Erysipelas is a superficial bacterial skin infection that begins on the face but can spread to the extremities. The ancient name for this infection is St. Anthony's Fire. Erysipelas presents as a painful, macular, fiery red rash with well-defined margins. This disorder presents abruptly and spreads rapidly.

177. The correct answer is (C). Chronic thrombocytopenia will rarely resolve spontaneously like the acute version of thrombocytopenia. Chronic thrombocytopenia is classically treated with high doses of prednisone.

178. The correct answer is (D). The pneumococcal polysaccharide vaccine is indicated for individuals over the age of 65 who have a chronic illness that puts them at increased risk of community-acquired pneumonia. This vaccine is also indicated in children aged 2-5 years of age who have not previously been immunized.

179. The correct answer is (C). Broad-spectrum antibiotics such as cefipime, peperacillin, or meropenem are indicated for the treatment of nosocomial, or hospital-acquired, pneumonia until the causative agent is found. Once the causative organism is identified, appropriate therapy based on the culture results can be initiated.

180. The correct answer is (E). Wolff-Parkinson-White (WPW) syndrome is defined as the pre-excitation of the ventricles due to an accessory pathway known as the bundle of Kent. WPW is classically exhibited electrocardiographically by a short PR interval and a delta wave.

181. The correct answer is (A). Bronchitis is very difficult to distinguish from pneumonia. Patients present with cough with or without sputum, dyspnea, fever, sore throat, headaches, and muscle aches. Auscultation of the chest will reveal expiratory rhonchi or wheezes. Chest X-ray will be normal, which is the only way to distinguish bronchitis from pneumonia.

182. The correct answer is (B). Cardiogenic shock is a type of shock that can arise from myocardial infarctions, arrythmia, heart failure, valvular abnormalities, myocarditis, cardiac contusions, and myocardiopathies. Shock can cause low blood pressure, tachycardia, orthostatic changes, and altered mental status. The electrocardiogram reveals an acute myocardial infarction.

183. The correct answer is (A). Atrial bigeminy is the condition of the heart having a premature atrial conduction after every normal heartbeat. Patients in atrial bigeminy will often experience heart palpitations.

184. The correct answer is (D). Keratoderma is a condition characterized by a thickening of the horny layer of the epidermis. This condition can successfully be treated with liquid nitrogen. Mild acid treatments have also been proven effective for treatment of this condition.

185. The correct answer is (A). Cryoprecipitate is a frozen blood product prepared from plasma. Each unit of cryoprecipitate contains 250 mg of fibrinogen, which is essential for treatment of disseminated intravascular coagulopathy.

186. The correct answer is (D). In order to evaluate for viable myocardial tissue post acute myocardial infarction, a series of myocardial perfusion SPECT images must be obtained using Thallium-201. The redistributive properties of Thallium-201 allow this particular isotope to reveal viable myocardium when a series of myocardial perfusion images is obtained over 24 hours.

187. The correct answer is (B). Squamous cell lung carcinoma is a form of non-small cell lung carcinoma. Patients with this type of carcinoma will present with cough, hemoptysis, chest pain, and weight loss. Squamous cell carcinoma is bronchial in origin and a centrally located mass will appear on a chest X-ray.

188. **The correct answer is (E).** Malingering is a disorder of exaggerating or fabricating pain or illness for secondary purposes such as avoiding school, avoiding work, obtaining drugs, or obtaining lighter criminal sentences. Patients with this disorder will insist they are ill even when a physical exam does not confirm illness. Patients will not accept a clean bill of health from a physician.

189. **The correct answer is (D).** Insulin is the only medicinal treatment approved for gestational diabetes. Insulin will stay in the mother's bloodstream and not cross into the child's bloodstream. Glyburide and metformin have not yet received FDA approval for gestational diabetes. Glyburide does not cross the placenta, but metformin crosses the placenta in small amounts. Medications for gestational diabetes should only be used if dietary changes fail to address the condition.

190. **The correct answer is (E).** The majority of cases of Meniere's disease can be treated with diuretics and salt restriction. If symptoms persist and do not respond to diuretic treatment, surgical intervention may be required for resolution of this disorder.

191. **The correct answer is (D).** Melancholia is characterized by not being able to find pleasure anywhere in life, even during pleasurable experiences. Patients may exhibit suicidal ideations, agitation, anorexia, weight loss, depression, feelings of guilt, and sleep disturbances.

192. **The correct answer is (C).** Pyogenic granulomas are commonly referred to as capillary hemangiomas. These benign neoplasms appear as red, raspberry-like nodules that primarily occur on the exposed areas of the body such as neck, arms, fingers, hands, and legs. These nodules normally appear after injury or surgery but may appear spontaneously.

193. **The correct answer is (C).** Desmopressin acetate is the most effective medication in treatment of Von Willebrand disease. This medication is usually used in conjunction with factor VIII concentrates for maximum benefit.

194. **The correct answer is (A).** Betamethisone is given to ensure fetal lung maturity when a hypertensive pregnant female must give birth early. Betamethisone increases the level of surfactant within the lungs of the unborn child, which is critical for lung maturity.

195. **The correct answer is (C).** Macular degeneration is a disorder characterized by permanent central vision loss. Macular degeneration may simply be caused by old age or by the toxic effects from cholorquine or phenothiazine medications, such as thorazine or compazine.

196. **The correct answer is (A).** On a standard electrocardiogram, leads I, aVL, V5, and V6 represent the lateral wall of the heart muscle. Any electrocardiographic abnormalities seen in these leads correspond to the area of the heart that is affected. For example, S-T elevation in lead V5 indicates a myocardial infarction occurring in the lateral wall of the heart.

197. **The correct answer is (B).** Chronic obstructive pulmonary disease, or COPD, includes the disorders of emphysema and chronic bronchitis. Patients will present with progressively worsening shortness of breath, excessive cough, and sputum production. Auscultation of the lungs will reveal decreased breath sounds and early inspiratory crackles. Percussion yields increased resonance. Chest X-ray reveals hyperinflation of the lungs and flat diaphragms.

198. **The correct answer is (E).** Septic shock is a type of distributive shock that is caused by poorly regulated blood volume. Septic shock is most associated with Gram-negative sepsis in patients who are of advanced age, diabetic, immunosuppressed, and who have recently undergone an invasive procedure.

199. **The correct answer is (B).** The copper-T intrauterine device can be effective for up to ten years. This device reduces the viability and number of sperm that reach the egg and also decreases the movement and number of eggs that reach the uterus. The continuous release of copper from the IUD is thought to enhance the contraceptive effect.

200. **The correct answer is (C).** Myasthenia gravis is an autoimmune neuromuscular disease that leads to fluctuating muscle weakness and fatigue. This condition is commonly treated with cholinesterase

inhibitors. Cholinesterase inhibitors prevent the breakdown of acetylcholine, which increases the levels of the acetylcholine neurotransmitter available to muscle cells.

201. **The correct answer is (B).** Bunions are the most common deformity of the metatarsophalangeal joint and are more common in women than in men. Patients will complain of toe or foot pain, deformities of the toes, and inability to find shoes that fit properly. X-rays will reveal a deformity of the proximal phalanx at an angle greater than 15 degrees.

202. **The correct answer is (E).** Dacryocystitis is an inflammation of the lacrimal gland usually caused by obstruction. Treatment for this disorder includes warm compresses along with antibiotics.

203. **The correct answer is (C).** On a standard electrocardiogram, leads V3 and V4 represent the anterior wall of the heart muscle. Any electrocardiographic abnormalities seen in these leads correspond to the area of the heart that is affected. For example, S-T depression in lead V4 indicates the presence of myocardial ischemia in the anterior wall of the heart.

204. **The correct answer is (D).** Pulmonary embolism presents clinically with pleuritic chest pain, dyspnea, and hemoptysis. Cough and diaphoresis may also be present. Physical examination reveals tachycardia, tachypnea, low-grade fever, crackles, and accentuation of the pulmonary component of the second heart sound. Chest X-ray will often be normal with pulmonary embolism. However, some cases will exhibit a "Hampton's hump," a wedge-shaped, pleural-based consolidation that reveals a pulmonary infarct resulting from the embolism.

205. **The correct answer is (E).** Classic criteria for primary hypertension are a systolic pressure greater than 140 mmHg or a diastolic pressure greater than 90 mmHg. These readings must be consistent over separate blood pressure readings. Most patients are asymptomatic. However, the most common complaint is a nonspecific headache.

206. **The correct answer is (D).** A 72-hour fecal fat test is commonly used to diagnose the disorder of malabsorption. This test is an evaluation of the function of the liver, gallbladder, pancreas, and intestines. Improper fat absorption can cause stools to change color, known as steatorrhea.

207. **The correct answer is (D).** Implanon is a form of contraception that requires the implantation of a single rod that releases etonorgestrel at a rate of about 40 mcg/day. This form of contraception may be useful for up to three years. Etonorgestrel is a progesterone analog, which inhibits ovulation and changes the cervical mucous and uterine lining.

208. **The correct answer is (B).** Blepharitis is a condition characterized by chronic inflammation of the eyelid margins. Rims of the eyelid are red and eyelashes will adhere. Dandruff-like deposits and fibrous scales may be present. Treatment for this condition should include eyelid scrubs with diluted baby shampoo on cotton-tipped swabs. If infection is suspected, topical antibiotics can also be added to the treatment regimen.

209. **The correct answer is (C).** The patient's presentation of dull pain, swelling, redness, and tenderness of the left leg is suspicious for deep venous thrombosis. Deep venous thrombosis can be effectively evaluated through an ultrasound exam with Doppler.

210. **The correct answer is (E).** A tension pneumothorax is secondary to a sucking chest wound or pulmonary laceration. It is characterized by chest pain and shortness of breath. Chest X-ray will reveal an accumulation of air in the pleural space with mediastinal shift to the opposite side. Physical exam will reveal impaired ventilation leading comprised cardiac function.

211. **The correct answer is (B).** Left-sided congestive heart failure occurs when the left side of the heart begins to fail and fluid begins to accumulate in the lungs. It can lead to symptoms such as exertional dyspnea, non-productive cough, orthopnea, and exercise intolerance. Auscultation of the chest should reveal bilateral rales and gallops. Auscultation of the chest reveals a parasternal lift, enlarged apical impulse, diminished first heart sound, an S3 gallop, and an S4 gallop. Chest X-ray should reveal cardiomegaly, bilateral pleural effusions, and perivascular or interstitial edema.

212. **The correct answer is (C).** Intussesception is defined as the invagination of a proximal segment

of the bowel into the portion just distal to it. For pediatric patients with this disorder, a sausage-like mass may be appreciated with an abdominal examination.

213. **The correct answer is (B).** Methotrexate can be used to treat up to 80% of ectopic pregnancies. Criterion for methotrexate treatment is a serum hCG level under 5,000 mU. Patients with ectopic pregnancies and serum hCG over 5,000 mU should be treated laparoscopically.

214. **The correct answer is (C).** Gardasil is the vaccine that will prevent against all four strains of the human papilloma virus (HPV). Strains 6 and 11 of HPV are associated with the development of genital warts. Strains 16 and 18 of HPV are associated with the development of cervical cancer. The other HPV vaccine, Cervarix, only prevents against strains 16 and 18 of HPV.

215. **The correct answer is (A).** Diazepam is the indicated course of treatment for individuals who suffer from acute episodes of vertigo. Diazepam should be administered intravenously or rectally for most effective treatment. Bed rest may also be required with acute episodes of vertigo.

216. **The correct answer is (A).** A d-dimer level is a blood test result that indicates the level of protein fragments present in the blood after a blood clot has been degraded by fibrinolysis. A negative d-dimer level will rule out blood clots immediately, regardless of the symptoms the patient is experiencing.

217. **The correct answer is (E).** Ranson's criteria is a commonly used formula to evaluate acute pancreatitis. These criteria are based on several factors such as age, WBC count, blood glucose level, serum lactate dehydrogenase level, AST, serum calcium, and blood urea nitrogen.

218. **The correct answer is (B).** The d-dimer lab test is used to confirm the diagnosis of thrombosis, or blood clots. D-dimer is a small fragment of protein that remains after a blood clot has been degraded by fibrinolyis. A negative lab test for d-dimer completely rules out the possibility of pulmonary embolism.

219. **The correct answer is (C).** Deep venous thrombosis, also known as thrombophlebitis, is a partial or complete obstruction of a vein in the legs. This disorder most commonly occurs in the long saphenous vein. Patients will present with dull pain in one leg, accompanied by swelling, redness, and tenderness. A d-dimer level greater than 500 ng/dL is an indicating factor for deep venous thrombosis.

220. **The correct answer is (A).** Methotrexate can be used for treatment of ectopic pregnancies if the ectopic mass is less than 3.5 cm. Patients with ectopic pregnancies with fetal masses in excess of 3.5 cm should be treated laparoscopically.

221. **The correct answer is (C).** For individuals who suffer from severe motion sickness associated with severe vertigo, scopolamine is the most effective treatment. Scopolamine is most often administered via transdermal patch, which releases a dose of 330 mcg per day.

222. **The correct answer is (C).** A temporal artery biopsy is required to positively confirm a diagnosis of giant cell arteritis. Giant cell arteritis is a systemic, inflammatory condition of the medium and large vessels.

223. **The correct answer is (B).** Endometriosis is the condition in which the endometrial glands and stroma are found outside the endometrial cavity. Patients may present with dysmenorrhea, painful sexual intercourse, painful bowel movements, and intermittent spotting. Diagnosis can be made with ultrasonography and laparoscopy or laparotomy.

224. **The correct answer is (C).** Perioral dermatitis is primarily found in young women. This disorder is characterized by redness, inflammation, burning, and eruptions of the skin around the mouth.

225. **The correct answer is (A).** Laparotomy is a form of surgical removal of the ectopic gestation that is only indicated for patients with significant abdominal adhesions and those who are hemodynamically unstable.

226. **The correct answer is (E).** The most effective method to avoid the occurrence of decubitus ulcers (bed sores) in nursing home patients is to reposition, or turn, the patients periodically throughout the day. This method will eliminate pressure and friction on any single area of the body for a prolonged period of time, which will inhibit the formation of

decubitus ulcers. Meticulous hygiene and proper nutrition also help.

227. The correct answer is (A). Adenomyosis is a disorder characterized by the extension of the endometrial glands into the uterine musculature. Patients with this disorder will present with severe secondary menorrhea and menorrhagia. Physical exam will reveal a symmetrically enlarged uterus. Pregnancy should be ruled out to confirm diagnosis of this disorder.

228. The correct answer is (B). Pityriasis rosea is characterized by a herald patch that precedes symmetrical papular eruption. A herald patch is a solitary round or oval pink plaque with a raised border and fine scales in the margin. The associated rash will appear as round or oval salmon-colored lesions approximately 1 cm in diameter.

229. The correct answer is (B). The disorder of labyrinthitis is commonly treated with meclizine. Promethazine or dimenhydrinate may also be used. Meclizine is a common medication prescribed for the treatment of dizziness caused by disorders of the inner ear, and is available in regular and chewable tablets. The underlying cause of labyrinthitis is unknown but it is believe to be caused by an otitis or viremia.

230. The correct answer is (B). A barium swallow is the most appropriate diagnostic procedure for the diagnosis of hiatal hernia. It is used to examine the upper gastrointestinal tract and the stomach. To obtain this evaluation, the patient must ingest a barium solution, which will line the esophagus and stomach and enable the evaluation.

231. The correct answer is (B). Cholangitis, a potentially life-threatening condition, is characterized by common bile duct obstruction with ascending infection and can be diagnosed by Charcot's triad. Charcot's triad consists of right upper quadrant pain, jaundice, and fever.

232. The correct answer is (B). Creatinine phosphokinase, normally referred to as CPK, is an enzyme found primarily in the brain, heart, and skeletal muscle. An elevation of this enzyme is indicative of damage to a muscle. Myocardial infarction causes damage to the heart muscle, which in turn

will cause an elevation in creatinine phosphokinase levels.

233. The correct answer is (B). Chronic venous insufficiency is characterized by loss of venous wall tension, resulting in stasis of venous blood. This disorder is common in individuals with a history of deep venous thrombosis, varicose veins, or a leg injury. Patients may present clinically with edema in the lower extremities, ulcers just above the ankle, itching and dull leg pain when standing, and shiny, thin, discolored skin in the lower extremities.

234. The correct answer is (B). Cervical cerclage is indicated to reduce the risk of miscarriage if the pregnant female has a history of cervical incompetence. Cervical cerclage is defined as closure of the cervix by mechanical means. This technique involves placing a strong suture into and around the cervix and is normally performed during weeks 12 to 14 of pregnancy. The suture is removed later in the pregnancy when the risk of miscarriage has passed and the fetus is full term.

235. The correct answer is (B). Recombinant tissue plasminogen activator is a protein involved in the breakdown of blood clots. Types of recombinant tissue plasminogen activators include alteplase, reteplase, and tenecteplase. Recombinant tissue plasminogen activators are the indicated form for treatment of acute ischemic strokes.

236. The correct answer is (A). A Mallory-Weiss tear is most often associated with alcoholism. A Mallory-Weiss tear is a linear mucosal tear in the esophagus, generally at the gastroesophageal junction.

237. The correct answer is (E). Nonseminomatous testicular tumors are radio-resistant, which means they will not respond to radiation therapy. Treatment for this type of tumor, depending on the stage of the disease, includes retroperitoneal lymph node dissection, chemotherapy, and surgery.

238. The correct answer is (D). Pulmonic stenosis is a congenital anomaly that usually presents during infancy or childhood. Adults can present with stenosis resulting from rheumatic scarring or connective tissue disease. Adults with pulmonic stenosis will complain of exercise intolerance. Auscultation will reveal a systolic murmur between the second and third left intercostal space, radiating to the left shoulder and neck. Auscultation also reveals early pulmonic ejection sound.

239. **The correct answer is (A).** An abdominal aortic aneurysm, commonly referred to as "triple A," is a weakness and dilatation of the wall of the abdominal aorta. Patients with abdominal aortic aneurysm are commonly asymptomatic. However, some patients can experience abdominal pain, back pain, and sensations of a pulsing mass in the center of the stomach.

240. **The correct answer is (A).** Amniocentesis can be performed to assess fetal lung maturity. Amniocentesis is most often performed between the 32nd and 36th week of pregnancy. For women with gestational diabetes, this may be performed into the 39th week due to the fact that gestational diabetes can inhibit fetal lung development.

241. **The correct answer is (E).** Sunscreen is imperative to slow the progression of vitiligo. Sunscreen will offer protection to the hypopigmented macules, which are associated with and are characteristic of vitiligo.

242. **The correct answer is (B).** Felbatol, scientifically known as Felbamate, is an anti-convulsant medication commonly prescribed for epileptics whose seizures have not improved with other treatments. This medication is also used when serious side effects, such as aplastic anemia and hepatic failure, occur with other combinations of treatments.

243. **The correct answer is (C).** Esophageal varices are normally caused by portal hypertension that is caused by cirrhosis from alcoholism or chronic viral hepatitis. Esophageal varices are dilatations of the veins of the esophagus. Varices normally occur at the distal end of the esophagus.

244. **The correct answer is (C).** Osteomalacia is a disorder characterized by bone softening due to a deficiency of vitamin D. Individuals with this disorder will experience fractures from very minor injuries. Other causes may include deficiencies of calcium or phosphate, or aluminum toxicity.

245. **The correct answer is (C).** Mitral stenosis impedes the flow of blood between the left atrium and ventricle of the heart. Patients will present with dyspnea, fatigue, cough, nocturnal dyspnea, hemoptysis, or hoarseness. Auscultation of the chest reveals a mid-diastolic murmur at the apex with little radiation. Auscultation also reveals S1 accentuated opening snap following S2.

246. **The correct answer is (D).** Infectious esophagitis is a rare disorder; however, it is most common in immunosuppressed patients. Patients with infectious esophagitis will complain of difficult and painful swallowing. Endoscopy will reveal lesions in the esophagus that vary according to the causing virus. Infection with cytomegalovirus will cause large deep ulcers, while herpes simplex virus will cause multiple shallow ulcers and a candida (yeast) infection will reveal white plaques.

247. **The correct answer is (C).** Antipsychotic drugs such as haldol and seroquel are commonly used to control hostility associated with a variety of psychological disorders. These medications are tranquilizers that block the dopamine pathways of the brain.

248. **The correct answer is (E).** Generalized non-convulsive seizures are commonly treated by administration of valproic acid. This medication also serves as a mood stabilizer used for disorders such as bipolar disorder and depression.

249. **The correct answer is (A).** A urea breath test is useful for indicating the presence of *Helicobacter pylori* in the stomach due to the fact that urea is the by-product of *H. pylori* metabolism.

250. **The correct answer is (E).** Light therapy, otherwise known as phototherapy or heliotherapy, has proven successful for patients who suffer from seasonal affective disorder. Light therapy consists of exposure to daylight or to specific wavelengths of light from light-emitting diodes or fluorescent lamps. Light therapy treatments are administered for a prescribed amount of time and/or administered a certain time of day.

251. **The correct answer is (B).** Daily use of sunscreens is indicated for treatment of hyperpigmented macules associated with melasma. Ultraviolet radiation from sunlight can make hyperpigmented macules darker and more noticeable. Sunscreens should be worn everyday whether it be winter

or summer, indoors or outdoors because ultraviolet radiation can penetrate through clouds and windows.

252. **The correct answer is (C).** Relapses of moderate or severe attacks stemming from multiple sclerosis are most effectively treated with interferon-b. Mild attacks are generally treated with daily subcutaneous injections of glatiramer acetate.

253. **The correct answer is (A).** Zollinger-Ellison syndrome is characterized by a gastrin-secreting tumor called a gastrinoma. It causes hypergastrinemia that results in a resistant form of peptic ulcer disease. A fasting gastrin level greater than 150 pg/mL indicates hypergastrinemia.

254. **The correct answer is (B).** Hypercalcemia is a common result of hyperparathyroidism. Hypercalcemia is the result of excess release of parathyroid hormone (PTH) associated with hyperparathyroidism.

255. **The correct answer is (B).** Aortic stenosis narrows the aortic valve opening, which impedes the ejection fraction of the left side of the heart. Patients with aortic stenosis present with dyspnea, fatigue, cough, nocturnal dyspnea, hemoptysis, or hoarseness. Auscultation will reveal mid-systolic murmur at the second right intercostal space radiating to the neck and left sternal border.

256. **The correct answer is (B).** Patients with esophageal dysmotility classically present with difficulty swallowing or complaints of "food not going down properly." Barium swallow can reveal both motor and structural abnormalities of the esophagus. Achalasia, a global esophageal motor disorder, is characterized by the esophagus resembling a parrot's beak because of a dilated esophagus tapering to the distal obstruction.

257. **The correct answer is (E).** Verenicline, most commonly known as Chantix, is a medication marketed as a smoking cessation aid. This medication blocks the brain from the pleasant effects obtained from smoking. Buproprion, commonly known as Zyban, is another medication in the class of smoking-cessation aids.

258. **The correct answer is (B).** Amantadine is commonly prescribed to individuals with multiple sclerosis in order to lessen fatigue associated with the disorder. Amantadine is also useful in the treatment of Parkinson's disease and respiratory infections caused by the influenza A virus.

259. **The correct answer is (B).** Methyldopa, commonly referred to as Aldomet, is the medication of choice for the management of pregnancy-induced hypertension. Methyldopa is in the FDA category B which means it is unlikely to cause harm to the unborn baby.

260. **The correct answer is (C).** *Legionella pneumoniae* occurs as a result of exposure to contaminated water droplets from cooling and ventilation systems. This form of pneumonia is associated with acute onset of high fever, dry cough, and dyspnea.

261. **The correct answer is (D).** Ovarian cysts are primarily asymptomatic. When ovarian cysts cause symptoms, the symptoms can be delay in menstrual cycle and abdominal pain associated with uterine hemorrhaging. The hemorrhaging is the result of the cysts rupturing. Diagnosis is confirmed with pelvic ultrasound. Ovarian cysts that occur in post-menopausal women are considered malignant until proven otherwise.

262. **The correct answer is (B).** Symptoms of Huntington's disease do not appear until after 30 years of age. Mental symptoms include irritability, moodiness, antisocial behavior, and dementia. Physical signs may include restlessness, fidgeting, and quick, involuntary muscle movements of the hand and feet.

263. **The correct answer is (E).** Minoxidil's ability to slow or stop hair loss and promote regrowth is due to its antihypertensive and vasodilatory properties. This medication is the safest, most effective treatment for male pattern baldness. Finasteride may also be effective to treat male pattern baldness; however, loss of libido and erectile dysfunction may occur with use of finasteride.

264. **The correct answer is (D).** An abdominal angiogram is the only diagnostic exam proven to accurately depict vascular invasion of the pancreas and confirm a diagnosis of pancreatic cancer. Research is currently being performed to evaluate other modalities' accuracy in diagnosing pancreatic cancer; however, the results of the research is currently inconclusive.

265. **The correct answer is (C).** Ceftriaxone is the treatment of choice for men and women infected with gonorrhea. Gonorrhea is resistant to several other common medications, such as penicillin, tetracyclines, and fluoroquinolones; therefore, ceftriaxone is the drug of choice.

266. **The correct answer is (A).** Achilles tendonitis can be viewed on a standard lateral X-ray, which will show a soft tissue shadow and calcifications along the Achilles tendon and its insertions. MRI of the lower leg can evaluate for rupture of the Achilles tendon.

267. **The correct answer is (A).** Hypoparathyroidism can cause neuromuscular irritability and increased deep tendon reflexes. Chvostek's sign is commonly associated with hypoparathyroidism. Chvostek's sign is due to hyperirritability of a facial nerve, resulting in pain and facial muscle contraction after tapping.

268. **The correct answer is (B).** Aortic regurgitation results from volume overload of the left ventricle. Patients with aortic regurgitation present with dyspnea, fatigue, cough, nocturnal dyspnea, hemoptysis, or hoarseness. Auscultation also reveals a soft systolic and diastolic decrescendo from the second to the fourth left intercostal space radiating to the apex and right sternal border.

269. **The correct answer is (E).** Most small bowel obstructions are due to adhesions or hernias. Patients with small bowel obstructions present with abdominal pain, distention, vomiting of partially digested food, and obstipation. Auscultation of the abdomen will reveal high-pitched bowel sounds that come in rushes. Bloodwork can reveal dehydration and electrolyte imbalances.

270. **The correct answer is (A).** Disulfiram, most commonly referred to as Antabuse, is commonly prescribed for treatment of chronic alcoholism. Antabuse will cause unpleasant reactions when even small amounts of alcohol are consumed. The unpleasant symptoms may include flushing of the face, headache, nausea, vomiting, chest pain, blurred vision, sweating, shortness of breath, and anxiety.

271. **The correct answer is (D).** Xenical is a member of the class of medications called lipase inhibitors.

Xenical is currently the only FDA-approved long-term anti-obesity medication. This medication reduces intestinal fat absorption by inhibiting the production of pancreatic lipase, which breaks down fats.

272. **The correct answer is (D).** For individuals who have been diagnosed with hookworms, pyrantel is an effective medication for any patient over 5 years of age. Pyrantel should not be administered to individuals under the age of 5. Children under the age of 5 who develop hookworms should be treated with mebendazole instead.

273. **The correct answer is (B).** Acetowhitening is used primarily to evaluate warts on genital skin and mucous membranes, including the uterine cervix, in order to identify areas of squamous cell change for biopsy.

274. **The correct answer is (B).** Peripheral nerve abnormalities are common among individuals with diabetes. Neuropathy is generally related to the duration and severity of the diabetic condition. Individuals with diabeteic peripheral neuropathy will present with numbness, burning, and pain in the lower extremities. The lower extremities are more commonly affected than the upper extremities.

275. **The correct answer is (A).** Acute herpetic gingivostomatitis typically occurs between the ages of 6 months and 5 years. Patients present with sudden onset of fever, anorexia, listlessness, and bleeding gums. Physical exam will reveal red, swollen mucosa. Vesicles will be noticed on oral mucosa, tongue, and lips.

276. **The correct answer is (E).** Restless leg syndrome affects women more often than men. Patients present with a subjective need to move their legs. Symptoms associated with restless leg syndrome include tingling, creeping and crawling sensations, itching, heaviness, coldness, or tension in the lower extremities.

277. **The correct answer is (D).** Naloxone is the medication that is used to counteract the effects of an overdose of opiates, such as heroin or morphine. This medication is specifically used to counteact the life-threatening depression of the central nervous system and respiratory system that is associated with overdose of opiates.

278. The correct answer is (D). Clomiphene citrate is commonly prescribed for anovulatory women to promote ovulation. A five-day regimen of 50 to 100 mg is administered beginning on day 3, 4, or 5 of the menstrual cycle.

279. The correct answer is (E). When evaluating causes of infertility among couples, a hysterosalpingography is useful to evaluate tubal patency as a cause of infertility. This exam can also evaluate any uterine abnormalities that may contribute to infertility.

280. The correct answer is (E). Hypoparathyroidism can commonly cause neuromuscular irritability and increased deep tendon reflexes. Trousseau's phenomenon is associated with hypoparathyroidism. It is a carpal muscle spasm that results from the muscles of the upper arm being compressed, such as with a blood pressure cuff.

281. The correct answer is (C). Hypertrophic cardiomyopathy is characterized by massive cardiac hypertrophy (particularly in the septum), small left ventricle, systolic anterior mitral motion, and diastolic dysfunction. This condition is exclusively transmitted genetically and is most common among individuals of Asian descent. Patients with this disorder usually present with shortness of breath and angina. Echocardiogram will reveal left ventricular hypertrophy, asymmetric septal hypertrophy, small left ventricle and diastolic dysfunction. Electrocardiogram reveals left ventricular hypertrophy and exaggerated septal Q-waves.

282. The correct answer is (D). Fecal impaction is the retention of a large mass of hard stool, normally in the rectum, but sometimes higher in the colon. Individuals with fecal impaction may experience abdominal pain, rectal discomfort, anorexia, nausea, and vomiting. Examination will reveal rock hard stool in the rectal vault and an abdominal mass may be palpable.

283. The correct answer is (D). A Milwaukee brace, also known as a cervico-thoraco-lumbo-sacral orthosis, is a back brace designed specifically to treat curvatures of the spine. These braces are custom made from a mold of the patient's torso. These braces are designed specifically to prevent against progression of the curvature. If curvature worsens despite the brace, surgical intervention may be required.

284. The correct answer is (B). Lithium is commonly used in the treatment and prevention of manic episodes in individuals diagnosed with bipolar disorder. Lithium is a member of the class of medications known as antimanic agents. This class of medications is used to decrease abnormal activity in the brain.

285. The correct answer is (D). Magnesium sulfate, or $MgSO_4$, is very effective is slowing or stopping pre-term uterine contraction due to the fact that it inhibits myometrial contractility mediated by calcium. Side effects include nausea, fatigue, and muscle weakness. Toxicity from magnesium sulfate can lead to decreased reflexes, respiratory depression, and cardiac collapse.

286. The correct answer is (A). Barotrauma is defined as the inablity to equalize barometric stress on the inner ear, resulting in pain. This disorder is caused by auditory tube dysfunction as a result of congenital narrowing or acquired mucosal edema. Barotrauma is commonly the result of airplane descent, rapid altitude changes, or underwater diving.

287. The correct answer is (C). McMurray's test, also known as McMurray's circumduction test, is used to evaluate for tears in the meniscus of the knee. A tear in the meniscus will cause a pedunculated tag, which would be palpable or even cause an audible click when the knee is extended.

288. The correct answer is (B). Acute herpetic pharygotonsillitis is common in adults manifesting initial herpes simplex virus-1 disease. Patients present with fever, malaise, headache, and sore throat. Physical examination reveals vesicles on the posterior pharynx and tonsils. In addition, a grayish exudate is appreciated over the posterior mucosa.

289. The correct answer is (C). Menopause is clinically confirmed when the level of follicle stimulating hormone exceeds 30 mIU/mL. The rise in follicular stimulating hormone levels is directly proportional to the diminishing production of estrogen by the ovaries.

290. The correct answer is (C). Morton's neuroma is an abnormal thickening of the nerve tissue that commonly occurs between the third and fourth toes. Pain associated with this disorder can commonly be treated with soft metatarsal pads in the shoes or steroid injections between the toes. If conservative treatment fails, surgical removal of the neuroma is warranted; however, this will cause permanent numbness of the third and fourth toes.

291. The correct answer is (E). Ridodrine is a member of a class of medications called beta-mimetic adrenergic agents, which are effective in slowing or stopping pre-term contractions by stimulating beta-receptors to relax smooth muscle. Side effects of these medications include maternal and fetal tachycardia, emesis, headaches, and pulmonary edema.

292. The correct answer is (E). Individuals who suffer from schizophrenia will show enlarged ventricles and cortical atrophy on a CT scan, indicative of chronic schizophrenic disease. CT scanning can be a useful tool for diagnosis of schizophrenia.

293. The correct answer is (C). The anterior choroidal, anterior cerebral, and middle cerebral arteries are responsible for the anterior circulation to the brain. Strokes involving any of these arteries can result in aphasia, apraxia, hemiparesis, hemisensory losses, and visual field defects.

294. The correct answer is (E). Restrictive cardiomyopathy results from fibrosis of the ventricular wall and is most commonly due to amyloidosis, radiation, or diabetes. Patients usually present with reduced exercise capacity and possibly right-sided congestive heart failure. Chest X-ray shows mildly enlarged cardiac silhouette. Echocardiogram reveals mildly reduced left ventricular function.

295. The correct answer is (B). Chronic pancreatitis is predominantly caused by alcohol abuse. Chronic pancreatitis will present as epigastric pain that radiates to the back and is relieved when patient leans forward or lies in the fetal position. This disorder differs from acute pancreatitis by the presence of fat malabsorption and steatorrhea. Serum amylase and lipase levels will be elevated.

296. The correct answer is (E). Individuals who experience pain associated with spinal stenosis can obtain relief following a lumbar epidural injection of corticosteroids. Approximately 25% of patients with spinal stenosis who undergo lumbar epidural corticosteroid injections experience sustained relief of their symptoms.

297. The correct answer is (D). Methotrexate, Ciclosporin, Rituximab, and Sulfasalazine are all examples of DMARDs, short for disease modifying antirheumatic drugs. These medications are indicated immediately following the diagnosis of rheumatoid arthritis. They will slow down the progression of rheumatoid arthritis, unlike NSAIDs, which treat inflammation but not the underlying disease.

298. The correct answer is (E). A nosebleed that occurs from the Woodruff's plexus is often arterial, which explains the presence of bright red blood. This disorder is a result of trauma. Blood will often be appreciated in the posterior pharynx.

299. The correct answer is (E). Gamekeeper's thumb is an injury to the ulnar collateral ligament. This injury is the result of a tear in the ulnar collateral ligament at the site of the proximal phalanx.

300. The correct answer is (B). Botulism is caused by ingestion of the *Clostridium botulinium* bacteria. This bacterial is typically found in the soil and may be found in home-canned, smoked, and commercial foods. Symptoms occur normally 12 to 36 hours after ingestion. Individuals with botulism can present with double vision, drooping eyelids, impaired extraocular movements, and fixed, dilated pupils. Other symptoms may include dry mouth, dysphagia, nausea, and vomiting.

301. The correct answer is (B). Calcium channel blockers effectively stop premature uterine contractions due to the fact that these medications inhibit smooth muscle contractility and relax the uterine muscles by decreasing intracellular calcium ions. Side effects associated with calcium channel blockers include hypotension and tachycardia.

302. The correct answer is (C). Pick's disease is a form of dementia that only affects the frontal and temporal lobes of the brain. Individuals with this disorder have abnormal substances called Pick cells or Pick bodies inside the nerve cells of the affected areas.

303. The correct answer is (D). Infective endocarditis is a form of endocarditis caused by a bacterium. Patients present with fever, cough, dyspnea, joint pain, back or flank pain, and gastrointestinal complaints. Classic features are palatal, conjunctival, or subungual petechiae; splinter hemorrhages; painful lesion of the fingers, toes, and feet; painless red lesions of the palms or soles; and exudative lesions on the retina. Positive blood cultures and intracardiac movement are also classic indicators for this disorder.

304. The correct answer is (E). Primary sclerosing cholangitis is a chronic thickening of the bile duct walls. This disorder is commonly found in individuals with inflammatory bowel disease, such as Crohn's disease and ulcerative colitis. Patient may present with jaundice, itching, fatigue, malaise, and weight loss. Physical exam may yield hepatomegaly and/or splenomegaly. Liver enzymes will be elevated.

305. The correct answer is (B). Any patient whose presentation is suspicious for a scaphoid fracture should be treated as a fracture in a long-arm thumb spica cast, even when X-rays prove negative for scaphoid fracture. Patients should remain in a cast until an MRI or bone scan can be obtained to confirm or rule out a scaphoid fracture.

306. The correct answer is (D). Magnesium sulfate is administered to pregnant women who are experiencing premature labor in order to slow down or stop uterine contractions. Signs of magnesium sulfate overdose or toxicity include respiratory depression and loss of deep tendon reflexes. If an individual exhibits these signs of overdose, calcium gluconate can be administered.

307. The correct answer is (E). Rickets is classically noted on a plain chest radiograph with a rachitic rosary or "string of beads" appearance. This appearance is due to the thickening of costochondral margins that is associated with Rickets.

308. The correct answer is (B). A carbuncle is an infection of more than one hair follicle as a conglomerate mass. The lesions commonly present as red, hard, tender lesions in the hair-bearing regions of the head, neck, and body. An infection of a single hair follicle is a furuncle, commonly referred to as a boil.

309. The correct answer is (D). Osgood-Schlatter disease is apophysitis of the tibial tubercle associated with overuse or trauma. This disease primarily occurs in boys 8-15 years of age. Patients present with anterior knee pain with swelling over the tibial tubercle. Lateral knee X-ray will most often be normal, but fragmentation of the tibial tubercle may be seen.

310. The correct answer is (D). Pyloric stenosis is a congenital disorder in which the gastric outlet is obstructed by pyloric hypertrophy. Patients with this disorder will present with projectile vomiting, weight loss, and dehydration. Affected infants will still be hungry and want to be fed even though they are experiencing projectile vomiting. Upper GI series will show a "string sign."

311. The correct answer is (C). Golfer's elbow is known as medial epicondylitis. This disorder causes pain on the inner side, or medial aspect, of the arm and elbow. A medial counterforce brace should be worn to maintain stability of the elbow and reduce pain associated with this disorder.

312. The correct answer is (E). Biphosponate medications, such as Boniva and Fosamax, are currently approved for maintenance therapy of osteoporosis. These medications are referred to as antiresorptive medications, which means they slow or stop the process of bone degradation. These medications offer prevention against the development of osteoporosis and slow the progression if osteoporosis has already developed.

313. The correct answer is (E). Betamethisone will cause the lungs of a premature infant to produce surfactant, which enhances the infant's ability to breathe on its own with less respiratory treatment. Betamethisone is administered to women who are further than 24 weeks and less than 34 weeks into gestation, within seven days of delivery. Betamethisone is administered via two injections, 24 hours apart.

314. The correct answer is (B). A crescent sign on a lateral hip radiograph is a classic finding for avascular necrosis. Avascular necrosis of the hip is a result of inadequate blood supply to the trabecular bone, which will ultimately cause collapse of the femoral head.

315. The correct answer is (B). Petechiae are defined as minute hemorrhagic spots that cannot be blanched by diascopy. Petechiae are commonly caused by minor trauma such as hard coughing, vomiting, or crying. This disorder may also be a sign of thrombocytopenia.

316. The correct answer is (D). Paget's disease is characterized by localized dysplastic bone formation. Most cases of Paget's disease are asymptomatic and diagnosed by an abnormally high alkaline phosphatase level. This disorder primarily occurs in the spine, pelvis, femur, humerus, tibia and skull. X-rays may reveal kyphosis and bowed femurs.

317. The correct answer is (E). A vericocele is the formation of a varicose vein in the spermatic vein. This disorder will present with a chronic, non-tender mass on the left side of the scrotum. The lesion will have the consistency of a "bag of worms," will increase in size with Valsalva, and will decrease in size with elevation of the testicles or by lying in the supine position.

318. The correct answer is (E). For individuals diagnosed with non-small cell carcinoma, surgery is a viable treatment option. Non-small cell lung carcinomas such as squamous cell carcinoma, adenocarcinoma, and large cell carcinoma grow slowly and have a greater chance of treatment via surgery than small cell carcinoma. The 5-year survival rate after surgery is 35%-40%.

319. The correct answer is (A). Oxytocin, more commonly known as Pitocin, is administered intravenously to induce labor when the cervix is dilated more than 1 cm and some effacement has occurred. Dosages of oxytocin are increased periodically until strong contractions occur approximately every 3 minutes.

320. The correct answer is (C). A Hampton's hump sign on a chest radiograph is classically indicative of pulmonary embolism. Hampton's hump is denoted by a shallow wedge-shaped opacity along the periphery of the lung. This sign results from a pulmonary embolism causing an infarct at the site of the embolism.

321. The correct answer is (A). Retinopathy primarily occurs secondary to systemic disorders such as diabetes, hypertension, and HIV disease. This disorder is the leading cause of blindness in the U.S. Examinations can reveal venous dilatation, microaneurysms, retinal hemorrhages, retinal edema, hard exudates, or vitreous hemorrhages.

322. The correct answer is (B). Kyphosis is defined as an increased convex curvature of the thoracic spine. Approximately one-third of patients with kyphosis will also develop scoliosis.

323. The correct answer is (C). Gastroenteritis is the most common form of Salmonella infection. Symptoms normally begin 8 to 48 hours after consuming contaminated food or beverage. Patients with gastroenteritis typically present with fever, nausea, vomiting, abdominal cramps, and bloody diarrhea for three to five days. Diagnosis is made via stool culture positive for Salmonella.

324. The correct answer is (A). Selective estrogen receptor modulators, such as raloxifene and lasofoxifene, are currently prescribed for many disorders such as osteoporosis, breast cancer, and menopausal symptoms. These medications, although effective for these disorders, increase the risk of blood clots developing.

325. The correct answer is (C). Foods that contain the amino acid tyramine are contraindicated for individuals who are prescribed monoamine oxidase inhibitors (MAOI). Serious side effects, such as a hypertensive crisis, may occur if tyramine is ingested while on these medications. Some common foods that contain tyamine include wine, beer, nearly all cheeses, aged foods, and smoked meats.

326. The correct answer is (A). A greenstick fracture is a very common injury among children. This type of fracture is classically defined as a fracture in which one side of the bone is broken while the other side is bent.

327. The correct answer is (D). Leiomyomata is the clinical, medical term used to refer to the disorder of uterine fibroids. Women who have leiomyomata have a fourfold increase in risk of developing endometrial cancer.

328. The correct answer is (B). Hodgkin's lymphoma refers to a group of cancers characterized by enlargement of lymphoid tissue, spleen, and liver. Hodgkin's lymphoma usually arises in a single area and spreads to neighboring lymph nodes. When alcohol is consumed, pain can occur in the affected nodes.

329. The correct answer is (D). Diabetes mellitus is a disorder characterized by an abnormal level of blood glucose. Type II diabetes occurs primarily in middle-aged, obese individuals. Patients with this disorder can present with fatigue, itching, skin infections, blurred vision, and poor wound healing. Classic diagnostic lab values for this disorder include random glucose levels over 200 mg/dL and/or fasting glucose levels greater than 125 mg/dL. It is caused by overproduction of and subsequent resistance to insulin.

330. The correct answer is (A). Buproprion is contraindicated for treatment of anorexia nervosa because it may exacerbate the anorexic condition and lower the seizure threshold for patients with anorexia. This medication, commonly marketed as Wellbutrin, is an antidepressive medication most commonly used as a smoking cessation aid as well as for treatment of other psychological disorders.

331. The correct answer is (E). Patients with polycystic ovary syndrome will have enlarged polycystic ovaries bilaterally. This disorder is classically diagnosed by a "string of pearls" appearance on an ultrasound examination.

332. The correct answer is (A). Inhaled corticosteroids offer the greatest anti-inflammatory results and allow for best management of chronic asthma. These medications are the first choice for everyday, maintenance therapy for chronic asthma. Beta-adrenergic agonists should be available as rescue medication as they provide greatest bronchodilation during acute attacks of asthma.

333. The correct answer is (B). Sympathomimetic drugs have an anorexic effect, which make them a preferred treatment for binge eating. Medications included in this class of drug are amphetamine, detxroamphetamine, phentermine, phendimetrazine, and benzphetamine. Sympathomimetic drugs mimic the effects of the sympathetic nervous system. These types of medications are commonly used to treat cardiac arrest and low blood pressure, and to delay preterm labor.

334. The correct answer is (D). A boot-shaped heart on a chest radiograph is a common clinical finding with the tetralogy of Fallot. Tetralogy of Fallot is

actually four congenital heart abnormalities that commonly occur together. The four abnormalities include pulmonary stenosis, ventricular septal defect, overriding aorta, and right ventricular hypertrophy.

335. The correct answer is (C). Endometriosis is characterized by endometrial glands and stroma found outside the endometrial cavity. This disorder most commonly occurs in women in their late 20's or early 30's who have never been pregnant.

336. The correct answer is (C). Leukoplakia is characterized by a painless white area that occurs on the tongue, inside the cheek, on the lower lip, or on the floor of the mouth. This is a common occurrence for patients who chew smokeless tobacco, smoke cigarettes, are HIV positive, or abuse alcohol.

337. The correct answer is (D). Type I diabetes mellitus occurs most often in young people, often prepubescent children. This disorder is characterized by weight loss with normal or increased appetite, polydipsia, polyuria, and/or nocturia. Individuals with this disorder may experience blurred vision, itching, weakness, and orthostatic hypotension. This disease is classically diagnosed by a random glucose level over 200 mg/dL in a pre-pubescent child. It is caused by the failure of the Islets of Langerhans of the pancreas to produce insulin.

338. The correct answer is (A). Pregbalin, commonly known as Lyrica, is the only FDA-approved drug for the treatment of fibromyalgia pain. Fibromyalgia symptoms can include pain, muscle stiffness, muscle tenderness, fatigue, difficulty falling asleep, and difficulty staying asleep.

339. The correct answer is (D). Testicular torsion is defined as a twisting of the spermatic cord, which cuts off blood supply to the testicles. A classic diagnostic sign for testicular torsion is the doughnut sign on a nuclear medicine testicular scan. A doughnut sign is defined as increased uptake of radioactive tracer surrounding a photopenic testicle.

340. The correct answer is (C). Anticholinergic medications, such as ipratropium or tiotropium, are superior to beta-adrenergic agonists in achieving bronchodilation for individuals suffering from chronic obstructive pulmonary disease (COPD). Short-acting bronchodilators should be on hand to treat acute exacerbations of dyspnea.

341. The correct answer is (E). SSRIs function to regulate serotonin levels and regulate sleep patterns, thus alleviating symptoms associated with fibromyalgia. Studies have shown that patients with fibromyalgia have low levels of serotonin. Patients with fibromyalgia also have disturbed sleep, which leads to fatigue and increased pain.

342. The correct answer is (C). Torsades de Pointes is a lethal form of ventricular tachycardia. Torsades de Pointes is a polymorphic form of ventricular tachycardia that occurs with an underlying QTc interval.

343. The correct answer is (B). Individuals who suffer from avoidant personality disorder often exhibit an inferiority complex and extreme sensitivity to rejection, and have intense social anxiety and feelings of inadequacy.

344. The correct answer is (B). Migraines are caused by a intracranial vasospasm followed by extracranial vasodilatation. They are characterized by unilateral throbbing or pulsing headaches accompanied with nausea, vomiting, photophobia, and visual aura.

345. The correct answer is (C). Postpartum thyroiditis is a painless inflammation of the thyroid gland that can occur 2 to 6 months following childbirth. This disorder is more prevalent in individuals with a history of thyroiditis or type I diabetes. Patients with this disorder will experience symptoms associated with hyperthyroidism such as rapid heartbeat, unexplained weight loss, and nervousness. Bloodwork will confirm hyperthyroidism with decreased TSH and increased T3 and T4.

346. The correct answer is (D). Salagen, scientifically known as pilocarpine, is used to increase salivary flow for patients who experience dry mouth as a result of Sjogren's syndrome. This medication is used when other therapies, such as artifical tears, artificial saliva, and increasing oral fluid intake, fail to provide adequate relief.

347. The correct answer is (D). Urinalysis for proteinuria is the proper lab test to obtain when evaluating for kidney damage. Normal, healthy kidneys will not allow proteins to enter into the urine. If kidneys are damaged, the filters or glomeruli allow proteins to leak out of the blood and into the urine.

348. The correct answer is (D). Chemotherapy is the treatment of choice for small cell lung carcinoma, also called oat cell carcinoma. Oat cell carcinoma is more likely to spread early and surgery is rarely successful. Chemotherapy has proven to increase survival, although patients rarely live 5 years after diagnosis. Surgical intervention is required for non-small cell carcinomas and carcinoid tumors.

349. The correct answer is (D). Septic arthritis is characterized by yellow-to-green joint fluid and a white blood cell count greater than 50,000 /µl. Results of 75% polymorphonucleocytes and a positive culture also indicate this disorder.

350. The correct answer is (E). Tension headaches are the most common type of headache. They are characterized by steady, aching, band-like pain around the head not associated with nausea, vomiting, or photophobia. These headaches normally occur bilaterally. Sleep deprivation, hunger, stress, and eyestrain are common causes for tension headaches.

351. The correct answer is (D). Hypothyroidism is clinically diagnosed as an underactive thyroid gland. Patients with this disorder will present with fatigue, depression, muscle stiffness, peripheral edema, weight gain, dry skin, cold intolerance, and/or thinning hair. Bloodwork will reveal elevated thyroid stimulating hormone along with low T3 and T4 levels.

352. The correct answer is (D). Calcium channel blockers act to reduce systemic arterial pressure for individual suffering from pulmonary hypertension. Other medical treatments may include an oral anticoagulant and a potent pulmonary vasodilator called prostacyclin.

353. The correct answer is (B). Bactrim is a combination of sulfamethoxazole and trimethoprim, and is commonly prescribed for treatment of confirmed pneumocystis pneumonia and for prevention against occurrence of pneumocystis pneumonia in immunosuppressed patients.

354. The correct answer is (C). A woman who was treated for breast cancer is at increased risk of developing endometrial cancer. Breast cancer is commonly treated with the drug tamoxifen, which increases the risk of developing endometrial cancer. Women who fall in this group should have a yearly pelvic exam and report any and all vaginal bleeding.

355. The correct answer is (D). Malignant pleural effusions occur when lung cancer causes abnormal fluid collection to build up between the outside of the lung and the chest cavity. Once the effusions are drained, a procedure called pleurodesis should be performed. Pleurodesis is a surgical procedure that adheres the lining on the outside of the lung to the lining of the chest wall to inhibit fluid collecting in this space.

356. The correct answer is (A). Ribavirin is indicated as treatment for bronchiolitis with the presence of respiratory syncytial virus (RSV). A 3- to 7-day regimen of ribavirin has been proven to reduce mortality, length of hospitalization, and duration of mechanical ventilation for patients with RSV-induced bronchiolitis.

357. The correct answer is (D). Rheumatoid arthritis is characterized by yellow to opalescent joint color and a white blood count of 3,000-50,000 /μl, 25-50% polymorphonucleocytes, and a negative culture.

358. The correct answer is (E). Vascular dementia, also referred to as multi-infarct dementia, occurs more often in men than in women. It is associated with hypertension, with or without transient ischemic attacks. This disorder commonly presents with forgetfulness and inattentiveness in the absence of depression. Social graces will remain intact with vascular dementia.

359. The correct answer is (A). Acute lymphocytic leukemia is primarily diagnosed in children 3 to 7 years of age. Children with this disorder may present with fatigue, fever, lethargy, headache, and bone pain in the sternum, tibia, and femur. Bloodwork will reveal pancytopenia with circulating blasts. Terminal deoxynucleotidyl transferase is present is 95% of acute lymphocytic leukemia cases. Chest X-ray can reveal a mediastinal mass.

360. The correct answer is (E). A tension pneumothorax is a medical emergency. If a tension pneumothorax is suspected, immediate decompression with a large-bore needle is required to allow air to move out of the chest. Once the tension pneumothorax has been decompressed, a chest tube should be inserted to ensure proper inflation of the lung.

Appendices

···

Recertification Information

THE PHYSICIAN ASSISTANT NATIONAL RECERTIFYING EXAM (PANRE)

After a physician assistant (PA) is initially certified, the PA must maintain an active PA certification.

The Physician Assistant National Recertifying Exam (PANRE) is the only recertification exam that must be taken by PAs who currently hold a National Commission on Certification of Physician Assistants (NCCPA) certification. The certification cycle for a physician assistant is 6 years. After 6 years, the certificate is no longer valid. For a PA to remain certified, he or she must complete 100 hours of continuing medical education every 2 years. Every 6 years, the PA must pass the PANRE.

The PANRE is a computer-based exam that contains 300 multiple-choice questions that must be answered in 5 hours. PAs must submit an application to take the exam and pay a fee of $350. It's administered at testing centers throughout the United States. Examinees may not use any reference materials while taking the exam. The exam is designed to reevaluate and assess the PA's current knowledge and skills in medical surgery.

Prior to 2011, PAs who needed to take the recertification exam had two choices: the PANRE and the Pathway II. The Pathway II was an exam that was completed from home. It had the same number of questions as the PANRE, but examinees had 6 weeks to complete it and were allowed to use reference materials. This exam is no longer offered and PAs are now required to take the PANRE for recertification.

PANRE ELIGIBILITY

Physician assistants can take the PANRE either during their fifth or sixth year of their certificate cycle. PAs can only take the exam twice in their fifth year and twice in their sixth year, meaning they have up to four attempts to pass the PANRE. PAs in their sixth year should note that they only have two tries to pass the PANRE and a 90-day waiting period between exam dates.

To determine eligibility, visit the National Commission on Certification of Physician Assistants Web site at www.nccpa.net. If an illegible PA takes the exam, his or her scores will be rescinded and the PA will be responsible for retaking the test once he or she becomes eligible. Fees will not be refunded in these types of cases.

PAs who have let their certification lapse can regain their certification by taking the PANRE. If a PA's certification lapsed because he or she didn't finish required continuing medical education (CME) hours or failed to make all payments within the 6-year time frame, the PA can pay a reinstatement fee of $250 and finish his or her hours within 6 months of the end of the certification cycle.

To regain certification once it expires, the PA must log 300 hours of CME, 100 of which must be earned during the 2 years leading up to the submission of the application for the exam. Also, 150 of the total required CME hours must be Category I and 50 of these must be earned within the 2 years leading up to the submission of the application for the exam.

Category I includes live or attendance-based activities, such as national conferences, workshops, seminars, or scientific meetings, and enduring materials, such as printed, recorded, audio, or video activities.

The PA can also regain certification by retaking the PANCE exam. No CME hours are required to retake the PANCE exam.

THE PRACTICE-FOCUSED COMPONENT

As of 2009, the PANRE is offered with practice-focused content in one of three specialized areas:

1. Adult medicine
2. Primary care
3. Surgery

Sixty percent of the questions focus on general medical information and the additional 40 percent of questions are based on an area of the PA's choice. This practice-focused content allows PAs to choose which types of questions they would like to see on the PANRE based on their area of practice. Even though the PA is allowed to choose the type of content he or she wants on the PANRE, it doesn't really make a difference because it doesn't make the material on the exam any easier or change the exam format. The PANRE is still scored in the same way and the chosen area of focus on the exam will not show up on the score report.

The following are some of the subjects covered on the PANRE:

- Anatomy/ Physiology
- Bleeding Disorders
- CDC Prevention Isolation Guidelines
- Dementia
- HIV and AIDS
- Immune System
- Liver Function
- Maslow's Hierarchy of Needs
- Multiple Sclerosis
- Obstetrics/ Gynecology
- Pharmacology
- Surgical Terminology

APPLYING FOR THE PANRE

If a PA is in his or her fifth or sixth year of the certificate cycle, he or she should schedule a date to take the take the PANRE as soon as possible. The PA should submit an online application through the National Commission on Certification of Physician Assistants (www.nccpa.net) and pay a fee of $350.

Once the PA is deemed eligible to take the PANRE, he or she can schedule to take the exam at any time during the 180-day time frame given by the NCCPA. If the PA fails to take the exam during this time, he or she will have to reapply and pay the fee again. If the PA decides that he or she can't take the test during this time frame or needs to reschedule, he or she must submit a request of withdrawal in writing to NCCPA at least 24 hours before the exam. If this is not done, the PA will have to reapply and pay the exam fee again.

The Americans with Disabilities Act (ADA) requires the NCCPA to provide qualified examinees with special accommodations during the exam, if needed.

TAKING THE PANRE

On the day of the exam, the examinee should arrive at the testing center at least 30 minutes prior to the exam. If the examinee doesn't adhere to this cut-off time, he or she will not be admitted to the test and will have to reapply and pay the exam fee again. The examinee should bring two valid forms of identification to the exam. The first form of ID must contain a photograph, a printed name, and signature, such as a driver's license, student ID, or passport. The other must have the examinee's printed name and a signature, such as a Social Security card or credit card. Note, the examinee's names must match on both forms of ID or the examinee will be prevented from taking the exam. See exceptions at www.nccpa.net.

Once the examinee begins the exam, he or she cannot stop in the middle, cancel, or reschedule, unless there is a valid emergency. If there is an emergency, the examinee must file an examination grievance to the NCCPA in writing within 3 days of the exam.

The exam will be monitored at all times by a staff member. If the examinee fails to follow the staff member's instructions or acts in a way that is deemed irregular, the examinee may be disqualified from taking the exam or he or she may be given an invalid test score. The following are some examples of irregular behavior:

- Seeking access to the PANRE exam prior to start of exam
- Copying answers or allowing someone else to copy answers
- Taking notes during the exam
- Possessing recording devices, cameras, reference materials, etc.
- Copying, memorizing, printing, or e-mailing any part of the exam
- Stealing exam materials
- Impersonating an examinee

If there is evidence that an examinee has participated in irregular behavior, the NCCPA can revoke the examinee's existing certification, suspend his or her certification, declare the exam scores invalid, impose fines, or pursue legal action.

Examinees are not allowed to bring food, drinks, or any personal items into the testing area and will be given a locker for these items. Some of these items may be accessed during breaks. If the examinee is found to be in possession of any of the following items, they will be confiscated and returned after the exam is over:

- Cell phones
- Laptops
- PDAs
- BlackBerry® devices
- Exam notes
- Reference books
- Study guides

Once the PANRE is scored, the NCCPA will notify the examinee of his or her scores by e-mail. This should take approximately two weeks. If the examinee needs a printed copy of his or her scores, he or she must contact the NCCPA. Sometimes a score is deemed invalid due to circumstances beyond the examinee's control, such as the way the exam was administered, or due to circumstances in the control of the examinee, such as irregular behavior. The NCCPA reserves the right to invalidate PANRE scores. The examinee can refute an invalid score by filing a written appeal to the NCCPA.

Other Careers in Medicine

AUDIOLOGIST

Audiologists specialize in detecting and treating hearing, balance, and other ear problems. Sometimes, audiologists may even see patients with symptoms of sensory or neurological issues. These specialists assess their patients' conditions and diagnose their problems by measuring the level at which their patients begin to hear sound and their abilities to distinguish sounds. They may also use specialized equipment to diagnose balance disorders. Oftentimes, audiologists collaborate with physicians, occupational therapists, and physical therapists.

Once audiologists diagnose the problem, they determine which treatments are most appropriate for their patients. They may choose to clean their patients' ear canals or fit them for hearing aids or cochlear implants. They may recommend the use of home amplification devices, as well. Many times, audiologists choose to counsel their patients as a part of their treatment. They offer advice on how to live with hearing loss, how to use specific instruments and devices, and how to communicate with others, no matter the location.

Audiologists may choose to work for a health-care organization or start a private practice. They can specialize in working with children, the elderly, or those with special needs in addition to hearing loss. They may also choose to conduct research on the causes of hearing loss and types of treatments or they may work on developing or inventing new technology to use in treating those suffering from hearing loss.

DIETITIAN

Dietitians generally plan nutrition programs and supervise the preparation and serving of meals. They often promote healthy eating habits and recommend dietary modifications to prevent or treat others' illnesses. Depending on the field a dietitian enters, he or she may be responsible for teaching healthy eating habits, managing food service systems, or conducting research.

Dietitians can choose to specialize in a variety of fields. Clinical dietitians work for hospitals and nursing homes. They may manage the food service department of the institution or may be responsible for developing nutritional programs for patients and residents. Community dietitians may work for public health clinics, health maintenance organizations, or home health agencies. They may work to teach community members how to shop for healthy groceries and prepare nutritional meals for their families.

In recent years, nutritionists and dietitians have been heavily sought after due to the rise in childhood obesity. Food manufacturers and marketing or advertising agencies typically employ many dietitians, as well.

EMERGENCY MEDICAL TECHNICIAN

When people suffer a medical illness or traumatic injury outside of a hospital, they often request the help of emergency medical technicians (EMTs). EMTs treat the patient at the scene to the best of their abilities and knowledge and then transport the patient to a medical facility.

EMTs often work together on the scene of an emergency and during transport. As one partner assesses a patient, the other may complete the focused history while talking to the patient's family members or witnesses. As one completes an ongoing assessment during transport, the other may drive the ambulance. Once they reach the hospital, EMTs record the treatment they provided the patient and complete the appropriate documents.

EMTs don't only transfer patients who need emergency care. They may also assist in moving patients between hospitals or special facilities for treatments.

According to the National Registry of Emergency Medical Technicians (NREMT), there are five levels of EMTs: first responders, EMT-Basics, EMT-Intermediates 1985, EMT-Intermediates 1999, and paramedics.

HOME HEALTH AIDE

Home health aides help people live at home even when they can no longer care for themselves. Patients may be chronically ill, disabled, cognitively impaired, or elderly. Aides may even assist people outside the home who wish to continue to work or attend school. Most aides, however, work with physically or mentally disabled or elderly clients whose families cannot give them the care they need.

In general, aides do light housekeeping like laundry, food shopping, and cooking. They may also help bathe and groom their clients. Many are trained to check the patient's pulse, temperature, and respiratory rate. Some give massages, change bandages and dressings, and maintain medical equipment. They often counsel their patients and give them both advice and support. If the families are active in their patients' lives, they may give them advice on meal preparation, cleanliness, and living or coping with their loved one's condition.

Depending on where the home health aide is employed, he or she may spend all day with one patient or they may see up to six patients each day. If a client needs 24-hour home health, three or four aides may rotate their shifts to accommodate that patient.

LABORATORY TECHNICIAN

Clinical laboratory technicians are often responsible for performing the tests necessary for determining whether patients have diseases or disorders. They also perform tests that track the progress of both the spread and treatment of diseases.

Technicians complete these tests by examining and analyzing cells and bodily fluids such as urine, blood, or spinal fluid. They may also count cells, keeping track of abnormal growth or loss. Tests that laboratory technicians perform may be immunologic, biological, chemical, microscopic, hematological, or bacteriological.

Chemical lab technologists typically supervise technicians as they prepare specimen and run automatic analyzers or manual tests. Both technologists and technicians can choose to specialize in a given area. Specialized positions include phlebotomists, histotechnicians, and cytotechnologists.

MEDICAL ASSISTANT

Medical assistants may assist in either administrative or clinical capacities. Administrative medical assistants help keep many offices operating smoothly. They arrange hospital and lab services, fill out insurance forms, and file medical records. They may also answer phones, schedule patient visits, pay bills, and greet patients.

Clinical medical assistants play a more active role in patient care than administrative medical assistants. They may take medical histories, assess vital signs, prepare patients for exams, and explain treatment options and medication side effects in the physician's absence. They may also prepare and perform lab tests, draw blood, change dressings, and remove stitches. Depending on the state in which they live, clinical medical assistants can often renew prescriptions and administer medications, as well.

As in many other medical professions, medical assistants can choose to specialize in an area. Examples include ophthalmic medical assistants, podiatric medical assistants, and optometric assistants. Responsibilities of specialized medical assistants range from keeping a physician's office neat and orderly to assisting with surgeries.

OCCUPATIONAL THERAPIST

Occupational therapists help patients develop and improve their basic motor skills and reasoning abilities. Occupational therapists' main goal is to re-teach the mentally, physically, developmentally, and emotionally challenged how to perform tasks independently at home, school, or in a work environment.

They may work with their patients to teach them how to eat, dress, and move around their homes on their own. They may provide advice about time- and money-management, shopping, and homemaking. They may work with their clients to develop computer skills, as well. Some occupational therapists then use computer programs to teach problem-solving, decision-making, abstract-reasoning, and perceptual skills. They may also help their clients improve their memory and coordination.

If a patient has recently been assigned to use adaptive equipment in his or her everyday life, occupational therapists may work with him or her to ensure that they know how to properly use and care for the equipment. Examples of adaptive equipment include wheelchairs, eating aids, and dressing aids.

Occupational therapists may choose to specialize in working with particular age groups, disabilities, or disorders. Some work with infants and toddlers, while others find joy in teaching the elderly how to remain independent at home and on the road. Occupational therapists may also work with patients who abuse alcohol or drugs or suffer from mood, eating, or stress disorders.

PHYSICAL THERAPIST

Physical therapists diagnose and treat patients with medical issues and serious injuries that may affect their abilities to move efficiently. Physical therapists assess their patients, diagnose the issue, and then work with their patients to develop fitness and wellness programs. These programs help to treat the patients' pain, prevent a loss of function, and restore mobility and confidence in performing physical tasks. Oftentimes, physical therapists teach their patients exercises and ask them to perform these movements at their homes between sessions.

Physical therapists may work with patients who have suffered loss of mobility or function due to arthritis, stroke, amputations, sprains/fractures, and back and neck injuries. Interventions for these injuries may include manual therapy techniques, therapeutic exercise, physical agents, electrotherapeutic modalities, and the use of assistive/adaptive equipment such as wheelchairs or crutches.

Physical therapists may specialize in working with children, the elderly, athletes, or people with specific disabilities or disorders. They may also participate in home health, visiting their clients at their homes and helping them perform therapeutic exercises in a comfortable and familiar environment.

PHYSICIAN

There are two types of physicians: Medical Doctors, known as MD's, and Doctors of Osteopathic Medicine, known as DO's. Both types diagnose illnesses and treat injuries and diseases. They embrace methods of treatment such as surgery and prescribed drugs. DO's, however, often look to the musculoskeletal system for answers, prescribe preventative medicine, and recommend holistic patient care.

Physicians can specialize in a number of fields and may be referred to as anesthesiologists, family and general physicians, general internists, general pediatricians, obstetricians and gynecologists, psychiatrists, and surgeons.

RADIOLOGIC TECHNICIAN

Radiologic technicians are responsible for performing diagnostic imaging exams, such as X-rays. X-ray films, or radiographs, allow physicians to further examine, diagnose, and treat their patients.

Radiologic technicians often prepare patients for procedures or exams that may expose them to radiation. They explain the tests and help position the patient so they capture the correct area in the X-ray. They are also responsible for ensuring limited expose to radiation for patients and other coworkers. They may keep patient records, maintain equipment, or even manage radiology departments.

Radiologic technicians can advance to titles such as radiologic technologist, cardiovascular technologists and technicians, diagnostic medical sonographers, and nuclear medicine technologists.

REGISTERED NURSE

Depending on the setting and specialization, responsibilities of registered nurses, or RNs, may differ. Generally, however, all RNs record patient medical histories and symptoms, assist in the performance of diagnostic tests, administer treatments and medications, and provide emotional support and advice to patients and their families. RNs may also start IVs, check dosage, and observe patient status.

Many nurses are also in charge of organizing and running public health screenings, immunization clinics, blood drives, or public seminars. They may visit schools or nursing homes to promote healthy diets and exercise programs, as well.

RNs may specialize in numerous areas including: perioperative, diabetes management, dermatology, pediatric oncology, ambulatory care, critical care, emergency or trauma, transport, home health care, hospice and palliative care, long-term care, medical-surgical, occupational health, perianesthesia, psychiatric-mental health, radiology, rehabilitation, transplant, addictions, intellectual and developmental disabilities, HIV/AIDs, oncology, cardiovascular, gastroenterology, gynecology, nephrology, neuroscience, ophthalmic, orthopedic, otorhinolaryngology, respiratory, and urology.

SPEECH-LANGUAGE PATHOLOGIST

Speech-language pathologists work to diagnose and treat patients experiencing difficulty communicating due to speech, language, voice, fluency, cognitive, or swallowing issues. These patients may have speech rhythm and fluency problems, voice disorders, problems understanding and producing language, cognitive impairments, swallowing disorders, or may simply wish to improve communication skills through modification of an accent.

Speech-language pathologists use specific instruments to diagnose the severity of their patients' problems. Many times, they know the cause of their patients' speech difficulties upon their initial meeting; many patients have cerebral palsy, mental retardation, or hearing loss. Others may have a developmental or learning disorder, a cleft palate, or may have experienced a stroke or brain injury.

Each patient receives an individualized plan of care tailored to his or her needs and abilities. Speech-language pathologists may work with their patients to develop sign language skills, improve their voices, and strengthen muscles. They may also help patients improve their written communication skills. Many times speech-language pathologists will counsel patients and their families about living with communication issues.

Physician Assistant Programs

| Program | State | Health-Care Experience | REQUIRED FOR ADMISSION | | DEGREES OFFERED | | | |
			Some College	Bachelor's Completed	Associate	Bachelor's	Certificate	Master's
Albany Medical College	NY	Required		Yes				Yes
Alderson-Broaddus College	WV		Yes					Yes
Anne Arundel CC	MD	Recommended		Yes			Yes	Option
Arcadia University	PA	Required		Yes				Yes
Arcadia University-DE	DE	Required		Yes				Yes
Arizona School of Health Sciences	AZ	Recommended		Yes				Yes
Augsburg College	MN	Recommended		Yes			Yes	Yes
Barry University	FL	Required		Yes			Yes	Yes
Baylor College of Medicine	TX	Recommended		Yes				Yes
Bethel College	TN	Required		Yes				Yes
Butler University	IN	Recommended	Yes					Yes
Central Michigan University	MI	Required		Yes				Yes
Charles Drew University	CA	Recommended	Yes			Yes	Yes	
Chatham University	PA			Yes				Yes
CUNY/Sophie Davis School	NY	Recommended	Yes			Yes	Yes	
Cuyahoga CC	OH	Required	Yes	Yes			Yes	Yes
D'Youville College	NY	Required				Yes		Yes
Daemen College	NY	Required		Yes		Yes		Yes
Des Moines University	IA	Required		Yes			Yes	Yes
DeSales University	PA	Required		Yes				Yes
Drexel University	PA	Required	Yes				Yes	Yes
Duke University	NC	Required		Yes			Yes	Yes
Duquesne University	PA	Recommended	Yes					Yes
East Carolina University	NC			Yes				Yes

Program	State	Health-Care Experience	Some College	Bachelor's Completed	Associate	Bachelor's	Certificate	Master's
Emory University	GA	Required		Yes				Yes
Gannon University	PA	Recommended		Yes				Yes
George Washington University	DC	Recommended		Yes			Yes	Yes
Grand Valley State University	MI	Required	Yes	Yes				Yes
Harding University	AR	Recommended		Yes				Yes
Hofstra University	NY	Required	Yes			Yes	Yes	
Howard University	DC	Recommended	Yes			Yes	Yes	
Idaho State University	ID			Yes				Yes
Interservice PA Program	TX		Yes			Yes	Yes	Yes
James Madison University	VA	Required		Yes				Yes
Jefferson College	VA	Required	Yes	Yes				Yes
Malcolm X College	IL	Required	Yes		Yes		Yes	Option
Keck School of USC	CA	Recommended		Yes				Yes
Kettering College	OH	Recommended		Yes				Yes
King's College	PA	Required		Yes				Yes
Le Moyne College	NY	Required	Yes	Yes				Yes
Lock Haven University of PA	PA	Recommended		Yes			Yes	Yes
Loma Linda University	CA	Required		Yes				Yes
Long Island University	NY	Required	Yes			Yes	Yes	
LA University Health Sciences Center	LA	Required	Yes			Yes		
Marietta College	OH	Recommended		Yes				Yes
Marquette University	WI	Required	Yes					Yes
Marywood University	PA	Required		Yes				Yes
MCPHS-Boston	MA	Recommended		Yes				Yes
MCPHS-Manchester	NH	Recommended		Yes				Yes
MCPHS-Worcester	MA	Recommended		Yes				Yes
Medical College of Georgia	GA	Recommended	Yes					Yes
Medical University of SC	SC	Recommended	Yes					Yes
Mercer University	GA	Required		Yes				Yes
Mercy College	NY	Recommended	Yes			Yes		Yes
Methodist University	NC	Required		Yes				Yes
Midwestern University-Downers Grove	IL	Required		Yes				Yes

Program	State	Health-Care Experience	REQUIRED FOR ADMISSION		DEGREES OFFERED			
			Some College	Bachelor's Completed	Associate	Bachelor's	Certificate	Master's
Mount Union College	OH	Recommended		Yes				Yes
Mountain State University	WV	Required	Yes			Option		Yes
NY Institute of Technology	NY	Required		Yes				Yes
Northeastern University	MA	Required		Yes				Yes
Nova SE University-Fort Lauderdale	FL	Recommended	Yes					Yes
Nova SE University-Naples	FL	Recommended	Yes					Yes
Nova SE University-Orlando	FL	Recommended	Yes					Yes
OR Health and Science University	OR	Required		Yes				Yes
Our Lady of the Lake College	LA	Required		Yes				Yes
Pace University-Lenox Hill	NY	Required		Yes			Yes	Yes
Pacific University	OR	Required	Yes	Yes				Yes
PA College of Optometry	PA	Required		Yes				Yes
PA College of Technology	PA	Required	Yes			Yes		Option
Philadelphia College	PA	Required		Yes			Yes	Yes
Philadelphia University	PA	Required	Yes	Yes				Yes
Quinnipiac University	CT	Required		Yes			Yes	Yes
Red Rocks CC	CO	Required		Yes			Yes	Option
Riverside CC	CA	Required	Yes		Option		Yes	
Rochester Institute of Tech.	NY	Recommended				Yes		
Rocky Mountain College	MT	Recommended	Yes					Yes
Rosalind Franklin University	IL	Recommended		Yes				Yes
Saint Francis University	PA	Recommended		Yes				Yes
St. John's University	NY	Recommended		Yes		Yes	Yes	
Saint Louis University	MO	Required		Yes				Yes
Samuel Merritt College	CA	Recommended		Yes				Yes
San Joaquin Valley College	CA	Required	Yes		Yes	Option		Option
Seton Hall University	NJ	Required		Yes				Yes
Seton Hill University	PA	Required		Yes				Yes
Shenandoah University	VA	Recommended		Yes				Yes
South College	TN	Recommended		Yes				Yes
South University	GA	Recommended		Yes				Yes
Southern IL University-Carbondale	IL	Required		Yes				Yes

Program	State	Health-Care Experience	REQUIRED FOR ADMISSION		DEGREES OFFERED			
			Some College	Bachelor's Completed	Associate	Bachelor's	Certificate	Master's
Springfield College	MA	Required				Yes		Yes
Stanford University	CA	Required	Yes		Yes	Option	Yes	Option
SUNY Downstate Medical Center	NY	Required	Yes			Yes		
Stony Brook University	NY	Required		Yes				Yes
Texas Tech University	TX	Recommended	Yes					Yes
Touro College of Health	NY	Required	Yes			Yes		
Touro College-Manhattan	NY	Required	Yes			Yes		Yes
Touro College-Winthrop University	NY	Required	Yes			Yes		
Touro University-California	CA	Required		Yes				Yes
Touro University-Nevada	NV	Recommended		Yes				Yes
Towson University-Essex	MD	Required		Yes			Yes	Yes
Trevecca Nazarene University	TN	Recommended		Yes				Yes
Union College	NE	Required	Yes	Yes			Yes	Yes
University of AL at Birmingham	AL	Recommended		Yes				Yes
University of CA-Davis	CA	Recommended	Yes				Yes	Option
University of CO Denver	CO			Yes				Yes
University of Detroit Mercy	MI	Required		Yes				Yes
University of Findlay	OH		Yes			Yes		
University of Florida	FL	Recommended		Yes			Yes	Yes
University of Iowa	IA	Required		Yes			Yes	Yes
University of Kentucky	KY	Recommended		Yes				Yes
University of MD-Eastern Shore	MD	Recommended	Yes			Yes		
University of Medicine and Dentistry of NJ	NJ	Recommended	Yes	Yes		Yes		Yes
University of NE Medical Center	NE	Recommended		Yes				Yes
University of New England	ME	Recommended		Yes			Yes	Yes
University of New Mexico	NM	Recommended	Yes			Yes	Yes	
University of North Dakota	ND	Required		Yes				Yes
University of North Texas-Fort Worth	TX	Recommended	Yes					Yes
University of Oklahoma	OK	Recommended	Yes					Yes
University of Oklahoma-Tulsa	OK	Recommended		Yes				Yes
University of Saint Francis (IN)	IN	Required		Yes				Yes

www.facebook.com/CareerResource

Program	State	Health-Care Experience	REQUIRED FOR ADMISSION		DEGREES OFFERED			
			Some College	Bachelor's Completed	Associate	Bachelor's	Certificate	Master's
University of St. Francis (NM)	NM	Required		Yes				Yes
University of Southern Alabama	AL	Required		Yes				Yes
University of Texas Medical Branch	TX			Yes				Yes
University of Texas Pan American	TX	Recommended	Yes	Yes			Yes	Yes
University of Texas-San Antonio	TX	Recommended	Yes					Yes
University of Texas Southwestern Medical Center	TX	Recommended		Yes				Yes
University of Toledo	OH	Recommended		Yes				Yes
University of Utah	UT	Recommended		Yes			Yes	Yes
University of Washington MEDEX	WA	Required	Yes	Yes		Option	Yes	Option
University of Wisconsin-LaCrosse-Gundersen-Mayo	WI	Required		Yes			Yes	Yes
University of Wisconsin-Madison	WI	Required	Yes			Yes		
Wagner College	NY	Recommended	Yes	Yes		Yes	Yes	Yes
Wake Forest University	NC	Required		Yes				Yes
Wayne State University	MI	Required		Yes				Yes
Weill Cornell Medical College	NY	Required		Yes			Yes	
Western Michigan University	MI	Required		Yes				Yes
Western University	CA			Yes				Yes
Wichita State University	KS	Recommended		Yes				Yes
Wingate University	NC	Required		Yes				Yes
Yale University	CT	Recommended		Yes				Yes
York College of the CUNY	NY	Required				Yes		

Adapted from the Physician Assistant Education Association Web site:
http://www.paeaonline.org/index.php?ht=d/sp/i/242/pid/242

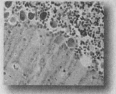

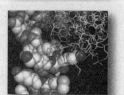
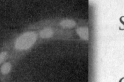

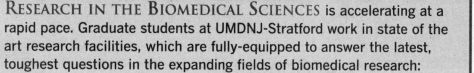

+ AMIT SOOD | sports business major
BE A BILLIKEN
Find out how the breadth and depth of the fully accredited undergraduate and graduate programs at Saint Louis University's JOHN COOK SCHOOL OF BUSINESS will give you the knowledge and tools necessary for success in today's global and highly technical business world.
+ Visit BeABilliken.com for more information on our undergraduate business programs and to see what life is like as a Billiken.
To learn about our graduate business programs, attend an open house or visit gradbiz.slu.edu. +
SAINT LOUIS UNIVERSITY
CONCENTRATIONS IN THE JOHN COOK SCHOOL OF BUSINESS
Accounting
Economics
Entrepreneurship
Finance
Information Technology Management
International Business
Leadership and Change Management
Marketing
Sports Business
GRADUATE PROGRAMS IN THE JOHN COOK SCHOOL OF BUSINESS
One-Year MBA
Part-Time MBA
Master of Supply Chain Management
Master of Accounting
Executive Master of International Business
Post-MBA Certificate

NOTES

NOTES

NOTES

NOTES